2024

RAND McNALLY®

Road Atlas

Contents

Celebrating 100 Years on the Open Road

The Rand McNally *Road Atlas* has been an essential tool on the Great American Road Trip since the publication of 1924's *Auto Chum*, the predecessor of today's atlas. Take a trip down memory lane with a nostalgic look back at 100 years of roadside culture, cars, and the highway system that shaped the open road with this 2024 Collector's Edition.

2294	1072	1641	861	2618	1264	1390
1916	662	1573	620	2210	1049	1370
536	1806	289	2142	940	684	1310
1046	2878	1823	3306	660	2079	2844
300	2143	1078	2566	101	1327	2099
1448	1652	668	1930	1844	602	354
584	1435	478	1835	937	493	1379
1017	1688	237	2048	1412	432	793
744	2182	434	2528	1146	968	1225
1068	1026	749	1372	1421	209	1036
1251	2646	905	2992	1659	1431	1688

Mileage Chart

Driving distances between 90 North American cities and national parks.

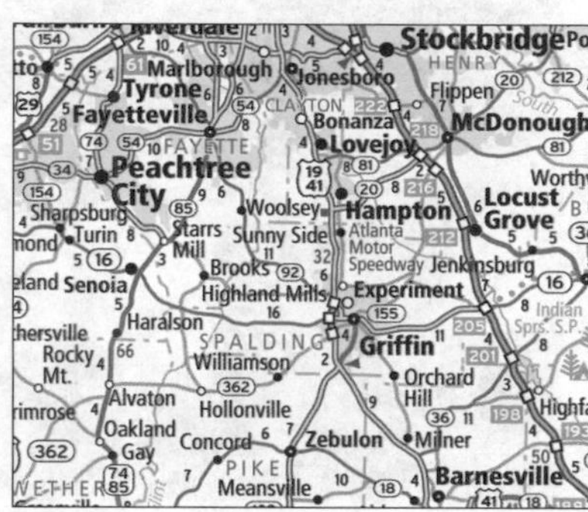

Maps

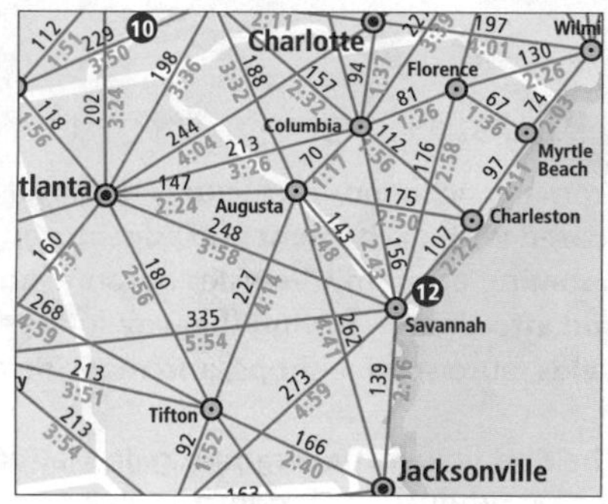

Mileage and Driving Times Map

Distances and driving times between hundreds of North American cities and national parks.

Published and printed in U.S.A.

If you have a comment, suggestion, or even a compliment, please visit us at randmcnally.com/tellrand.

RAND McNALLY PUBLISHING

1 2 3 WR 24 23

Celebrating 100 Years on the Open Road

Back in 1924, long-distance road trips required not only a true sense of adventure, but also lots of time (sometimes weeks, rather than days!), determination, and a packing list geared toward self-sufficiency.

Roadside amenities were rare; breakdowns and punctured tires were not. Travel was slow along a hodgepodge of routes—some marked, others not; some paved, others gravel or hard-packed dirt that was dusty in dry weather and muddy after rain. You might not encounter another person for days, and you were bound to get lost. Unless, of course, you had the Rand McNally *Auto Chum*.

The predecessor of Rand McNally's iconic atlas revolutionized road-travel navigation, and the company continues this tradition 100 years later. Although today's road trips are faster and more comfortable, a good one still requires a true sense of adventure—and a thoughtful packing list that includes a Rand McNally *Road Atlas*.

To help celebrate the atlas centennial, following are some highlights of the open road and Rand McNally through the decades.

1920s: Modernity for the Masses

From music to motion pictures to motor cars, the 1920s roared with excitement and adventure, all fueled by a booming economy. Vehicles became more drivable—and affordable—paving the way for new jobs in the oil fields, auto service shops, and roadside amenities.

The End is Just the Beginning. In May of 1927, Ford ceased production (begun in 1908) of the beloved Model T. The company's moving assembly line and other innovations enabled more than 15 million customers to afford the so-called Tin Lizzie and, essentially, launched the automotive and road-travel industries.

RMC MILE • MARKER **May of 1927 was also when Charles Lindbergh successfully completed a solo, nonstop flight across the Atlantic Ocean, marking a first in aviation history. He used Rand McNally maps to navigate over land.**

New Roads to Adventure. Many of the routes that were funded and developed during the previous decade's grassroots Good Roads Movement were well-established by the 1920s. Among them was the Lincoln Highway, America's first transcontinental route (from New York City to San Francisco) dedicated to auto travel.

It was the 1926 adoption of the U.S. Highway System that really made inroads, though, by setting uniform naming conventions and construction standards, with asphalt and cement becoming more common paving materials. Though some of the earlier auto routes became obsolete, others served as the basis for U.S. Highways. Portions of the Lincoln Highway, for instance, became U.S. Route 30.

Fueling Cars and Culture. Prior to 1905, when the first self-measuring gasoline-storage pump was invented, the chances to "fill 'er up" were few and far between. In the 1920s, though, rough-and-ready refuel and repair shops and curb-side pumps were being replaced by more-sophisticated filling stations. Some featured English Cottage, Tudor, Colonial, and other residential architectural styles. Others took the form of whimsical shapes, from teapots to windmills—the earliest examples of the loveable kitsch adopted by many roadside businesses.

1929 Philadelphia, PA.

1930s Shell gas station at night.

RMC MILE • MARKER When Rand McNally's cartographers struggled to fit cumbersome names on maps, a contest was held to find a solution. The numbering system developed by the winner, a draftsman named John Brink, became the model for what was (and still is) used for U.S. Highways.

1930s: Great Depression Recovery Efforts Pave the Way

American life went from boom to bust with the 1929 stock market crash. Building more roads became part of the federal Works Progress Administration (WPA) plan for boosting the economy during the Great Depression. By 1939, the country had nearly 1.4 million miles of paved roads—and more amenities catering to the needs of drivers.

Good Grub on the Go. In the 1920s, with iconic chains like KFC (1952) and McDonald's (1954) still decades in the future, finding a good roadside eatery was hard. That changed in 1929, when word first got out about Howard Johnson's—a down-home restaurant in Quincy, MA, that served 28 flavors of ice cream, hot dogs, chicken pot pies, baked beans, and soft drinks. In the 1930s, as its popularity grew, "HoJos" added locations and introduced its hallmark orange roofs with cupolas and weathervanes. By the 1960s and '70s, it was America's largest restaurant chain, with more than 1,000 company owned and franchised outlets.

Road Shows. In 1932, Richard Hollingshead, Jr. was awarded U.S. Patent 01909537, leading to the development of drive-in movie theaters. By 1958, America had an estimated 5,000 of them. Rising land values and changing tastes and technology have since reduced that number to about 300, including the oldest one in continuous operation: Shankweiler's (1934) in Orefield, PA.

Airstream Blows In. Wally Byam had been designing and building camping trailers in his backyard and selling his plans to thousands of do-it-yourselfers, when, in 1931 his wife, Marion, insisted that he incorporate a working kitchen. Until then, he hadn't thought beyond his original teardrop-shape, two-tone-painted, Masonite camper.

Inspired by an airplane fuselage, Eyam created the skinned, riveted-aluminum, aerodynamic Clipper—the original Airstream Trailer Company design. Early standard features included not only that storied kitchen but also a side door, pressurized water, a toilet, and holding tanks for water and waste. Airstreams were also the first fully contained trailers inside which an adult could stand fully upright.

A Hollywood, CA, drive-in circa 1951.

RMC MILE • MARKER **In 1937, the first Rand McNally Map & Travel Store opened in New York City. The chain would grow to 29 outlets. Within 24 hours of Germany's invasion of Poland in 1939, stores across the U.S. sold out of Rand McNally's Europe maps. Throughout WW II, company presses operated around the clock to keep up with demand for maps of the theaters of battle.**

Bumper-to-bumper 1940s freeway traffic in California.

1940s–1950s: War-Time Austerity, Post-War Prosperity

Within months of the December 7, 1941, attack on Pearl Harbor, road construction and automobile production all but stopped. During WW II, gasoline was rationed, and more people used public transit. The postwar years, however, saw an economic recovery, and the Greatest Generation began to hit the road with their Baby Boomers in tow. In addition, a prewar plan to connect American cities became a reality—so did the suburbs.

The Highway That's the Best. Built atop earlier auto trails, one of the first U.S. Highways, the beloved Route 66, was initially used by migrants fleeing the Dust Bowl for California during the Depression and by military trucks transporting troops and materiel during WW II.

In postwar America, however, it was favored by vacationers, who followed it, as the famous song says, "from Chicago to LA / More than 2,000 miles all the way." It was soon lined with myriad roadside amenities, more and more of which adopted the colorful, kitschy twists—an unusual shape structure, a giant statue, a flashing sign—that we associate with the Golden Days of American road travel.

A Bad Trip Leads to Inn-Sight. By the 1930s, you could pull off the road into a mom-and-pop motor court and, for a few dollars, step into a cabin with electricity, plumbing, and (hopefully) a clean bed. Over time, amenities—maybe a filling station, a restaurant, and a store—were added.

In 1951, Memphis contractor Kemmons Wilson—irked by the hit-and-miss quality of motor courts during a family vacation to Washington, DC—sketched out a concept for a better hotel experience. Draftsman Eddie Bluestone cleaned up Wilson's sketches, and, having just watched the 1942 Bing Crosby film *Holiday Inn*, wrote the name on his plans. It stuck. Wilson then hired a theater-marquee company to create an illuminated sign. Done in green, gold, and red and shaped (roughly) like America, it caught the attention of drivers and the nation.

Iconic Holiday Inn sign.

The first Holiday Inn's success led to three more—each a day's drive from the other. As it grew, the chain over-delivered with now-standard touches like free ice, vending machines, TVs, phones, pools, and a kids-stay-free policy. By 1958, Wilson had opened 50. That number reached 500 by 1964 and surpassed 1,000 by 1968.

Paving the Nation. Just as the U.S. Highway System made earlier routes like the Lincoln Highway obsolete, so, too, did interstates make some highways, like Route 66, obsolete. The origin of what would become the Dwight D. Eisenhower National System of Interstate and Defense Highways, named for the president who spearheaded it, was the Federal Highway Act of 1956, which earmarked $30 billion for a comprehensive network of roads with 12-foot-wide lanes, 10-foot-wide paved right shoulders, 4-foot-wide paved left shoulders, and curves—all allowing for speeds of 50–70 mph.

"See the USA / in Your Chevrolet . . . ." It was 1952 when Dinah Shore first belted out her sponsor's zippy tune to end her weekly NBC variety show. Chevy continued its small-screen prominence when, in 1960, CBS launched the popular Friday night show, *Route 66*, featuring the adventures of two guys traveling in a Corvette convertible. The 116-episode series ran until 1964—doing a lot to promote road travel and Chevy!

Fast forward to 2005. The show? CW Network's cult-classic *Supernatural* (which ended in 2020). The travelers? Two brothers who traverse rural America battling supernatural forces along the way. What do they drive? A vintage (1967), black, Chevy Impala, of course.

Bob's Gasoline Alley on historic Route 66 in Missouri.

RMC MILE • MARKER In some episodes of the TV series, *Supernatural*, the protagonists use Rand McNally maps! It's just one of many TV shows and movies in which the company's maps and atlases have cameos. Keep an eye out.

Dinosaur Park roadside attraction in South Dakota, 1950s.

1960s–1970s: From Cheap Fuel and Big Cars to Gas Shortages and Economy Cars

By 1960, 61 million cars were registered in the U.S., and interstate construction was booming. Gas was 31 cents per gallon, and a luxury car cost about $2,600. Young people were buying new cars; more than 600,000 Ford Mustangs were sold in 1966 alone.

In the 1970s, OPEC's oil embargo led to gas shortages and price increases. Americans turned to smaller, more fuel-efficient Japanese cars. Throughout both decades, people also began to question the aesthetic and environmental effects of the "superhighway."

Greener and Cleaner. Toll ways and freeways built in the '50s and '60s meant cars could go faster than ever on bigger, straighter roads. However, interstates were also monotonous; separated drivers from their surroundings; and infamous for their smog, noise pollution, and roadside trash.

In 1965, First Lady "Ladybird" Johnson was instrumental in rallying support for the Highway Beautification Act. Five years later, the Federal-Aid Highway Act addressed environmental concerns, including noise and air quality. In 1974, an international oil embargo led to the need for fuel conservation. This, in turn, resulted in a new maximum national speed limit of 55 mph (where it stayed until 1995)—not to mention Sammy Hagar's hit song, "I Can't Drive 55."

That's a Big 10-4, Good Buddy: In the 1970s, two-way CB (citizens band) radios became a popular (though not very private) way to keep in touch with others out on the road. The craze began with truckers, who shared information on gas stations with good supplies of fuel (not always a given during the oil crisis), alerted each other to speed traps, and organized convoys and blockades protesting things like the 55-mph national speed limit.

Songs like C.W. McCall's 1975 hit "Convoy" and movies such as 1977's *Smokey and the Bandit* introduced a mainstream audience to the life of the long-distance trucker. Noncommercial drivers began using CBs, adopting creative call signs, or "handles," and learning the equally creative lingo. Celebrities also got in on the act: First Lady Betty Ford's handle was "Big Mama." James Earl Jones reportedly signed on as "Darth" and Mel Blanc as "Daffy" or "Bugs," with both men using character voices to match their handles.

OPEC's oil embargo led to gas shortages during the 1970s.

Fuel's Gold

Gas prices always seem to be on rise, sometimes increasing between the time you head to work and the time you drive home! Was fuel always so expensive? Relatively speaking, yes.

Year	Estimated Average Cost per Gallon*	Cost Adjusted for Inflation
1920	0.30	$4.47
1930	0.20	$3.57
1940	0.18	$3.83
1950	0.27	$3.44
1960	0.31	$3.12
1970	0.36	$2.77
1980	$1.19	$4.30
1990	$1.15	$2.62
2000	$1.51	$2.61
2010	$2.79	$3.81
2020	$2.17	$2.50

*Source: the U.S. Department of Energy.

RMC **MILE • MARKER** **The company's first full-color *Road Atlas* premieres in 1960.**

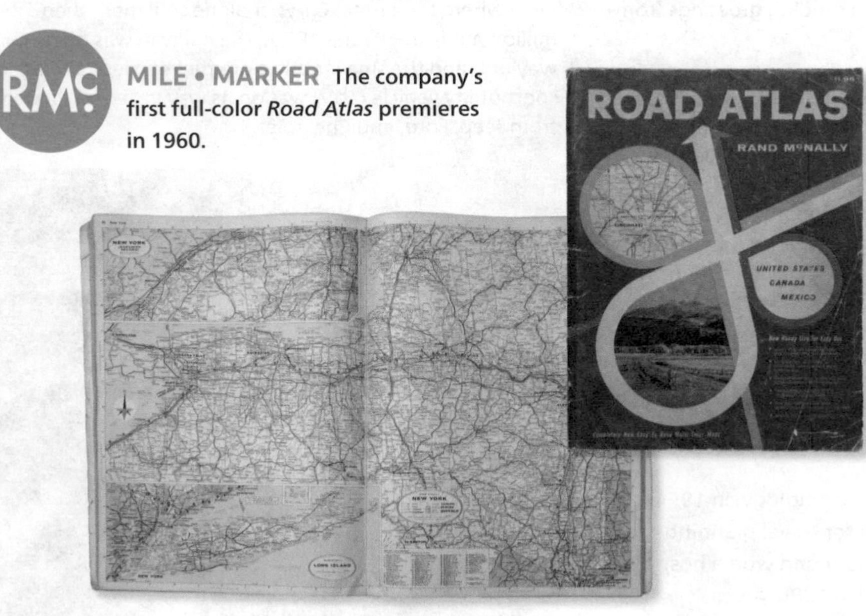

Classic Car Colors

Thanks to traditional sensibilities (holdovers from the days of carriages and stage coaches) and practicality (oh, those muddy roads), most early automobiles came in black or very dark colors, like burgundy or hunter green. The palette became increasingly varied after WW II. Here's a rundown on the most popular colors from the 1950s onward.

1950s
Blue (with chrome trim) is popular, as are two-tone schemes, with one part of the body painted a dark color, and the roof or other areas painted a lighter color, usually white.

1960s
Blue and green are tied, though some sports cars stand out in red. Bright yellow and violet also debut.

1970s
Brown, beige, and cream rise to the top as increasingly environmentally aware Americans begin a love affair with earth tones. Olive green also makes the scene, as does that classic VW chartreuse.

1980s
Black and red lead this slick decade, though blue continues as a favorite, too.

1990s
The color of choice is green in all hues. Aqua adds still more depth to the palette.

The New Millennium
Silver earned the top spot in the first decade, when high-tech went into overdrive. It has since been overtaken by white with gray, black, and blue toward the top of the list as well. Thanks to the environmental-movement reboot, though, earth tones like burnt orange and olive green are on the uptick.

Classic colors (above top to bottom):
1958 Pontiac Laurentian Safari Wagon, 1970 Cadillac DeVille, 1981 Pontiac Firebird Trans Am.

Motorola leads the mobile-phone way—first with a "brick" and then with a "flip."

Before there were minivans, families piled into station wagons. Above: Ford's Country Squire and Chevrolet's Caprice faux "woodies."

1980s–1990s: The Future Looks Brighter as Technology Blooms

In the 1980s, a stronger economy and renewed national pride made exploring the United States popular, and the introduction of minivans made road travel more comfortable. By the 1990s, most major interstates were complete, and 80% of U.S. travel was by car.

The decade also saw auto technology make giant strides, with things like airbags, onboard diagnostics, LED headlamps, and smart keys. The world wide web arrived, and telecommunications, Geographic Information Systems (GIS), and navigation technology accelerated.

Greetings From . . . . In the early days, most road trippers kept in touch with home using postcards, telegrams, or payphones. That began to change in 1983, when Motorola introduced the first of its commercially produced, hand-held mobile phones. Before complaining about any aspect of today's smartphones, consider this: the DynaTAC 8000X, nicknamed "the brick," weighed just under 2 pounds, was 13 inches long, took about 10 hours to fully charge, and allowed roughly 30 minutes of talk time—for a cost of 24 cents (off peak) or 40 cents (peak) per minute.

Such rates were comparable to those for long-distance land-line calls, but the DynaTAC 8000X also came with a price tag befitting the ostentatious 1980s: around $4,000. At that time, it cost 10 cents to make a local payphone call and 13 cents to mail a postcard.

Although clunky versions of the car phone had been available to an elite few since the 1940s, in the late 1980s, they became sleeker and more reliable. Again, Motorola led the way, but, by 1987 (when postcard postage had risen to 15 cents), you could also pick one up at Radio Shack for about $1,400.

Nine years later, telecom advancements (and the arrival of cellular-service plans) enabled Motorola to release its revolutionary, wallet-size, 3-ounce, hand-held StarTAC "clamshell" or "flip" phone. It cost about $1,000, and roughly 60 million were sold. By then, it cost 20 cents to mail a postcard and 25 cents to make a local payphone call. But who needed either when sending greetings from the road was easier than ever?

From the Station Wagon to the SUV: Until the 1980s, the station wagon was the darling of family travel. As early as 1909, innovative car jockeys had modified Henry Ford's Model T, giving it a larger body, often using wood, to accommodate more people or cargo. These vehicles, popular for transporting passengers to and from railroad stations, were dubbed "depot hacks," "woodies" and, of course, "station wagons." Car manufacturers took note, including Ford (Model A, 1929); Chevrolet (Suburban, 1935); and Chrysler (Town and Country, 1941).

After WW II, wagons hit the road in a big way. Though Ford's Country Squires, known for their faux-wood steel-panel siding, were popular, all the major manufacturers had models that made trips to the grocery store, Sunday drives, and camping getaways easy thanks to colossal rear cargo areas. Anything that didn't fit in the back was simply tied to the roof rack.

Volkswagen's 1950 Microbus and Chevy's 1961 Corvan (part Corvair, part cargo van) were early forerunners of the family minivan, though the first such vehicles as we know them (sliding side doors, higher seats and more of them) didn't roll off assembly lines till 1983. Soccer moms everywhere took note; Chrysler alone sold more than 12 million minivans. By the 1990s, the minivan was on its way out, and the smaller but more fuel-efficient and agile sport utility vehicle (SUV) was on its way in, led by models from Jeep, Ford, and Chevrolet.

In the 1990s, sport utility vehicles (SUVs) began replacing minivans as the family vehicle of choice.

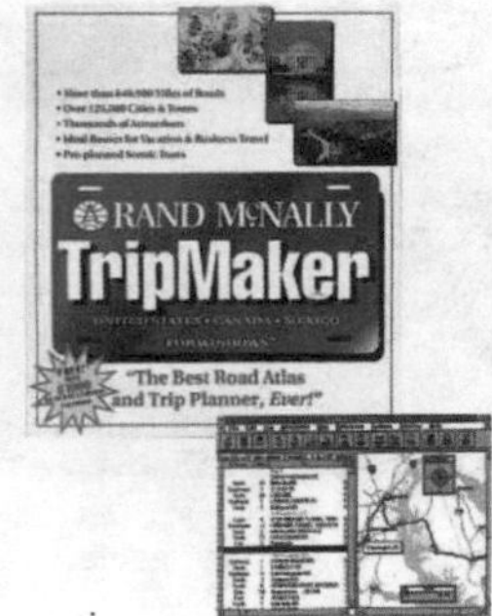

RMC **MILE • MARKER Keeping up with evolving technology, in 1994, Rand McNally introduced TripMaker® software for travel planning on personal computers. It became a market leader and won a host of awards. StreetFinder® street navigation software followed in 1996. A year later, randmcnally.com was launched, offering up-to-date information on road construction and weather, online reservations, shopping, and other services.**

Because of the pandemic, RV sales and rentals skyrocketed, as did national park visitation. Above, Arches National Park, UT.

The New Millennium: Technology Booms and Road Travel Zooms

Technological advances continue to drive the auto industry. Smartphones, in-car Wi-Fi and Bluetooth technology, and electric and hybrid vehicles have given road travelers more options to navigate, stay connected, and save on fuel costs (while helping to save the planet).

The country has also turned its attention back to a few road-travel basics. The 2021 Bipartisan Infrastructure Law has allocated billions of dollars to upgrades and improvements, including much-needed road and bridge repairs and the installation of electric-vehicle charging stations across the nation. The timing is perfect: because of the COVID-19 pandemic, more Americans have discovered the joys of road trips.

Road Travel Renaissance. After months of lockdown, Americans found that road trips were the best way to break free while maintaining social distance. Bookings on RVshare, a leading rental marketplace, rose by 650% in 2020, and the Recreational Vehicle Industry Association reported that 2021 manufacturer shipments of RVs for sale increased by 40%. National Park visitation also skyrocketed, with several parks setting or breaking annual records.

The demographics have shifted, too. Prior to the pandemic, lack of time prevented Gen Xers and Millennials from taking road trips. Remote work, however, has enabled them to join their retiree counterparts out on the open road—often more than once a year for journeys that last longer and go farther than was previously possible. The road travel Renaissance continues.

A sign of the times.

The Sky's the Limit... For Now

Electric, hybrid, driver-assisted. . . what about flying cars? Well, the most promising versions are quite small—not to mention ultra-expensive—so taking a family road trip in an airborne automobile is still a distant dream. But it's no longer mere fiction, as depicted in books, movies, and TV shows for decades.

The Jetsons. In the 1962–63 prime-time animated comedy about a space-age all-American family, George Jetson's flying vehicle was the ultimate compact car: it folded up into a briefcase!

Chitty-Chitty Bang Bang. You're probably familiar with the 1968 movie musical named for a beloved flying car, but did you know it was based on a 1964 children's book written by Ian Fleming?

The Man With the Golden Gun. Speaking of Ian Fleming . . . at one point in this 1974 flick featuring his James Bond character, villain-assassin Francisco Scaramanga eludes 007 in a flying AMC Matador Coupe.

Back to the Future. This popular movie franchise—with releases in 1985, '89, and '90—did a lot for the image of the DeLorean DMC-12, which is what Doc Brown used to create his flux-capacitor-equipped time machine.

Agents of S.H.I.E.L.D. In the Marvel comics TV series (2013–20), Stark Industries took a retro approach with Agent Phil Coulson's flying car—a red 1967 Chevy Corvette nicknamed Lola. And she was a beauty!

RMC MILE • MARKER **Sure, GPS is nice, but what if you lose your signal? Or you want more geographic context than what's shown on a small screen? Or you're feeling nostalgic and want your kids to learn about maps and atlases? You wouldn't be alone. Throughout the pandemic, the 2021 and 2022 editions of the Rand McNally *Large Scale Road Atlas* were on the *Publisher's Weekly* Top 25 List, reaching #9 in August of 2021. After 100 years and more than 200 million copies sold, the Rand McNally *Road Atlas* is still going strong!**

Mileage Chart

This handy chart offers more than 2,400 mileages covering 90 North American cities and U.S. national parks. Want more mileages? Visit randmcnally.com/MC and type in any two cities or addresses.

	Albuquerque, NM	Amarillo, TX	Atlanta, GA	Baltimore, MD	Billings, MT	Birmingham, AL	Boise, ID	Boston, MA	Branson, MO	Brownsville, TX	Buffalo, NY	Charleston, SC	Charleston, WV	Charlotte, NC	Cheyenne, WY	Chicago, IL	Cincinnati, OH	Cleveland, OH	Columbus, OH	Dallas, TX	Denver, CO	Des Moines, IA	Detroit, MI	El Paso, TX	Fargo, ND	Grand Junction, CO	Hartford, CT	Houston, TX	Indianapolis, IN	Jackson, MS	Jacksonville, FL	Kansas City, MO	Las Vegas, NV	Little Rock, AR	Los Angeles, CA	Louisville, KY	Memphis, TN	Miami, FL	Milwaukee, WI	Minneapolis, MN	Mobile, AL	Montpelier, VT	Nashville, TN	New Orleans, LA	New York, NY	Norfolk, VA	Oklahoma City, OK	Omaha, NE	Orlando, FL	Philadelphia, PA	Phoenix, AZ	Pittsburgh, PA	Portland, ME	Portland, OR	Raleigh, NC	Rapid City, SD	Reno, NV	Saint Louis, MO	Salt Lake City, UT	San Antonio, TX	San Diego, CA	San Francisco, CA	Savannah, GA	Seattle, WA	Spokane, WA	Tampa, FL	Washington, DC	Wichita, KS
Acadia N.P., ME	2490	2206	1366	671	2507	1448	2935	283	1704	2469	728	1241	1014	1112	2198	1254	1142	911	1034	2035	2242	1570	997	2626	1900	2484	372	2115	1208	1683	1417	1692	2988	1718	3256	1249	1583	1760	1348	1667	1698	293	1370	1791	478	840	1949	1707	1559	577	2952	841	172	3360	972	2171	3154	1453	2636	2310	3317	3371	1285	3325	3045	1613	710	1884
Albuquerque, NM		284	1386	1887	998	1241	938	2219	864	990	1782	1703	1543	1626	546	1333	1387	1598	1457	647	446	983	1570	260	1318	380	2118	884	1279	1047	1636	784	572	877	786	1300	1008	1952	1354	1225	1234	2203	1219	1165	2001	1910	542	863	1730	1924	462	1641	2315	1363	1761	843	1019	1037	599	712	810	1086	1634	1438	1320	1746	1885	591
Amarillo, TX	284		1102	1602	965	957	1243	1935	580	788	1498	1419	1259	1342	515	1049	1103	1314	1173	363	424	765	1286	407	1002	607	1834	589	995	762	1352	570	857	593	1072	1016	720	1668	1132	1009	949	1919	932	881	1716	1632	256	647	1446	1640	746	1357	2031	1669	1474	714	1304	752	883	510	1097	1370	1350	1743	1505	1462	1600	382
Anchorage, AK	3672	3641	4338	4321	2660	4284	2707	4495	3788	4430	4155	4532	4111	4389	3128	3617	3914	3965	3975	4097	3227	3450	3905	3940	2935	3288	4513	4339	3804	4302	4689	3572	3424	3959	3412	3919	4093	5004	3545	3165	4486	4318	4093	4485	4428	4506	3894	3391	4782	4380	3681	4082	4443	2448	4436	2995	3026	3825	3006	4152	3532	3084	4585	2276	2387	4798	4319	3736
Atlanta, GA	1386	1102		682	1831	146	2177	1095	652	1145	894	317	502	244	1439	715	461	714	567	780	1404	902	722	1418	1361	1643	996	794	533	380	346	800	1959	515	2174	420	379	661	809	1127	328	1165	248	468	882	558	844	992	440	780	1844	684	1192	2603	408	1508	2396	555	1878	986	2138	2472	247	2649	2369	451	637	955
Baltimore, MD	1887	1602	682		1952	780	2378	400	1079	1801	372	571	361	442	1644	699	513	369	409	1368	1673	1015	524	2003	1346	1916	300	1448	584	1017	744	1068	2420	1050	2670	604	914	1082	792	1112	1003	498	703	1124	192	228	1346	1153	889	98	2349	246	496	2804	302	1616	2599	829	2081	1642	2695	2816	605	2770	2491	942	39	1260
Big Bend N.P., TX	592	470	1344	1929	1393	1201	1530	2325	973	625	1939	1661	1610	1588	938	1442	1495	1755	1614	561	838	1182	1678	325	1525	949	2226	637	1388	964	1505	988	1043	880	1128	1400	1015	1820	1525	1427	1102	2395	1226	981	2128	1912	650	1102	1598	2028	757	1794	2422	1956	1753	1190	1491	1145	1191	404	1050	1507	1558	2021	1912	1614	1892	807
Billings, MT	998	965	1831	1952		1780	620	2236	1241	1758	1786	2132	1742	1990	453	1246	1546	1596	1606	1425	551	946	1535	1257	607	662	2143	1652	1435	1688	2182	1026	971	1407	1240	1539	1477	2497	1173	838	1874	2207	1586	1868	2041	2132	1203	845	2275	2011	1210	1713	2333	891	2067	323	956	1278	552	1480	1301	1173	2078	818	540	2291	1951	1064
Birmingham, AL	1241	957	146	780	1780		2126	1177	507	1020	908	463	564	390	1386	660	464	716	569	636	1329	848	724	1274	1307	1573	1078	668	478	237	434	749	1814	370	2029	366	234	746	754	1072	258	1247	192	343	960	715	699	939	534	880	1700	748	1274	2551	555	1456	2262	501	1826	861	1994	2327	393	2597	2318	537	744	810
Boise, ID	938	1243	2177	2378	620	2126		2660	1588	1928	2214	2473	2123	2336	736	1693	1943	2020	2013	1702	830	1360	1960	1205	1227	620	2566	1930	1835	2048	2528	1372	624	1786	842	1877	1825	2844	1732	1461	2236	2636	1925	2216	2465	2525	1497	1225	2622	2435	914	2137	2761	428	2444	942	422	1622	339	1651	958	639	2418	503	425	2638	2375	1338
Boston, MA	2219	1935	1095	400	2236	1177	2660		1433	2198	453	970	744	841	1927	983	870	638	763	1764	1970	1299	724	2373	1629	2210	101	1844	937	1412	1146	1421	2714	1447	2983	978	1312	1482	1074	1396	1427	179	1099	1520	207	569	1678	1436	1288	306	2681	570	110	3086	702	1900	2881	1182	2365	2039	3046	3098	1014	3054	2774	1342	439	1613
Branson, MO	864	580	652	1079	1241	507	1588	1433		1005	995	968	755	868	851	545	601	808	668	435	806	400	784	985	816	1049	1327	602	493	432	968	209	1437	172	1651	510	274	1284	630	643	620	1417	464	597	1201	1158	323	402	1062	1138	1326	851	1529	2013	1003	920	1806	249	1288	708	1675	1950	900	2059	1780	1078	1078	292
Brownsville, TX	990	788	1145	1801	1758	1020	1928	2198	1005		1853	1459	1525	1388	1303	1474	1409	1669	1528	547	1213	1230	1673	814	1614	1370	2099	354	1379	793	1225	1036	1550	794	1630	1314	929	1538	1557	1475	821	2268	1140	700	1981	1716	738	1192	1319	1900	1259	1708	2294	2354	1556	1515	1998	1177	1589	274	1552	2010	1320	2428	2296	1329	1765	896
Buffalo, NY	1782	1498	894	372	1786	908	2214	453	995	1853		866	435	656	1478	533	434	190	326	1378	1521	849	273	1908	1180	1762	397	1499	500	1125	1037	984	2266	1061	2535	540	922	1385	630	946	1166	428	712	1248	395	569	1242	987	1184	388	2245	216	553	2639	637	1450	2433	746	1915	1654	2596	2650	909	2604	2325	1235	382	1176
Calgary, AB	1542	1511	2357	2332	541	2305	747	2615	1783	2299	2165	2542	2122	2400	998	1627	1925	1976	1985	1967	1096	1461	1915	1809	956	1154	2524	2209	1814	2239	2703	1567	1284	1958	1557	1930	2028	3018	1555	1221	2481	2380	2116	2419	2438	2516	1763	1386	2797	2390	1524	2093	2505	787	2446	865	1276	1820	869	2021	1617	1500	2620	678	424	2833	2330	1606
Charleston, SC	1703	1419	317	571	2132	463	2473	970	968	1459	866		471	207	1740	908	620	721	636	1099	1706	1199	826	1734	1557	1946	871	1105	726	697	235	1103	2276	831	2491	613	696	583	1002	1323	602	1068	549	742	768	437	1160	1293	380	668	2165	654	1066	2904	278	1811	2698	856	2180	1300	2459	2789	106	2950	2671	433	530	1272
Charleston, WV	1543	1259	502	361	1742	564	2123	744	755	1525	435	471		264	1389	491	196	250	162	1049	1355	788	352	1684	1136	1595	644	1171	312	801	642	752	2099	732	2330	244	597	990	589	902	816	813	388	908	530	403	1002	943	792	466	2005	225	840	2554	322	1410	2342	506	1829	1324	2354	2564	514	2560	2281	840	362	945
Charlotte, NC	1626	1342	244	442	1990	390	2336	841	868	1388	656	207	264		1600	769	477	514	426	1023	1566	1057	616	1662	1414	1810	742	1038	583	624	379	961	2199	754	2414	470	619	728	867	1180	571	928	407	712	641	328	1084	1151	526	539	2088	446	938	2761	168	1670	2555	714	2037	1230	2381	2712	251	2808	2528	578	398	1092
Cheyenne, WY	546	515	1439	1644	453	1386	736	1927	851	1303	1478	1740	1389	1600		960	1210	1288	1281	971	100	628	1227	807	787	340	1834	1202	1104	1316	1792	634	829	1055	1102	1144	1091	2107	1000	865	1504	1899	1192	1488	1733	1792	720	492	1885	1703	1008	1405	2024	1161	1712	298	956	888	437	1025	1162	1172	1687	1225	993	1901	1642	608
Chicago, IL	1333	1049	715	699	1246	660	1693	983	545	1474	533	908	491	769	960		289	342	354	926	1002	332	280	1455	641	1242	888	1085	181	738	1068	526	1746	650	2015	296	531	1381	90	408	917	954	469	923	787	878	792	470	1153	757	1795	459	1079	2118	816	912	1913	296	1398	1202	2080	2130	951	2063	1785	1166	697	724
Cincinnati, OH	1387	1103	461	513	1546	464	1943	870	601	1409	434	620	196	477	1210	289		248	106	934	1187	580	259	1569	937	1427	767	1055	108	686	796	584	1932	617	2172	97	482	1127	381	703	721	855	273	804	637	605	846	722	905	571	1849	288	967	2369	521	1208	2163	348	1647	1210	2196	2380	664	2363	2084	916	512	779
Cleveland, OH	1598	1314	714	369	1596	716	2020	638	808	1669	190	721	250	514	1288	342	248		142	1194	1330	659	168	1721	990	1570	562	1315	315	937	892	799	2073	868	2342	347	729	1240	434	756	973	611	525	1057	460	551	1057	797	1043	428	2060	131	736	2446	572	1260	2240	560	1725	1457	2407	2458	764	2414	2135	1091	367	992
Columbus, OH	1457	1173	567	409	1606	569	2013	763	668	1528	326	636	162	426	1281	354	106	142		1039	1261	653	191	1578	1000	1501	661	1174	176	790	812	657	2004	724	2244	206	587	1164	445	766	826	747	378	910	533	570	917	792	954	468	1920	184	859	2439	486	1270	2234	421	1718	1314	2269	2451	680	2424	2144	1007	407	851
Crater Lake N.P., OR	1307	1595	2580	2772	1033	2528	422	3054	1990	2305	2609	2866	2515	2736	1129	2086	2336	2413	2406	1976	1223	1753	2353	1473	1640	972	2959	2212	2227	2375	2931	1775	754	2178	738	2270	2235	3246	2126	1874	2562	3038	2318	2494	2858	2917	1889	1618	3025	2828	1039	2530	3156	250	2837	1351	310	2015	691	2028	858	410	2810	422	493	3041	2768	1731
Dallas, TX	647	363	780	1368	1425	636	1702	1764	435	547	1378	1099	1049	1023	971	926	934	1194	1039		880	683	1163	635	1079	1124	1665	228	873	402	992	489	1220	319	1437	836	453	1307	1010	928	589	1824	664	519	1548	1350	204	656	1086	1467	1066	1221	1861	2128	1191	1061	1668	630	1403	276	1359	1734	996	2193	1964	1102	1332	361
Denver, CO	446	424	1404	1673	551	1329	830	1970	806	1213	1521	1706	1355	1566	100	1002	1187	1330	1261	880		670	1270	707	873	243	1876	1035	1083	1226	1756	603	747	965	1015	1109	1097	2069	1042	913	1414	1942	1158	1398	1775	1758	631	534	1851	1732	908	1447	2067	1256	1678	397	1051	854	533	935	1077	1268	1651	1320	1091	1860	1671	519
Des Moines, IA	983	765	902	1015	946	848	1360	1299	400	1230	849	1199	788	1057	628	332	580	659	653	683	670		599	1124	475	909	1206	938	474	828	1253	193	1413	573	1682	586	617	1567	371	242	998	1270	656	1008	1105	1196	545	137	1339	1074	1445	777	1395	1786	1107	626	1581	354	1065	960	1747	1798	1150	1764	1484	1354	1014	391
Detroit, MI	1570	1286	722	524	1535	724	1960	724	784	1673	273	826	352	616	1227	280	259	168	191	1163	1270	599		1702	930	1508	668	1319	288	945	1002	764	2013	885	2281	361	742	1354	374	696	978	718	534	1066	613	704	1029	736	1144	583	2032	285	825	2385	677	1200	2180	533	1664	1439	2346	2397	870	2353	2075	1178	522	964
El Paso, TX	260	407	1418	2003	1257	1274	1205	2373	985	814	1908	1734	1684	1662	807	1455	1569	1721	1578	635	707	1124	1702		1370	642	2300	744	1398	1038	1619	929	718	954	796	1474	1089	1934	1497	1377	1215	2347	1300	1095	2201	1986	660	1004	1712	2102	424	1774	2455	1630	1826	1110	1166	1157	866	554	718	1175	1632	1705	1587	1728	1966	730
Fargo, ND	1318	1002	1361	1346	607	1307	1227	1629	816	1614	1180	1557	1136	1414	787	641	937	990	1000	1079	873	475	930	1370		1115	1538	1321	825	1265	1708	600	1579	988	1848	944	1054	2025	569	235	1451	1601	1116	1445	1438	1529	875	420	1807	1405	1780	1107	1726	1497	1460	550	1564	841	1160	1343	1908	1781	1609	1424	1147	1813	1344	685
Grand Canyon N.P., AZ	400	684	1786	2294	1072	1641	861	2618	1264	1390	2182	2102	1943	2025	774	1729	1786	1997	1857	1047	676	1344	1969	600	1546	433	2518	1284	1679	1446	2036	1184	275	1277	490	1699	1408	2351	1716	1586	1634	2603	1619	1565	2406	2314	942	1208	2130	2324	218	2041	2715	1286	2160	1070	722	1436	522	1112	551	788	2033	1351	1243	2146	2285	990
Grand Junction, CO	380	607	1643	1916	662	1573	620	2210	1049	1370	1762	1946	1595	1810	340	1242	1427	1570	1501	1124	243	909	1508	642	1115		2115	1279	1324	1470	1994	844	506	1207	774	1349	1340	2308	1282	1152	1657	2184	1397	1638	2014	1997	870	774	2095	1975	571	1686	2309	1046	1917	639	799	1095	283	1092	835	968	1890	1121	1002	2099	1914	759
Grt. Smoky Mts. N.P., TN	1440	1151	189	536	1806	289	2142	940	684	1310	705	333	313	190	1408	585	293	548	406	882	1375	873	561	1522	1230	1614	843	962	399	528	510	771	2010	567	2224	286	430	862	682	996	520	1015	220	633	716	485	896	964	624	637	1903	496	1042	2577	326	1479	2371	527	1852	1151	2249	2528	378	2624	2344	640	502	908
Halifax, NS	2865	2581	1742	1046	2878	1823	3306	660	2079	2844	1103	1616	1390	1488	2569	1624	1517	1286	1409	2410	2612	1940	1335	3042	2271	2854	747	2490	1583	2059	1792	2067	3358	2093	3627	1624	1958	2145	1724	2037	2073	668	1745	2166	853	1216	2324	2078	1935	952	3328	1216	550	3731	1348	2541	3524	1828	3006	2685	3688	3741	1661	3695	3416	1988	1085	2259
Hartford, CT	2118	1834	996	300	2143	1078	2566	101	1327	2099	397	871	644	742	1834	888	767	562	661	1665	1876	1206	668	2300	1538	2115		1745	834	1313	1047	1318	2619	1348	2888	877	1213	1385	980	1304	1328	198	1000	1421	108	470	1577	1345	1189	207	2580	469	197	2992	602	1808	2786	1080	2271	1940	2930	3004	915	2960	2682	1242	340	1512
Houston, TX	884	589	794	1448	1652	668	1930	1844	602	354	1499	1105	1171	1038	1202	1085	1055	1315	1174	228	1035	938	1319	744	1321	1279	1745		1021	439	871	732	1457	439	1550	960	575	1186	1163	1171	468	1914	786	347	1632	1362	437	898	965	1547	1178	1354	1940	2356	1202	1291	1904	784	1634	197	1472	1929	971	2431	2192	980	1411	595
Indianapolis, IN	1279	995	533	584	1435	478	1835	937	493	1379	500	726	312	583	1104	181	108	315	176	873	1083	474	288	1398	825	1324	834	1021		671	874	482	1828	583	2068	113	464	1198	272	591	733	921	287	818	707	720	739	613	968	643	1742	359	1034	2260	628	1100	2056	243	1541	1149	2089	2273	770	2253	1973	984	582	674
Jackson, MS	1047	762	380	1017	1688	237	2048	1412	432	793	1125	697	801	624	1316	738	686	937	790	402	1226	828	945	1038	1265	1470	1313	439	671		590	664	1620	261	1838	586	209	905	830	1040	188	1482	414	183	1198	948	603	852	683	1115	1466	971	1509	2473	789	1371	2067	491	1749	635	1759	2133	580	2537	2229	699	980	707
Jacksonville, FL	1636	1352	346	744	2182	434	2528	1146	968	1225	1037	235	642	379	1792	1068	796	892	812	992	1756	1253	1002	1619	1708	1994	1047	871	874	590		1152	2210	832	2421	772	677	349	1163	1474	403	1245	596	547	939	613	1160	1343	141	844	2050	825	1243	2954	449	1860	2748	906	2229	1066	2343	2723	135	3000	2720	198	706	1272
Kansas City, MO	784	570	800	1068	1026	749	1372	1421	209	1036	984	1103	752	961	634	526	584	799	657	489	603	193	764	929	600	844	1318	732	482	664	1152		1349	381	1616	507	451	1466	565	436	850	1405	555	844	1196	1155	348	187	1246	1127	1246	840	1518	1797	1074	704	1591	250	1073	766	1597	1808	1048	1844	1564	1252	1066	193
Key West, FL	2099	1815	809	1251	2646	905	2992	1659	1431	1688	1544	742	1149	886	2256	1534	1275	1399	1325	1455	2222	1726	1515	2082	2178	2466	1560	1334	1348	1053	507	1617	2673	1294	2884	1238	1159	162	1632	1944	866	1758	1063	1010	1446	1120	1623	1807	387	1357	2514	1332	1756	3417	956	2326	3211	1370	2693	1529	2806	3186	642	3464	3185	402	1213	1735
Las Vegas, NV	572	857	1959	2420	971	1814	624	2714	1437	1550	2266	2276	2099	2199	829	1746	1932	2073	2004	1220	747	1413	2013	718	1579	506	2619	1457	1828	1620	2210	1349		1450	270	1854	1581	2525	1786	1656	1808	2688	1792	1739	2518	2486	1112	1278	2303	2480	285	2190	2813	1022	2334	1039	447	1600	419	1272	331	569	2206	1128	1138	2319	2428	1164
Little Rock, AR	877	593	515	1050	1407	370	1786	1447	172	794	1061	831	732	754	1055	650	617	868	724	319	965	573	885	954	988	1207	1348	439	583	261	832	381	1450		1665	520	137	1147	724	815	449	1506	348	425	1230	1035	335	574	925	1150	1340	905	1543	2211	889	1093	1898	345	1488	594	1676	1963	763	2275	1948	941	1014	446
Los Angeles, CA	786	1072	2174	2670	1240	2029	842	2983	1651	1630	2535	2491	2330	2414	1102	2015	2172	2342	2244	1437	1015	1682	2281	796	1848	774	2888	1550	2068	1838	2421	1616	270	1665		2085	1794	2735	2055	1925	2014	2957	2006	1894	2787	2707	1326	1546	2515	2713	370	2428	3082	963	2548	1312	470	1821	688	1357	120	380	2422	1134	1215	2525	2670	1377
Louisville, KY	1300	1016	420	604	1539	366	1877	978	510	1314	540	613	244	470	1144	296	97	347	206	836	1109	586	361	1474	944	1349	877	960	113	586	772	507	1854	520	2085		384	1085	390	710	620	962	174	705	740	649	759	699	858	676	1762	388	1074	2310	568	1214	2104	263	1586	1111	2109	2321	658	2357	2077	872	606	701
Memphis, TN	1008	720	379	914	1477	234	1825	1312	274	929	922	696	597	619	1091	531	482	729	587	453	1097	617	742	1089	1054	1340	1213	575	464	209	677	451	1581	137	1794	384		1012	622	831	382	1369	212	394	1094	898	466	641	778	1014	1471	768	1408	2245	753	1160	2029	283	1524	727	1819	2095	626	2299	2018	779	879	577
Mexico City, DF	1392	1332	1718	2372	2301	1592	2330	2768	1548	570	2424	2029	2095	1962	1846	2017	1979	2239	2098	1090	1756	1790	2254	1124	2158	1772	2669	924	1963	1364	1796	1598	1755	1364	1839	1884	1500	2111	2100	2032	1392	2838	1710	1272	2571	2286	1282	1735	1889	2471	1469	2279	2865	2756	2126	2139	2202	1721	1991	821	1700	2218	1906	2830	2711	1905	2335	1440
Miami, FL	1952	1668	661	1082	2497	746	2844	1482	1284	1538	1385	583	990	728	2107	1381	1127	1240	1164	1307	2069	1567	1354	1934	2025	2308	1385	1186	1198	905	349	1466	2525	1147	2735	1085	1012		1475	1791	719	1587	913	861	1288	950	1476	1658	229	1180	2362	1173	1585	3260	797	2173	3063	1221	2544	1379	2656	3038	483	3315	3035	255	1044	1587
Milwaukee, WI	1354	1132	809	792	1173	754	1732	1074	630	1557	630	1002	589	867	1000	90	381	434	445	1010	1042	371	374	1497	569	1282	980	1163	272	830	1163	565	1786	724	2055	390	622	1475		336	1011	1054	564	1015	879	969	875	509	1258	849	1817	551	1176	2062	914	840	1953	379	1437	1285	2118	2170	1045	1990	1712	1260	788	763
Minneapolis, MN	1225	1009	1127	1112	838	1072	1461	1396	643	1475	946	1323	902	1180	865	408	703	756	766	928	913	242	696	1377	235	1152	1304	1171	591	1040	1474	436	1656	815	1925	710	831	1791	336		1224	1367	881	1223	1204	1295	788	372	1573	1171	1687	874	1492	1727	1227	575	1818	563	1308	1205	1986	2040	1374	1655	1377	1578	1110	634
Mobile, AL	1234	949	328	1003	1874	258	2236	1427	620	821	1166	602	816	571	1504	917	721	973	826	589	1414	998	978	1215	1451	1657	1328	468	733	188	403	850	1808	449	2014	620	382	719	1011	1224		1497	447	144	1202	887	791	1038	497	1101	1643	1000	1523	2661	737	1557	2255	645	1936	662	1936	2320	502	2727	2478	509	965	894
Montpelier, VT	2203	1919	1165	498	2207	1247	2636	179	1417	2268	428	1068	813	928	1899	954	855	611	747	1824	1942	1270	718	2347	1601	2184	198	1914	921	1482	1245	1405	2688	1506	2957	962	1369	1587	1054	1367	1497		1160	1589	306	668	1662	1408	1387	405	2666	612	220	3061	800	1871	2854	1166	2336	2096	3018	3071	1113	3025	2746	1440	538	1597
Montréal, QC	2129	1845	1218	548	2099	1299	2523	310	1342	2311	393	1118	822	980	1790	847	824	578	714	1722	1832	1163	560	2261	1496	2072	328	1884	847	1517	1294	1330	2576	1451	2845	931	1314	1646	938	1262	1549	133	1105	1640	381	717	1588	1302	1436	454	2591	603	258	2948	850	1766	2743	1092	2228	1998	2912	2960	1162	2916	2638	1490	587	1529
Nashville, TN	1219	932	248	703	1586	192	1925	1099	464	1140	712	549	388	407	1192	469	273	525	378	664	1158	656	534	1300	1116	1397	1000	786	287	414	596	555	1792	348	2006	174	212	913	564	881	447	1160		532	884	688	677	747	683	802	1682	560	1196	2357	542	1262	2151	310	1633	939	2030	2306	495	2404	2124	700	666	688
New Orleans, LA	1165	881	468	1124	1868	343	2216	1520	597	700	1248	742	908	712	1488	923	804	1057	910	519	1398	1008	1066	1095	1445	1638	1421	347	818	183	547	844	1739	425	1894	705	394	861	1015	1223	144	1589	532		1304	1026	722	1032	641	1222	1523	1090	1616	2642	878	1551	2186	675	1920	541	1816	2252	642	2716	2409	651	1087	880
New York, NY	2001	1716	882	192	2041	960	2465	207	1201	1981	395	768	530	641	1733	787	637	460	533	1548	1775	1105	613	2201	1438	2014	108	1632	707	1198	939	1196	2518	1230	2787	740	1094	1288	879	1204	1202	306	884	1304		370	1460	1245	1089	97	2463	369	304	2891	502	1708	2685	954	2170	1822	2809	2902	811	2858	2580	1138	228	1391
Norfolk, VA	1910	1632	558	228	2132	715	2525	569	1158	1716	569	437	403	328	1792	878	605	551	570	1350	1758	1196	704	1986	1529	1997	470	1362	720	948	613	1155	2486	1035	2707	649	898	950	969	1295	887	668	688	1026	370		1366	1335	755	270	2373	425	666	2962	183	1799	2744	911	2238	1557	2730	2973	481	2949	2671	808	189	1349
Oklahoma City, OK	542	256	844	1346	1203	699	1497	1678	323	738	1242	1160	1002	1084	720	792	846	1057	917	204	631	545	1029	660	875	870	1577	437	739	603	1160	348	1112	335	1326	759	466	1476	875	788	791	1662	677	722	1460	1366		452	1254	1384	1005	1100	1775	1922	1218	857	1563	496	1200	468	1351	1627	1092	1948	1710	1270	1343	158
Omaha, NE	863	647	992	1153	845	939	1225	1436	402	1192	987	1293	943	1151	492	470	722	797	792	656	534	137	736	1004	420	774	1345	898	613	852	1343	187	1278	574	1546	699	641	1658	509	372	1038	1408	747	1032	1245	1335	452		1436	1212	1325	914	1533	1650	1266	525	1445	439	930	920	1613	1662	1239	1663	1383	1445	1151	298
Orlando, FL	1730	1446	440	889	2275	534	2622	1288	1062	1319	1184	380	792	526	1885	1153	905	1043	954	1086	1851	1339	1144	1712	1807	2095	1189	965	968	683	141	1246	2303	925	2515	858	778	229	1258	1573	497	1387	683	641	1089	755	1254	1436		986	2145	975	1385	3048	597	1956	2841	999	2323	1160	2436	2816	280	3093	2814	84	849	1365
Philadelphia, PA	1924	1640	780	98	2011	880	2435	306	1138	1900	388	668	466	539	1703	757	571	428	468	1467	1732	1074	583	2102	1405	1975	207	1547	643	1115	844	1127	2480	1150	2713	676	1014	1180	849	1171	1101	405	802	1222	97	270	1384	1212	986		2387	304	402	2861	399	1675	2656	888	2140	1742	2738	2873	703	2828	2550	1040	137	1319
Phoenix, AZ	462	746	1844	2349	1210	1700	914	2681	1326	1259	2245	2165	2005	2088	1008	1795	1849	2060	1920	1066	908	1445	2032	424	1780	571	2580	1178	1742	1466	2050	1246	285	1340	370	1762	1471	2362	1817	1687	1643	2666	1682	1523	2463	2373	1005	1325	2145	2387		2104	2778	1332	2224	1305	733	1499	653	985	352	749	2091	1414	1381	2153	2348	1053
Pittsburgh, PA	1641	1357	684	246	1713	748	2137	570	851	1708	216	654	225	446	1405	459	288	131	184	1221	1447	777	285	1774	1107	1686	469	1354	359	971	825	840	2190	905	2428	388	768	1173	551	874	1000	612	560	1090	369	425	1100	914	975	304	2104		666	2563	499	1378	2357	604	1842	1495	2452	2574	697	2530	2252	1023	244	1035
Portland, ME	2315	2031	1192	496	2333	1274	2761	110	1529	2294	553	1066	840	938	2024	1079	967	736	859	1861	2067	1395	825	2455	1726	2309	197	1940	1034	1509	1243	1518	2813	1543	3082	1074	1408	1585	1176	1492	1523	220	1196	1616	304	666	1775	1533	1385	402	2778	666		3186	798	1996	2979	1279	2461	2136	3143	3196	1111	3150	2871	1438	535	1710
Portland, OR	1363	1669	2603	2804	891	2551	428	3086	2013	2354	2639	2904	2554	2761	1161	2118	2369	2446	2439	2128	1256	1786	2385	1630	1497	1046	2992	2356	2260	2473	2954	1797	1022	2211	963	2310	2245	3260	2062	1727	2661	3061	2357	2642	2891	2962	1922	1650	3048	2861	1332	2563	3186		2897	1214	578	2050	765	2076	1083	635	2844	172	351	3064	2800	1764
Québec, QC	2283	1999	1372	694	2257	1455	2681	396	1497	2472	552	1264	979	1134	1948	1004	979	735	870	1876	1991	1320	715	2416	1650	2230	427	2123	1001	1676	1440	1484	2734	1606	3003	1086	1470	1792	1096	1417	1703	259	1262	1795	524	863	1742	1457	1582	600	2745	760	275	3107	996	1921	2901	1246	2386	2152	3067	3119	1308	3074	2795	1636	733	1683
Raleigh, NC	1761	1474	408	302	2067	555	2444	702	1003	1556	637	278	322	168	1712	816	521	572	486	1191	1678	1107	677	1826	1460	1917	602	1202	628	789	449	1074	2334	889	2548	568	753	797	914	1227	737	800	542	878	502	183	1218	1266	597	399	2224	499	798	2897		1735	2690	830	2172	1397	2551	2847	322	2885	2605	648	262	1227
Rapid City, SD	843	714	1508	1616	323	1456	942	1900	920	1515	1450	1811	1410	1670	298	912	1208	1260	1270	1061	397	626	1200	1110	550	639	1808	1291	1100	1371	1860	704	1039	1093	1312	1214	1160	2173	840	575	1557	1871	1262	1551	1708	1799	857	525	1956	1675	1305	1378	1996	1214	1735		1167	959	649	1242	1372	1384	1756	1141	862	1960	1615	699
Regina, SK	1284	1253	1904	1882	472	1850	1092	2090	1321	2046	1721	2066	1674	1937	740	1151	1445	1503	1510	1510	838	1016	1441	1551	513	1080	2080	1753	1337	1805	2220	1104	1443	1525	1712	1454	1594	2570	1078	743	2009	1914	1659	1985	1994	2037	1307	927	2348	1946	1682	1619	2039	1120	2002	532	1428	1360	1024	1774	1773	1645	2117	1046	767	2360	1878	1149
Reno, NV	1019	1304	2396	2599	956	2262	422	2881	1806	1998	2433	2698	2342	2555	956	1913	2163	2240	2234	1668	1051	1581	2180	1166	1564	799	2786	1904	2056	2067	2748	1591	447	1898	470	2104	2029	3063	1953	1818	2255	2854	2151	2186	2685	2744	1563	1445	2841	2656	733	2357	2979	578	2690	1167		1844	518	1720	558	217	2644	720	793	2857	2595	1558
Saint Louis, MO	1037	752	555	829	1278	501	1622	1182	249	1177	746	856	506	714	888	296	348	560	421	630	854	354	533	1157	841	1095	1080	784	243	491	906	250	1600	345	1821	263	283	1221	379	563	645	1166	310	675	954	911	496	439	999	888	1499	604	1279	2050	830	959	1844		1326	906	1845	2061	802	2096	1817	1008	827	442
Salt Lake City, UT	599	883	1878	2081	552	1826	339	2365	1288	1589	1915	2180	1829	2037	437	1398	1647	1725	1718	1403	533	1065	1664	866	1160	283	2271	1634	1541	1749	2229	1073	419	1488	688	1586	1524	2544	1437	1308	1936	2336	1633	1920	2170	2238	1200	930	2323	2140	653	1842	2461	765	2172	649	518	1326		1311	750	735	2125	839	720	2339	2079	1042
San Antonio, TX	712	510	986	1642	1480	861	1651	2039	708	274	1654	1300	1324	1230	1025	1202	1210	1457	1314	276	935	960	1439	554	1343	1092	1940	197	1149	635	1066	766	1272	594	1357	1111	727	1379	1285	1205	662	2096	939	541	1822	1557	468	920	1160	1742	985	1495	2136	2076	1397	1242	1720	906	1311		1278	1736	1161	2150	2018	1170	1606	625
San Diego, CA	810	1097	2138	2695	1301	1994	958	3046	1675	1552	2596	2459	2354	2381	1162	2080	2196	2407	2269	1359	1077	1747	2346	718	1908	835	2930	1472	2089	1759	2343	1597	331	1676	120	2109	1819	2656	2118	1986	1936	3018	2030	1816	2809	2730	1351	1613	2436	2738	352	2452	3143	1083	2551	1372	558	1845	750	1278		501	2356	1256	1468	2447	2693	1401
San Francisco, CA	1086	1370	2472	2816	1173	2327	639	3098	1950	2010	2650	2789	2564	2712	1172	2130	2380	2458	2451	1734	1268	1798	2397	1175	1781	968	3004	1929	2273	2133	2723	1808	569	1963	380	2321	2095	3038	2170	2040	2320	3071	2306	2252	2902	2973	1627	1662	2816	2873	749	2574	3196	635	2847	1384	217	2061	735	1736	501		2720	807	874	2832	2812	1775
Sault Ste. Marie, ON	1777	1493	1040	852	1273	1014	1893	923	991	1918	514	1156	683	947	1411	471	577	496	521	1370	1428	710	347	1910	665	1692	904	1527	540	1180	1333	951	2196	1089	2465	649	972	1685	398	538	1268	740	823	1355	921	1037	1236	850	1475	911	2240	614	871	2165	1007	1118	2364	740	1848	1646	2502	2581	1201	2090	1812	1492	851	1150
Savannah, GA	1634	1350	247	605	2078	393	2418	1014	900	1320	909	106	514	251	1687	951	664	764	680	996	1651	1150	870	1632	1609	1890	915	971	770	580	135	1048	2206	763	2422	658	626	483	1045	1374	502	1113	495	642	811	481	1092	1239	280	703	2091	697	1111	2844	322	1756	2644	802	2125	1161	2356	2720		2896	2616	333	575	1202
Seattle, WA	1438	1743	2649	2770	818	2597	503	3054	2059	2428	2604	2950	2560	2808	1225	2063	2363	2414	2424	2193	1320	1764	2353	1705	1424	1121	2960	2431	2253	2537	3000	1844	1128	2275	1134	2357	2299	3315	1990	1655	2727	3025	2404	2716	2858	2949	1948	1663	3093	2828	1414	2530	3150	172	2885	1141	720	2096	839	2150	1256	807	2896		278	3109	2768	1828
Shenandoah N.P., VA	1794	1488	556	119	1951	634	2399	519	1016	1655	382	516	260	317	1650	698	474	368	389	1223	1614	1014	523	1863	1345	1855	420	1306	563	872	687	1012	2359	904	2582	506	768	1035	798	1111	886	618	558	978	320	181	1233	1155	847	217	2238	245	616	2824	263	1615	2604	768	2107	1496	2586	2842	567	2769	2490	885	82	1207
Spokane, WA	1320	1505	2369	2491	540	2318	425	2774	1780	2296	2325	2671	2281	2528	993	1785	2084	2135	2144	1964	1091	1484	2075	1587	1147	1002	2682	2192	1973	2229	2720	1564	1138	1948	1215	2077	2018	3035	1712	1377	2478	2746	2124	2409	2580	2671	1710	1383	2814	2550	1381	2252	2871	351	2605	862	793	1817	720	2018	1468	874	2616	278		2830	2490	1600
Tampa, FL	1746	1462	451	942	2291	537	2638	1342	1078	1329	1235	433	840	578	1901	1166	916	1091	1007	1102	1860	1354	1178	1728	1813	2099	1242	980	984	699	198	1252	2319	941	2525	872	779	255	1260	1578	509	1440	700	651	1138	808	1270	1445	84	1040	2153	1023	1438	3064	648	1960	2857	1008	2339	1170	2447	2832	333	3109	2830		902	1381
Thunder Bay, ON	1566	1348	1376	1288	1049	1322	1670	1298	983	1830	942	1570	1118	1382	1210	656	949	932	957	1270	1253	583	784	1718	441	1492	1305	1522	840	1361	1728	776	1996	1156	2265	957	1153	2041	585	341	1547	1121	1130	1545	1349	1473	1127	720	1822	1339	2028	1049	1246	1938	1443	913	2006	870	1648	1547	2326	2224	1613	1866	1588	1828	1286	974
Toronto, ON	1800	1516	963	472	1771	968	2194	548	1014	1919	98	964	535	756	1462	519	493	290	426	1393	1504	834	232	1932	1167	1744	490	1551	518	1186	1135	1001	2247	1120	2517	601	983	1483	609	933	1222	465	774	1306	489	669	1259	974	1284	497	2262	316	592	2620	737	1438	2414	763	1899	1669	2583	2632	1007	2588	2310	1333	482	1188
Tucson, AZ	449	735	1732	2320	1326	1588	1030	2669	1314	1145	2233	2052	1994	1975	995	1784	1836	2048	1908	952	895	1433	2020	312	1769	687	2569	1066	1728	1353	1936	1234	401	1271	485	1749	1406	2250	1805	1675	1530	2654	1617	1410	2448	2303	990	1313	2029	2383	116	2092	2766	1447	2142	1293	848	1485	776	871	407	864	1949	1529	1496	2040	2283	1040
Vancouver, BC	1574	1878	2785	2906	953	2733	638	3188	2195	2564	2740	3086	2696	2944	1372	2198	2499	2548	2560	2338	1465	1900	2487	1841	1559	1256	3094	2565	2389	2675	3136	1980	1264	2421	1275	2493	2437	3451	2125	1790	2894	2982	2540	2851	2993	3084	2083	1799	3229	2963	1550	2665	3286	313	3021	1277	890	2232	973	2286	1398	947	3032	141	413	3245	2903	1973
Washington, DC	1885	1600	637	39	1951	744	2375	439	1078	1765	382	530	362	398	1642	697	512	367	407	1332	1671	1014	522	1966	1344	1914	340	1411	582	980	706	1066	2428	1014	2670	606	879	1044	788	1110	965	538	666	1087	228	189	1343	1151	849	137	2348	244	535	2800	262	1615	2595	827	2079	1606	2693	2812	575	2768	2490	902		1258
Wichita, KS	591	382	955	1260	1064	810	1338	1613	292	896	1176	1272	945	1092	608	724	779	992	851	361	519	391	964	730	685	759	1512	595	674	707	1272	193	1164	446	1377	701	577	1587	763	634	894	1597	688	880	1391	1349	158	298	1365	1319	1053	1035	1710	1764	1227	699	1558	442	1042	625	1401	1775	1202	1828	1600	1381	1258	
Winnipeg, MB	1538	1222	1582	1570	723	1532	1345	1729	1033	1834	1403	1779	1360	1638	1006	864	1158	1214	1222	1298	1092	699	1153	1590	222	1334	1760	1541	1049	1484	1932	817	1692	1208	1965	1164	1273	2252	791	456	1721	1552	1336	1664	1659	1749	1095	640	2029	1629	2000	1331	1677	1474	1684	745	1684	1062	1277	1562	2025	1912	1829	1401	1121	2047	1568	905
Yellowstone N.P., WY	963	977	1904	2145	175	1852	418	2410	1316	1813	1960	2207	1906	2076	469	1418	1710	1772	1787	1436	563	1094	1710	1229	782	632	2315	1664	1602	1826	2256	1100	769	1519	1037	1611	1624	2569	1345	1016	2014	2381	1658	1950	2213	2314	1182	958	2356	2182	1002	1892	2506	833	2178	497	755	1356	351	1535	1098	972	2151	760	481	2356	2142	1072
Yosemite N.P., CA	989	1289	2391	2695	1129	2246	594	2979	1868	1939	2529	2708	2403	2619	1051	2012	2264	2339	2335	1636	1045	1680	2279	1104	1735	802	2888	1858	2155	2052	2642	1649	415	1870	308	2159	2009	2957	2051	1922	2239	2950	2212	2162	2802	2811	1533	1547	2735	2754	678	2457	3075	751	2762	1263	214	1899	615	1665	429	189	2639	923	967	2751	2695	1564

Mileages in this chart are based upon the routes usually followed by motorists. Highway systems include interstate, U.S., and state highways.

RAND McNALLY®

2024

Road Atlas

Maps

Maps

Indexes

Photo credits:
Table of contents: ©Camille Van Den Heuvel/ EyeEm / Getty; p. ii (clockwise from top) ©Jupiter Images / Getty, ©pidjoe / Getty, ©Rand McNally, ©Stockbyte / Getty; p. iii (t) ©H. Armstron Roberts / Alamy, (middle l) ©Charles Phelps Cushing / Alamy, (middle r) ©Oliver Strewe / Image Bank / Getty, (bottom l) ©Kurt Hutton / Stringer / Getty, (bottom r) ©Rand McNally; p. iv (t to b) ©Archive Holdings Inc / Getty, ©Circa Images / Alamy, ©tomekbudujedomek / Getty, ©miroslav_1 / istockphoto / Getty, ©H. Armstrong Roberts / Alamy; p. v (clockwise from top l) ©H. Armstrong Roberts / Alamy, ©Matthew Richardson / Alamy, B Christopher / Alamy, ©kenmo / istockphoto / Getty, ©Rand McNally; p. vi (clockwise from upper l) ©Chris Wilson / Alamy, ©Kaarsten / istockphoto / Getty, ©Nigel Boulton / Alamy, ©Matthew Richardson / Alamy, ©Murat Turner / The Image Bank / Getty, ©Rand McNally; p.vii (t to b) ©Anjar Suwarno / Getty (2), ©Baxternator / Getty, ©csfotoimages / istockphoto / Getty, ©Cindy Giovagnoli / Getty; p. 5 ©Blazen Images / Getty; p. 7 ©skiserge 1 / Getty; p. 9 ©Mimi Ditchie Photography / Getty; p. 11 ©Wesley Hitt / Getty; p. 13 ©Mariusz Blach / Getty; p. 15 ©Matteo Colombo / Getty; p. 16 ©ETham Photo / Getty; p. 17 ©Santa Barbara Conference & Visitors Bureau and Film Commission/J. Sinclair; p. 18 ©Rand McNally; p. 19 ©Sitnic Sofia / EyeEm / Getty; p. 21 ©Michael Russell / Getty; p. 22 ©Shutter18 / Getty; p. 25 ©Buena Vista Images / Getty; p. 27 ©Damocean / Getty; p. 29 ©Sean Pavone / Getty; p. 33 ©Ron Thomas / Getty; p. 34 ©City of Chicago/Hedrich Blessing; p. 35 ©The Children's Museum of Indianapolis; p. 37 ©Stevegeer / Getty; p. 39 ©Teddi Yaeger Photography / Getty; p. 41 ©Shoemcfly / Getty; p. 43 ©Kentucky Tourism; p. 47 ©Remsberg Inc. / Design Pics / Getty; p. 49 ©Gregobagel / Getty; p. 51 ©ehrlif / Getty; p. 52 ©Robert J. Eovaldi; p.53 ©Walker Art Center; p. 55 ©Wildnerdpix / Getty; p. 57 ©MO Div. of Tourism; p. 59 ©Eric Bowers Photo / Getty; p. 61 ©Matt Anderson / Getty; p. 63 ©zrf photo / Getty; p. 67 ©Aneese / Getty; p. 71 ©Getty; p. 72 ©Photodisc; p. 73 ©Getty; p. 75 ©NC Div of Tourism Film & Sports Dev.; p. 76 ©tonda / Getty; p. 79 ©Drnadig / Getty; p. 81 ©Holly Hildreth / Getty; p. 83 ©Getty; p. 85 ©zschnepf / Getty; p. 87 ©zrfphoto / Getty; p. 89 ©GPTMC; p. 90 ©f11photo / Getty; p. 95 ©FangXiaNuo / Getty; p. 96 ©Kingsport CVB; p. 97 ©S. Greg Panosian / Getty; p. 99 ©eric foltz / Getty; p. 101 ©ejesposito / Getty; p. 103 ©Getty; p. 105 ©wmay / Getty; p.107 ©Pam Susemiehl / Getty; p. 109 ©Christopher Kimmel / Getty; p. 110 ©Rene Frederick / Getty; p. 113 ©Kenosha Area CVB; p. 116 ©Wisconsin Dept. of Tourism; p. 123 ©Benedek / Getty; p. 125 ©Posnov / Getty.

Quick Map References

State & Province Maps

Selected City Maps

This list contains only 70 of more than 350 detailed city maps in the Road Atlas. To find more city maps, consult the state & province map list to the left and turn to the pages indicated.

National Park System Maps

If you have a comment, suggestion, or even a compliment, please visit us at randmcnally.com/tellrand.

Published and printed in U.S.A.

1 2 3 WR 24 23

Capital: Washington, G-17
Land area: 3,532,316 sq. mi.

Selected National Park Service locations

- Acadia National Park C-20
- Arches National Park G-6
- Badlands National Park E-9
- Big Bend National Park L-8
- Biscayne National Park M-18
- Bryce Canyon National Park. G-5
- Canyonlands National Park G-6
- Capitol Reef National Park. G-5
- Carlsbad Caverns National Park. J-7
- Channel Islands National Park H-1
- Congaree National Park. I-17
- Crater Lake National Park D-2
- Cuyahoga Valley National Park F-16
- Death Valley National Park G-3
- Denali National Park. L-4
- Dry Tortugas National Park M-17
- Everglades National Park. M-17
- Glacier Bay National Park. M-6
- Glen Canyon Nat'l Recreation Area . . G-
- Grand Canyon National Park. . . . . . . .H-
- Grand Teton National Park . . . . E-
- Great Sand Dunes Nat'l Park & Pres. . H-
- Great Smoky Mountains Nat'l Park. . H-1
- Guadalupe Mountains Nat'l Park . . . . J-

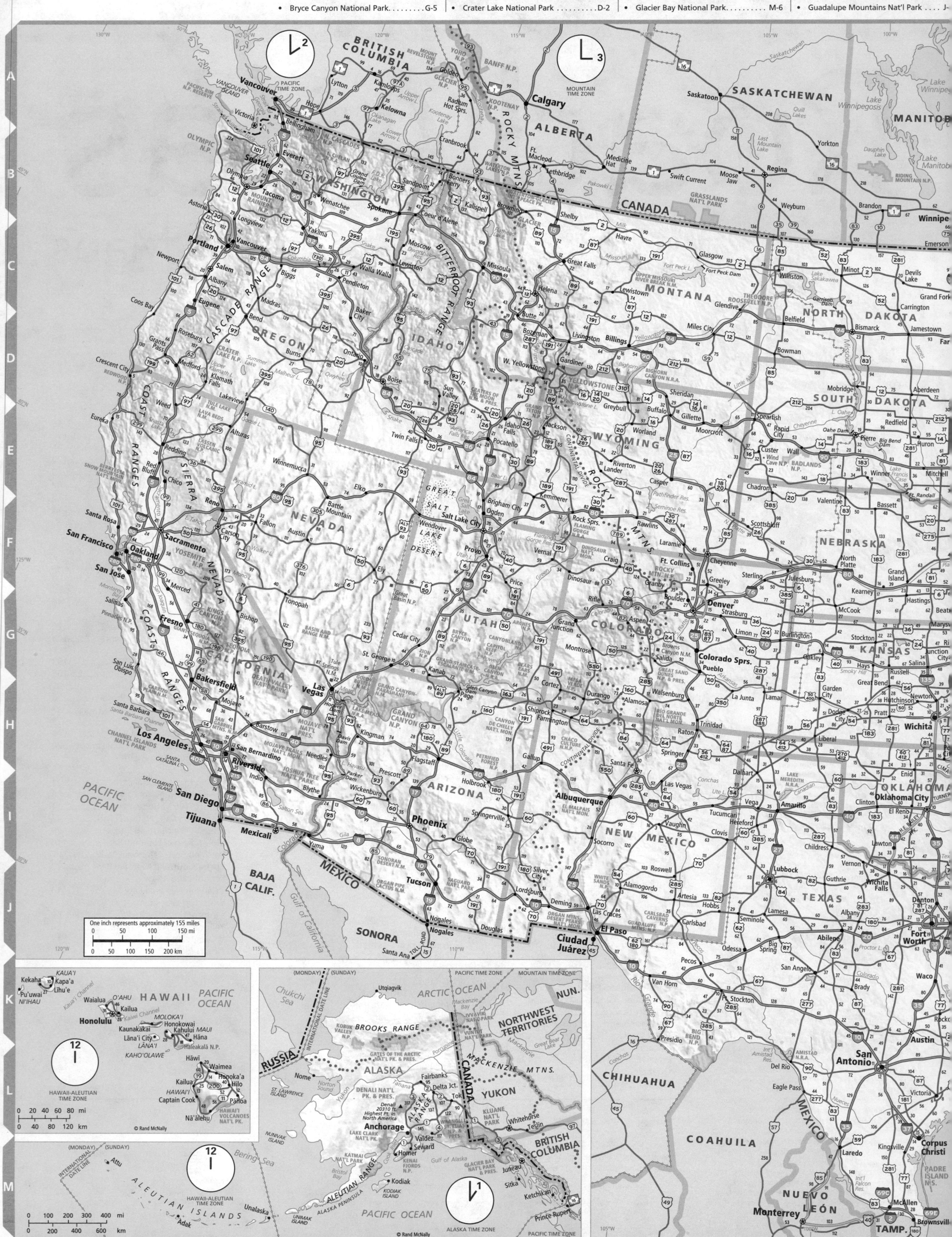

Population: 334,735,155
Largest city: New York, 8,804,190, E-18

Selected National Park Service locations

Haleakalā National Park............L-2	• Lassen Volcanic National Park.......E-2	• Petrified Forest National Park.......I-5	• Voyageurs National Park..........C-12
Hawai'i Volcanoes National Park L-2	• Mammoth Cave National Park H-14	• Redwood National Park............D-1	• Waterton-Glacier Int'l Peace Park....B-5
Hot Springs National Park I-12	• Mesa Verde National Park..........H-6	• Rocky Mountain National Park F-7	• Wind Cave National Park........... E-8
Isle Royale National Park C-13	• Mount Rainier National Park........B-3	• Sequoia National Park G-2	• Yellowstone National Park D-6
Kings Canyon National Park G-2	• North Cascades National Park.......B-4	• Shenandoah National Park G-17	• Yosemite National Park F-2
Lake Mead Nat'l Recreation Area....H-4	• Olympic National Park B-3	• Theodore Roosevelt National Park...D-8	• Zion National Park G-5

Alabama

Nickname: The Heart of Dixie
Capital: Montgomery, J-8
Land area: 50,633 sq. mi. (rank: 28th)
Population: 5,024,279 (rank: 24th)
Largest city: Huntsville, 215,006, B-7

Index of places Pg. 129

Travel planning & on-the-road resources

Tourism Information
Alabama Tourism Dept.: (800) 252-2262, (334) 242-4169; alabama.travel

Road Conditions & Construction
(888) 588-2848; algotraffic.com, www.dot.state.al.us

Toll Road Information
No tolls on state or federal highways

Determining distances along roads

Highway distances (segments of one mile or less not shown):
Cumulative miles (red): the distance between red arrows
Intermediate miles (black): the distance between intersections & plac

Interchanges and exit numbers
For most states, the mileage between interchanges may be determine by subtracting one number from the other.

Huntsville

Florence

Tennessee Pg. 94

Georgia Pg. 28

Mississippi Pg. 56

Mileages between cities	Andalusia	Anniston	Auburn	Birmingham	Chattanooga, TN	Columbus, GA	Dothan	Florence	Gadsden	Grove Hill	Huntsville	Meridian, MS	Mobile	Montgomery	Selma	Tuscaloosa
Atlanta, GA	252	90	108	146	117	106	206	263	119	294	181	289	328	160	210	201
Birmingham	181	64	109		146	141	196	118	61	155	102	146	258	90	87	58
Chattanooga, TN	322	119	221	146		219	319	166	89	300	102	291	399	232	228	203
Dothan	74	207	118	196	319	99		311	252	169	294	253	196	103	148	210
Huntsville	279	104	210	102	102	243	294	64	72	254		244	356	189	188	155
Mobile	123	280	222	258	399	256	196	376	313	82	356	133		168	159	203
Montgomery	91	110	54	90	232	87	103	205	148	134	189	153	168		50	104
Tuscaloosa	194	118	159	58	203	192	210	123	118	121	155	93	203	104	75	

Total mileages through Alabama

- I-10: 66 miles
- I-59: 241 miles
- I-20: 215 miles
- I-65: 367 miles

More mileages at randmcnally.com/MC

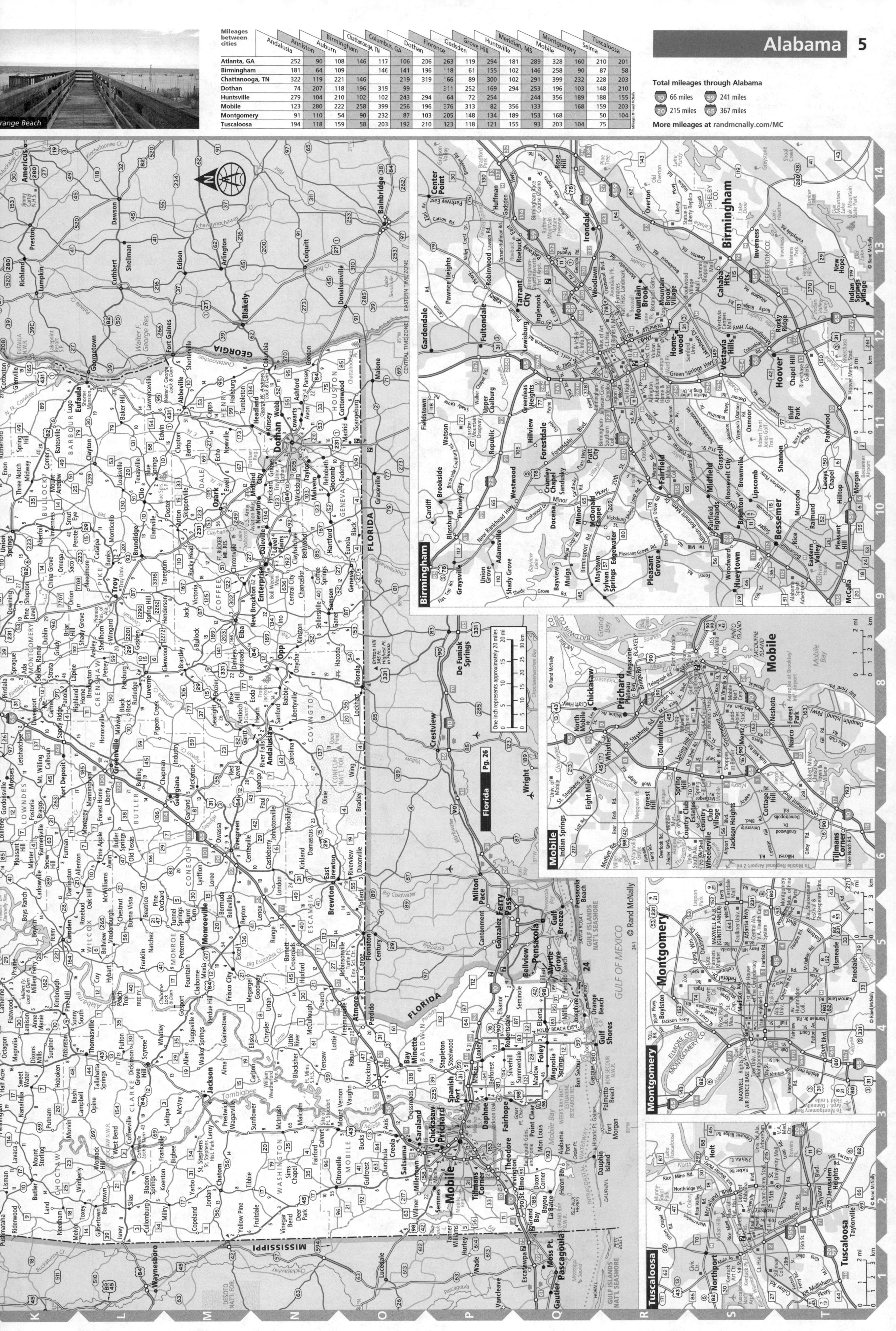

Alaska

Nickname: The Last Frontier
Capital: Juneau, H-12
Land area: 570,866 sq. mi. (rank: 1st)
Population: 733,391 (rank: 48th)
Largest city: Anchorage, 291,247, G-7

Index of places Pg. 129

Mileages between cities

	Anchorage	Denali N.P.	Fairbanks	Haines	Homer	Prince Rupert, BC	Tok	Valdez
Anchorage		236	358	756	221	1557	317	297
Fairbanks	358	122		640	578	1441	202	362
Haines	756	762	640		975	919	438	691
Homer	221	457	578	975		1776	537	277
Kenai	157	393	514	911	83	1713	473	213
Seward	126	362	483	880	168	1682	442	182
Tok	317	324	202	438	537	1240		252
Valdez	297	346	362	691	277	1493	252	

Total mileages through Alaska

① 408 miles ③ 325 miles
② 202 miles

More mileages at randmcnally.com/MC

Travel planning & on-the-road resources

Tourism Information
Alaska Travel Industry Association: www.travelalaska.com

Road Conditions & Construction
511, (866) 282-7577
dot.state.ak.us

Toll Road Information
Anton Anderson Memorial Tunnel: (907) 566-2244
dot.alaska.gov/creg/whittiertunnel/tolls.shtml

Determining Distances
(segments one mile or less not shown)
Cumulative miles (red): the distance between red arrows
Intermediate miles (black): the distance between intersections & places

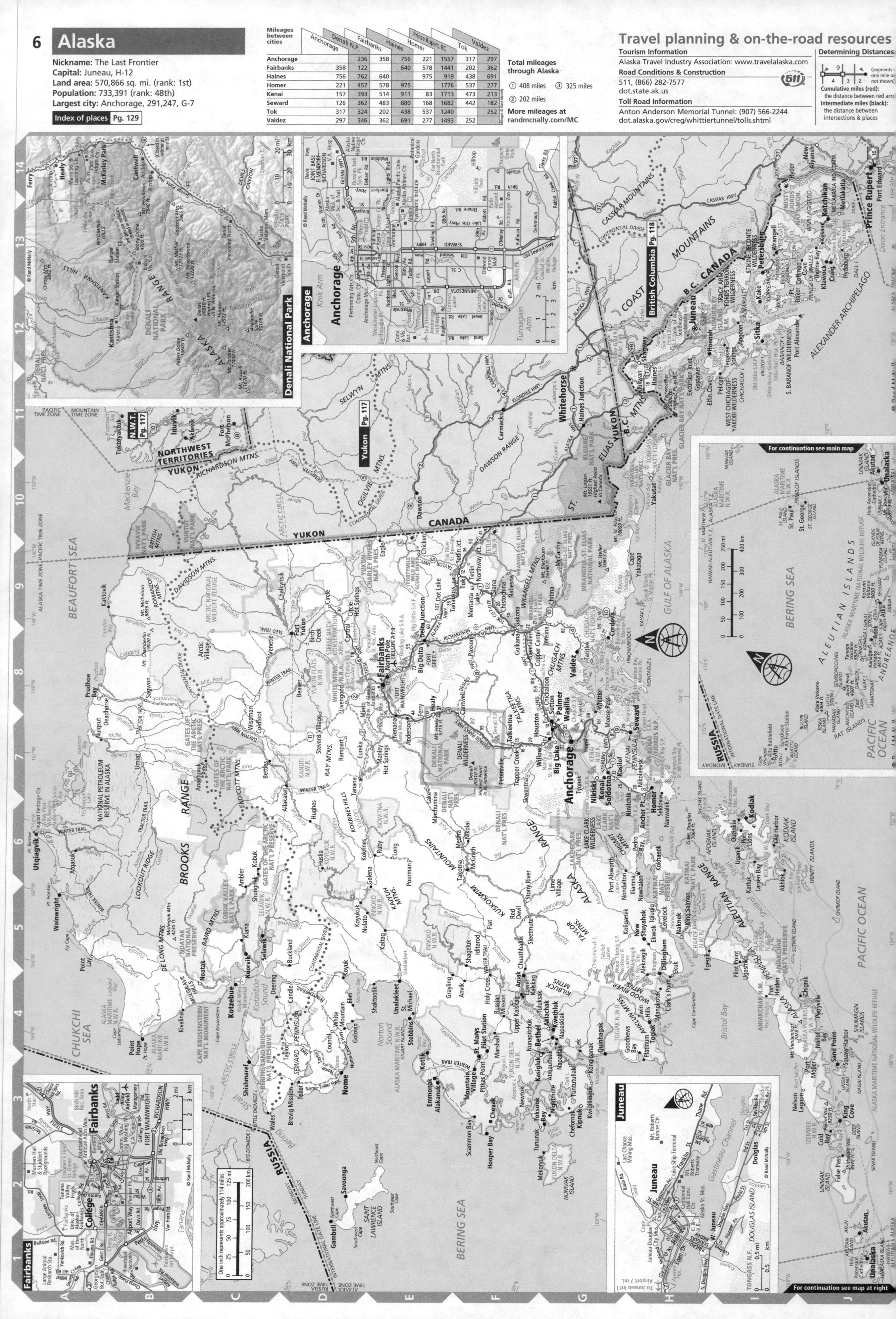

Havasu Falls

Sights to see

- Arizona Historical Society Sanguinetti House Museum, Yuma. L-6
- Arizona Museum of Natural History, Mesa. J-7
- Arizona Science Center, Phoenix M-3
- Arizona State Capitol, Phoenix M-1
- Heard Museum, Phoenix. L-2
- Painted Desert Inn Museum, Petrified Forest N.P. L-9
- Phoenix Art Museum, Phoenix. L-2
- Taliesin West, Scottsdale. H-7
- Tusayan Ruin and Museum, Grand Canyon N.P. D-9
- Yavapai Point Overlook, Grand Canyon N.P. B-1
- Yuma Territorial Prison State Historic Park, Yuma. L-6

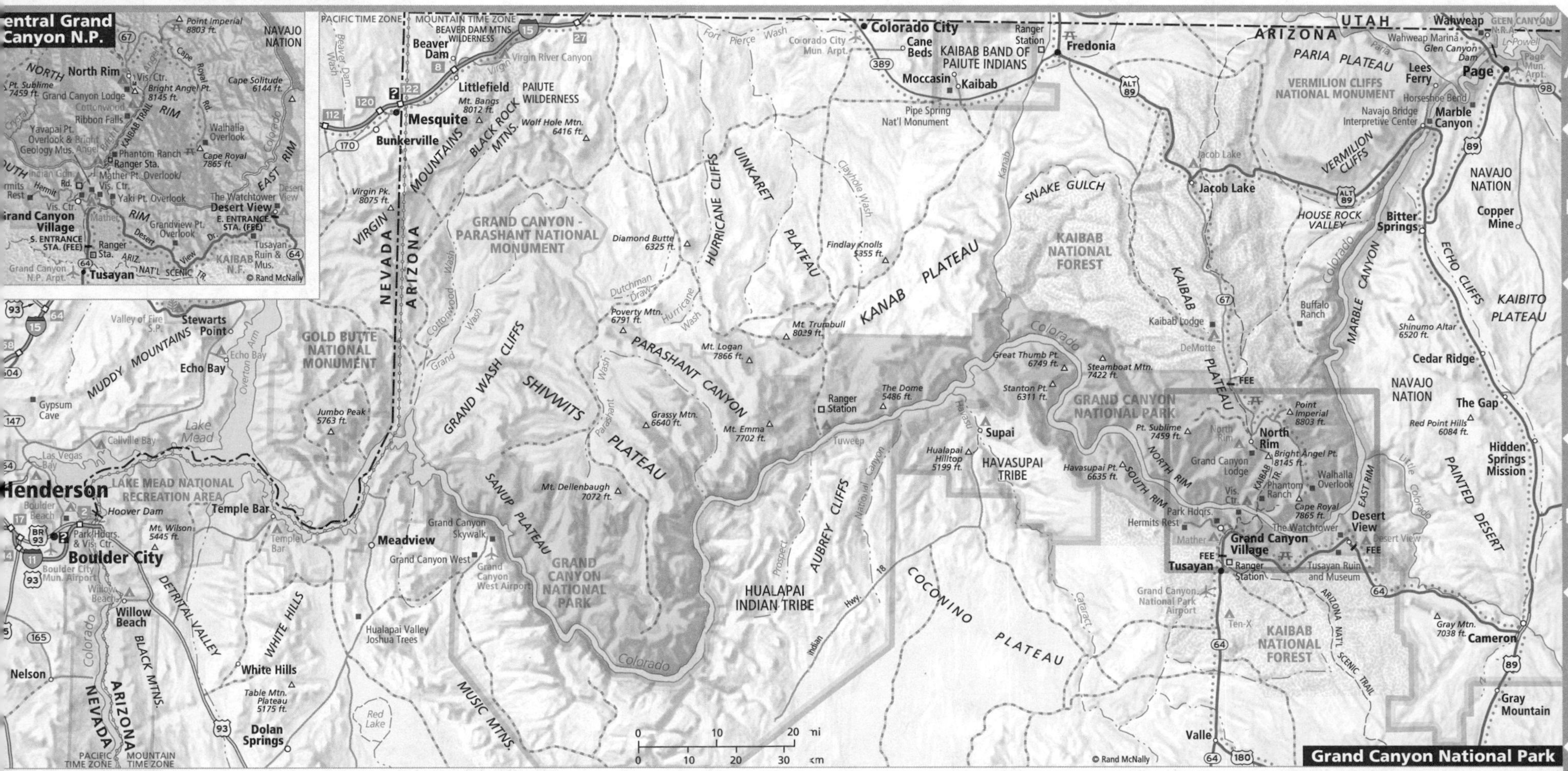

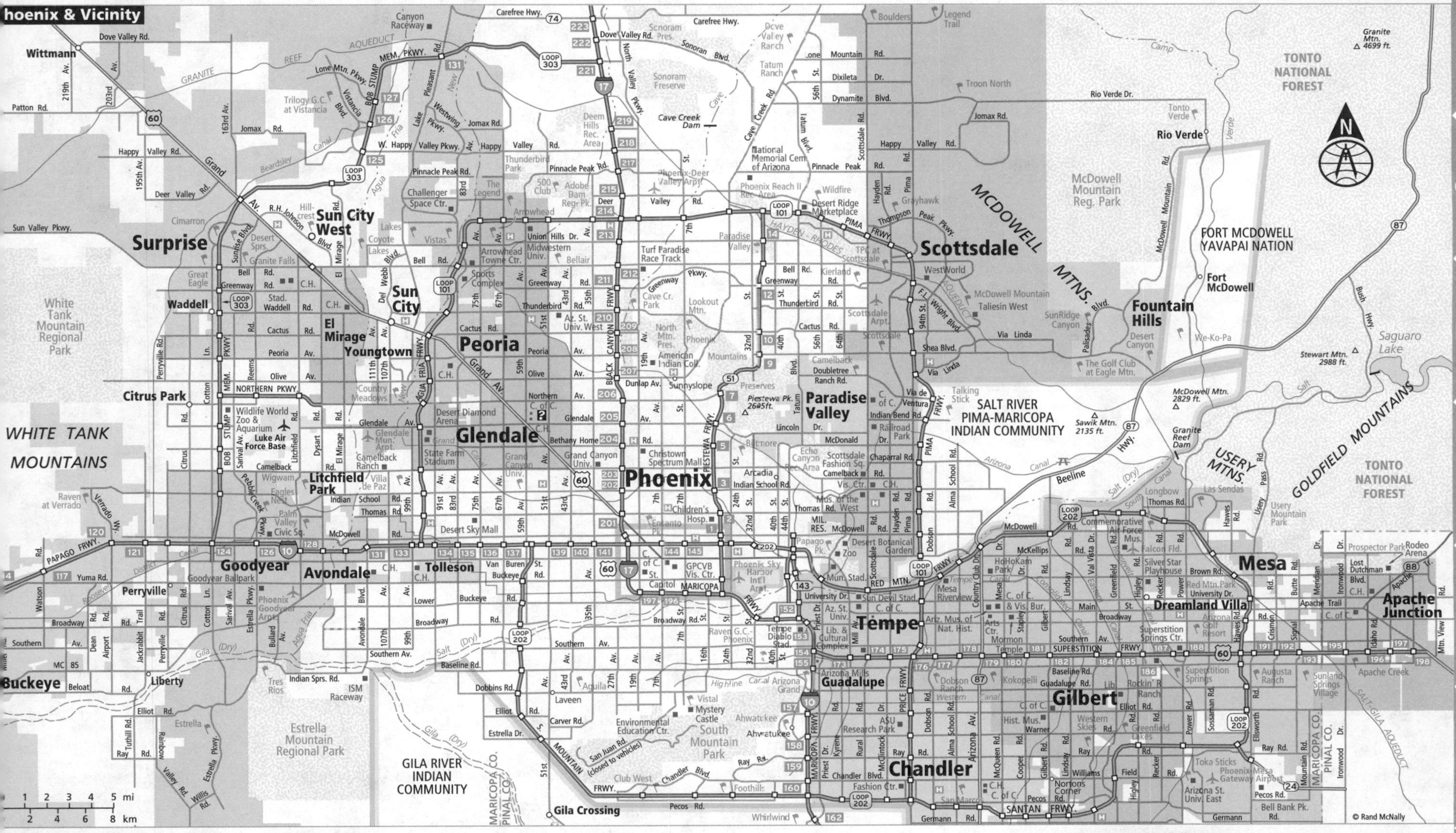

Central Grand Canyon N.P.

Grand Canyon National Park

Phoenix & Vicinity

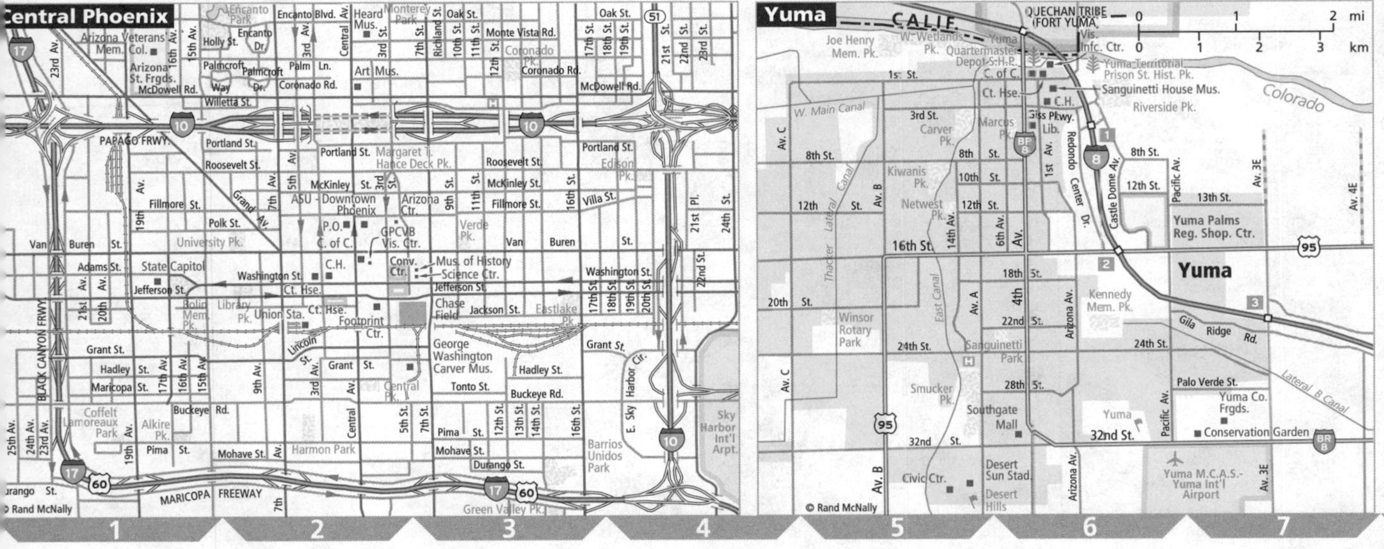

Arizona

Nickname: The Grand Canyon State
Capital: Phoenix, J-7
Land area: 113,623 sq. mi. (rank: 6th)
Population: 7,151,502 (rank: 14th)
Largest city: Phoenix, 1,608,139, J-7

Index of places Pg. 129

Travel planning & on-the-road resources

Tourism Information
Arizona Office of Tourism: (866) 275-5816, (602) 364-3700; www.visitarizona.com

Road Conditions & Construction
511, (888) 411-7623; www.az511.com, azdot.gov

Toll Road Information
No toll on state or federal highways

Determining distances along roads

Highway distances (segments of one mile or less not shown):
Cumulative miles (red): the distance between red arrows
Intermediate miles (black): the distance between intersections & places

Interchanges and exit numbers
For most states, the mileage between interchanges may be determined by subtracting one number from the other.

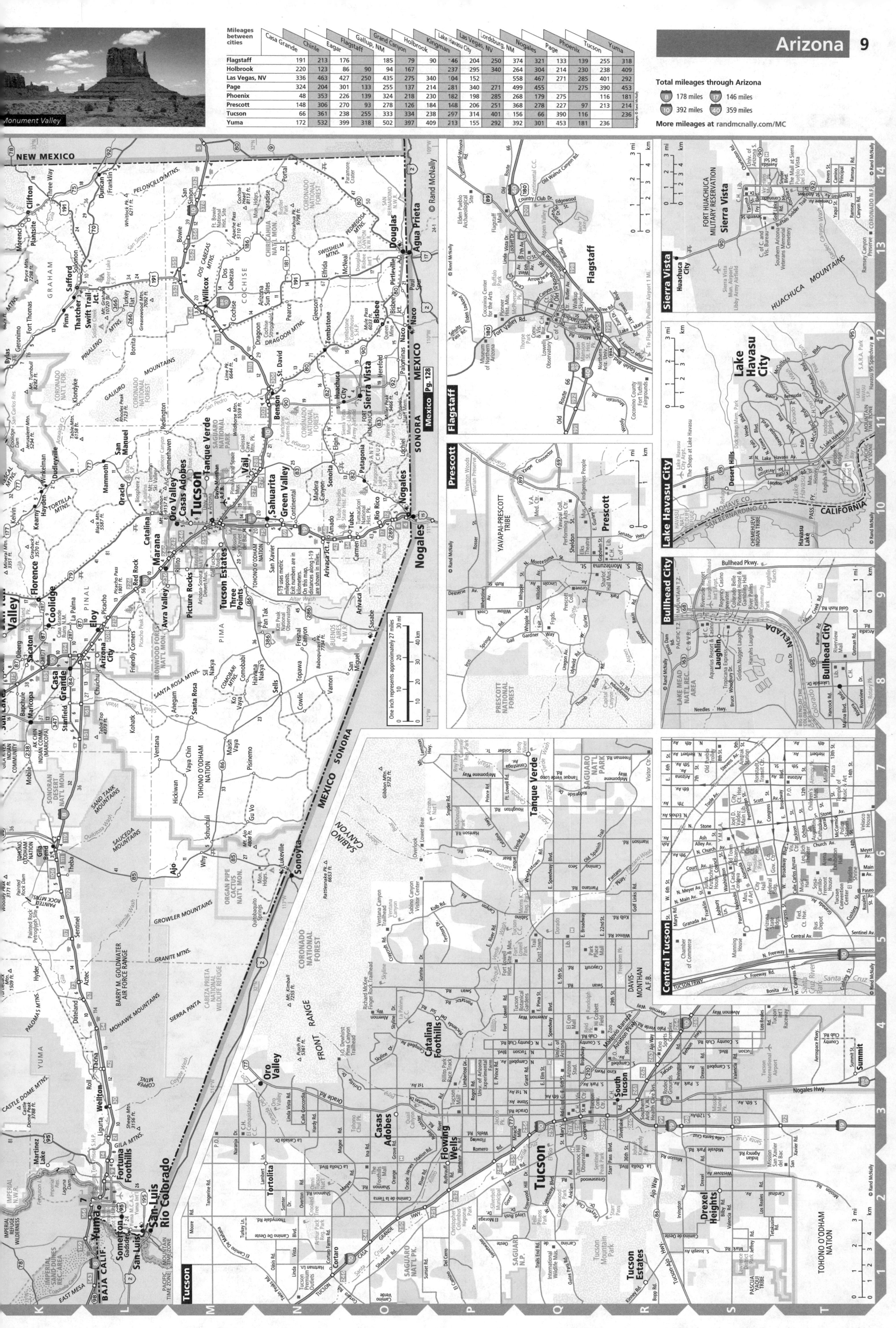

Mileages between cities	Casa Grande	Chinle	Eagar	Flagstaff	Gallup, NM	Grand Canyon	Holbrook	Kingman	Lake Havasu City	Las Vegas, NV	Lordsburg, NM	Nogales	Page	Phoenix	Tucson	Yuma
Flagstaff	191	213	176		185	79	90	146	204	250	374	321	133	139	255	318
Holbrook	220	123	86	90	94	167		237	295	340	264	304	214	230	238	409
Las Vegas, NV	336	463	427	250	435	275	340	104	152		558	467	271	285	401	292
Page	324	204	301	133	255	137	214	281	340	271	499	455		275	390	453
Phoenix	48	353	226	139	324	218	230	182	198	285	268	179	275		116	181
Prescott	148	306	270	93	278	126	184	148	206	251	368	278	227	97	213	214
Tucson	66	361	238	255	333	334	238	297	314	401	156	66	390	116		236
Yuma	172	532	399	318	502	397	409	213	155	292	392	301	453	181	236	

Total mileages through Arizona

- I-8: 178 miles
- I-17: 146 miles
- I-10: 392 miles
- I-40: 359 miles

More mileages at randmcnally.com/MC

Arkansas

Nickname: The Natural State
Capital: Little Rock, G-7
Land area: 52,024 sq. mi. (rank: 27th)
Population: 3,011,524 (rank: 33rd)
Largest city: Little Rock, 202,591, G-7

Index of places Pg. 129

Travel planning & on-the-road resources

Tourism Information
Arkansas State Tourism: (800) 628-8725, (501) 682-7777; www.arkansas.com

Road Conditions & Construction
(501) 569-2374; www.idrivearkansas.com, www.ardot.gov

Toll Road Information
No tolls on state or federal highways

Determining distances along roads

Highway distances (segments of one mile or less not shown):
Cumulative miles (red): the distance between red arrows
Intermediate miles (black): the distance between intersections & places

Interchanges and exit numbers
For most states, the mileage between interchanges may be determined by subtracting one number from the other.

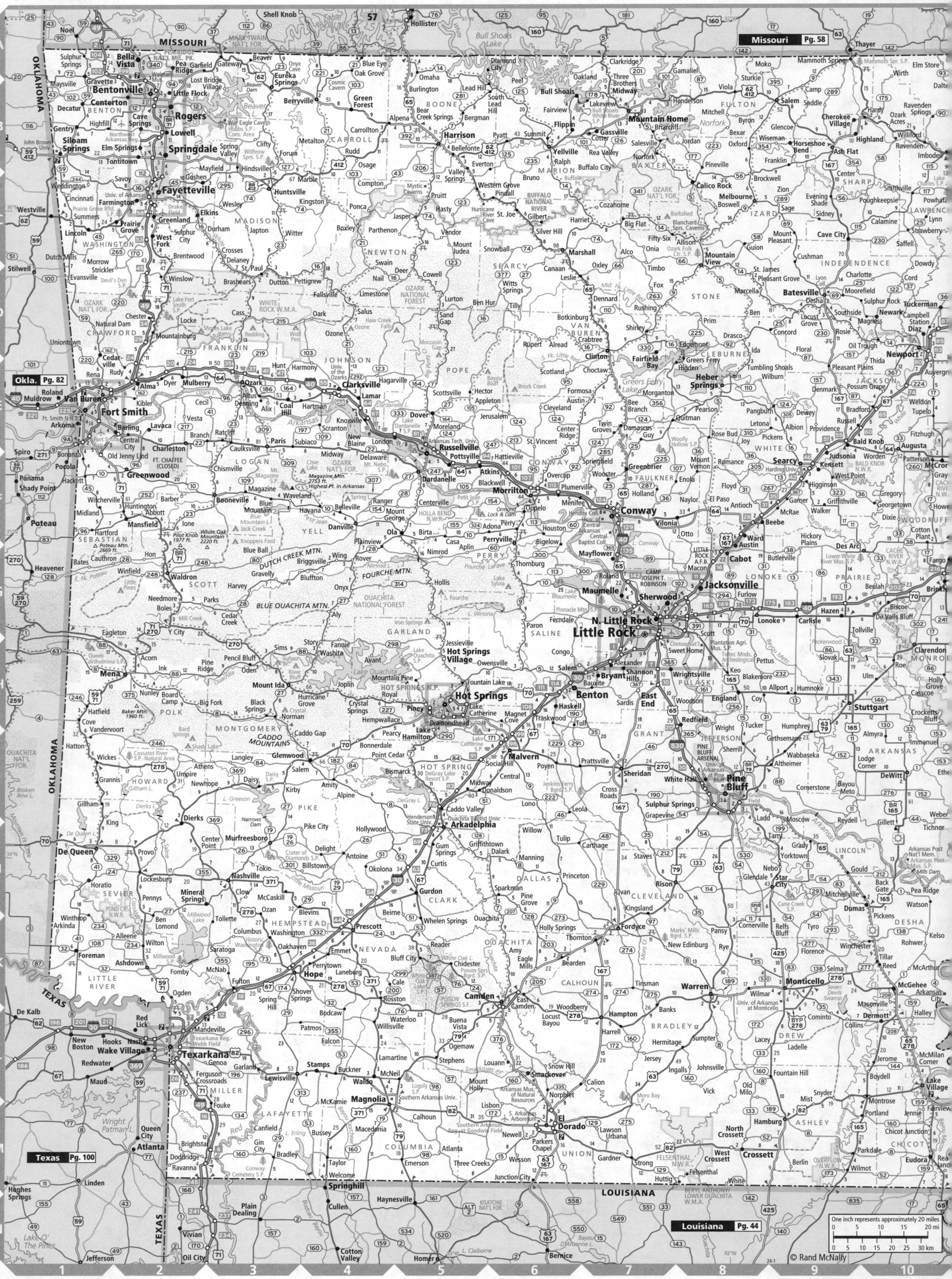

Missouri Pg. 58
Okla. Pg. 82
Texas Pg. 100
Louisiana Pg. 44

One inch represents approximately 20 miles

Mileages between cities	Batesville	Branson, MO	DeQueen	El Dorado	Fayetteville	Fort Smith	Greenville, MS	Hot Springs	Jonesboro	Little Rock	Memphis, TN	Mountain Home	Pine Bluff	Rogers	Russellville	Texarkana
El Dorado	209	287	141		304	227	109	121	245	118	250	268	91	325	190	88
Fayetteville	251	98	184	304		58	335	184	250	188	318	123	231	24	115	236
Fort Smith	219	158	130	227	58		304	130	261	158	286	187	199	81	84	182
Jonesboro	68	203	272	245	250	261	219	182		130	70	126	171	253	173	270
Little Rock	94	172	143	118	188	158	147	54	130		137	151	43	208	74	142
Memphis, TN	119	274	278	250	318	286	152	188	70	137		195	152	339	204	276
Mountain Home	78	83	287	268	123	187	298	198	126	151	195		194	126	125	287
Texarkana	234	306	54	88	236	182	198	110	270	142	276	287	152	258	209	

Total mileages through Arkansas

- 30: 143 miles
- 40: 284 miles
- 55: 72 miles
- 65: 309 miles

More mileages at randmcnally.com/MC

Jonesboro

Pine Bluff

Hot Springs/ Hot Springs National Park

Fayetteville / Springdale / Rogers

Fort Smith

Little Rock

Texarkana

Tenn. Pg. 94

Mississippi Pg. 56

Nickname: The Golden State
Capital: Sacramento, NK-7
Land area: 155,813 sq. mi. (rank: 3rd)
Population: 39,538,223 (rank: 1st)
Largest city: Los Angeles, 3,898,747, SJ-11

Index of places Pg. 129

Travel planning & on-the-road resources

Tourism Information
Visit California: (916) 444-4429; www.visitcalifornia.com

Toll Bridge Information
Golden Gate Bridge (San Francisco Bay area) *(FasTrak)*: (415) 921-5858, (415) 486-8655; www.goldengate.org
Bay Area Toll Authority (all other San Francisco Bay area bridges) *(FasTrak)*: (415) 778-6700, (415) 778-6757; mtc.ca.gov

Road Conditions & Construction
(800) 427-7623, (916) 654-2852; roads.dot.ca.gov, dot.ca.gov
Eastern Sierras/Bishop area: 511

Inland Empire region:	511, (877) 694-3511; go511.com
Los Angeles metro area:	511, (877) 224-6511; go511.com
Sacramento region:	511, sacregion511.org
San Diego area:	511, (855) 467-3511; www.511sd.com
San Francisco Bay area:	511, (888) 500-4636; 511.org
San Luis Obispo area:	511, (866) 928-8923

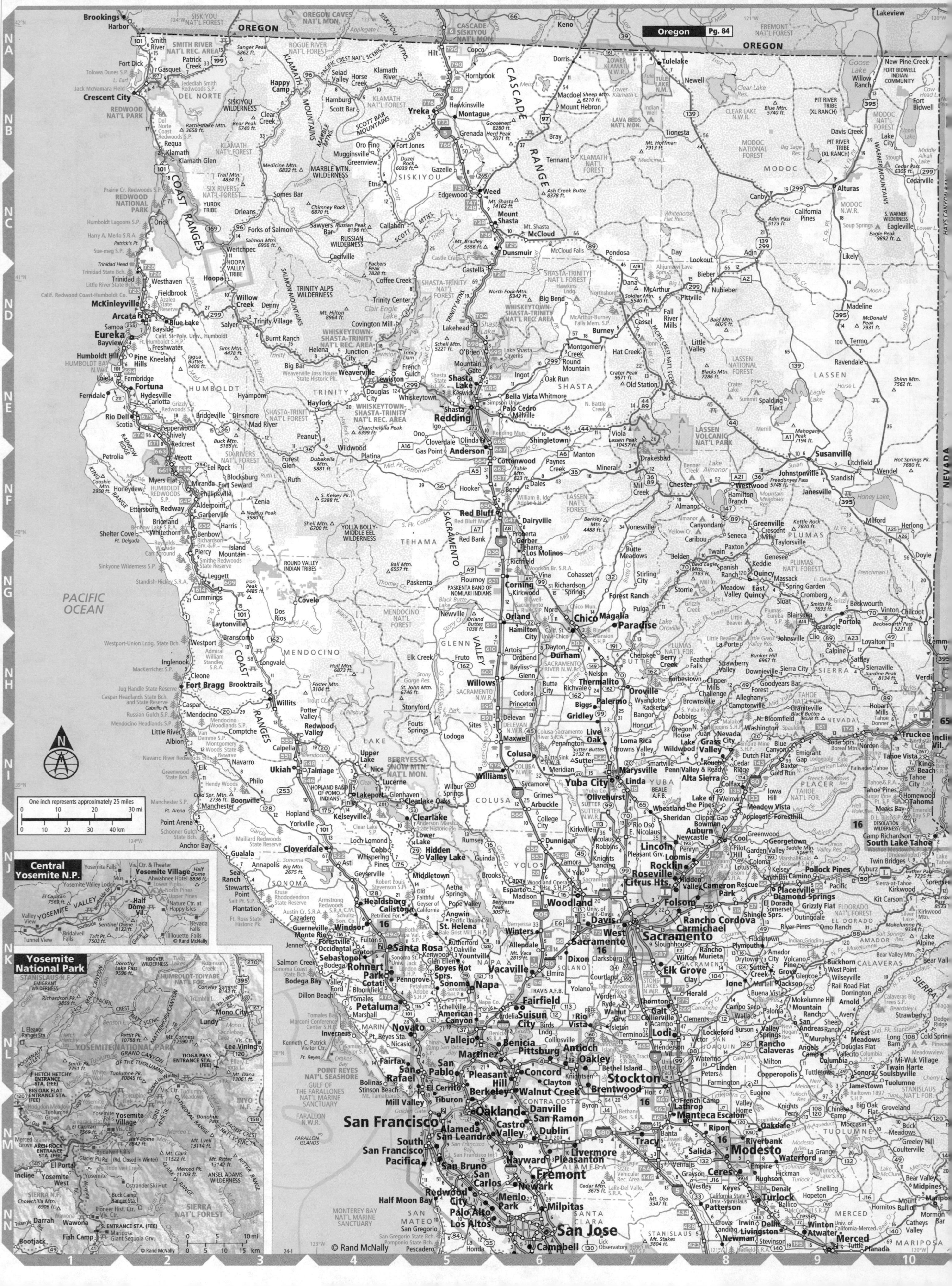

Oregon Pg. 84
OREGON
NEVADA
PACIFIC OCEAN
Central Yosemite N.P.
Yosemite National Park
One inch represents approximately 25 miles
San Francisco
Sacramento
San Jose
Oakland
Redding
Eureka
Stockton
Modesto
© Rand McNally

Mileages between cities	Bishop	Crescent City	Los Angeles	Oroville	Redding	Sacramento	San Francisco	San Jose	Santa Rosa	S. Lake Tahoe	Stockton	Susanville	Ukiah	Vallejo	Yosemite N.P.	Yreka
Alturas	371	280	648	225	144	302	357	385	365	228	349	103	330	329	392	176
Bishop		614	265	326	400	269	295	290	364	176	224	286	418	328	138	454
Eureka	546	81	644	222	146	289	272	315	217	392	325	259	158	262	454	198
Redding	400	208	544	94		161	216	244	198	264	209	112	188	187	332	98
Sacramento	269	372	383	68	161		87	115	95	100	47	217	145	58	160	257
San Francisco	295	355	380	150	216	87		45	55	187	82	303	115	30	189	312
San Jose	290	396	340	178	244	115	45		96	215	74	330	156	64	182	340
S. Lake Tahoe	176	472	445	157	264	100	187	215	195		147	143	248	159	189	311

Total mileages through California
5 797 miles 101 791 miles
80 199 miles

More mileages at randmcnally.com/MC

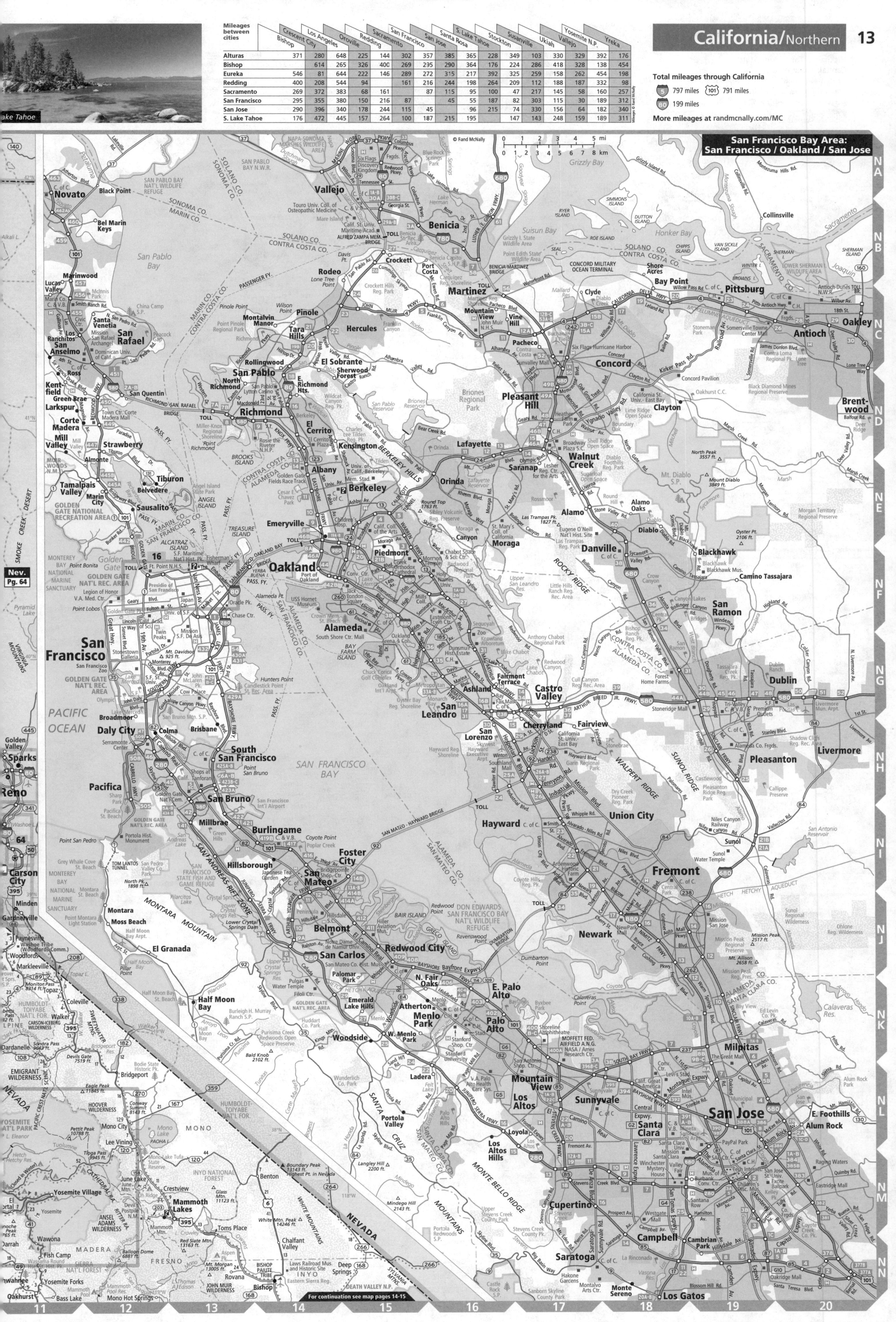

For continuation see map pages 14-15

Nickname: The Golden State
Capital: Sacramento, NK-7
Land area: 155,813 sq. mi. (rank: 3rd)
Population: 39,538,223 (rank: 1st)
Largest city: Los Angeles, 3,898,747, SJ-11

Index of places Pg. 129

Travel planning & on-the-road resources

Tourism Information	Toll Road Information (FasTrak)	Road Conditions & Construction (511)
Visit California: (916) 444-4429 visitcalifornia.com	91ExpressLanes (Orange Co.): (800) 600-9191; www.91expresslanes.com I-15 (San Diego Co.): (888) 889-1515; 511sd.com Metro Express Lanes (Los Angeles Co.): (877) 812-0022; www.metroexpresslanes.net South Bay Expwy. (San Diego Co.): (619) 661-7070; www.myfastrak.511sd.com/en/ The Toll Roads of Orange Co.: (949) 727-4800; www.thetollroads.com	(800) 427-7623, (916) 654-2852; roads.dot.ca.gov, dot.ca.gov Eastern Sierras/Bishop area: 511 Inland Empire region: 511, (877) 694-3511; go511.com Los Angeles metro area: 511, (877) 224-6511; go511.com Sacramento region: 511, sacregion511.org San Diego area: 511, (855) 467-3511; www.511sd.com San Francisco Bay area: 511, (888) 500-4636; 511.org San Luis Obispo area: 511, (866) 928-8923

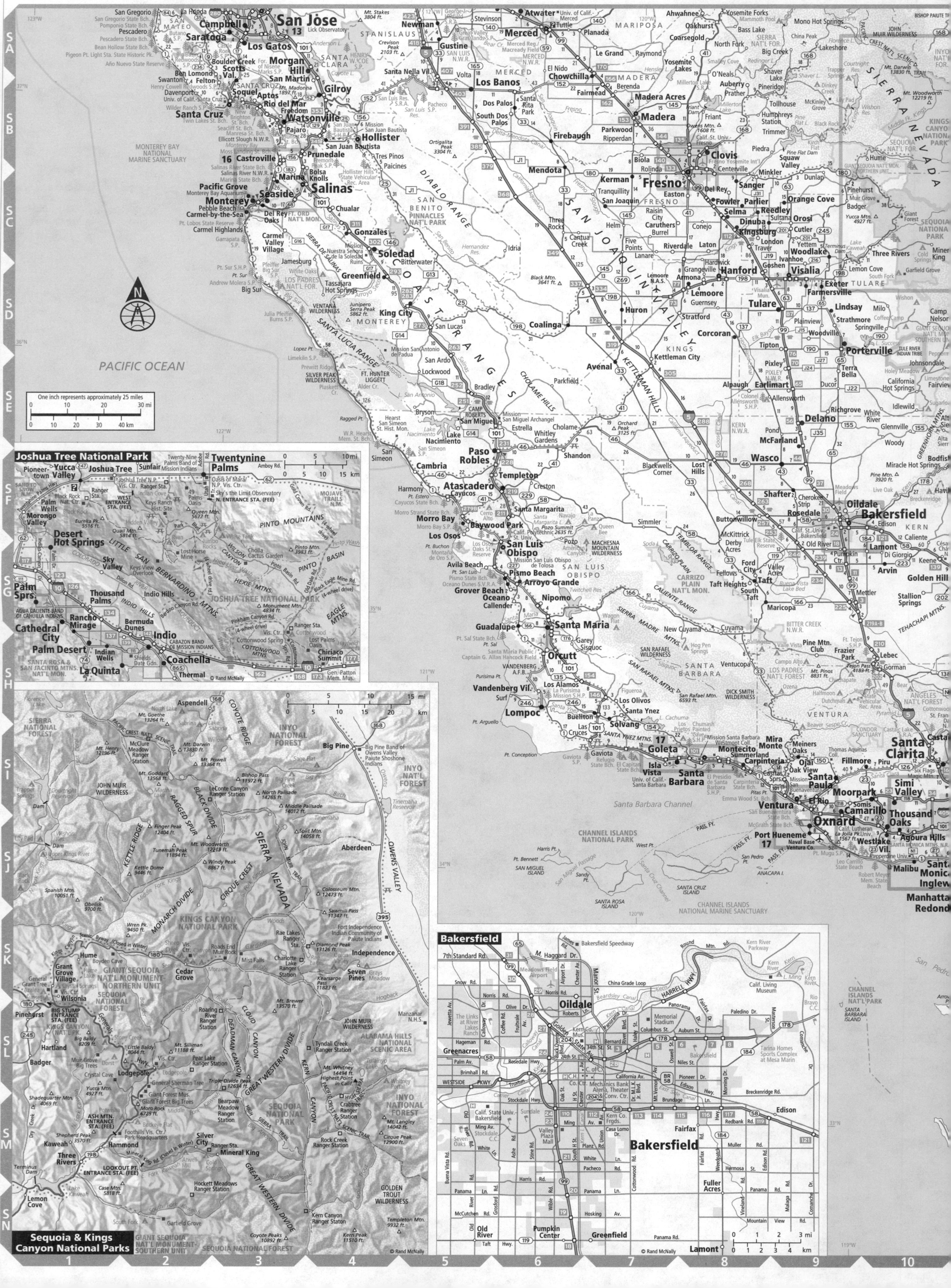

PACIFIC OCEAN

One inch represents approximately 25 miles

Joshua Tree National Park

Sequoia & Kings Canyon National Parks

Bakersfield

© Rand McNally

oshua Tree National Park

Mileages between cities	Bakersfield	Barstow	El Centro	Fresno	Las Vegas, NV	Los Angeles	Monterey	Needles	Palm Springs	Riverside	San Bernardino	San Diego	San Francisco	San Luis Obispo	Santa Barbara	Sequoia N.P.
Bakersfield		129	322	109	286	112	222	272	216	166	166	232	284	130	147	122
Fresno	109	239	429		395	218	150	381	323	271	273	339	183	130	254	77
Las Vegas, NV	286	156	312	395		270	507	110	278	234	225	331	569	415	358	410
Los Angeles	112	114	212	218	270		319	256	107	54	60	120	380	189	94	232
Monterey	222	350	530	150	507	319		494	424	372	373	439	112	142	237	226
Palm Springs	216	123	108	323	278	107	424	188		52	54	139	486	296	201	338
San Diego	232	176	113	339	331	120	439	317	139	97	106		501	313	214	352
Santa Barbara	147	203	306	254	358	94	237	345	201	148	150	214	325	94		268

Total mileages through California

- 5: 797 miles
- 10: 243 miles
- 15: 287 miles
- 40: 155 miles

More mileages at randmcnally.com/MC

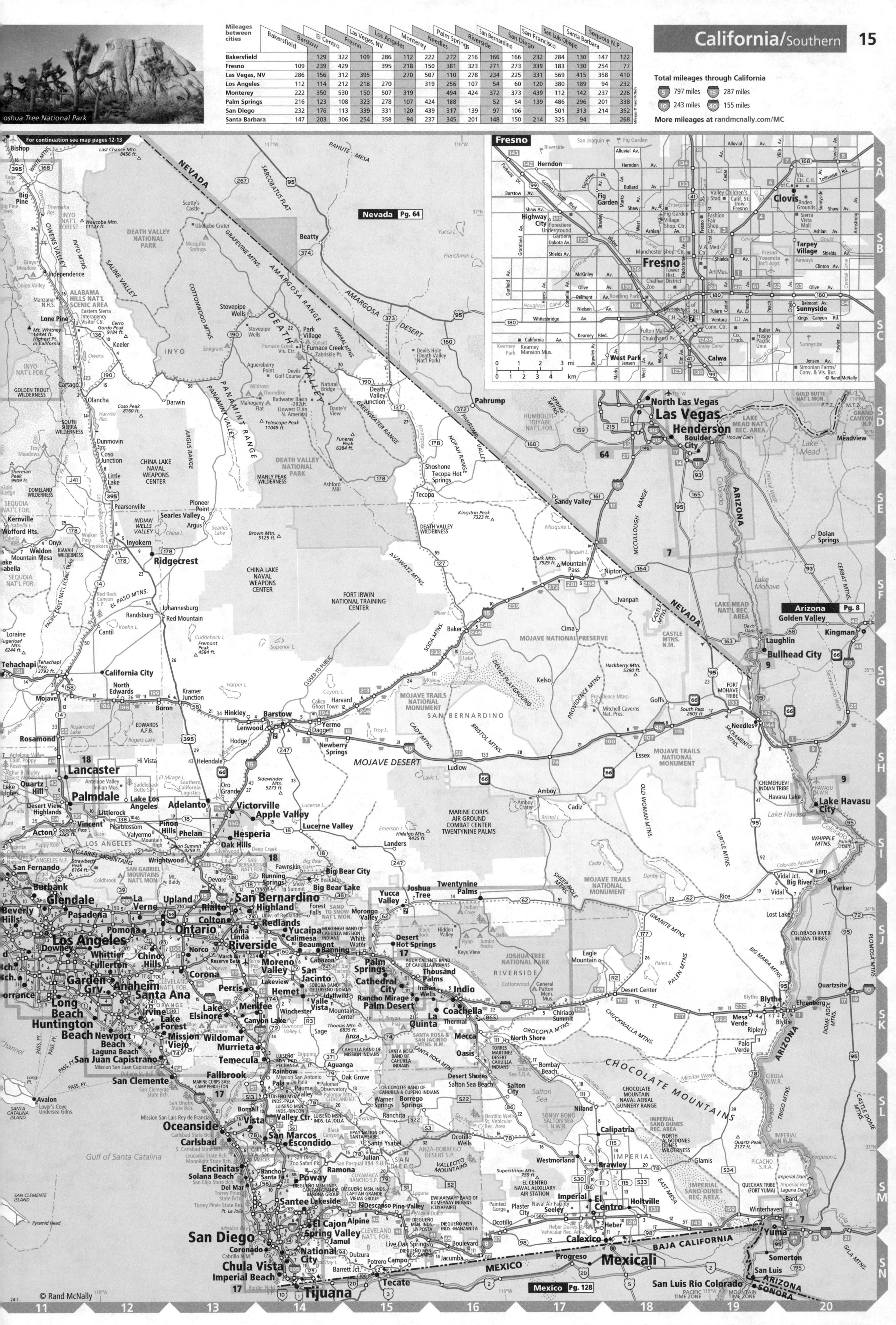

California/Northern cities

Sights to see

- California State Capitol, Sacramento I-6
- California State Railroad Museum, Sacramento H-6
- Chinatown, San Francisco C-8
- Coit Memorial Tower, San Francisco B-8
- Crocker Art Museum, Sacramento I-5
- Fisherman's Wharf, San Francisco A-7
- Ghirardelli Square, San Francisco B-7
- Golden Gate Bridge, San Francisco A-2
- Monterey Bay Aquarium, Monterey M-1
- Palisades Tahoe, Olympic Valley F-8
- Pier 39, San Francisco A-8
- San Francisco Cable Car Museum, San Francisco C-8

Santa Barbara harbor and coastline

Sights to see

- Balboa Park, San Diego K-10
- Birch Aquarium at Scripps Institute, San Diego G-1
- Cabrillo National Monument, San Diego K-1
- Gaslamp Quarter Historic District, San Diego........ M-9
- Legoland California, Carlsbad J-8
- The Living Desert Zoo and Gardens, Palm Desert ... G-10
- Museum of Contemporary Art, San Diego L-8
- Palm Springs Art Museum, Palm Springs............ E-7
- San Diego Air & Space Museum, San Diego K-9
- San Diego Zoo, San Diego J-3
- SeaWorld, San Diego............................ I-1
- Stearns Wharf, Santa Barbara B-5

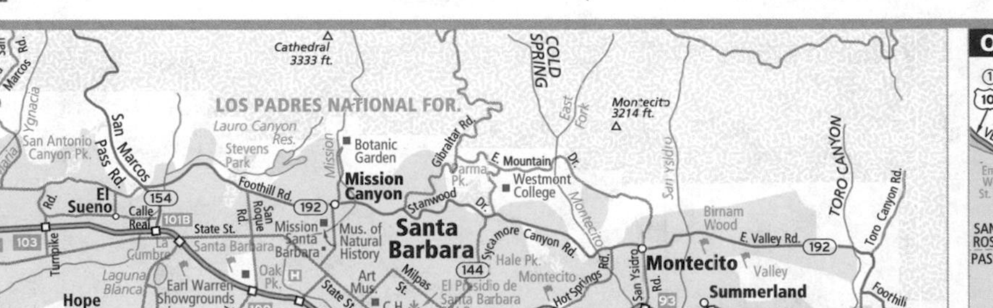

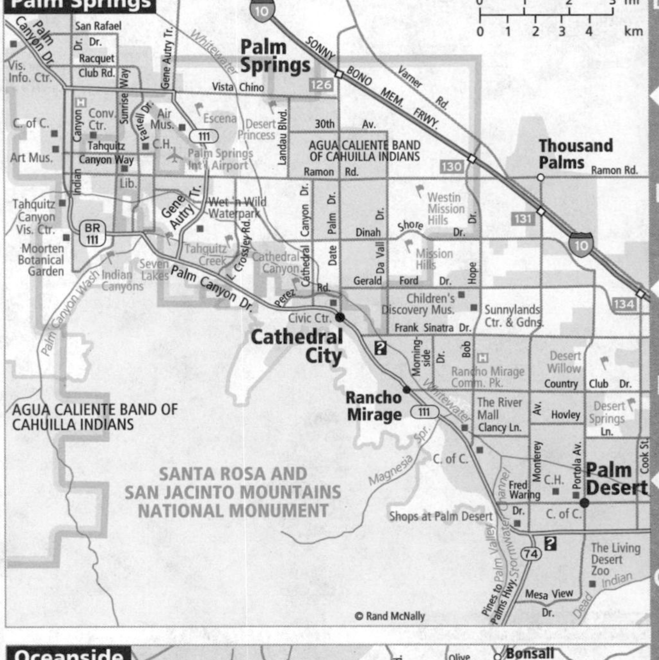

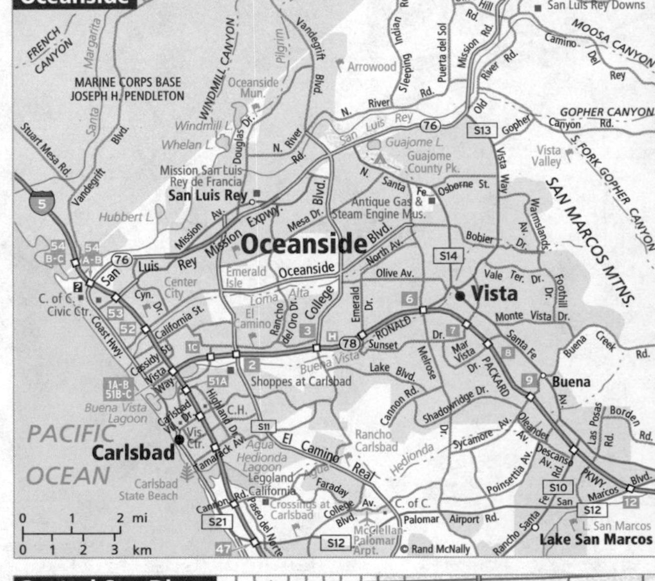

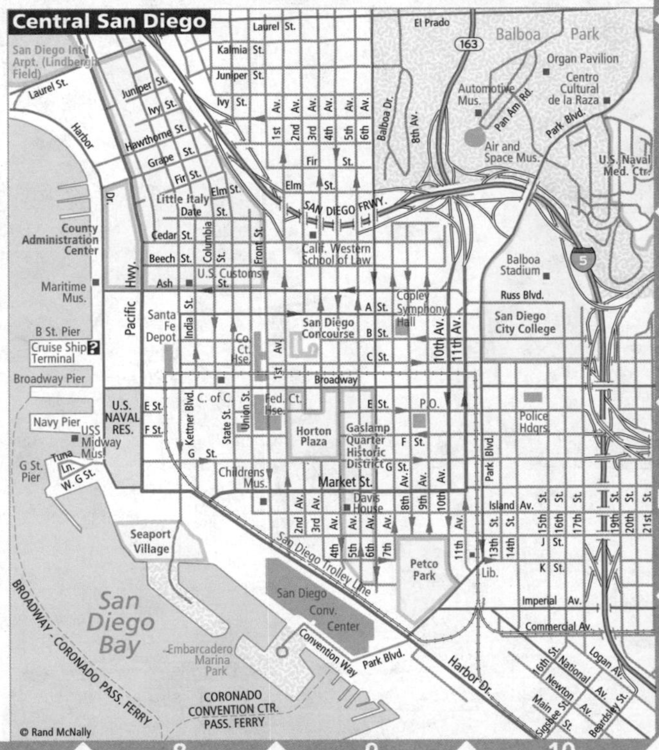

Sights to see
• Aquarium of the Pacific, Long Beach J-8
• Disneyland, Anaheim I-11
• Dodger Stadium................................. E-7
• El Pueblo de Los Angeles K-2
• Getty Center.................................... E-4
• Hollywood Bowl.................................D-6
• Huntington Library, San Marino D-8
• Japanese American National Museum K-3
• Knott's Berry Farm, Buena Park.................. H-10
• Los Angeles County Art Museum...................E-5
• Los Angeles Maritime Museum J-7
• Los Angeles Zoo and Botanical Gardens............D-6
Walt Disney Concert Hall
Los Angeles & Vicinity
Central Los Angeles
Lancaster / Palmdale
SANTA SUSANA MOUNTAINS
SAN GABRIEL MTNS. NAT'L MONUMENT
SAN GABRIEL MOUNTAINS
ANGELES NAT'L FOREST
SANTA MONICA MOUNTAINS
SANTA MONICA MOUNTAINS NATIONAL RECREATION AREA
SAN FERNANDO VALLEY
VERDUGO MTNS.
SIMI HILLS
Santa Clarita
Simi Valley
San Fernando
Thousand Oaks
Calabasas
Malibu
Los Angeles
Beverly Hills
West Hollywood
Santa Monica
Culver City
Burbank
Glendale
Pasadena
Altadena
Arcadia
Monrovia
Inglewood
Hawthorne
Torrance
Carson
Compton
Long Beach
Huntington Beach
Lakewood
Downey
Norwalk
Whittier
Cerritos
Cypress
Palmdale
Lancaster
Santa Monica Bay
PACIFIC OCEAN
© Rand McNally

Santa Monica Pier

Sights to see

- Mission San Juan Capistrano, San Juan Capistrano . . M-14
- Old Pasadena, Pasadena D-8
- Oldest Winery in California, Rancho Cucamonga . . . D-14
- The Queen Mary, Long Beach J-8
- Richard M. Nixon Library & Birthplace, Yorba Linda H-12
- Santa Monica Pier, Santa Monica F-4
- Universal City D-5
- Venice Boardwalk F-4
- Walt Disney Concert Hall K-1
- Warner Bros. Studio, Burbank .D-6
- Will Rogers State Historic Park, Pacific Palisades E-4

Nickname: The Centennial State
Capital: Denver, E-13
Land area: 103,610 sq. mi. (rank: 8th)
Population: 5,773,714 (rank: 21st)
Largest city: Denver, 715,522, E-13

Index of places Pg. 129

Travel planning & on-the-road resources

Tourism Information
Colorado Tourism Office: (800) 265-6723
www.colorado.com

Road Conditions & Construction
511, (800) 288-1047
www.cotrip.org, www.codot.gov

Toll Road Information
E-470 (Denver metro) ***(ExpressToll)***:
(888) 946-3470; www.expresstoll.com/Home
Express Lanes (CDOT) (Denver metro) ***(ExpressToll)***:
(303) 537-3470, www.codot.gov/programs/expresslanes
Northwest Parkway (Denver metro) ***(GOPASS)***:
(303) 533-1200; www.nwpky.com

Determining distances along roads
Highway distances (segments of one mile or less not shown):
Cumulative miles (red): the distance between red arrows
Intermediate miles (black): the distance between intersections & places
Interchanges and exit numbers
For most states, the mileage between interchanges may be determined by subtracting one number from the other.

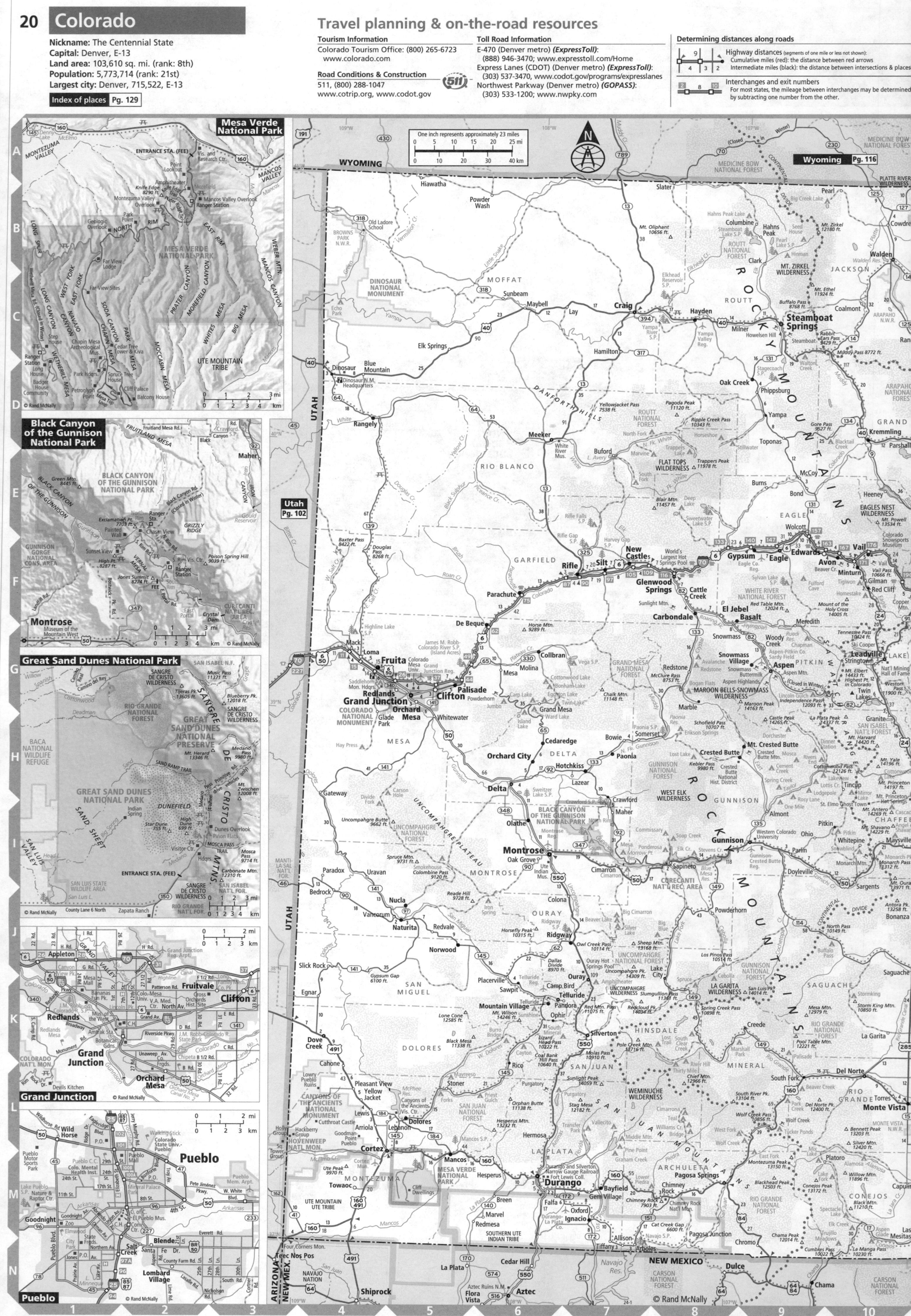

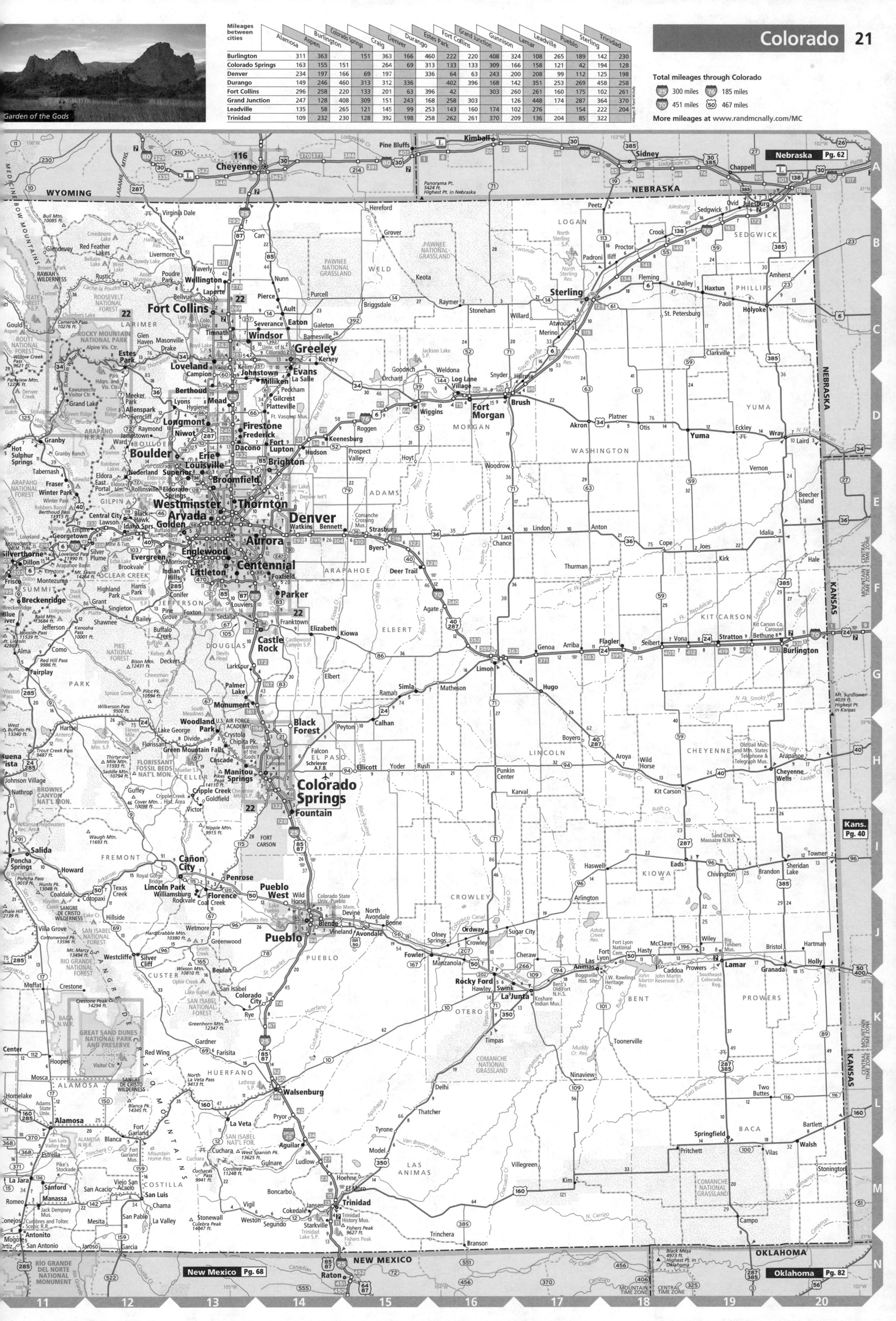

Mileages between cities	Alamosa	Aspen	Burlington	Colorado Springs	Craig	Denver	Durango	Estes Park	Fort Collins	Grand Junction	Gunnison	Lamar	Leadville	Pueblo	Sterling	Trinidad
Burlington	311	363		151	363	166	460	222	220	408	324	108	265	189	142	230
Colorado Springs	163	155	151		264	69	313	133	133	309	166	158	121	42	194	128
Denver	234	197	166	69	197		336	64	63	243	200	208	99	112	125	198
Durango	149	246	460	313	312	336		402	396	168	142	351	253	269	458	258
Fort Collins	296	258	220	133	201	63	396	42		303	260	261	160	175	102	261
Grand Junction	247	128	408	309	151	243	168	258	303		126	448	174	287	364	370
Leadville	135	58	265	121	145	99	253	143	160	174	102	276		154	222	204
Trinidad	109	232	230	128	392	198	258	262	261	370	209	136	204	85	322	

Sights to see

- Black American West Mus. & Heritage Ctr., Denver . . B-7
- Cave of the Winds, Colorado Springs L-8
- Colorado History Museum, Denver C-6
- Colorado State Capitol, Denver C-7
- Denver Art Museum, Denver C-6
- Denver Museum of Nature & Science, Denver I-5
- Garden of the Gods, Colorado Springs L-8
- National Center for Atmospheric Research, Boulder . . . F-1
- ProRodeo Hall of Fame, Colorado Springs K-9
- U.S. Air Force Academy, Colorado Springs J-9
- United States Mint, Denver C-6
- World Figure Skating Hall of Fame, Colorado Springs . . M-9

Denver Art Museum

Denver & Vicinity

Boulder · Longmont · Lafayette · Louisville · Broomfield · Thornton · Northglenn · Westminster · Arvada · Wheat Ridge · Golden · Lakewood · Denver · Aurora · Englewood · Littleton · Centennial · Highlands Ranch · Parker · Castle Rock · Commerce City · Brighton

© Rand McNally

0 1 2 3 4 5 mi
0 1 2 3 4 5 6 7 8 km

Central Denver

© Rand McNally

Rocky Mountain National Park

© Rand McNally

Fort Collins

© Rand McNally

0 1 2 mi
0 1 2 3 km

Colorado Springs

© Rand McNally

0 1 2 mi
0 1 2 3 km

ravel planning & on-the-road resources

ourism Information

onn. Tourism Office:
(888) 288-4748
(860) 500-2300
www.ctvisit.com

Road Conditions & Construction

(860) 594-2560
cttravelsmart.org
portal.ct.gov/dot
www.i-84waterbury.com

oll Road Information

o tolls on state or federal highways

Determining Distances

(segments of one mile or less not shown)

Cumulative miles (red): the distance between red arrows

Intermediate miles (black): the distance between intersections & places

Total mileages through Connecticut

84: 98 miles
95: 112 miles
91: 58 miles
395: 55 miles

More mileages at randmcnally.com/MC

Mileages between cities

	Bridgeport	Hartford	New Haven	New London	New York, NY	Putnam	Torrington	Waterbury
Bridgeport		55	18	64	54	107	50	30
Danbury	29	57	35	81	62	104	47	27
Hartford	55		38	45	108	47	26	30
New Haven	18	38		46	72	89	43	22
New London	64	45	46		118	47	79	63
Putnam	107	47	89	47	162		73	78
Torrington	50	26	43	79	109	73		20
Waterbury	30	30	22	63	89	78	20	

Connecticut

Nickname: The Constitution State
Capital: Hartford, C-9
Land area: 4,841 sq. mi. (rank: 48th)
Population: 3,605,944 (rank: 29th)
Largest city: Bridgeport, 148,654, H-5

Index of places Pg. 129

Hartford · Bridgeport / New Haven · Waterbury · Stamford / Greenwich · New London

Delaware/Florida cities

Nickname: The First State
Capital: Dover, G-2
Land area: 1,948 sq. mi. (rank: 49th)
Population: 989,948 (rank: 45th)
Largest city: Wilmington, 70,898, C-2

Index of places Pg. 129

Mileages between cities	Dover	Georgetown	Lewes	Milford	Philadelphia, PA	Salisbury, MD	Selbyville	Wilmington
Dover		36	40	20	80	56	55	50
Georgetown	36		15	16	114	27	20	85
Lewes	40	15		21	119	43	29	90
Middletown	26	62	66	46	56	84	81	27
Millville, NJ	94	124	128	108	45	147	143	53
Newark	46	80	85	64	43	102	99	14
Selbyville	55	20	29	36	133	24		104
Wilmington	50	85	90	70	29	107	104	

Mileages © Rand McNally

Total mileages through Delaware
95: 23 miles
1: 104 miles
13: 108 miles

More mileages at randmcnally.com/MC

Travel planning & on-the-road resources

Tourism Information
Delaware Tourism Office:
(866) 284-7483; www.visitdelaware.com

Road Conditions & Construction
(800) 652-5600, (302) 760-2080
www.deldot.gov

Toll Road Information *(all use E-ZPass)*
Delaware Department of Transportation:
(888) 397-2773, (302) 678-7000; www.ezpassde.com
Delaware River & Bay Authority (Del. Mem. Bridge & Lewes/Cape May Ferry):
(302) 571-6373; www.drba.net

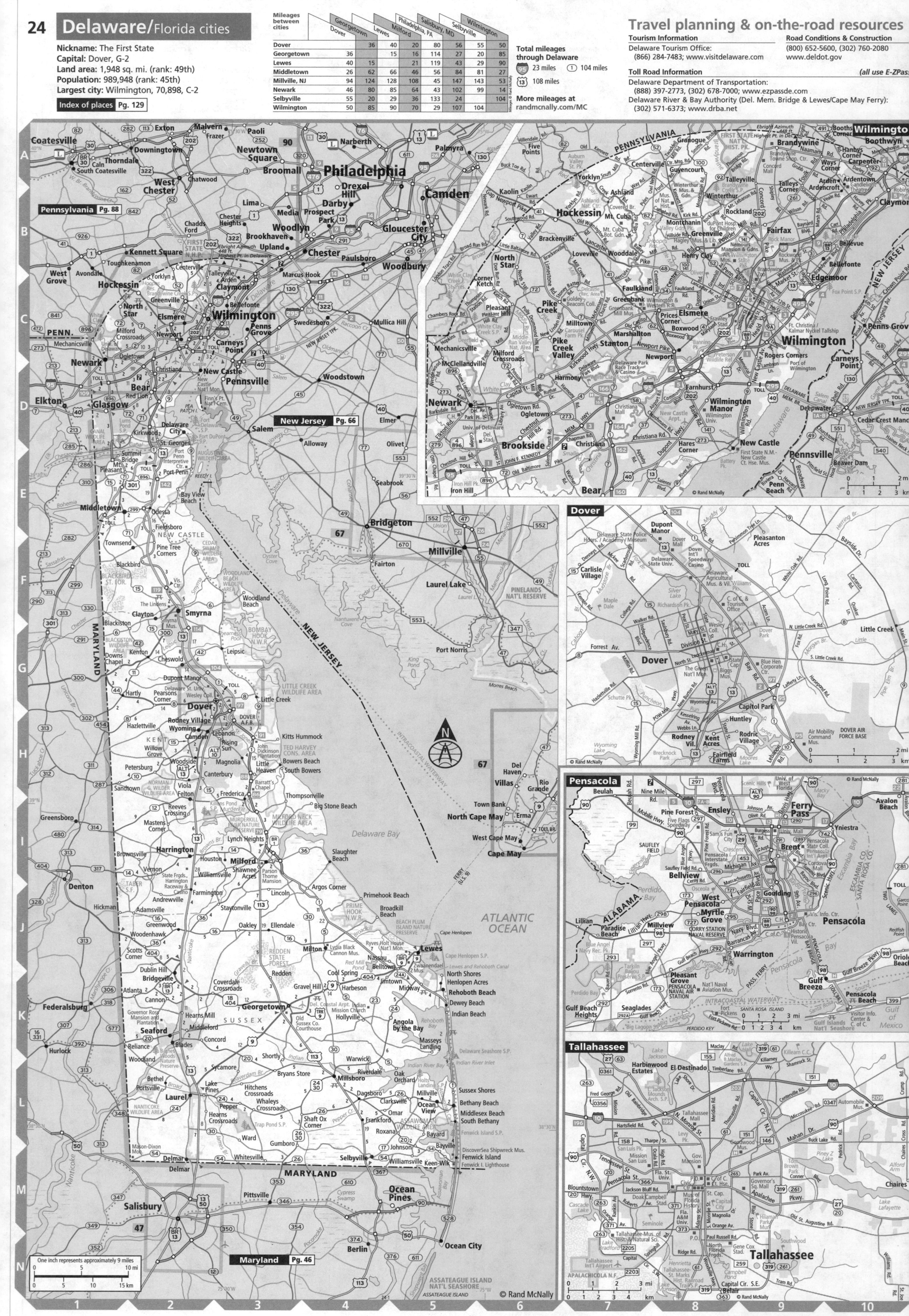

Art Deco Historic District, Miami Beach

Sights to see

- Art Deco National Historic District, Miami Beach...... L-9
- Busch Gardens, Tampa B-4
- Hugh Taylor Birch State Park, Fort Lauderdale H-9
- Marie Selby Botanical Gardens, Sarasota H-3
- Miami Seaquarium, Miami M-9
- Norton Museum of Art, Palm Beach B-10
- Ringling Center for the Cultural Arts, Sarasota G-3
- St. Petersburg Museum of History, St. Petersburg..... D-2
- Salvador Dali Museum, St. Petersburg.............. D-2
- Thomas A. Edison & Henry Ford Winter Estates, Fort Myers M-2
- Vizcaya Museum and Gardens, Miami M-8

Tampa / St. Petersburg / Sarasota

Miami / Fort Lauderdale & Vicinity

Lakeland / Winter Haven

Fort Myers / Cape Coral

Central Miami

© Rand McNally

Nickname: The Sunshine State
Capital: Tallahassee, B-2
Land area: 53,634 sq. mi. (rank: 26th)
Population: 21,538,187 (rank: 3rd)
Largest city: Jacksonville, 949,611, C-9

Index of places Pg. 129

Travel planning & on-the-road resources

Tourism Information
Visit Florida: (888) 735-2872
www.visitflorida.com

Road Conditions & Construction
511, (866) 511-3352
fl511.com, www.fdot.gov

Toll Road Information *(all use SunPass unless otherwise noted)*
Florida Express Lanes (FDOT): (850) 414-4100, www.fdot.gov/traffic/teo-divisions.shtm/cav-ml-stamp/managedlanes.shtm
Florida's Turnpike Enterprise: (407) 532-3999; floridasturnpike.com
Central Florida Expressway Authority (Greater Orlando) ***(also E-Pass)***: (800) 353-7277, (407) 823-7277; www.cfxway.com
Miami-Dade Expressway Authority: (855) 277-0848, (305) 637-3277; www.mdxway.com
Tampa Hillsborough Expressway Authority: (813) 272-6740; www.tampa-xway.com

Toll Bridge Info. *(all use SunPass*
Escambia Co. (Bob Sikes Br.): (844) 640-0088; myescambia.com
Santa Rosa Bay Br. Auth.: (800) 749-7453 floridasturnpike.com/tolls/toll-rates
Town of Bay Hbr. Islands (Broad Causeway) (305) 866-6241
www.bayharborislands-fl.gov

Coral reef near Key West

Mileages between cities	Daytona Beach	Fort Myers	Fort Pierce	Gainesville	Jacksonville	Key West	Miami	Orlando	Panama City	Pensacola	St. Petersburg	Sarasota	Tallahassee	Tampa	Titusville	West Palm Beach
Fort Myers	225		128	254	312	279	152	171	497	589	117	80	397	130	209	124
Jacksonville	92	312	227	72		507	349	141	264	355	222	253	164	198	136	284
Key West	414	279	284	483	507		162	387	727	821	390	352	627	402	371	231
Miami	256	152	123	336	349	162		229	579	663	262	225	479	255	213	68
Orlando	54	171	110	114	141	387	229		357	451	106	132	257	84	39	159
Pensacola	442	589	549	338	355	821	663	451	102		458	511	193	459	487	594
Tallahassee	253	397	364	148	164	627	479	257	96	193	257	328		273	295	413
Tampa	137	130	151	127	198	402	255	84	373	459	23	60	273		124	202

Total mileages through Florida

- 4: 132 miles
- 10: 362 miles
- 75: 471 miles
- 95: 382 miles

More mileages at randmcnally.com/MC

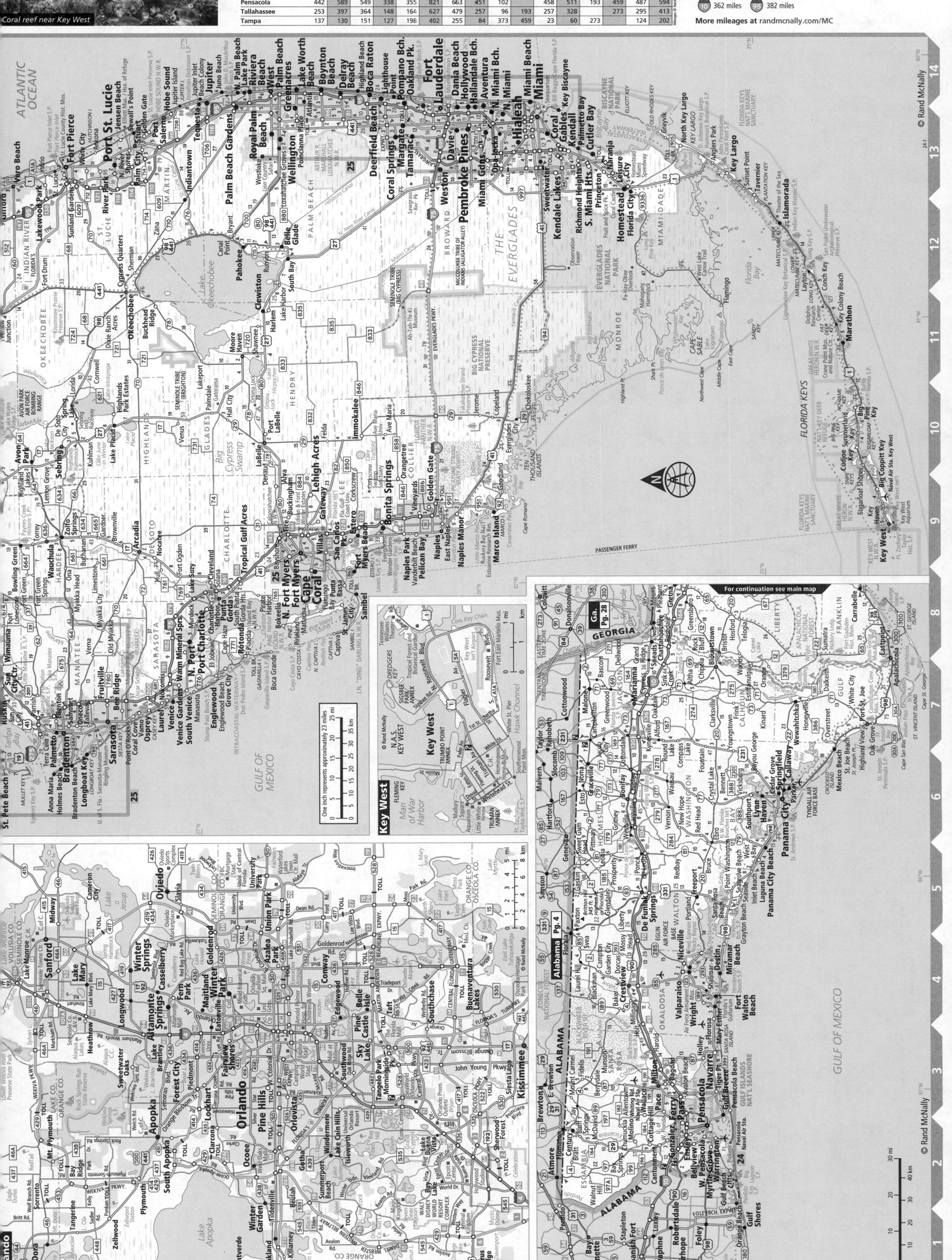

Georgia

Nickname: The Peach State
Capital: Atlanta, E-4
Land area: 57,701 sq. mi. (rank: 21st)
Population: 10,711,908 (rank: 8th)
Largest city: Atlanta, 498,715, E-4

Index of places Pg. 130

Travel planning & on-the-road resources

Tourism Information
Explore Georgia: (800) 847-4842; www.exploregeorgia.org

Road Conditions & Construction
511, (877) 694-2511; 511ga.org

Toll Road Information
State Road & Tollway Authority (Greater Atlanta) ***(Peach Pass):***
(404) 893-6100, (855) 724-7277; srta.ga.gov, peachpass.com

Determining distances along roads

Highway distances (segments of one mile or less not shown):
Cumulative miles (red): the distance between red arrows
Intermediate miles (black): the distance between intersections & places

Interchanges and exit numbers
For most states, the mileage between interchanges may be determined by subtracting one number from the other.

Augusta

Albany

S. Carolina Pg. 92

N. Carolina Pg. 74

Tennessee Pg. 94

Alabama Pg. 4

Forsyth Park, Savannah

Mileages between cities	Albany	Athens	Atlanta	Augusta	Bainbridge	Brunswick	Chattanooga, TN	Columbus	Gainesville	Jacksonville, FL	Macon	Rome	Savannah	Toccoa	Valdosta	Vidalia
Atlanta	182	69		148	240	275	117	106	54	346	82	70	247	94	228	172
Augusta	211	98	148		268	193	265	249	140	254	123	217	134	132	217	99
Chattanooga, TN	300	172	117	265	348	397		219	121	465	201	71	364	155	346	289
Columbus	85	171	106	249	128	258	219		161	292	98	144	249	201	173	175
Jacksonville, FL	198	310	346	254	204	66	465	292	396		270	416	135	375	121	164
Macon	106	91	82	123	163	193	201	98	132	270		152	165	143	152	90
Savannah	226	222	247	134	249	77	364	249	297	135	165	317		255	167	90
Valdosta	79	243	228	217	83	120	346	173	278	121	152	298	167	317		118

Total mileages through Georgia

- 20: 203 miles
- 75: 355 miles
- 85: 180 miles
- 95: 112 miles

More mileages at randmcnally.com/MC

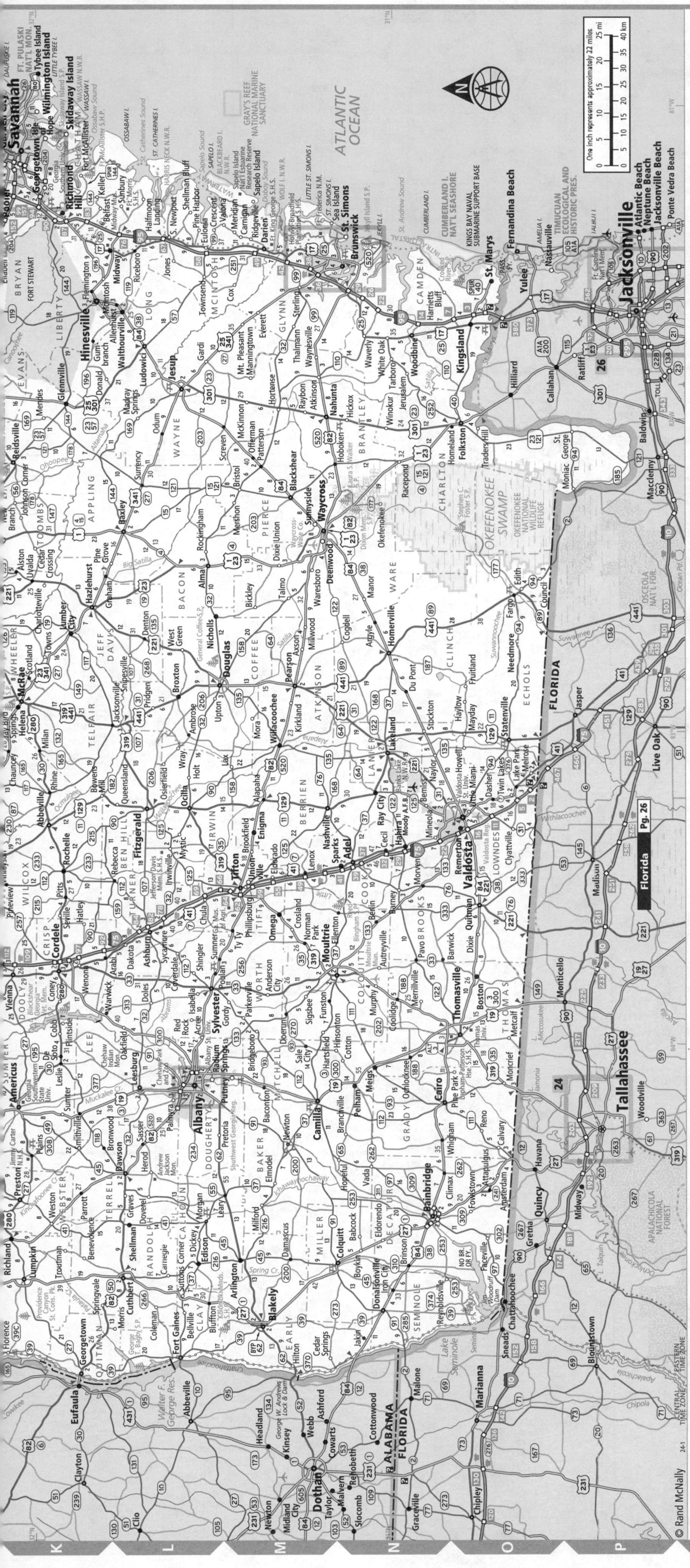

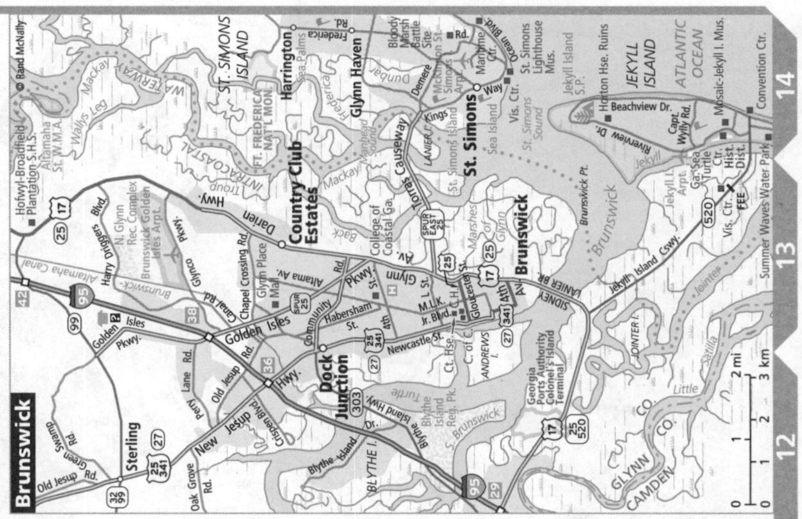

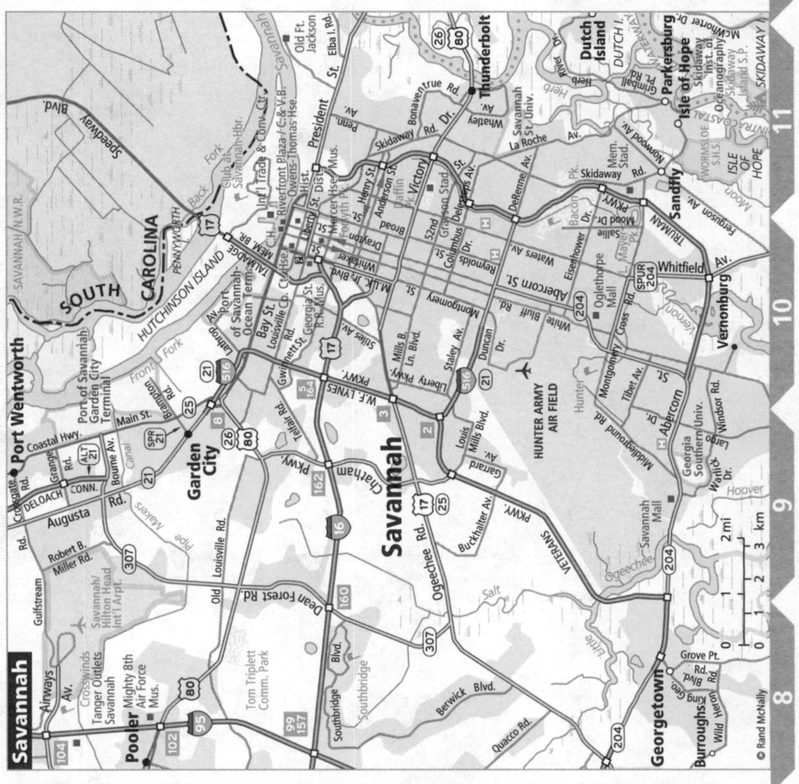

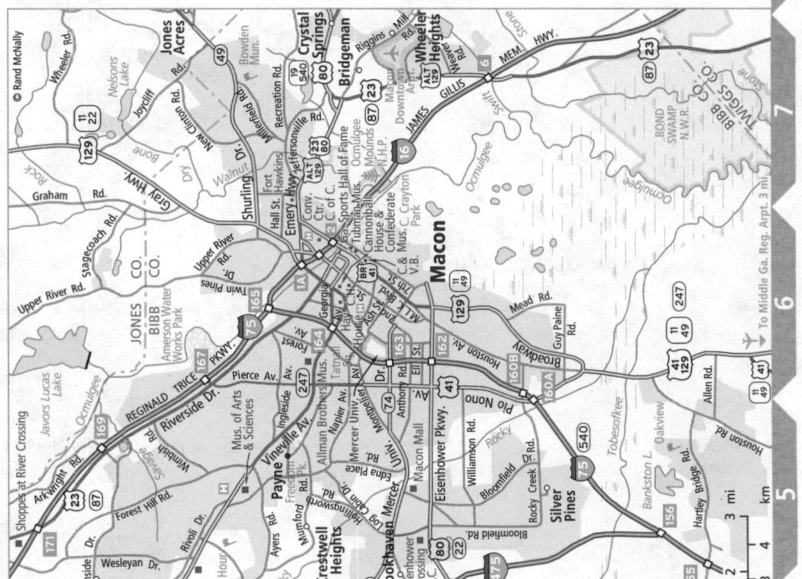

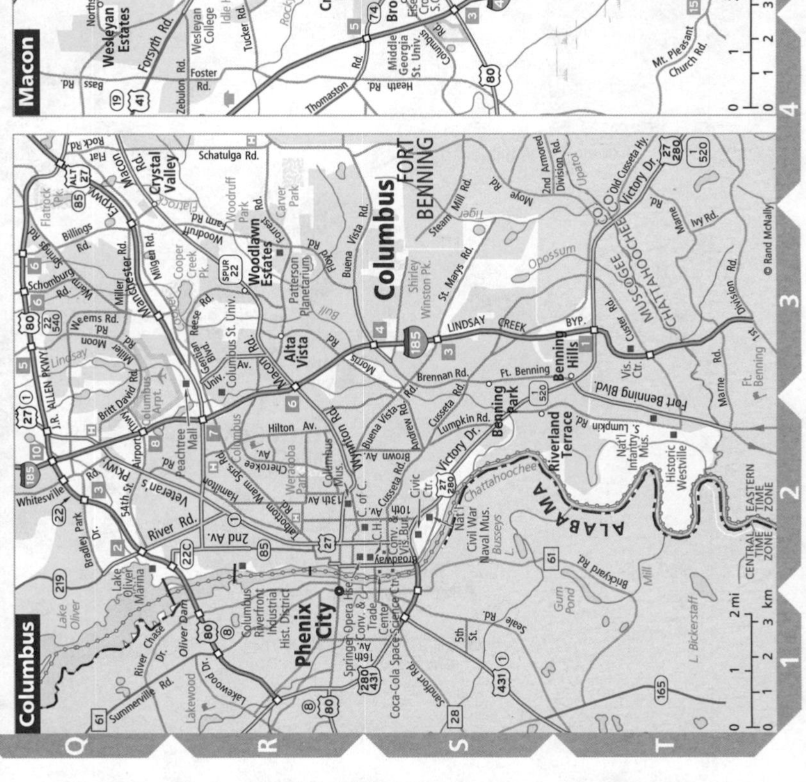

Hawaii/Georgia cities

Nickname: The Aloha State
Capital: Honolulu, N-4
Land area: 6,421 sq. mi. (rank: 47th)
Population: 1,455,271 (rank: 40th)
Largest city: Honolulu, 350,964, N-4

Index of places Pg. 130

Mileages between cities	Hilo	Honolulu	Kahului	Kailua	Kailua Kona	Kapa'a	Lahaina	Wahiawā
Hilo		225*	127*	237*	74	337*	149*	236*
Honolulu	225*		108*	11	177*	116*	130*	20
Kahului	127*	108*		22*	93*	214*	22	119*
Kailua Kona	74	177*	93*	188*		283*	116*	188*
Kapa'a	337*	116*	214*	128*	283*		236*	128*
Kaunakakai	177*	68*	55*	79*	144*	174*	77*	79*
Lahaina	149*	130*	22	43*	116*	236*		141*
Wahiawā	236*	20	119*	26	188*	128*	141*	

*Via plane

Mileages © Rand McNally

Total mileages through Hawaii
H1 27 miles
H3 15 miles
H2 8 miles

More mileages at randmcnally.com/MC

Travel planning & on-the-road resources

Tourism Information
Hawaii Tourism Authority:
(800) 464-2924
(888) 297-9472 (from Canada)
www.gohawaii.com

Toll Road Information
No tolls on state or federal highways

Road Conditions & Construction
(808) 587-2220
hidot.hawaii.gov/highways/roadwork
O'ahu: 511
www.goakamai.org

Determining Distances
(segments of one mile or less not shown)
Cumulative miles (red): the distance between red arrows
Intermediate miles (black): the distance between intersections & places

Travel planning & on-the-road resources

Tourism Information
Idaho Tourism:
(800) 847-4843; visitidaho.org

Road Conditions & Construction
511, (888) 432-7623
511.idaho.gov, www.itd.idaho.gov

Toll Road Information
No tolls on state or federal highways

Determining Distances
(segments of one mile or less not shown)
Cumulative miles (red): the distance between red arrows
Intermediate miles (black): the distance between intersections & places

Total mileages through Idaho
15: 196 miles
84: 276 miles
86: 63 miles
90: 74 miles

More mileages at randmcnally.com/MC

Mileages between cities	Boise	Coeur d'Alene	Lewiston	Missoula, MT	Mountain Home	Pocatello	Salmon	Twin Falls
Boise		383	268	367	44	234	247	128
Bonners Ferry	459	76	191	212	504	573	351	589
Coeur d'Alene	383		115	166	428	525	303	513
Idaho Falls	279	478	526	312	237	49	160	159
Lewiston	268	115		214	313	504	332	398
Pocatello	234	525	504	361	191		209	114
Salmon	247	303	332	138	287	209		247
Twin Falls	128	513	398	384	85	114	247	

Idaho

Nickname: The Gem State
Capital: Boise, K-2
Land area: 82,623 sq. mi. (rank: 11th)
Population: 1,839,106 (rank: 38th)
Largest city: Boise, 235,684, K-2

Index of places Pg. 130

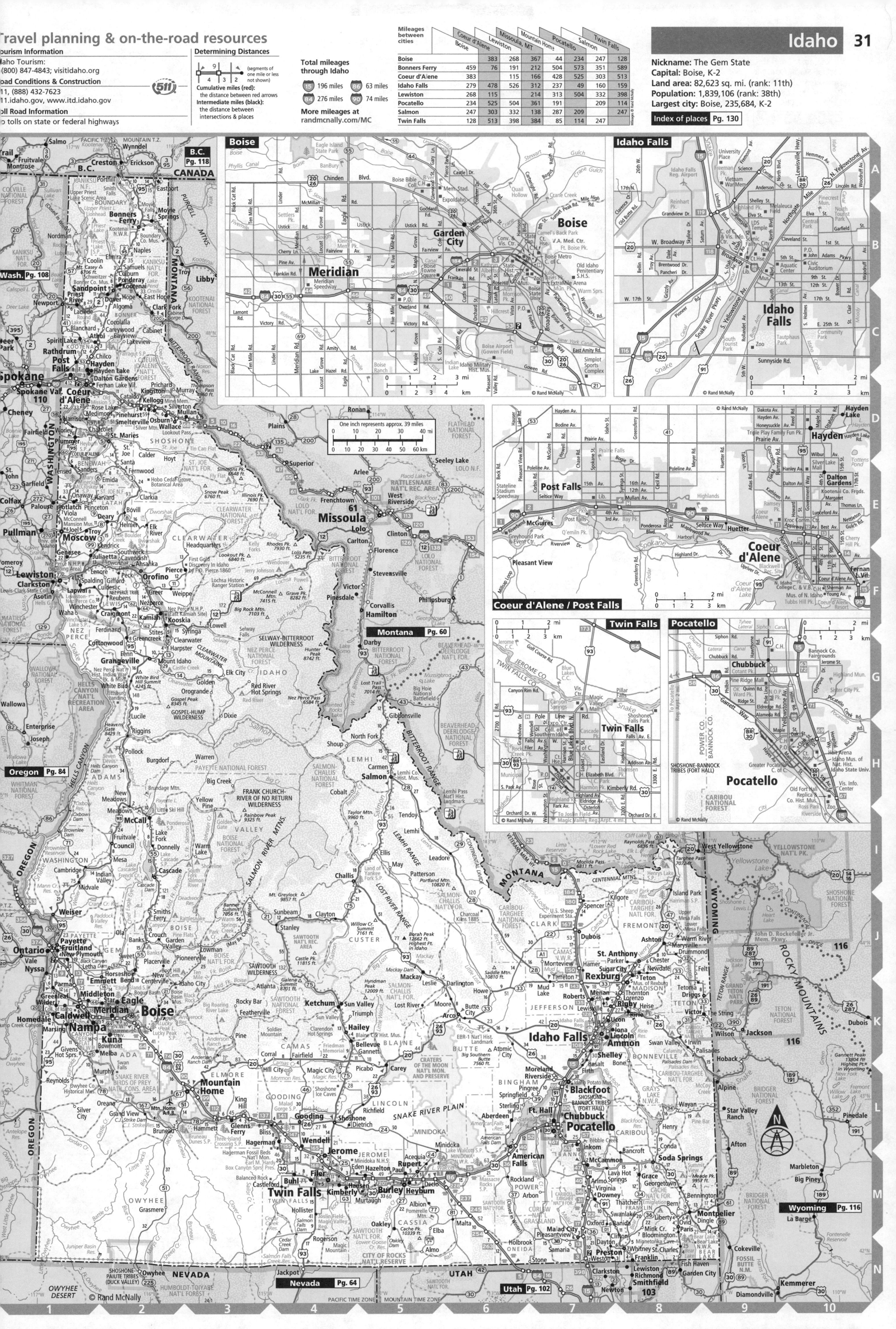

Nickname: Land of Lincoln
Capital: Springfield, J-8
Land area: 55,499 sq. mi. (rank: 24th)
Population: 12,812,508 (rank: 6th)
Largest city: Chicago, 2,746,388, C-13

Index of places Pg. 130

Travel planning & on-the-road resources

Tourism Information
Illinois Bureau of Tourism: (312) 814-4732; www.enjoyillinois.com

Road Conditions & Construction
(800) 452-4368; www.gettingaroundillinois.com, idot.illinois.gov

Toll Road/Bridge Information
Illinois Tollway (*I-Pass or E-ZPass*): (800) 824-7277; www.illinoistollway.com
Skyway Concession Co. (Chicago Skyway) (*I-Pass or E-ZPass*): (773) 356-5543; www.chicagoskyway.org

Determining distances along roads

Highway distances (segments of one mile or less not shown):
Cumulative miles (red): the distance between red arrows
Intermediate miles (black): the distance between intersections & places

Interchanges and exit numbers
For most states, the mileage between interchanges may be determined by subtracting one number from the other.

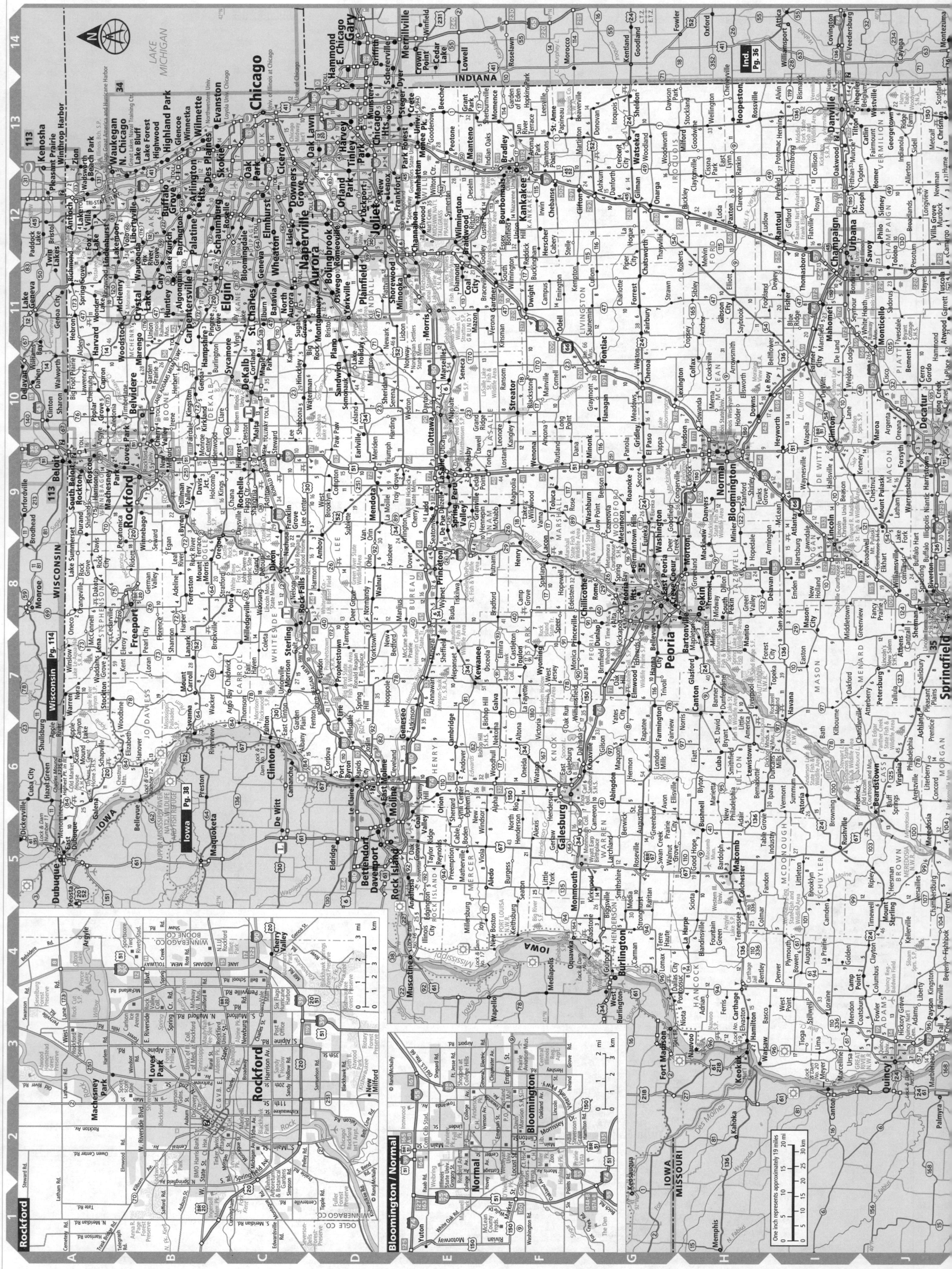

Rockford

Bloomington / Normal

One inch represents approximately 19 miles

Wisconsin Pg. 114
Iowa Pg. 38
Ind. Pg. 36

Navy Pier, Chicago

Mileages between cities	Bloomington	Carbondale	Champaign	Chicago	Decatur	Dubuque, IA	Kankakee	Lawrenceville	Moline	Mt. Vernon	Peoria	Quincy	Rockford	St. Louis, MO	Springfield	Waukegan
Carbondale	245		200	330	176	406	272	146	332	57	240	240	379	104	170	374
Champaign	51	200		135	48	256	78	130	182	147	89	194	185	180	85	180
Chicago	132	330	135		179	177	58	247	166	277	154	309	84	296	198	38
Moline	131	332	182	166	171	75	158	307		308	93	148	120	261	164	190
Peoria	38	240	89	154	78	167	108	214	93	215		130	138	168	71	184
Rockford	132	379	185	84	180	93	139	309	120	326	138	268		294	197	73
St. Louis, MO	162	104	180	296	135	335	252	144	261	79	168	139	294		98	326
Springfield	66	170	85	198	38	238	157	153	164	138	71	112	197	98		229

Total mileages through Illinois

55: 294 miles
57: 164 miles
70: 156 miles
90: 124 miles

More mileages at randmcnally.com/MC

Sights to see

- Adler Planetarium G-15
- Art Institute of Chicago.......... E-13
- Chicago Botanic Garden, Glencoe D-8
- Field Museum.......... G-14
- Frank Lloyd Wright Home & Studio, Oak Park.......... H-8
- John G. Shedd Aquarium G-14
- Lincoln Park Zoo H-9
- Millennium Park.......... E-13
- Museum of Science & Industry.......... J-10
- Navy Pier.......... D-14
- Willis Tower E-12
- Wrigley Field G-9

Chicago Cultural Center

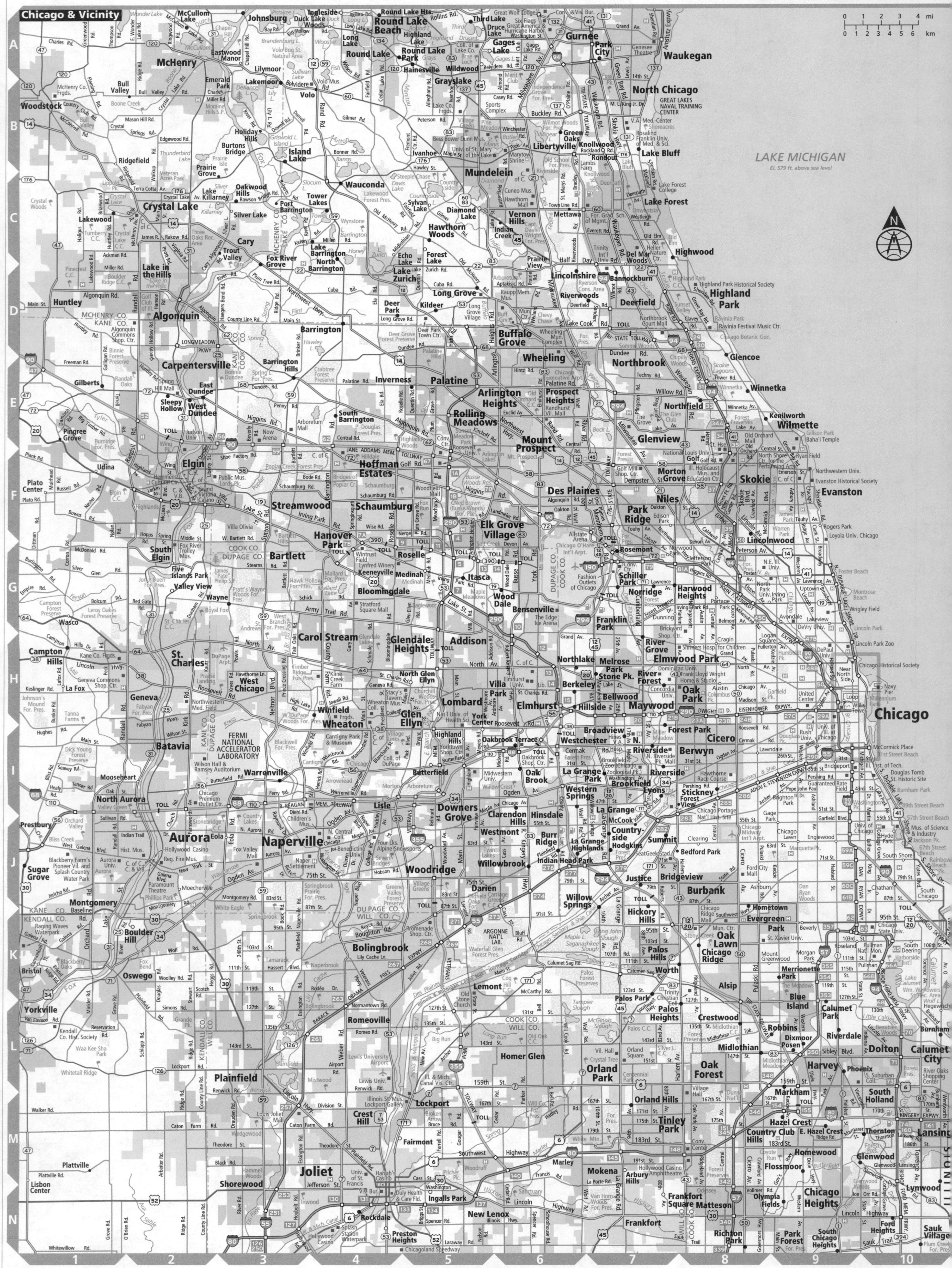

Chicago & Vicinity

LAKE MICHIGAN

El. 579 ft. above sea level

0 1 2 3 4 mi

0 1 2 3 4 5 6 km

Children's Museum of Indianapolis

Sights to see

- Abraham Lincoln Presidential Library & Museum, Springfield M-16
- Buckingham Fountain, Chicago F-13
- Children's Museum of Indianapolis, Indianapolis D-18
- Fort Wayne Children's Zoo, Fort Wayne L-19
- Illinois State Capitol Complex, Springfield M-16
- Indiana State Capitol, Indianapolis H-19
- Indiana State Museum, Indianapolis H-19
- Indianapolis Motor Speedway and Hall of Fame Museum, Indianapolis D-16
- NCAA Hall of Champions, Indianapolis H-18
- President Benjamin Harrison Home, Indianapolis F-20

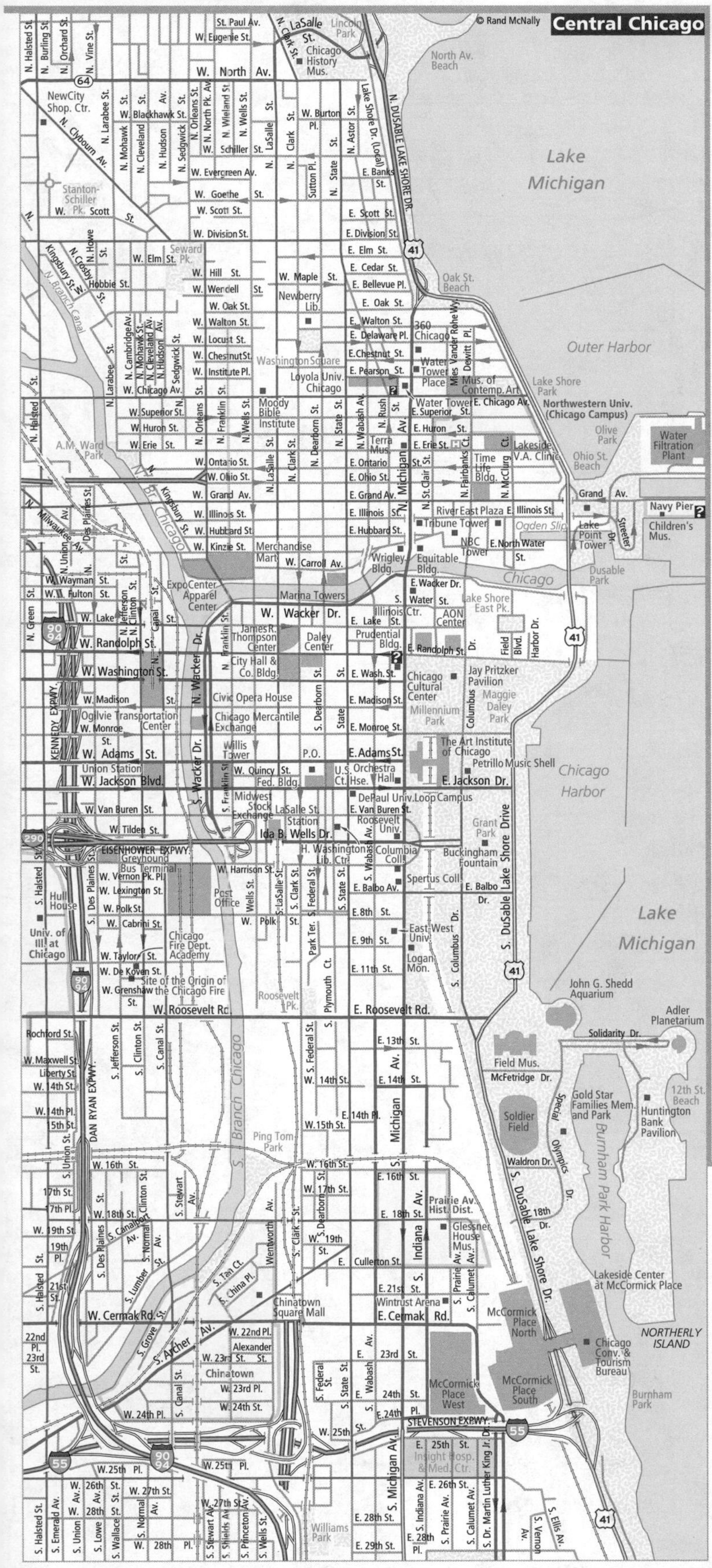

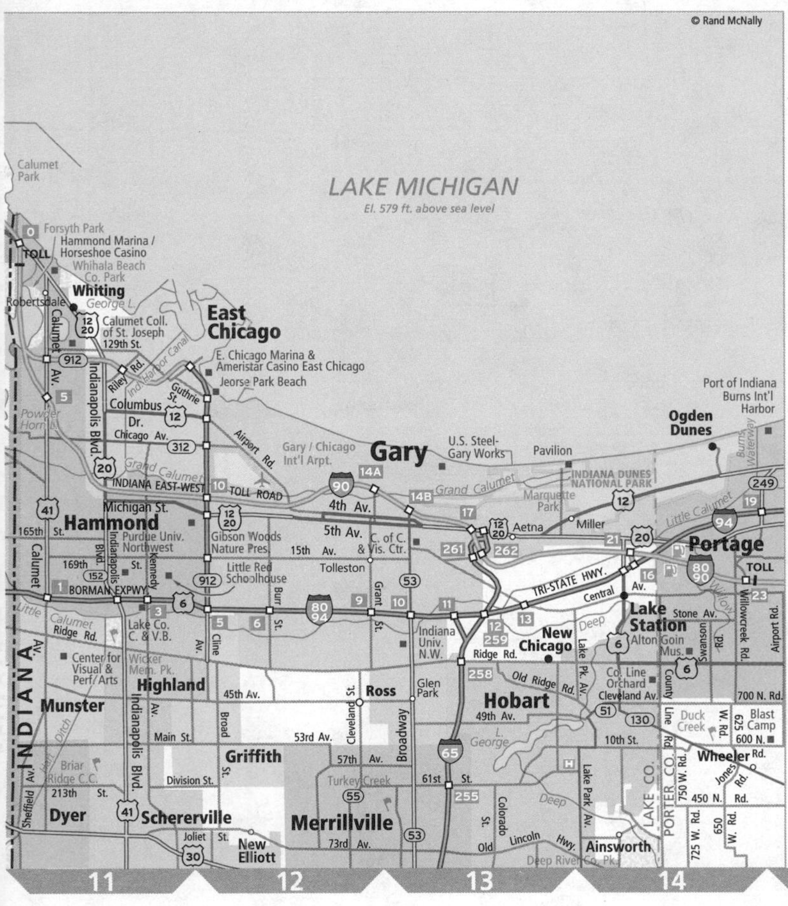

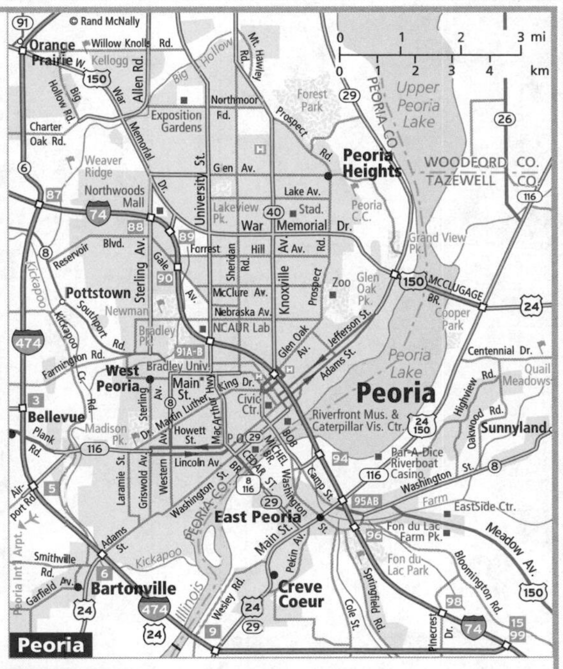

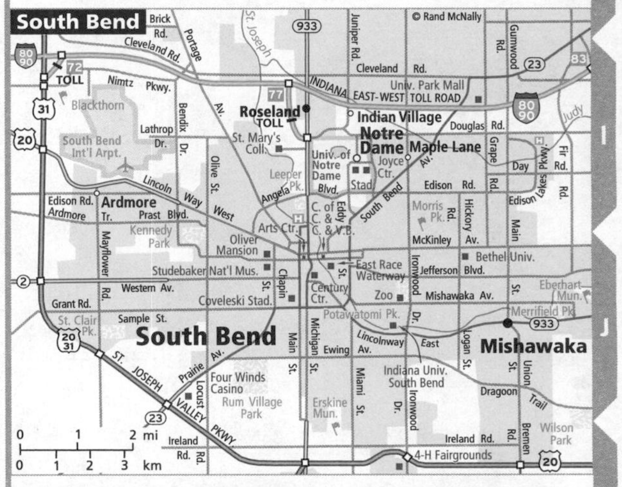

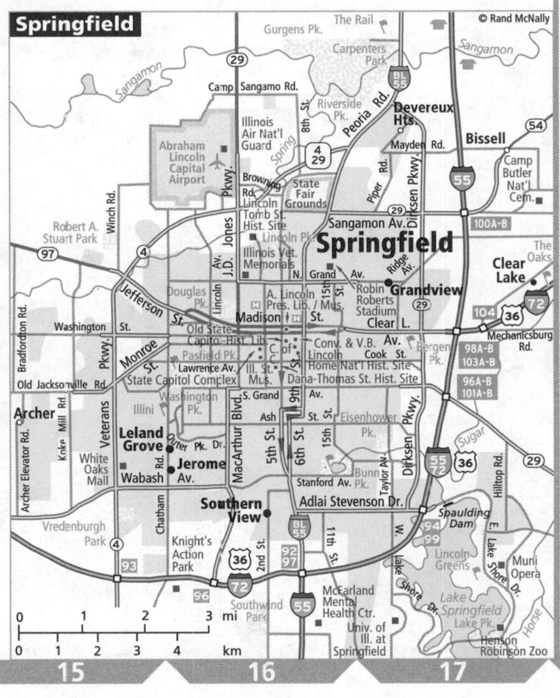

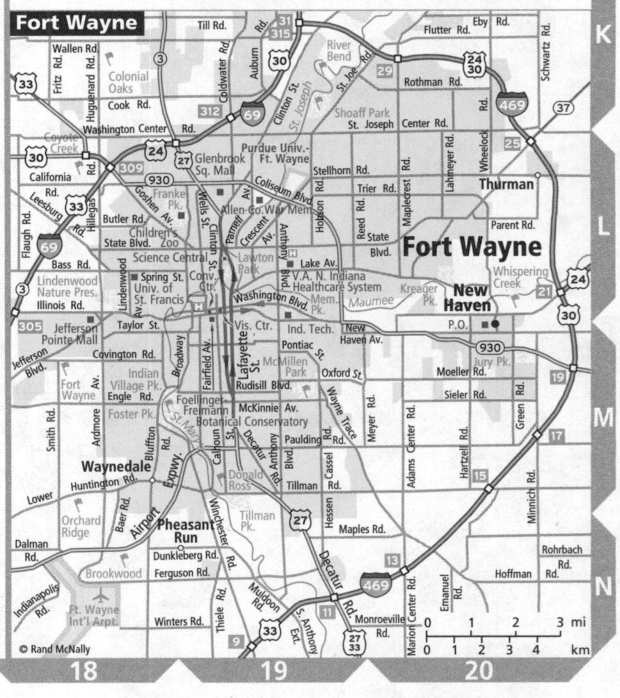

Central Chicago

© Rand McNally

Indianapolis

© Rand McNally

Central Indianapolis

Peoria

© Rand McNally

South Bend

© Rand McNally

Springfield

© Rand McNally

Fort Wayne

© Rand McNally

Nickname: The Hoosier State
Capital: Indianapolis, J-9
Land area: 35,817 sq. mi. (rank: 38th)
Population: 6,785,528 (rank: 17th)
Largest city: Indianapolis, 887,642, J-9

Index of places Pg. 130

Travel planning & on-the-road resources

Tourism Information
Indiana Office of Tourism Development: (317) 232-8860; visitindiana.com

Road Conditions & Construction
(800) 261-7623; 511in.org, pws.trafficwise.org/pws

Toll Road Information
Indiana Toll Road Concession Co. *(E-ZPass)*: (574) 675-4010; www.indianatollroad.org
RiverLink (Louisville area toll bridges) *(RiverLink or E-ZPass)*: (855) 748-5465; riverlink.com

Determining distances along roads

Highway distances (segments of one mile or less not shown):
Cumulative miles (red): the distance between red arrows
Intermediate miles (black): the distance between intersections & places

Interchanges and exit numbers
For most states, the mileage between interchanges may be determined by subtracting one number from the other.

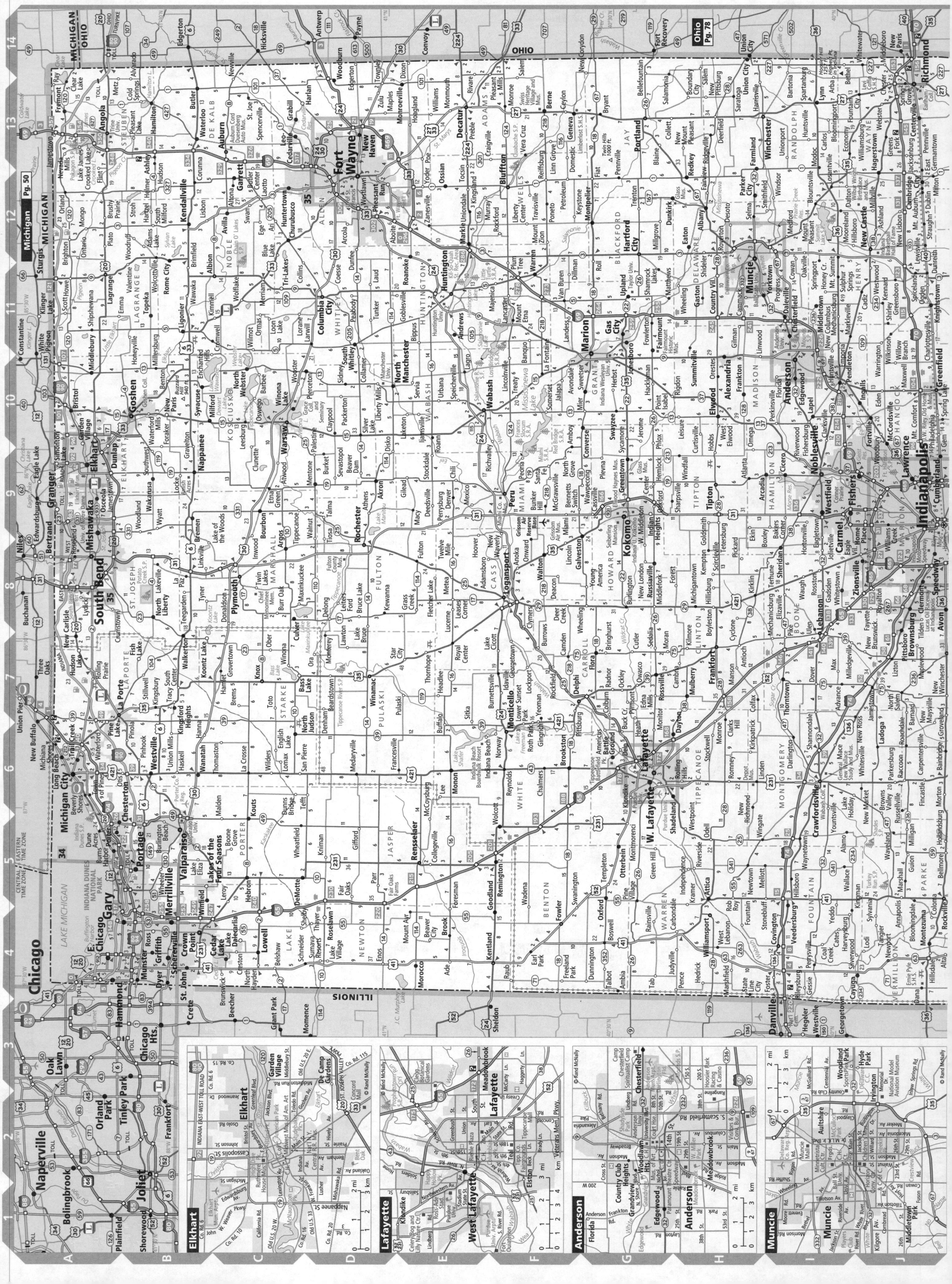

MICHIGAN
OHIO
ILLINOIS
LAKE MICHIGAN
Michigan Pg. 50
Ohio Pg. 78
Chicago
Indianapolis
Fort Wayne
South Bend
Elkhart
Lafayette
Anderson
Muncie

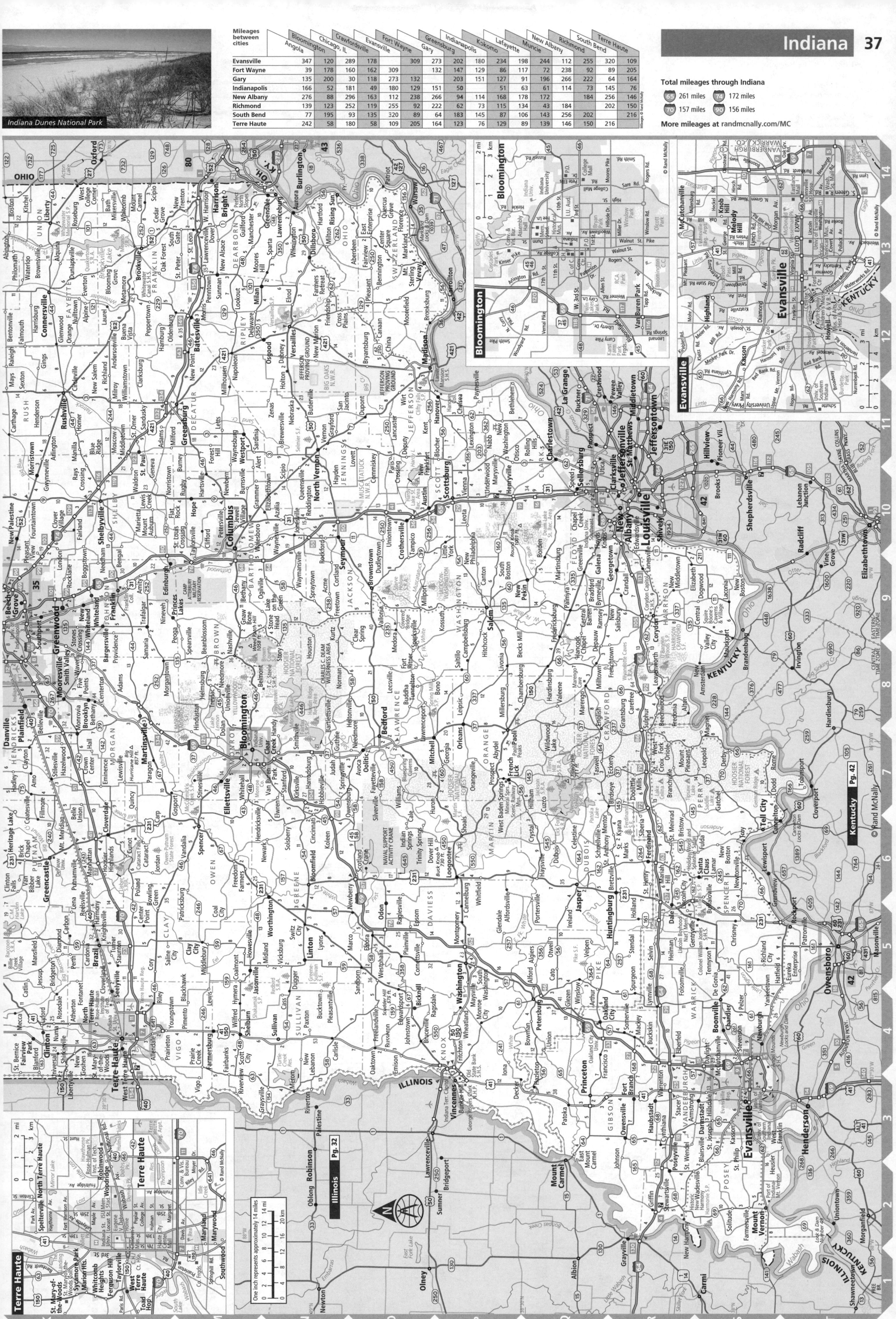

Mileages between cities	Angola	Bloomington	Chicago, IL	Crawfordsville	Evansville	Fort Wayne	Gary	Greensburg	Indianapolis	Kokomo	Lafayette	Muncie	New Albany	Richmond	South Bend	Terre Haute
Evansville	347	120	289	178		309	273	202	180	234	198	244	112	255	320	109
Fort Wayne	39	178	160	162	309		132	147	129	86	117	72	238	92	89	205
Gary	135	200	30	118	273	132		203	151	127	91	196	266	222	64	164
Indianapolis	166	52	181	49	180	129	151	50		51	63	61	114	73	145	76
New Albany	276	88	296	163	112	238	266	94	114	168	178	172		184	256	146
Richmond	139	123	252	119	255	92	222	62	73	115	134	43	184		202	150
South Bend	77	195	93	135	320	89	64	183	145	87	106	143	256	202		216
Terre Haute	242	58	180	58	109	205	164	123	76	129	89	139	146	150	216	

Iowa

Nickname: The Hawkeye State
Capital: Des Moines, I-10
Land area: 55,839 sq. mi. (rank: 23rd)
Population: 3,190,369 (rank: 31st)
Largest city: Des Moines, 214,133, I-10

Index of places Pg. 131

Travel planning & on-the-road resources

Tourism Information
Iowa Tourism Office: (800) 345-4692, www.traveliowa.com

Road Conditions & Construction
511, (800) 288-1047; www.511ia.org, iowadot.gov

Toll Road Information
BNSF Railway (Fort Madison Toll Bridge): en.wikipedia.org/wiki/Fort_Madison_Toll_Bridge

Determining distances along roads

Highway distances (segments of one mile or less not shown):
Cumulative miles (red): the distance between red arrows
Intermediate miles (black): the distance between intersections & places

Interchanges and exit numbers
For most states, the mileage between interchanges may be determined by subtracting one number from the other.

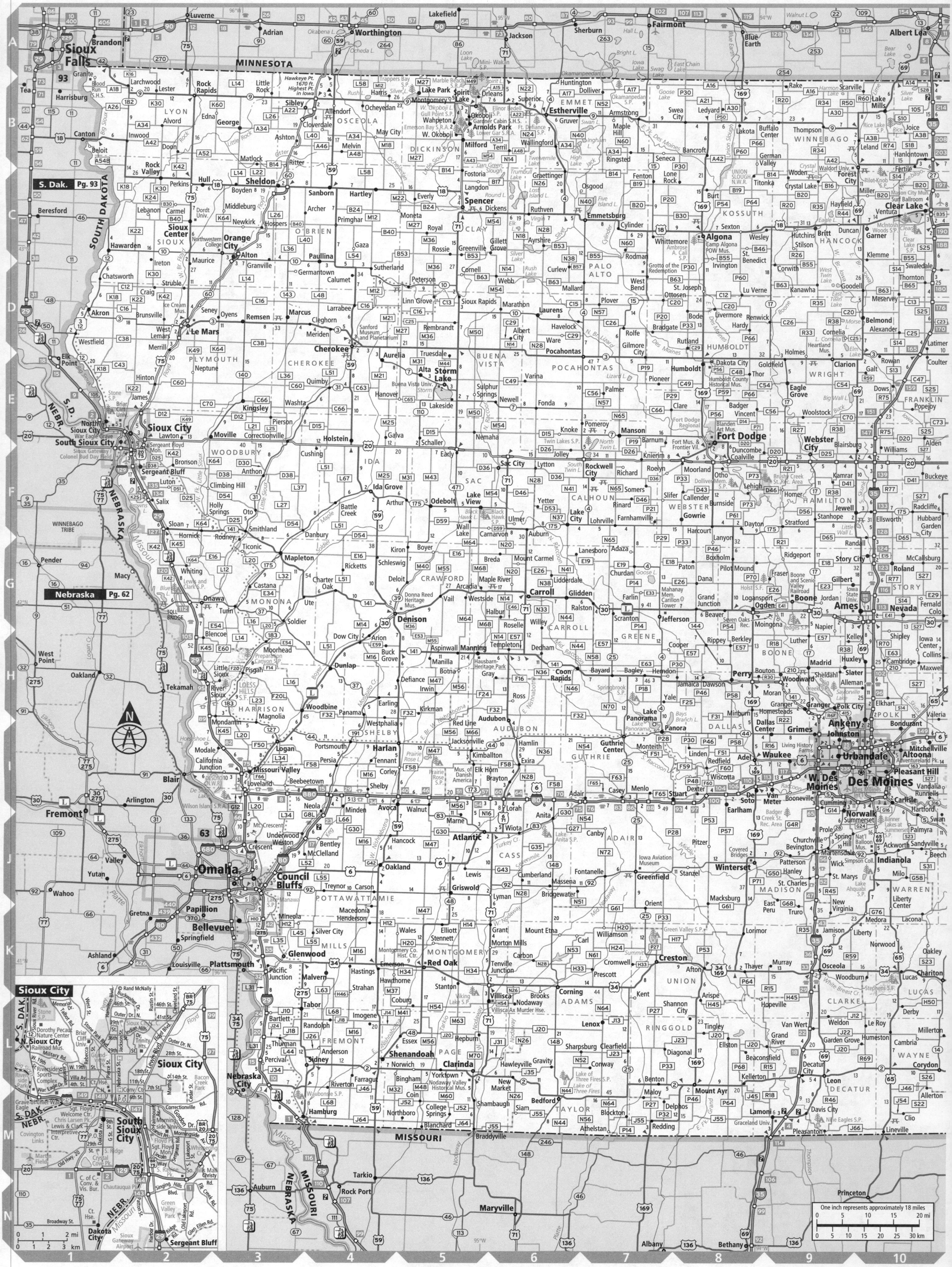

S. Dak. Pg. 93

Nebraska Pg. 62

Sioux City

One inch represents approximately 18 miles

Mileages between cities	Ames	Burlington	Cedar Rapids	Council Bluffs	Davenport	Decorah	Des Moines	Dubuque	Iowa City	Mason City	Ottumwa	Sioux City	Sioux Falls, SD	Spirit Lake	Storm Lake	Waterloo
Burlington	209		100	294	77	206	167	150	77	238	78	366	451	355	312	155
Cedar Rapids	108	100		253	82	105	126	70	28	136	110	268	357	252	212	53
Council Bluffs	160	294	253		295	328	127	327	241	246	213	94	180	176	122	253
Davenport	191	77	82	295		167	167	71	57	220	133	366	441	336	294	136
Des Moines	33	167	126	127	167	201		199	114	119	86	198	283	200	154	126
Dubuque	185	150	70	327	71	96	199		84	174	184	305	395	290	249	91
Mason City	91	238	136	246	220	88	119	174	165		203	200	222	118	135	83
Sioux City	175	366	268	94	366	304	198	305	312	200	285		85	109	78	218

Total mileages through Iowa

- 29: 155 miles
- 80: 303 miles
- 35: 218 miles
- 218: 257 miles

More mileages at randmcnally.com/MC

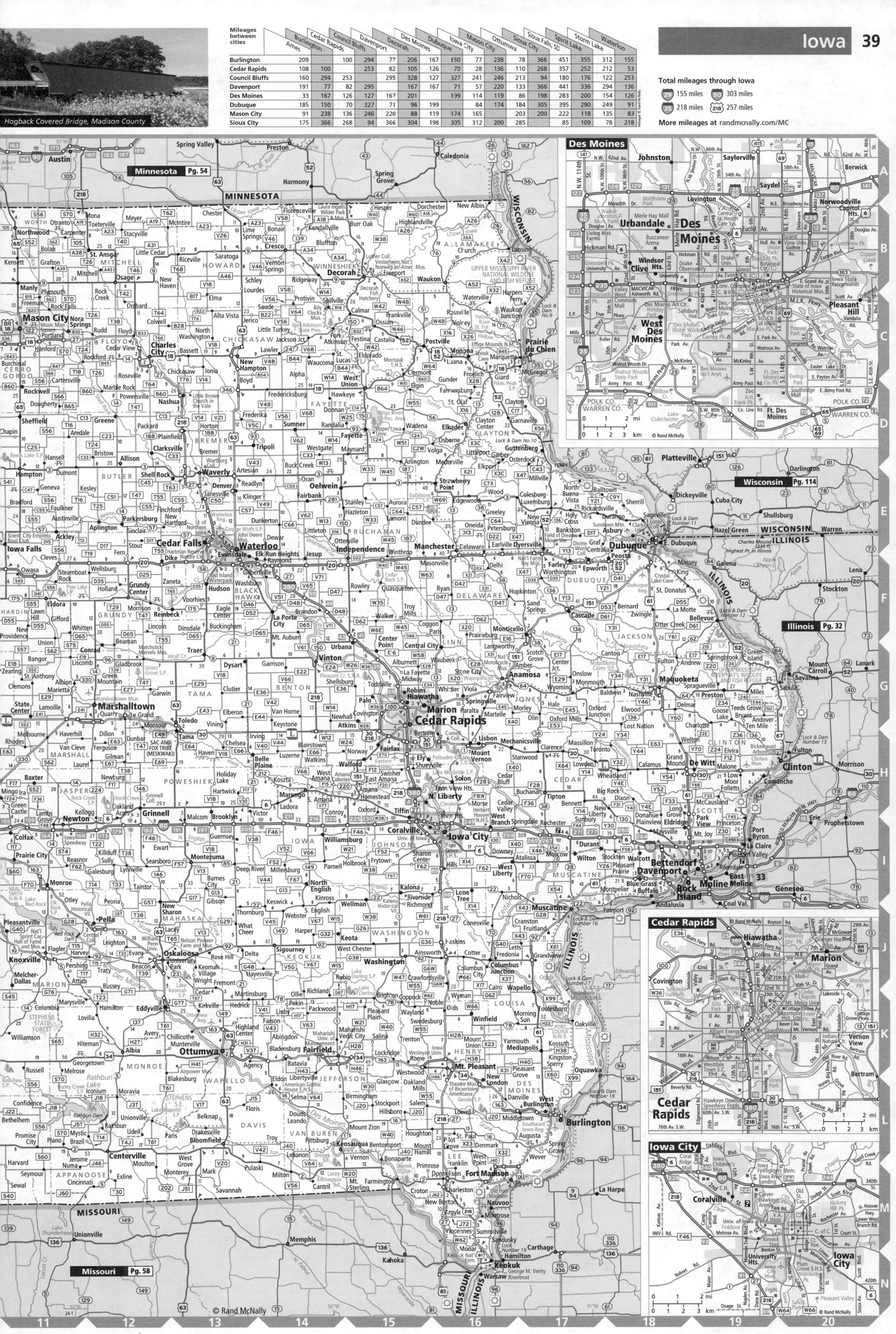

Kansas

Nickname: The Sunflower State
Capital: Topeka, D-16
Land area: 81,737 sq. mi. (rank: 13th)
Population: 2,937,880 (rank: 35th)
Largest city: Wichita, 397,532, H-13

Index of places Pg. 131

Travel planning & on-the-road resources

Tourism Information
Kansas Tourism Office: (785) 296-2009; www.travelks.com

Road Conditions & Construction
511, (866) 511-5368; www.kandrive.org, www.ksdot.org

Toll Road Information
Kansas Turnpike Authority (*K-TAG*): (800) 873-5824, (316) 682-4537; www.ksturnpike.com

Determining distances along roads

Highway distances (segments of one mile or less not shown):
Cumulative miles (red): the distance between red arrows
Intermediate miles (black): the distance between intersections & places

Interchanges and exit numbers
For most states, the mileage between interchanges may be determined by subtracting one number from the other.

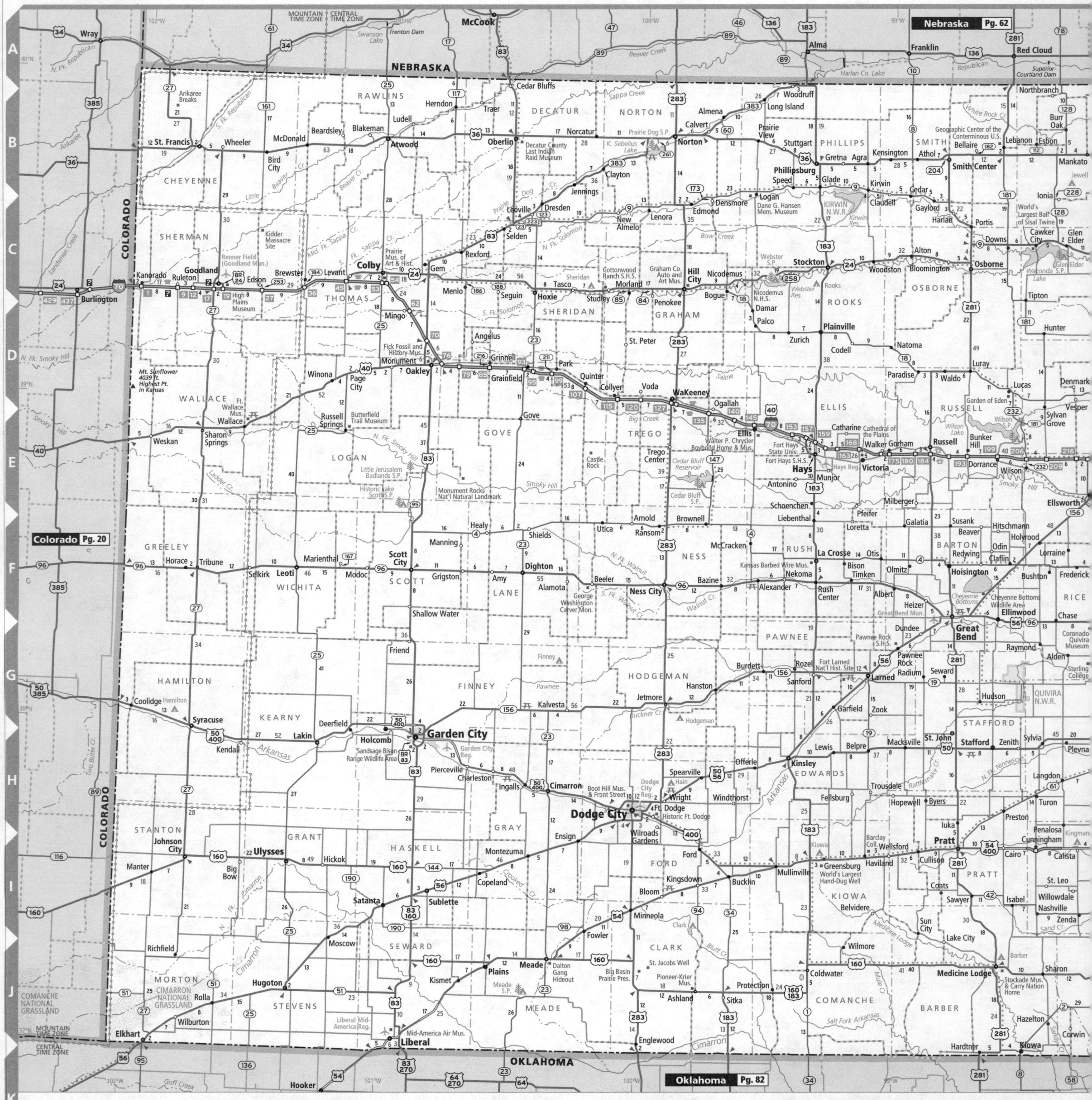
Nebraska Pg. 62
Colorado Pg. 20
Oklahoma Pg. 82
NEBRASKA
COLORADO
OKLAHOMA

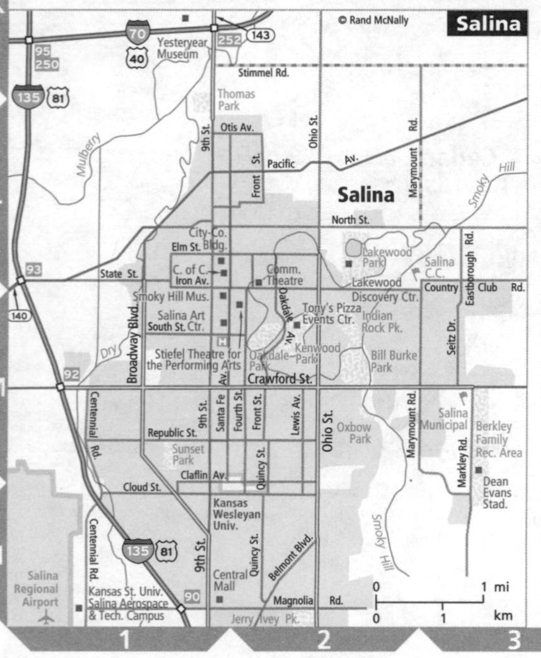
Salina

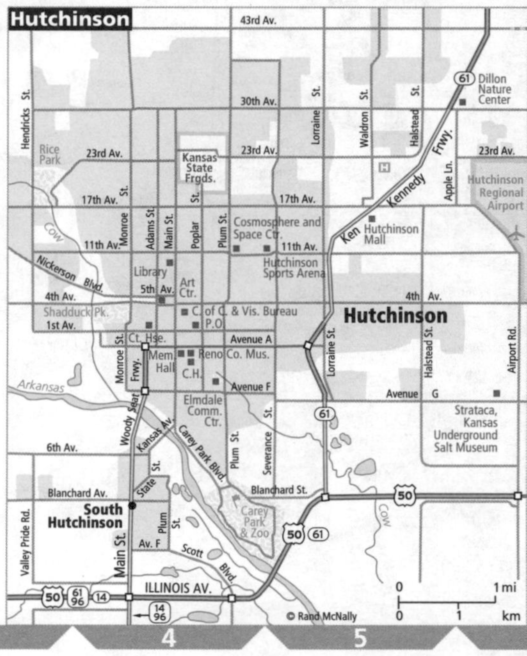
Hutchinson

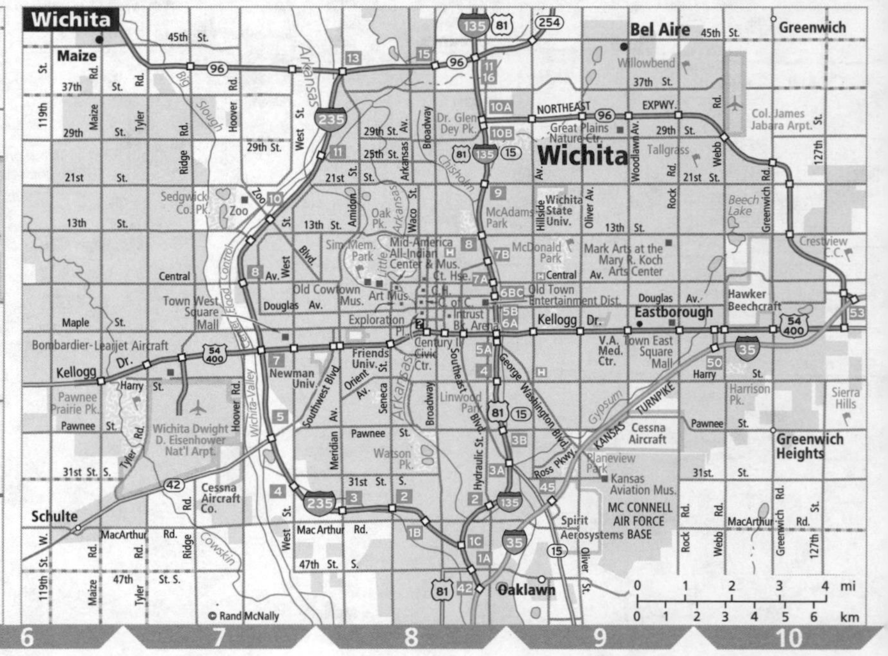
Wichita

Monument Rocks

Mileages between cities

	Arkansas City	Atchison	Coffeyville	Dodge City	Emporia	Fort Scott	Goodland	Hays	Hutchinson	Joplin, MO	Kansas City	Liberal	Manhattan	Salina	Topeka	Wichita
Dodge City	212	323	288		240	304	192	104	122	337	333	82	227	164	273	154
Goodland	384	395	455	192	349	472		144	268	505	406	209	299	235	344	323
Joplin, MO	150	196	65	337	177	60	505	366	233		154	395	252	274	196	183
Kansas City	228	58	172	333	109	94	406	266	220	154		406	117	173	62	196
Salina	151	160	224	164	117	238	235	96	65	274	173	246	65		109	90
Smith Center	266	213	338	195	231	342	175	91	155	387	263	277	150	117	206	205
Topeka	170	55	155	273	58	136	344	204	162	196	62	349	56	109		137
Wichita	61	188	134	154	85	149	323	183	51	183	196	212	130	90	137	

Total mileages through Kansas

- 35: 235 miles
- 56: 464 miles
- 70: 424 miles
- 81: 220 miles

More mileages at randmcnally.com/MC

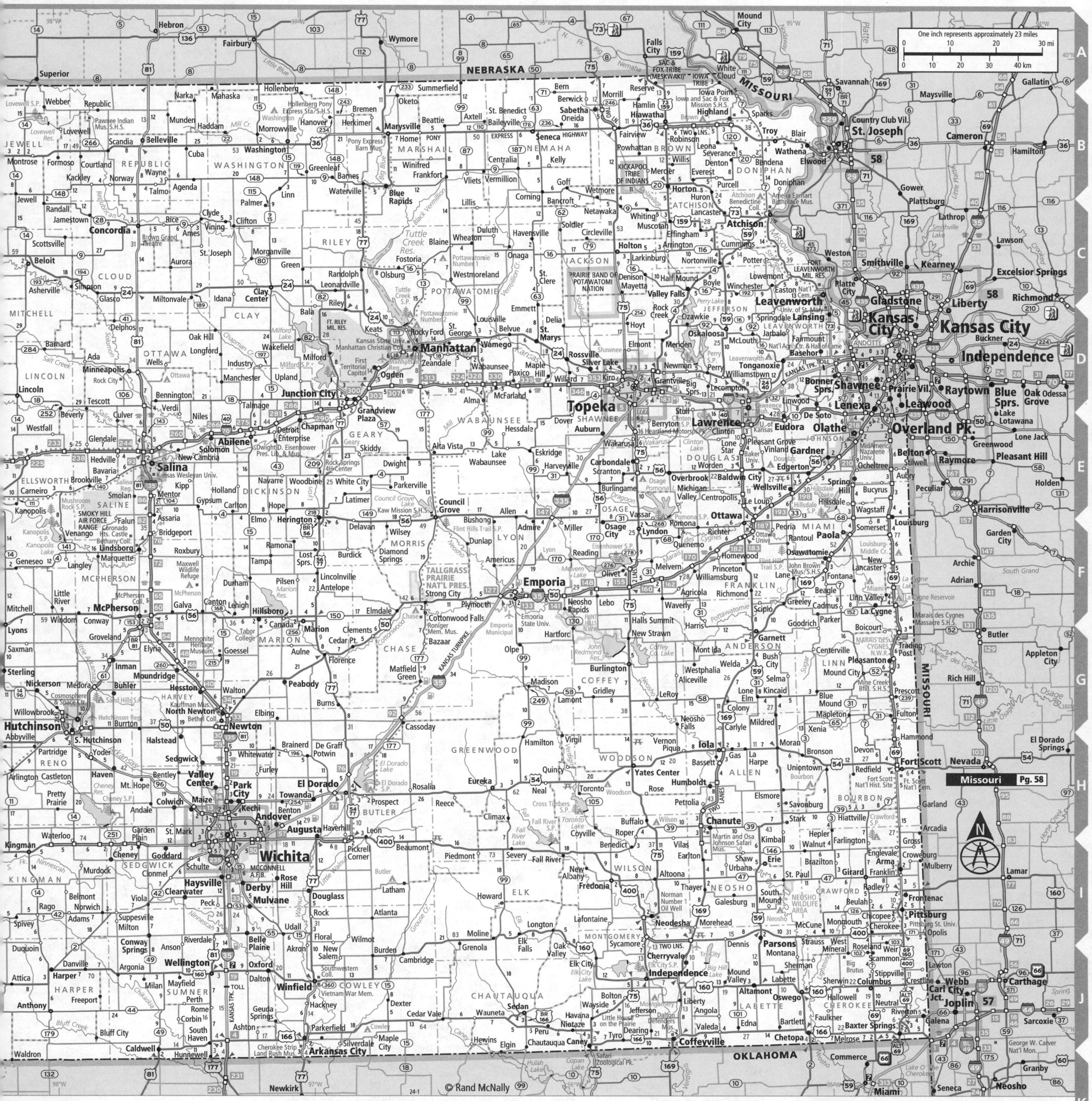

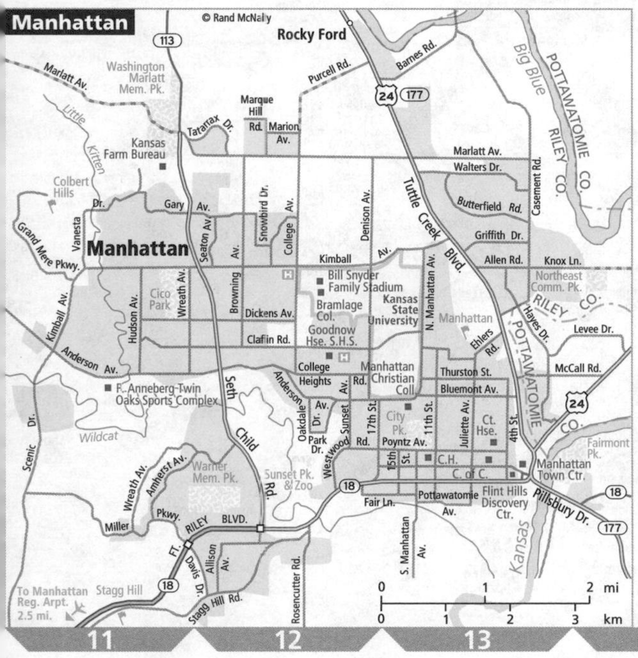

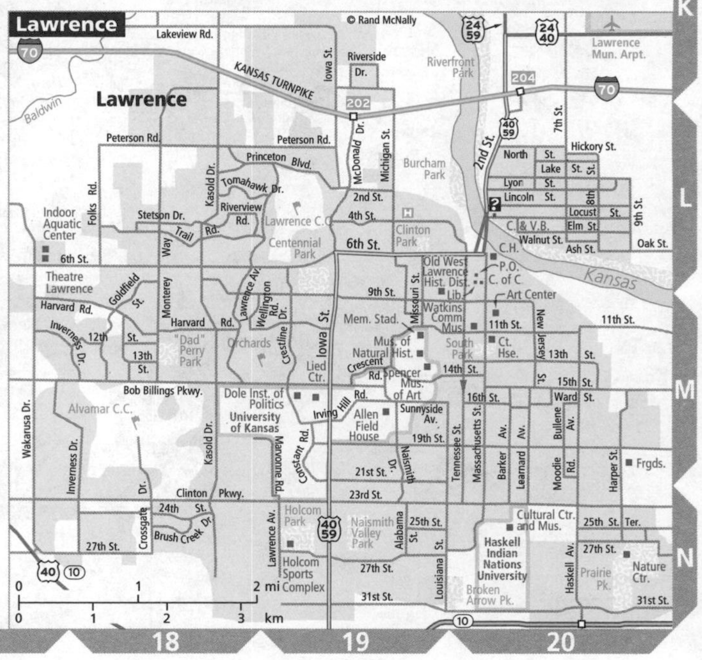

One inch represents approximately 23 miles

Missouri Pg. 58

NEBRASKA

MISSOURI

OKLAHOMA

Manhattan

Topeka

Lawrence

Kentucky

Nickname: The Bluegrass State
Capital: Frankfort, G-11
Land area: 39,481 sq. mi. (rank: 36th)
Population: 4,505,836 (rank: 26th)
Largest city: Louisville, 633,045, G-8

Index of places Pg. 131

Travel planning & on-the-road resources

Tourism Information
Kentucky Department of Tourism: (800) 225-8747, (502) 564-4930; www.kentuckytourism.com

Road Conditions & Construction
511, (866) 737-3767; transportation.ky.gov/sites/goky, drive.ky.gov

Toll Road Information
RiverLink (Louisville area toll bridges) *(RiverLink or E-ZPass)*: (855) 748-5465; www.riverlink.com

Determining distances along roads

Highway distances (segments of one mile or less not shown):
Cumulative miles (red): the distance between red arrows
Intermediate miles (black): the distance between intersections & places

Interchanges and exit numbers
For most states, the mileage between interchanges may be determined by subtracting one number from the other.

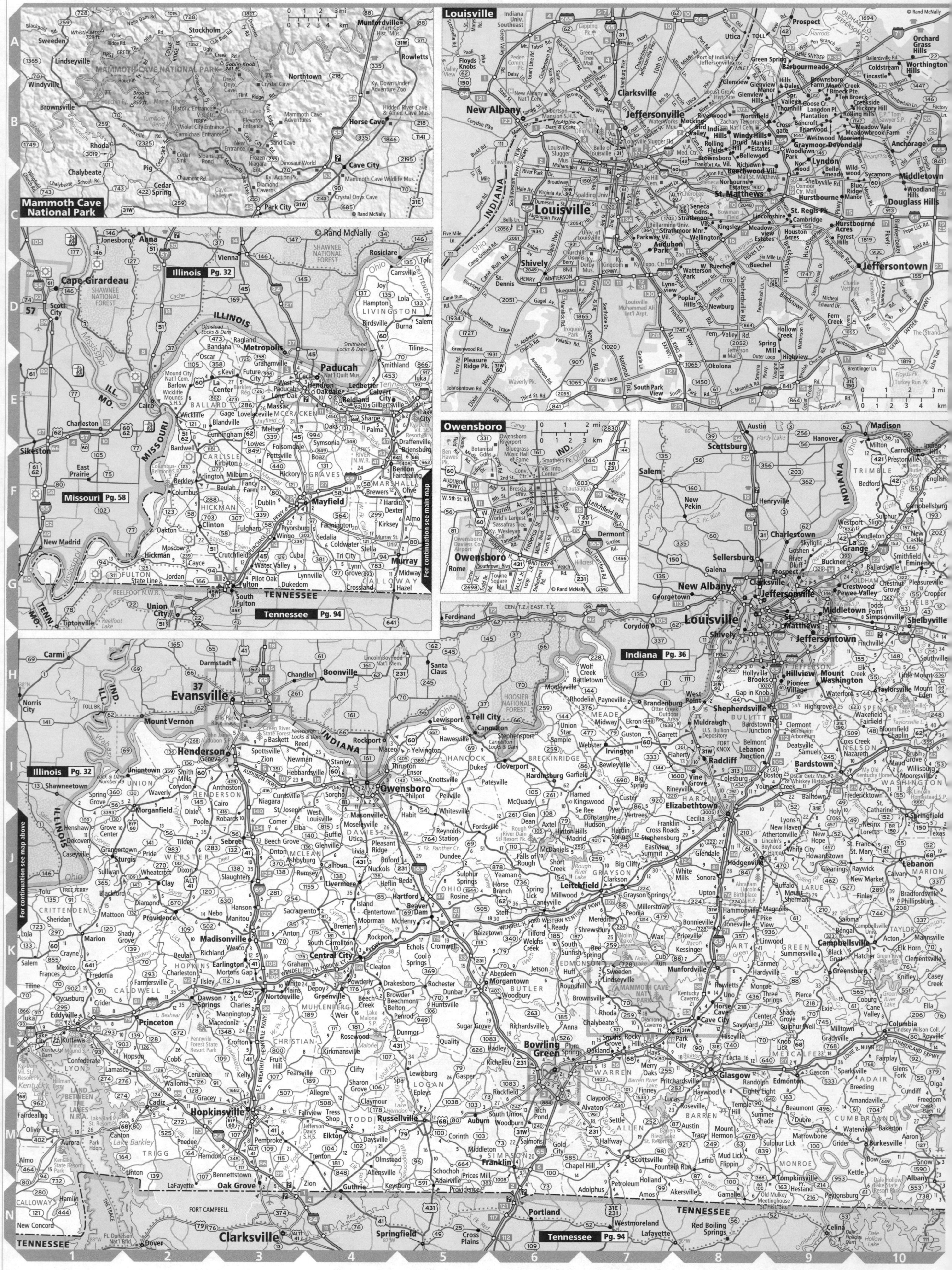
Mammoth Cave National Park
Louisville
Owensboro
Illinois Pg. 32
Missouri Pg. 58
Tennessee Pg. 94
Indiana Pg. 36
For continuation see main map
For continuation see map above
© Rand McNally
Paducah
Evansville
Henderson
Owensboro
Bowling Green
Hopkinsville
Clarksville
Elizabethtown
Louisville
Jeffersontown
Madisonville
Glasgow
TENNESSEE
INDIANA
ILLINOIS

Mileages between cities

	Ashland	Bowling Green	Cave City	Covington	Elizabethtown	Frankfort	Hopkinsville	Lexington	Louisville	Mayfield	Maysville	Middlesboro	Owensboro	Paducah	Pikeville	Somerset
Ashland		269	242	138	202	140	325	117	187	383	76	227	294	372	96	175
Bowling Green	269		31	209	70	147	64	151	113	160	216	198	71	151	265	109
Covington	138	209	181		140	78	265	81	97	322	59	208	203	312	216	157
Lexington	117	151	124	81	84	29	207		76	266	63	130	177	256	140	78
Louisville	187	113	85	97	44	50	170	76		227	133	203	106	216	211	124
Middlesboro	227	198	176	208	182	157	265	130	203	363	191		275	353	125	88
Owensboro	294	71	108	203	94	159	96	177	106	154	242	275		143	318	187
Paducah	372	151	186	312	172	250	72	256	216	24	319	353	143		396	265

Total mileages through Kentucky

64: 191 miles; 71: 97 miles; 65: 137 miles; 75: 192 miles

More mileages at randmcnally.com/MC

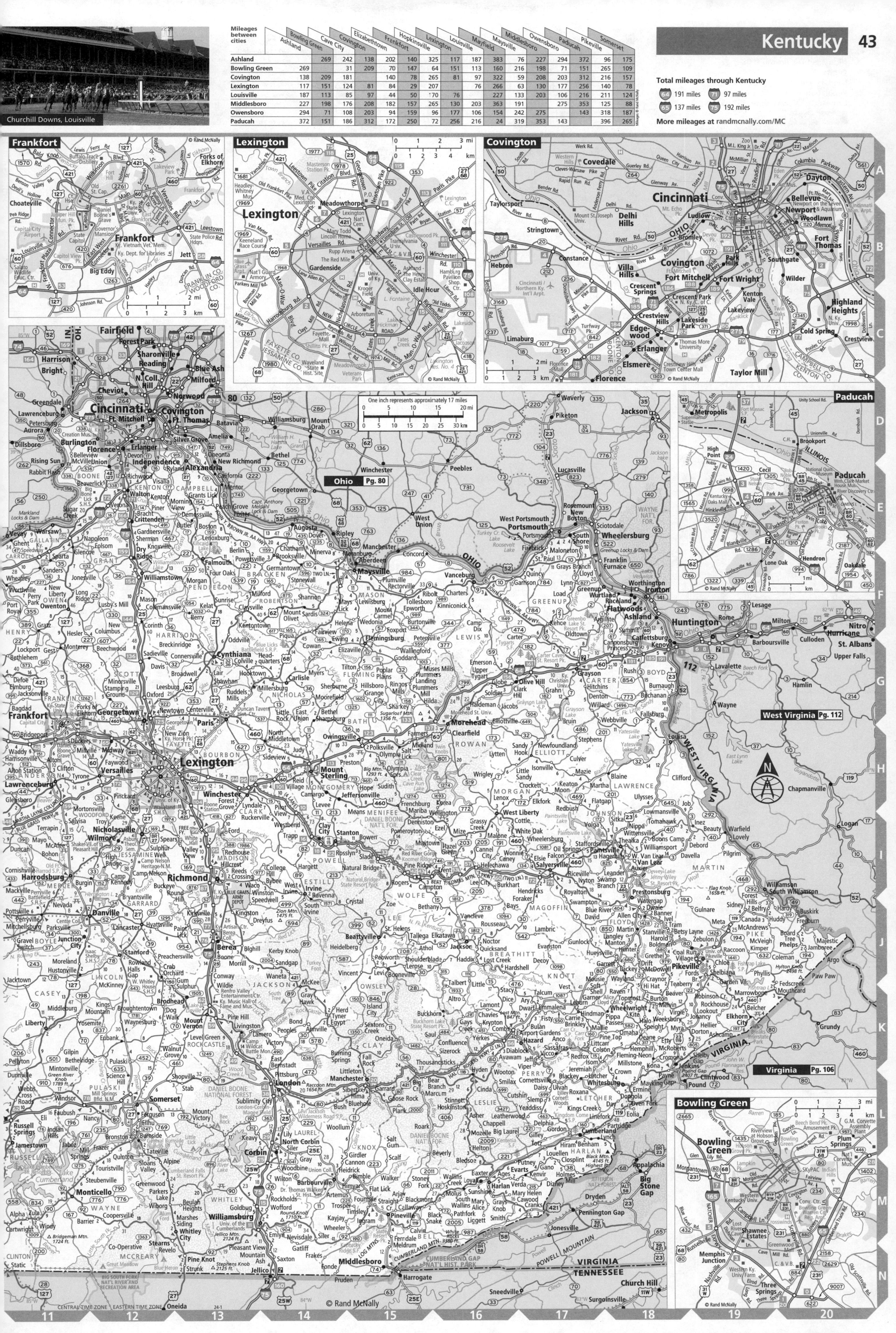

Louisiana

Nickname: The Pelican State
Capital: Baton Rouge, G-7
Land area: 43,193 sq. mi. (rank: 33rd)
Population: 4,657,757 (rank: 25th)
Largest city: New Orleans, 383,997, H-9

Index of places Pg. 131

Mileages between cities	Baton Rouge	Beaumont, TX	Houma	Lake Charles	Monroe	New Orleans	Shreveport	Vicksburg, MS
Alexandria	125	155	190	97	95	218	123	147
Baton Rouge		183	85	124	186	79	250	157
Gulfport, MS	134	318	131	258	276	78	375	201
Lafayette	55	133	102	73	182	134	211	212
Lake Charles	124	60	177		190	203	184	243
New Orleans	79	262	56	203	281		340	207
Shreveport	250	206	314	184	98	340		171
Vicksburg, MS	157	301	234	243	74	207	171	

Mileages © Rand McNally

Total mileages through Louisiana

10: 274 miles
20: 190 miles
49: 208 miles
55: 66 miles

More mileages at randmcnally.com/MC

Travel planning & on-the-road resources

Tourism Information
Louisiana Office of Tourism: (225) 342-8100; www.louisianatravel.com

Road Conditions & Construction
511, (888) 762-3511; www.511la.org, www.dotd.la.gov

Toll Bridges
Louisiana Dept. of Trans. & Development (La. Hwy. 1 Bridge) *(GeauxPass)*: (866) 662-8987; www.geauxpass.com
Lake Ponchartrain Causeway *(TollTag)*: (504) 835-3118; www.thecauseway.us

Travel planning & on-the-road resources

Tourism Information
Maine Office of Tourism:
(888) 624-6345
(207) 624-7483
visitmaine.com

Toll Road Information
Maine Turnpike Authority
(E-ZPass): (877) 682-9433
(207) 871-7771
www.maineturnpike.com

Road Conditions & Construction
511, (207) 624-3000; newengland511.org
www.maine.gov/mdot

Determining Distances
(segments of one mile or less not shown)

Cumulative miles (red): the distance between red arrows

Intermediate miles (black): the distance between intersections & places

Total mileages through Maine

95: 299 miles
2: 273 miles
1: 527 miles
201: 164 miles

More mileages at randmcnally.com/MC

Mileages between cities	Auburn	Bangor	Bar Harbor	Eastport	Houlton	Millinocket	Portland	Rangeley
Bangor	107		47	120	118	72	128	120
Eastport	226	120	118		115	125	247	242
Houlton	225	118	167	115		69	246	238
Madawaska	326	219	267	218	102	170	347	339
Portland	35	128	174	247	246	181		118
Portsmouth, NH	81	180	225	301	298	231	51	165
Rangeley	84	120	165	242	238	153	118	
Waterville	53	55	101	174	173	107	75	77

Nickname: The Pine Tree State
Capital: Augusta, F-4
Land area: 30,837 sq. mi. (rank: 39th)
Population: 1,362,359 (rank: 42nd)
Largest city: Portland, 68,408, H-3

Index of places Pg. 131

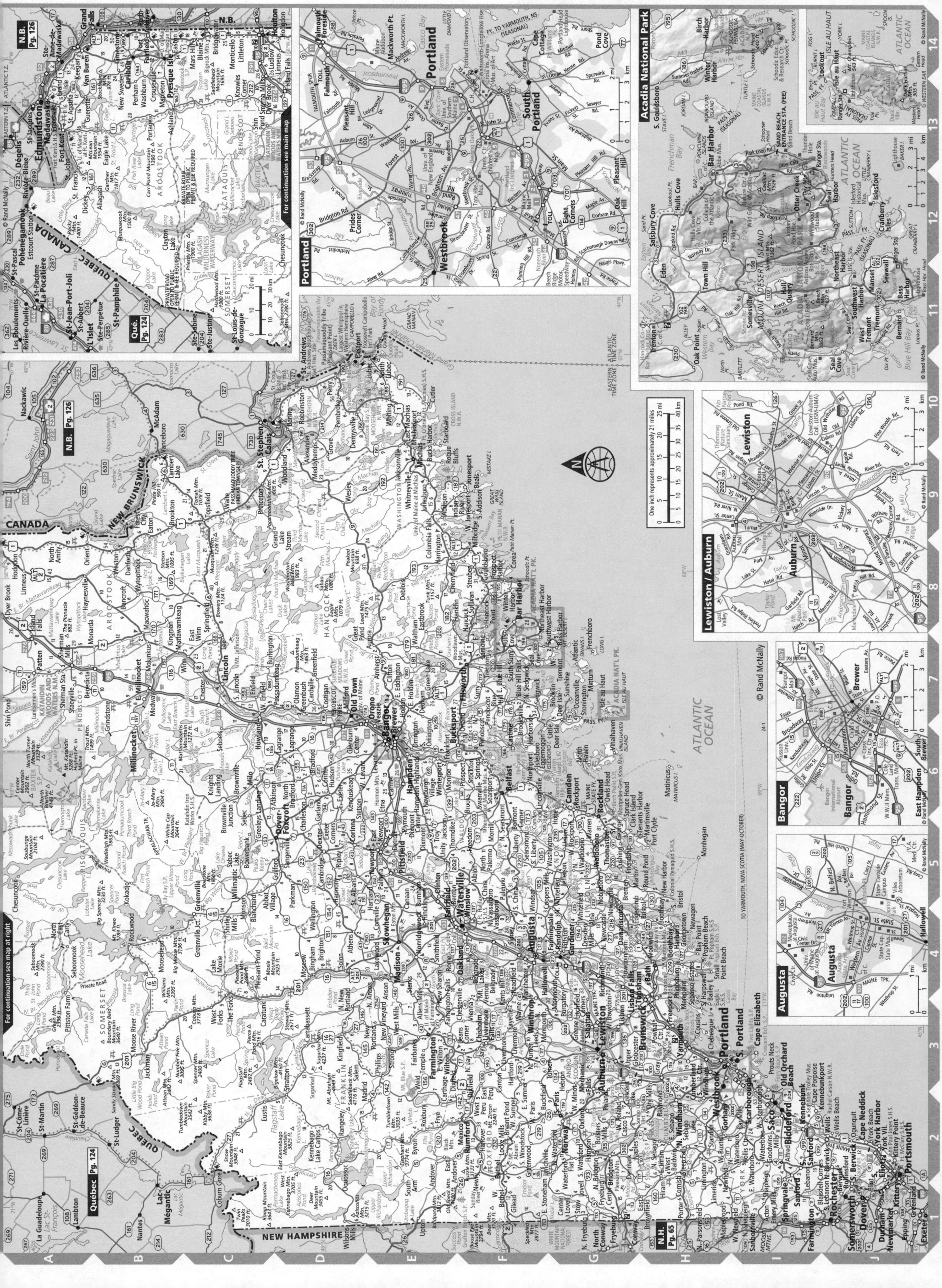

Maryland

Nickname: The Old Line State
Capital: Annapolis, E-14
Land area: 9,709 sq. mi. (rank: 42nd)
Population: 6,177,224 (rank: 18th)
Largest city: Baltimore, 585,708, C-13

Index of places Pg. 131

Travel planning & on-the-road resources

Tourism Information
Maryland Office of Tourism Development: (877) 209-5883; visitmaryland.org

Road Conditions & Construction
511, (855) 466-3511, (410) 582-5605; chart.maryland.gov, www.roads.maryland.gov

Toll Road Information
Maryland Transportation Authority (*E-ZPass*):
(866) 713-1596, (410) 537-1000; mdta.maryland.gov

Determining distances along roads

Highway distances (segments of one mile or less not shown):
Cumulative miles (red): the distance between red arrows
Intermediate miles (black): the distance between intersections & places

Interchanges and exit numbers
For most states, the mileage between interchanges may be determined by subtracting one number from the other.

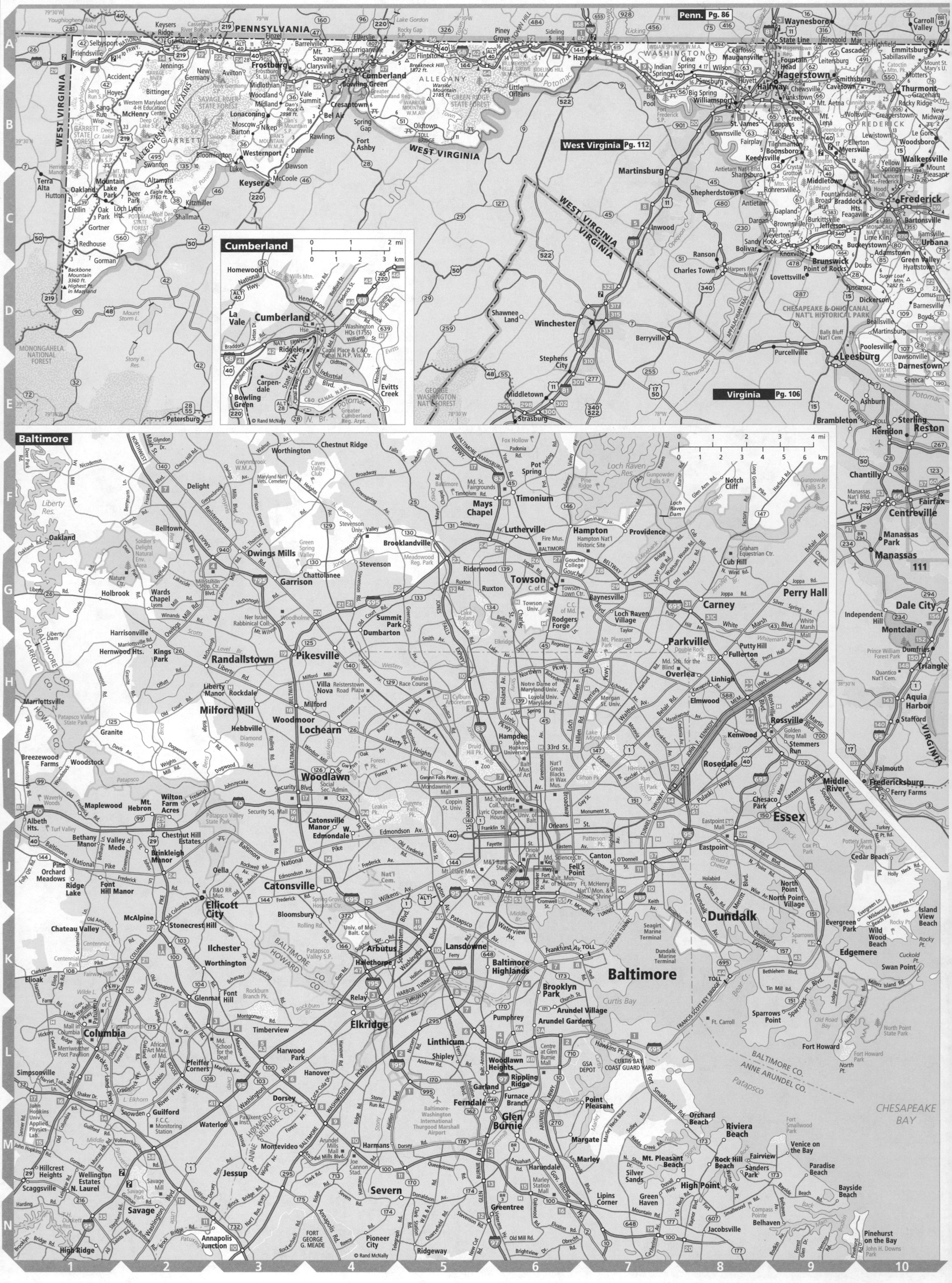

PENNSYLVANIA
WEST VIRGINIA
VIRGINIA
Penn. Pg. 86
West Virginia Pg. 112
Virginia Pg. 106
Cumberland
Baltimore
CHESAPEAKE BAY
© Rand McNally

Wild horses at Assateague Island National Seashore

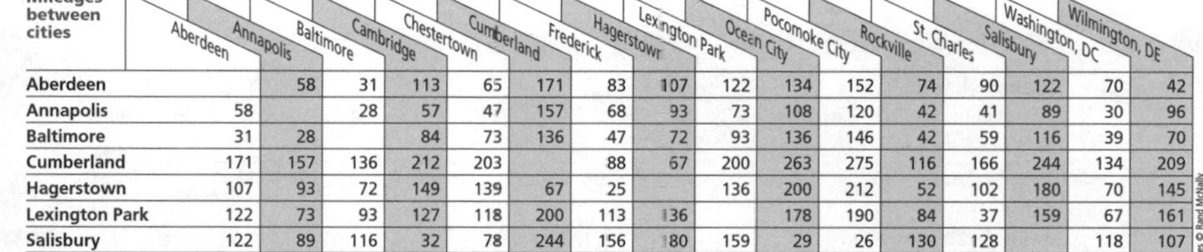

Mileages between cities	Aberdeen	Annapolis	Baltimore	Cambridge	Chestertown	Cumberland	Frederick	Hagerstown	Lexington Park	Ocean City	Pocomoke City	Rockville	St. Charles	Salisbury	Washington, DC	Wilmington, DE
Aberdeen		58	31	113	65	171	83	107	122	134	152	74	90	122	70	42
Annapolis	58		28	57	47	157	68	93	73	108	120	42	41	89	30	96
Baltimore	31	28		84	73	136	47	72	93	136	146	42	59	116	39	70
Cumberland	171	157	136	212	203		88	67	200	263	275	116	166	244	134	209
Hagerstown	107	93	72	149	139	67	25		136	200	212	52	102	180	70	145
Lexington Park	122	73	93	127	118	200	113	136		178	190	84	37	159	67	161
Salisbury	122	89	116	32	78	244	156	180	159	29	26	130	128		118	107
Washington, DC	70	30	39	86	76	134	48	70	67	139	148	19	30	118		109

Total mileages through Maryland

- 68: 81 miles
- 70: 94 miles
- 81: 12 miles
- 95: 110 miles

More mileages at randmcnally.com/MC

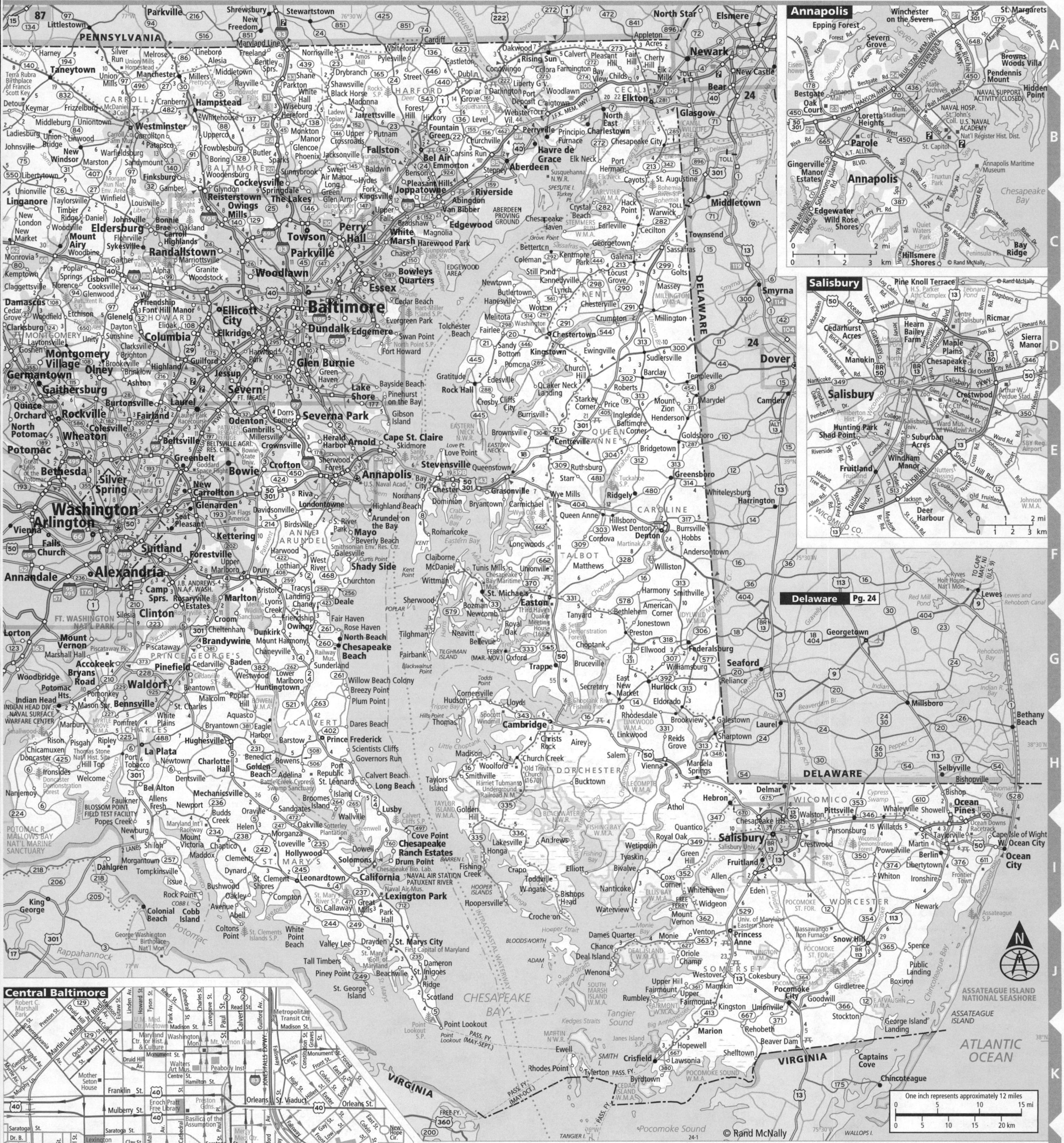

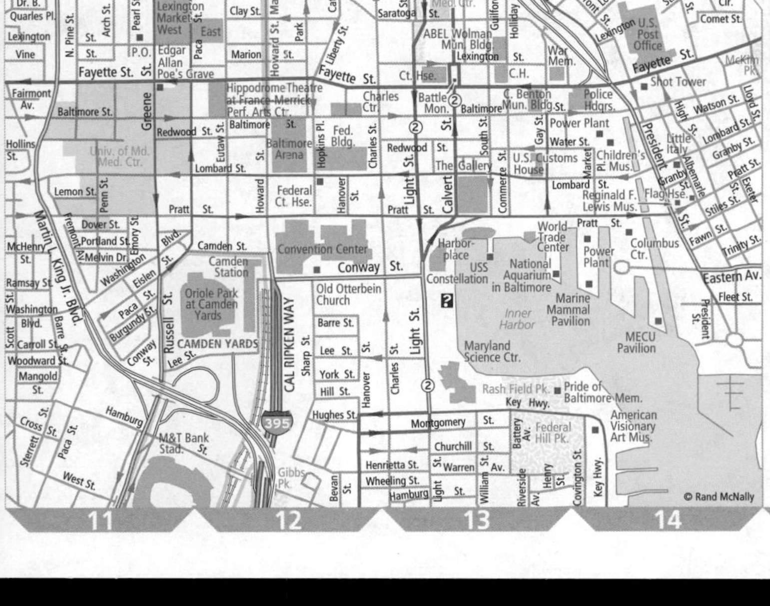

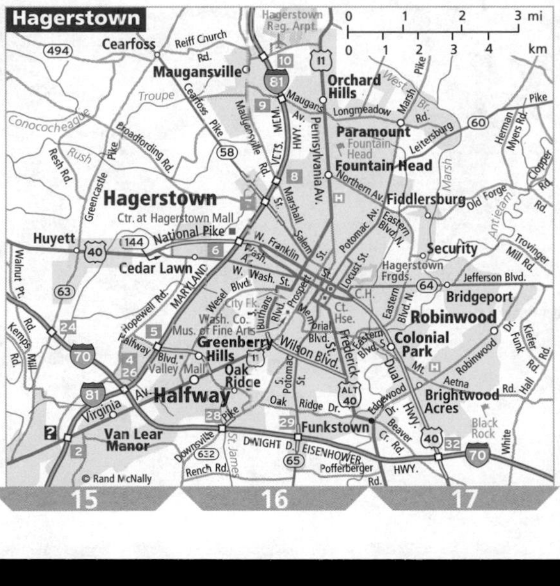

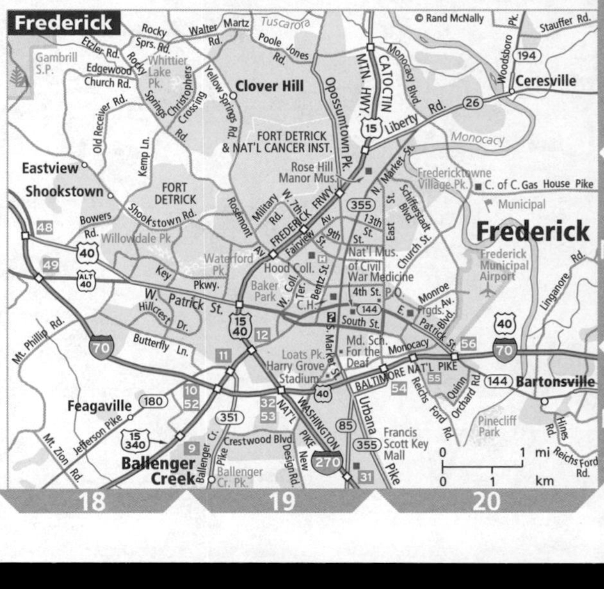

Annapolis

Salisbury

Delaware Pg. 24

Central Baltimore

Hagerstown

Frederick

One inch represents approximately 12 miles

Nickname: The Bay State
Capital: Boston, E-14
Land area: 7,799 sq. mi. (rank: 45th)
Population: 7,029,917 (rank: 15th)
Largest city: Boston, 675,647, E-14

Index of places Pg. 131

Travel planning & on-the-road resources

Tourism Information
Massachusetts Office of Travel & Tourism: (800) 227-6277, (617) 973-8500; www.visitma.com

Road Conditions & Construction
511, Metro Boston: (617) 986-5511, Central: (508) 499-5511, Western: (413) 754-5511
www.mass511.com

Toll Road Information
Massachusetts Department of Transportation (*E-ZPass*): (877) 627-7745; www.mass.gov/ezdrivema

Determining distances along roads

Highway distances (segments of one mile or less not shown):
Cumulative miles (red): the distance between red arrows
Intermediate miles (black): the distance between intersections & places

Interchanges and exit numbers
For most states, the mileage between interchanges may be determined by subtracting one number from the other.

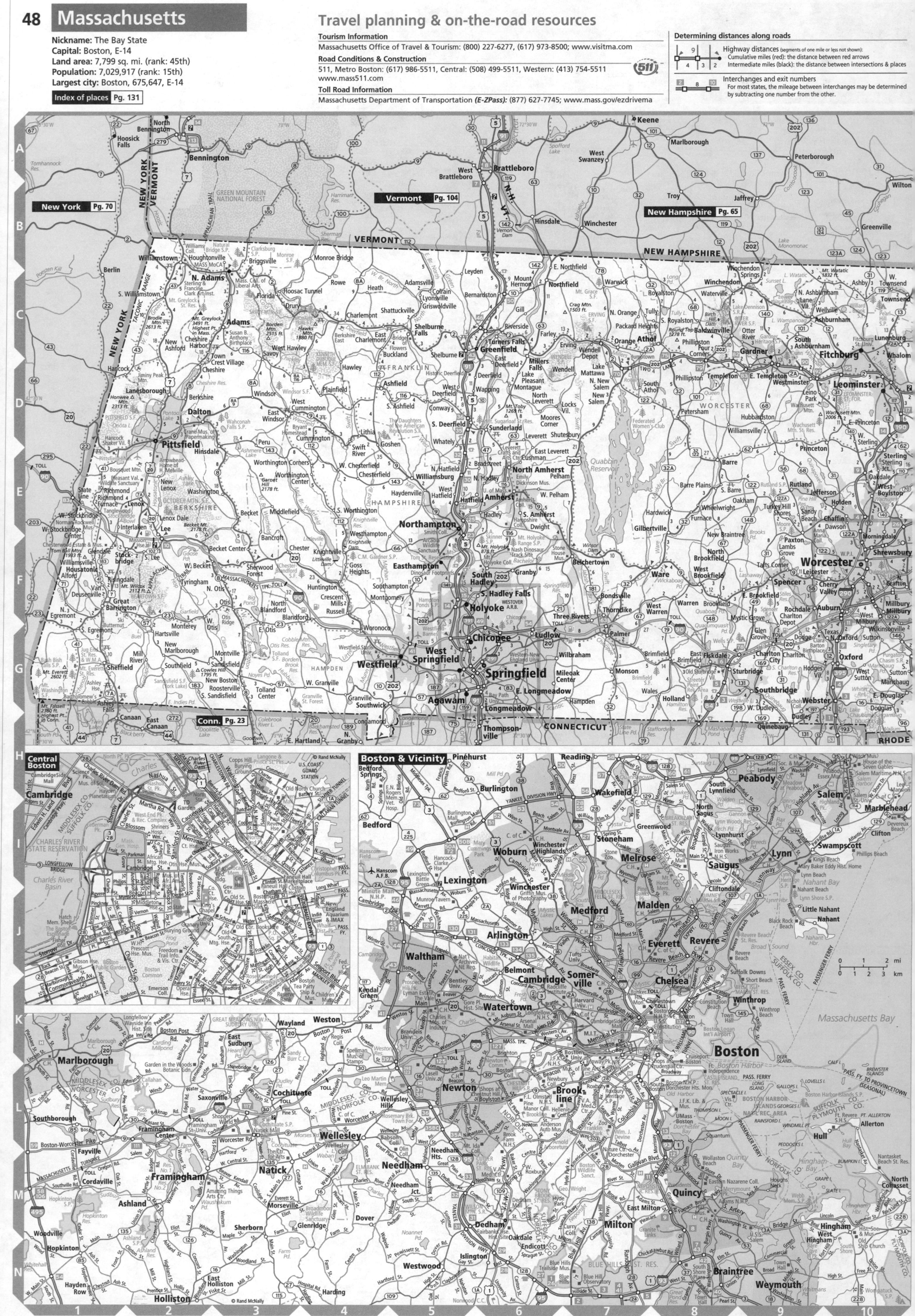

Faneuil Hall, Boston

Mileages between cities	Boston	Brockton	Falmouth	Fitchburg	Gloucester	Greenfield	Lowell	Nantucket	New Bedford	North Adams	Pittsfield	Plymouth	Providence, RI	Provincetown	Springfield	Worcester
Boston		24	76	47	39	94	29	101*	58	157	136	40	50	116	90	43
Gloucester	39	63	114	74		120	47	140*	97	157	169	78	90	154	122	75
Lowell	29	50	102	32	47	78		130*	84	115	139	69	69	145	92	41
New Bedford	58	37	40	94	97	148	84	77*		182	161	37	31	91	114	71
Pittsfield	136	150	189	124	169	79	139	226*	161	22		167	130	240	51	98
Provincetown	116	106	69	162	154	208	145	78*	91	262	240	77	119		194	146
Springfield	90	103	143	77	122	38	92	180*	114	73	51	121	83	194		51
Worcester	43	56	96	26	75	72	41	133*	71	120	98	74	40	146	51	

*Via ferry

Total mileages through Massachusetts

90: 136 miles; 95: 47 miles; 91: 55 miles; 93: 92 miles

More mileages at randmcnally.com/MC

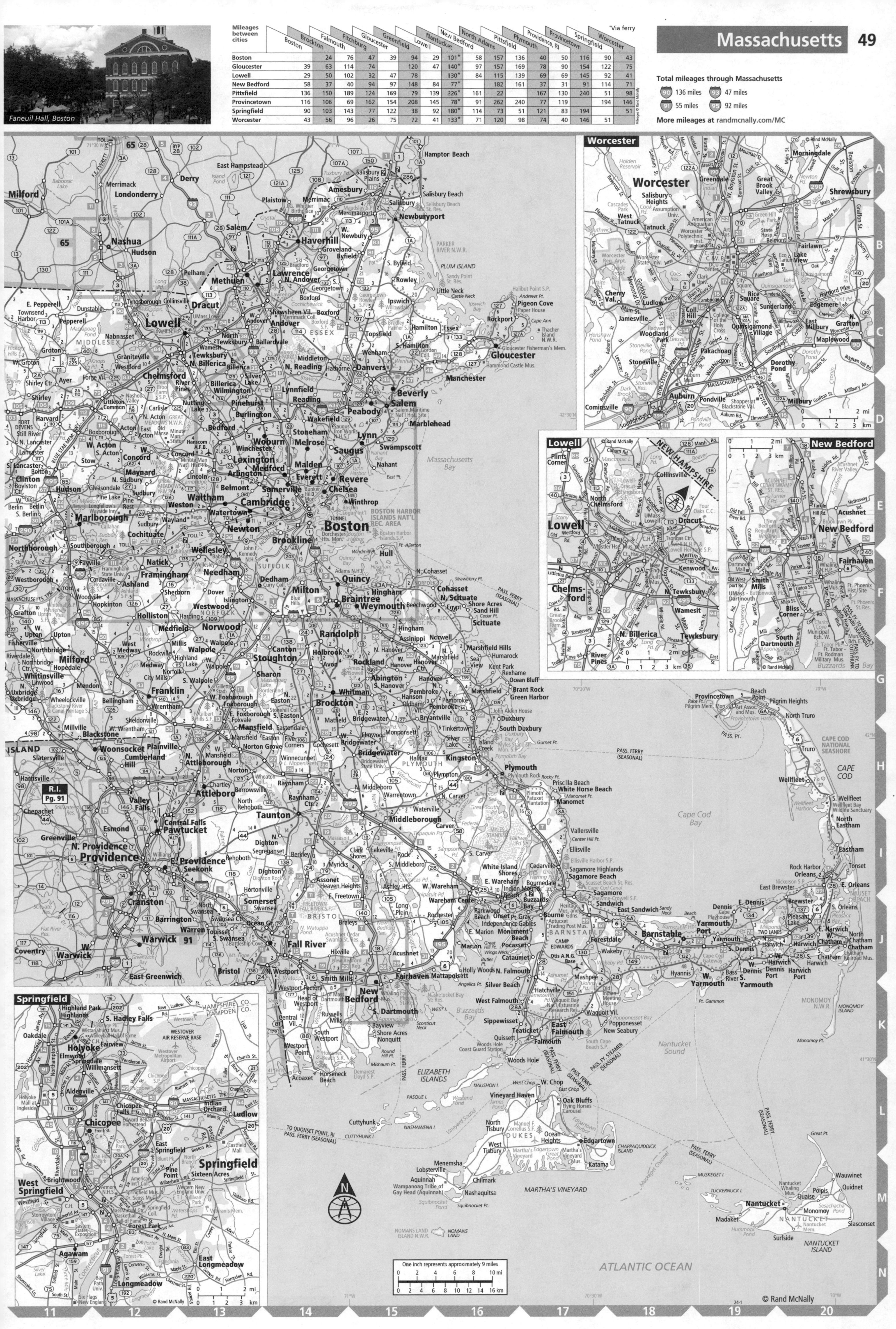

Nickname: The Great Lake State
Capital: Lansing, Q-9
Land area: 56,591 sq. mi. (rank: 22nd)
Population: 10,077,331 (rank: 10th)
Largest city: Detroit, 639,111, R-12

Index of places Pg. 131

Travel planning & on-the-road resources

Tourism Information
Pure Michigan:
(888) 784-7328; www.michigan.org

Road Conditions & Construction
(517) 241-2400
mdotjboss.state.mi.us/MiDrive/map
www.michigan.gov/mdot

International Toll Bridge/Tunnel Information
Michigan Department of Transportation: Blue Water Bridge (Port Huron): (810) 984-3131; www.michigan.gov/mdot
Ambassador Bridge (Detroit): www.ambassadorbridge.com
Detroit-Windsor Tunnel ***(NEXPRESS)***: (313) 567-4422 ext. 200, (519) 255-6100 ext. 6730; www.dwtunnel.com
International Bridge Administration (Sault Ste. Marie): (906) 635-5255, (705) 942-4345; www.saultbridge.com

Michigan Toll Bridge/Tunnel Information
Mackinac Bridge Authority ***(Mac Pass)***: (906) 643-7600; www.mackinacbridge.org

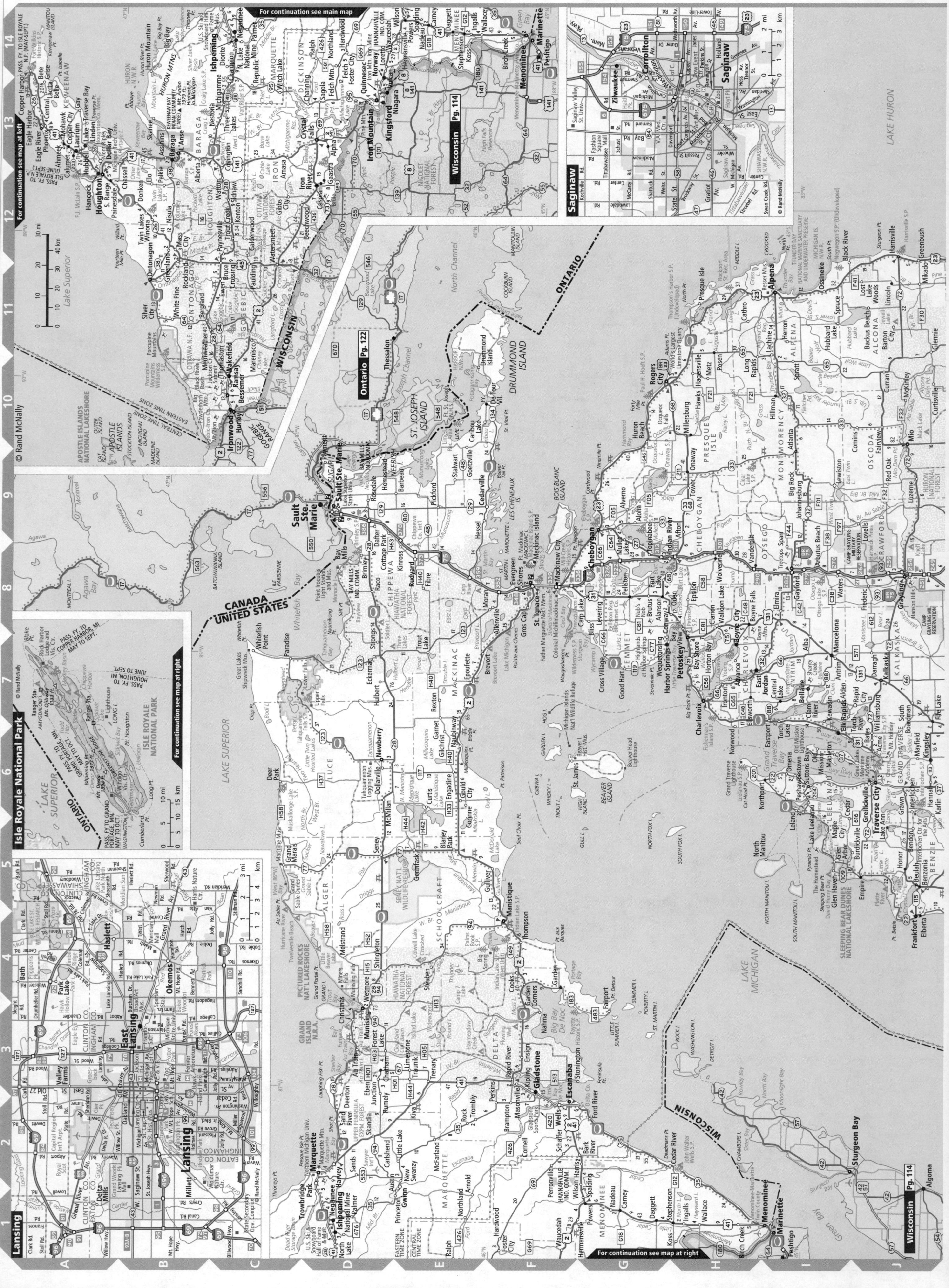

Eagle Harbor Lighthouse, Keweenaw Peninsula

Mileages between cities	Alpena	Chicago, IL	Detroit	Grand Rapids	Houghton	Ironwood	Kalamazoo	Ludington	Mackinaw City	Menominee	Muskegon	Port Huron	Saginaw	Sault Ste. Marie	Toledo, OH	Traverse City
Ann Arbor	227	240	43	132	538	584	98	228	272	473	172	102	86	329	51	238
Detroit	244	280		157	553	599	140	252	290	488	197	62	102	345	59	255
Flint	178	271	68	113	489	534	130	186	224	423	152	66	37	280	107	188
Grand Rapids	249	177	157		502	552	50	97	236	438	41	180	115	292	185	140
Ironwood	405	403	599	552	109		544	319	311	195	586	600	499	307	636	413
Kalamazoo	298	145	140	50	556	544		146	287	408	91	197	161	344	150	190
Lansing	228	216	90	68	494	539	75	162	228	429	107	122	88	284	118	180
Mackinaw City	94	412	290	236	266	311	287	218		200	251	290	188	56	327	102

Total mileages through Michigan

- 69: 199 miles
- 94: 275 miles
- 75: 396 miles
- 96: 192 miles

More mileages at randmcnally.com/MC

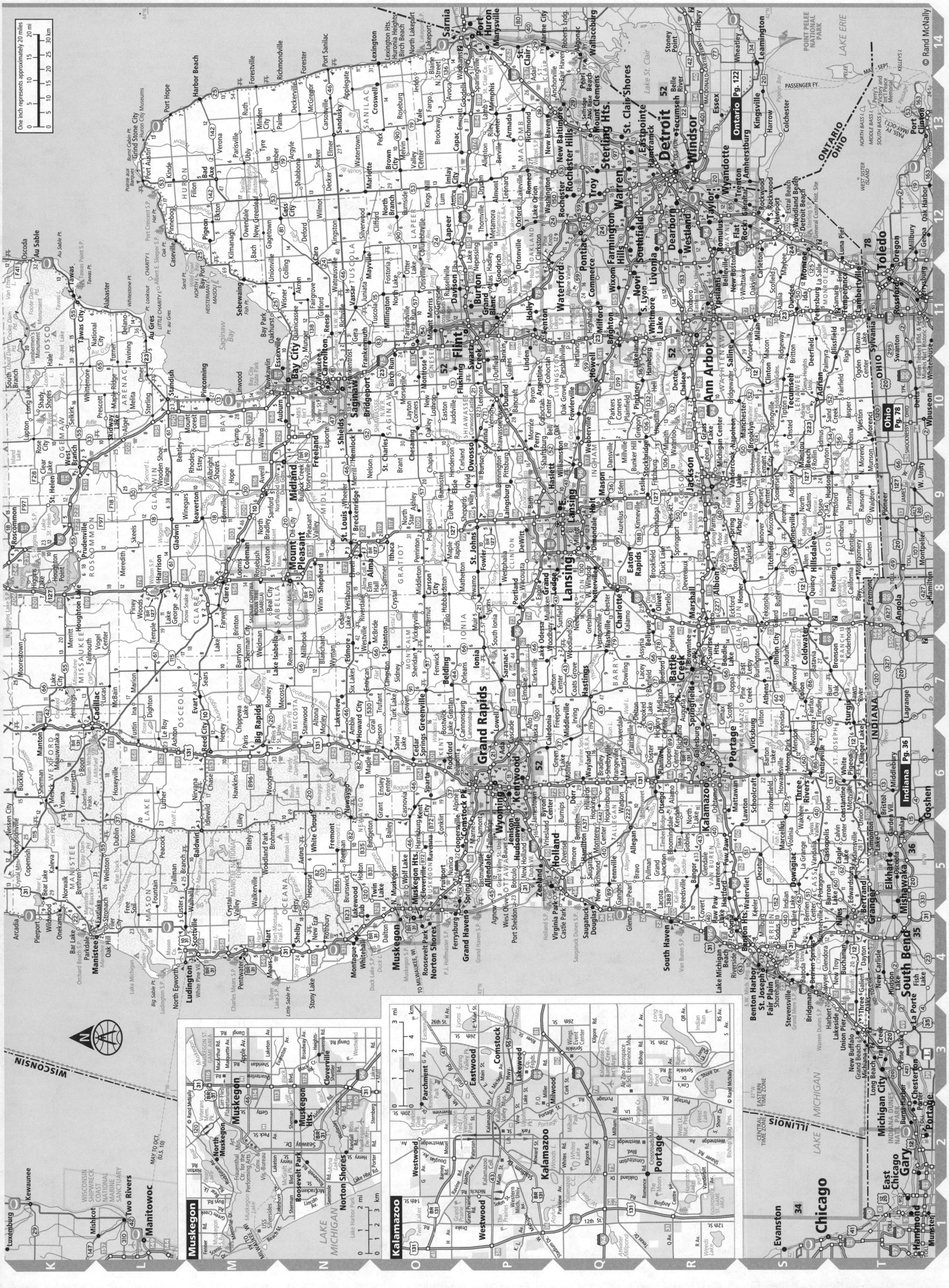

One inch represents approximately 20 miles

Muskegon

Kalamazoo

Ontario Pg. 122

Ohio Pg. 78

Indiana Pg. 36

Sights to see

- Cranbrook Art Museum, Bloomfield Hills D-5
- Detroit Zoo, Royal Oak E-6
- Edsel & Eleanor Ford House, Grosse Pointe Shores E-9
- Frederik Meijer Gardens, Grand Rapids. L-6
- Gerald R. Ford Museum, Grand Rapids L-5
- Gerald R. Ford Presidential Library, Ann Arbor M-10
- GM Renaissance Center, Detroit K-10
- Henry Ford Mus. of American Innovation, Dearborn . . H-5
- Michigan Science Center, Detroit. G-7
- Motown Historical Museum, Detroit. G-6
- Sloan Museum, Flint M-2
- University of Michigan, Ann Arbor M-9

Detroit Institute of Art

Detroit & Vicinity

Central Detroit

Flint

Grand Rapids

Ann Arbor

Walker Art Center, Minneapolis

Sights to see

- Bell Museum of Natural History, Minneapolis F-6
- Cathedral of St. Paul, St. Paul..................... M-7
- Frederick R. Weisman Art Museum, Minneapolis..... M-4
- Mall of America, Bloomington..................... I-5
- Mill City Museum, Minneapolis L-3
- Minneapolis Institute of the Arts, Minneapolis N-2
- Minneapolis Sculpture Garden, Minneapolis M-1
- Minnesota History Center, Minneapolis M-7
- Minnesota State Capitol, St. Paul.................. L-7
- Ordway Center for the Performing Arts, St. Paul..... M-7
- Science Museum of Minnesota, St. Paul M-7
- Walker Art Center, Minneapolis M-1

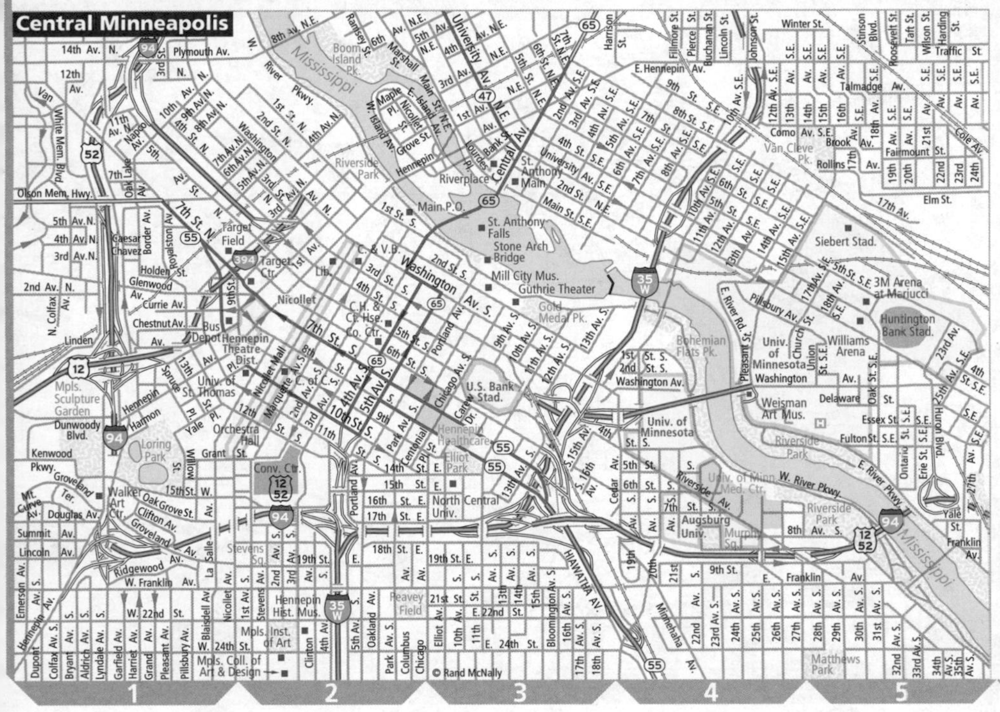

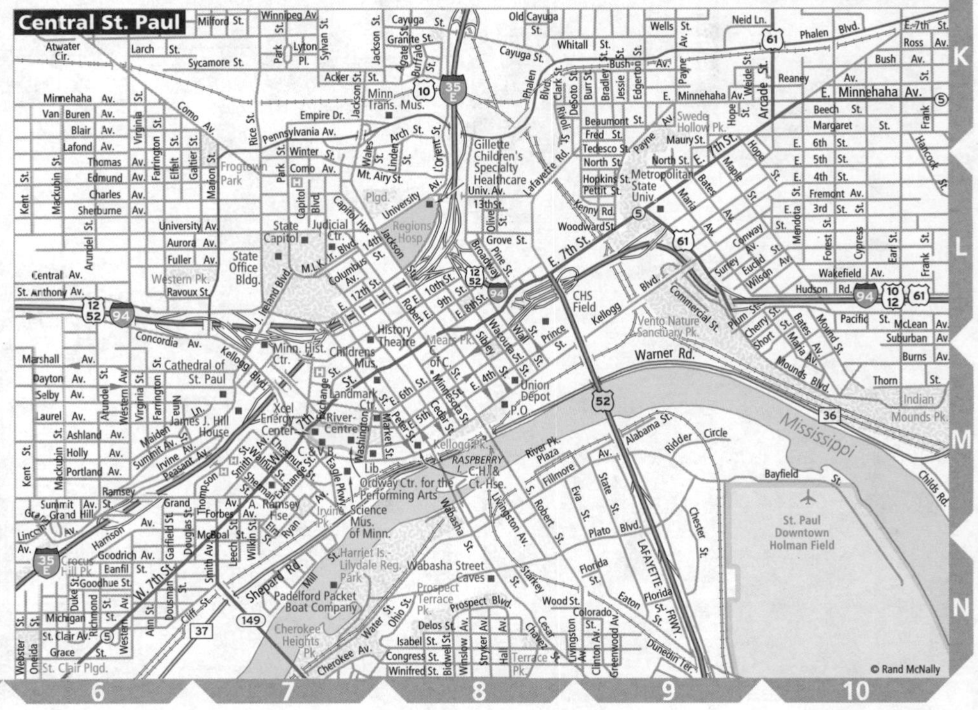

Minneapolis / St. Paul & Vicinity

Central Minneapolis

Central St. Paul

Minnesota

Nickname: The North Star State
Capital: St. Paul, O-10
Land area: 79,605 sq. mi. (rank: 14th)
Population: 5,706,494 (rank: 22nd)
Largest city: Minneapolis, 429,954, O-9

Index of places Pg. 132

Travel planning & on-the-road resources

Tourism Information
Explore Minnesota:
(888) 847-4866, (651) 556-8465; www.exploreminnesota.com

Road Conditions & Construction
511, (800) 542-0220
511mn.org, www.dot.state.mn.us

Toll Bridge Information
Boise Inc./Resolute Forest Products (Ft. Frances-International Falls Int'l Bridge):
recordsfinder.com/driving/usborder/border-crossings/mn/international-falls-fort-frances/

Toll Road Information
Minnesota Dept. of Transportation (Twin Cities metro) *(MnPass)*:
(800) 657-3774, (651) 296-3000; www.dot.state.mn.us/ezpassmn/

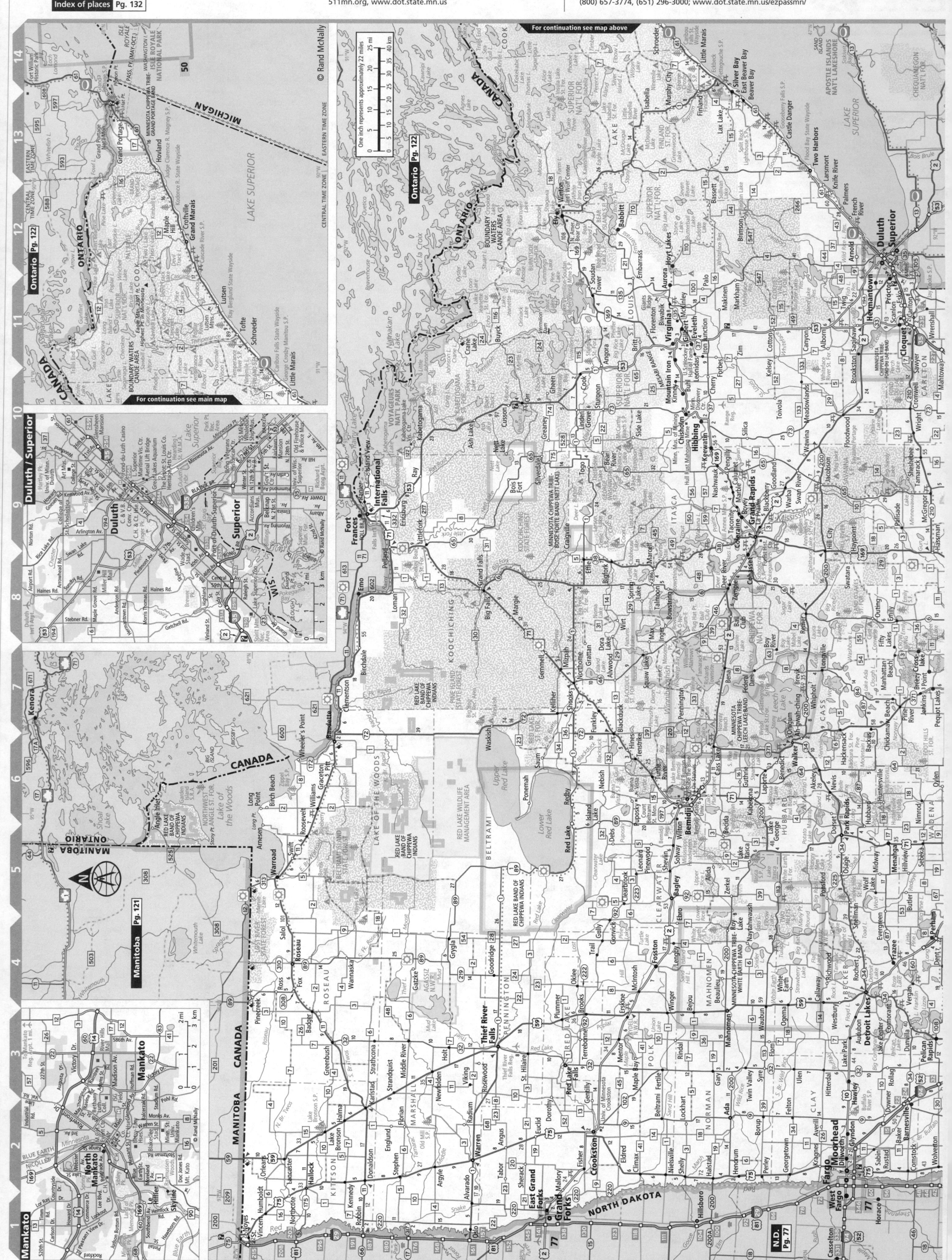

Boundary Waters Canoe Area

Mileages between cities	Albert Lea	Bemidji	Brainerd	Duluth	Grand Forks, ND	Grand Marais	Hibbing	International Falls	Mankato	Marshall	Minneapolis	Moorhead	Rochester	St. Cloud	Sioux Falls, SD	Willmar
Bemidji	316		97	151	114	259	105	112	290	258	222	135	306	151	380	188
Duluth	247	151	113		266	110	76	162	233	273	152	250	226	141	390	204
Minneapolis	96	222	130	152	314	262	208	293	80	153		233	86	65	236	93
Moorhead	328	135	136	250	82	361	212	249	303	206	233		321	170	244	172
Rochester	62	306	213	226	401	338	280	366	86	194	86	321		153	236	178
St. Cloud	160	151	63	141	251	253	173	251	135	130	65	170	153		220	62
St. Paul	98	230	137	149	325	260	204	290	87	159	9	243	78	75	241	102
Sioux Falls, SD	176	380	281	390	319	500	456	494	155	91	236	244	236	220		158

Total mileages through Minnesota

More mileages at randmcnally.com/MC

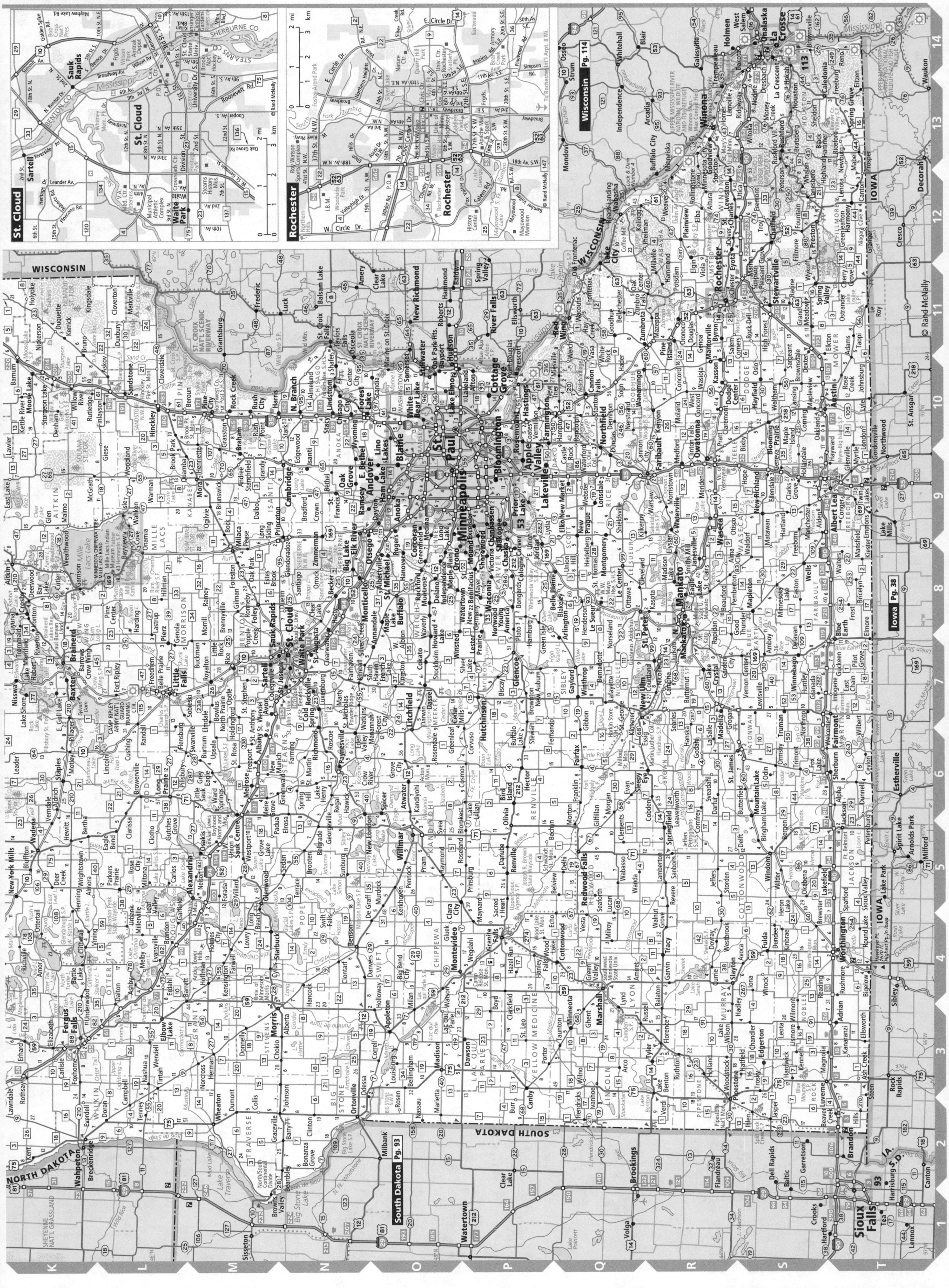

St. Cloud

Rochester

Mississippi

Nickname: The Magnolia State
Capital: Jackson, H-6
Land area: 46,913 sq. mi. (rank: 31st)
Population: 2,961,279 (rank: 34th)
Largest city: Jackson, 153,701, H-6

Index of places Pg. 132

Mileages between cities

	Batesville	Biloxi	Hattiesburg	Jackson	Memphis, TN	Natchez	Tupelo	Vicksburg
Biloxi	320		80	172	379	228	315	214
Greenville	112	293	210	121	152	152	177	91
Jackson	149	172	89		209	103	190	44
Memphis, TN	61	379	297	209		304	105	245
Meridian	176	172	89	91	234	194	142	134
New Orleans, LA	335	90	109	183	394	171	340	207
Tupelo	74	315	232	190	105	283		225
Vicksburg	188	214	131	44	245	70	225	

Total mileages through Mississippi

10: 77 miles
20: 169 miles
55: 290 miles
59: 172 miles

More mileages at randmcnally.com/MC

Travel planning & on-the-road resources

Tourism Information
Visit Mississippi:
(866) 733-6477, (601) 359-3129; visitmississippi.org

Road Conditions & Construction
(866) 521-6368
www.mdottraffic.com

Toll Road Information
No tolls on state or federal highways

Determining Distances

(segments of one mile or less not shown)
Cumulative miles (red): the distance between red arrows
Intermediate miles (black): the distance between intersections & places

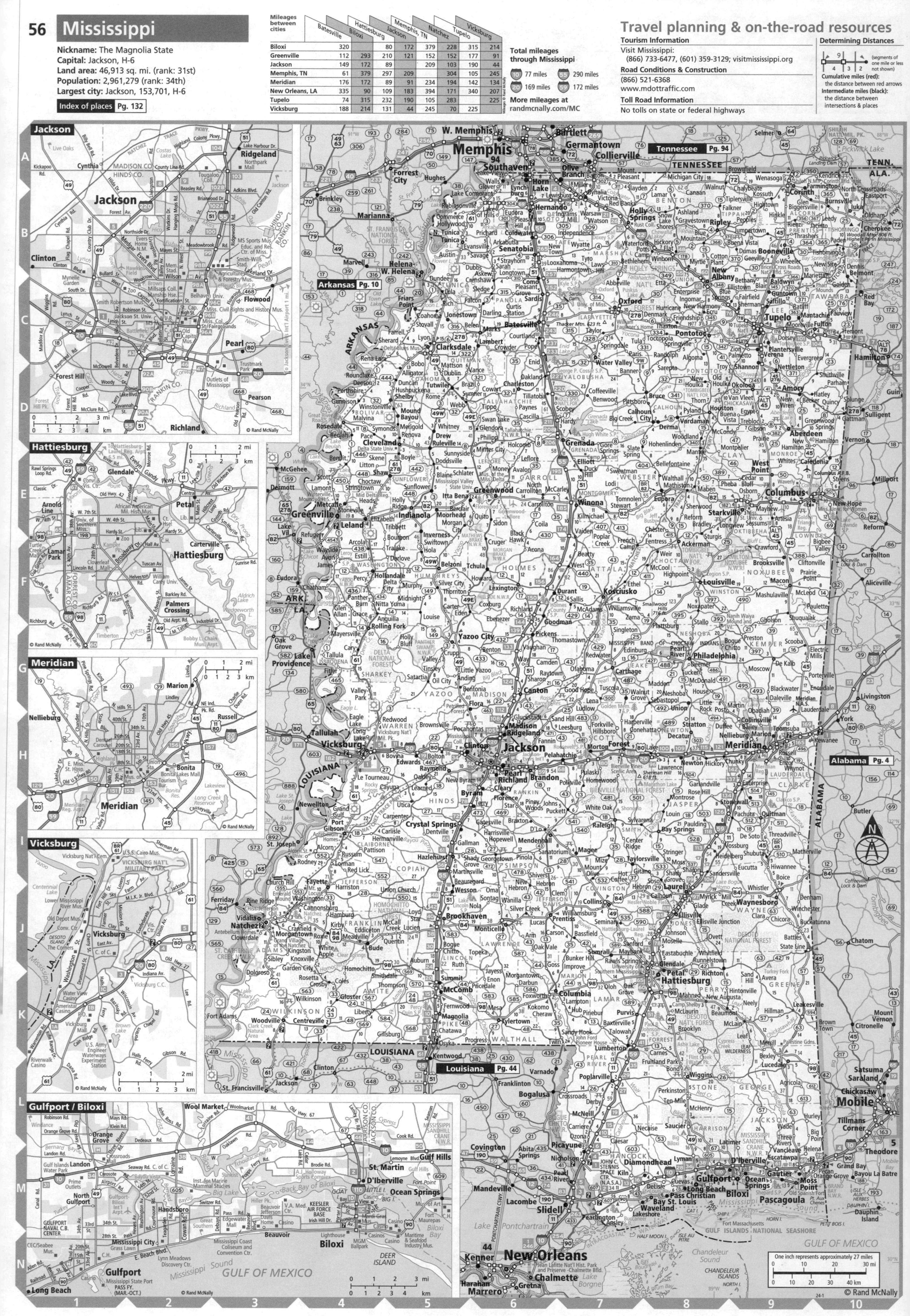

Gateway Arch, St. Louis

Sights to see

- Andy Williams Moon River Theatre, Branson M-8
- Anheuser-Busch Brewery, St. Louis . . . I-7
- Dolly Parton's Stampede, Branson M-9
- Gateway Arch Nat'l Park, St. Louis . . L-4
- Laumeier Sculpture Park, St. Louis . . J-4
- Magic House, Kirkwood I-4
- Missouri Botanical Garden, St. Louis . I-6
- St. Louis Art Museum, St. Louis H-6
- St. Louis Science Center, St. Louis . . . H-6
- St. Louis Zoo, St. Louis H-6
- Shepherd of the Hills, Branson K-6
- Shoji Tabuchi Theatre, Branson L-7
- White Water, Branson M-7
- Wonders of Wildlife Nat'l Museum & Aquarium, Springfield C-3

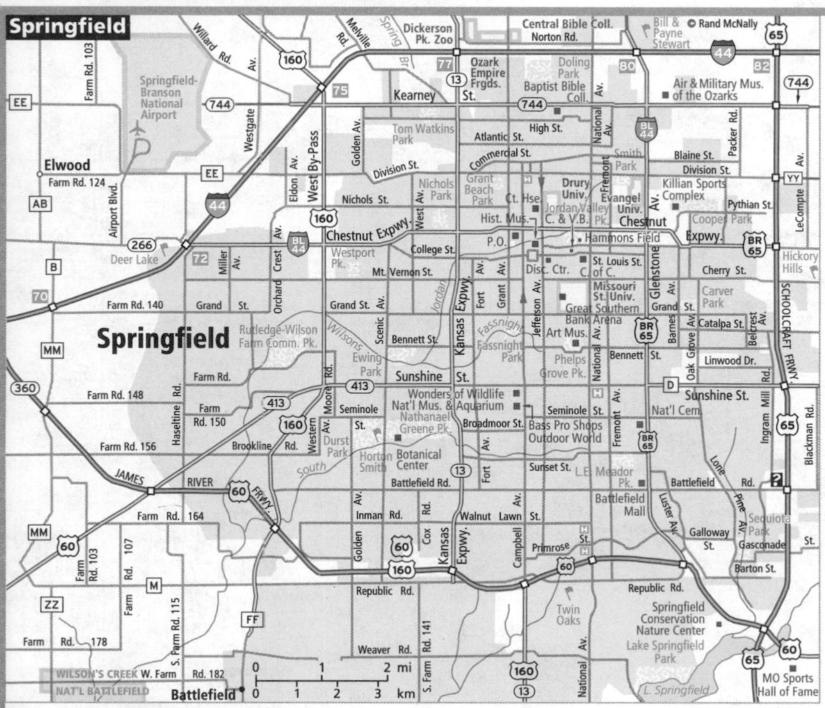

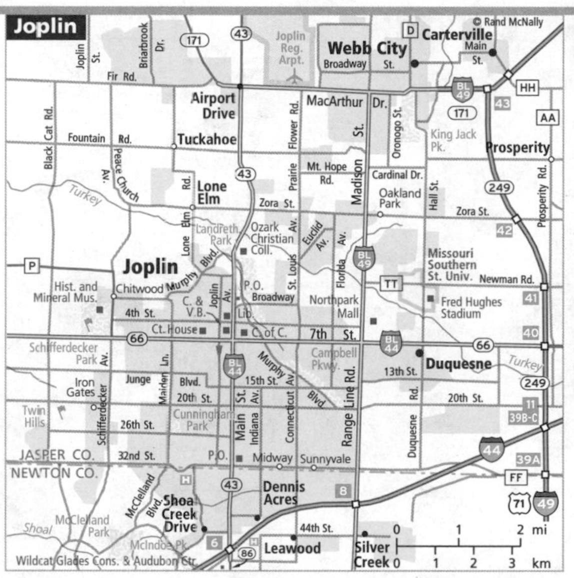

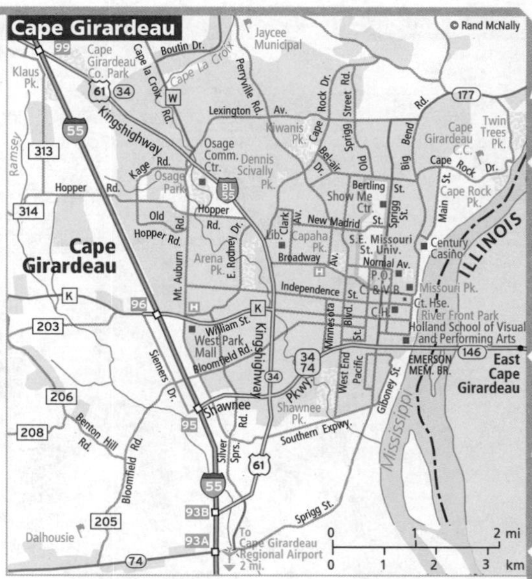

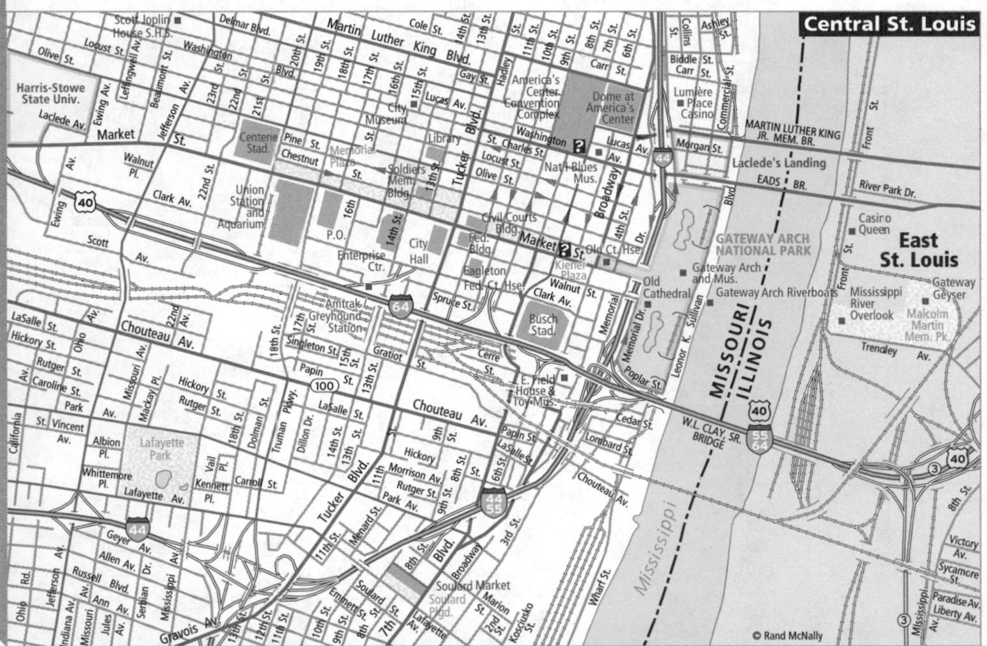

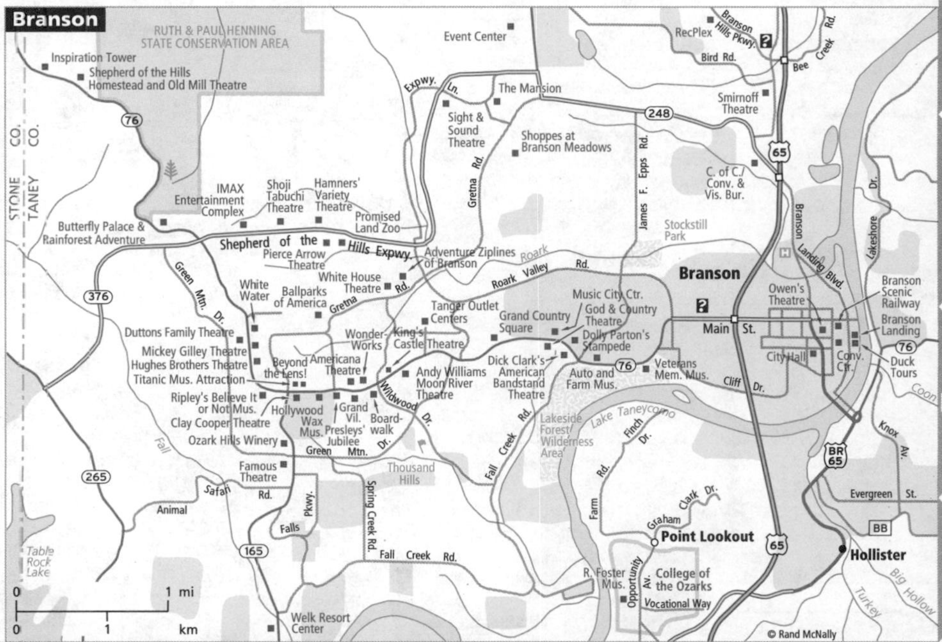

Springfield

Joplin

Cape Girardeau

St. Louis & Vicinity

Central St. Louis

Branson

Missouri

Nickname: The Show Me State
Capital: Jefferson City, G-14
Land area: 68,727 sq. mi. (rank: 18th)
Population: 6,154,913 (rank: 19th)
Largest city: Kansas City, 508,090, F-9

Index of places Pg. 132

Travel planning & on-the-road resources

Tourism Information
Missouri Division of Tourism: (573) 751-4133; www.visitmo.com

Road Conditions & Construction
(888) 275-6636, (866) 831-6277, (573) 751-2551; traveler.modot.org/map, www.modot.org

Toll Road Information
No tolls on state or federal highways

Determining distances along roads

Highway distances (segments of one mile or less not shown):
Cumulative miles (red): the distance between red arrows
Intermediate miles (black): the distance between intersections & places

Interchanges and exit numbers
For most states, the mileage between interchanges may be determined by subtracting one number from the other.

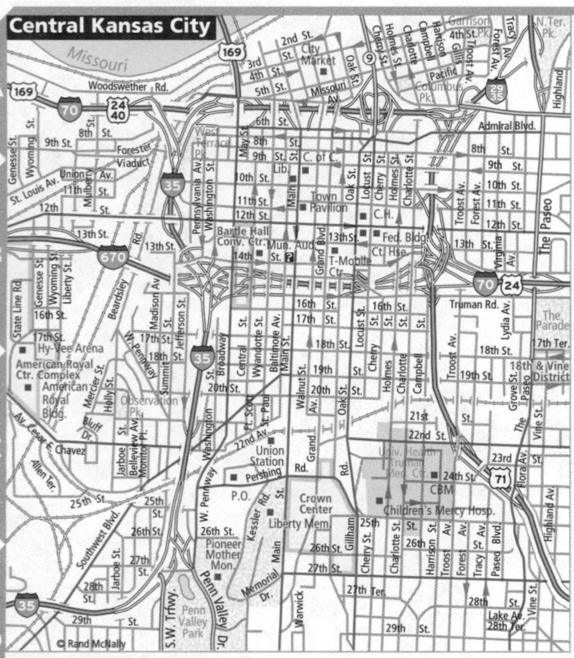

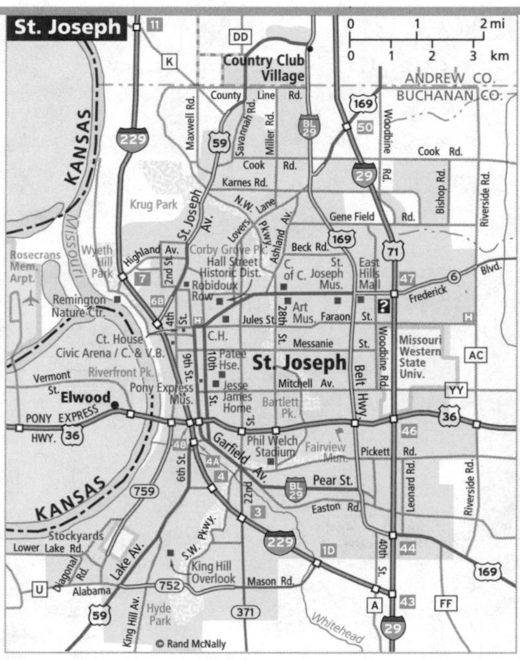

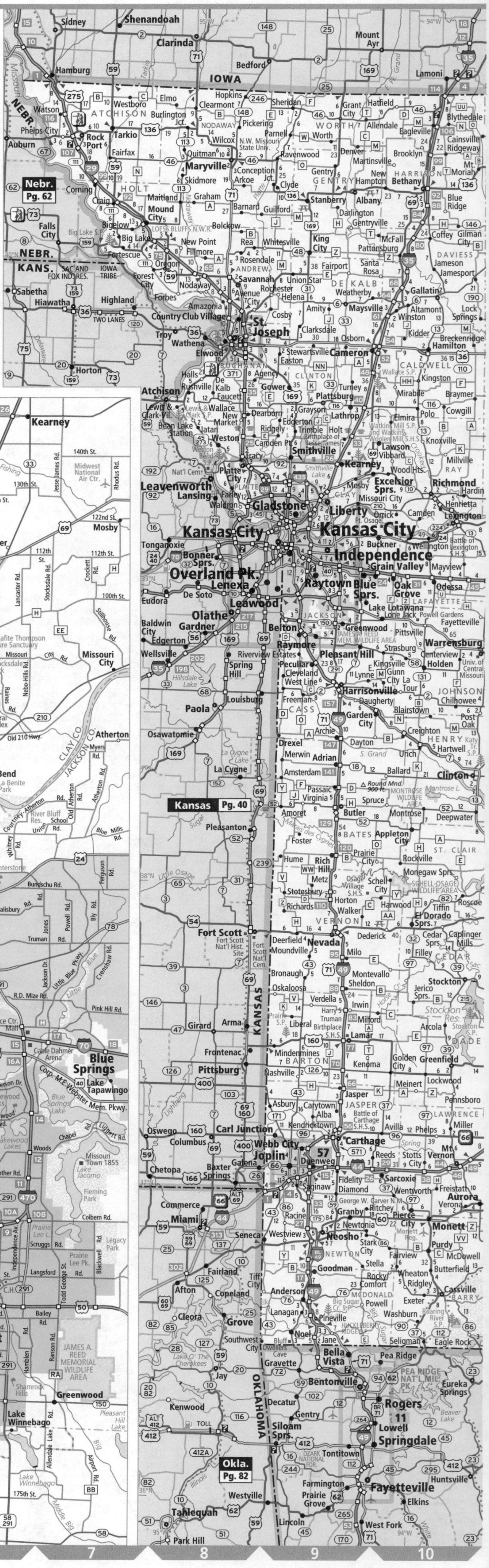

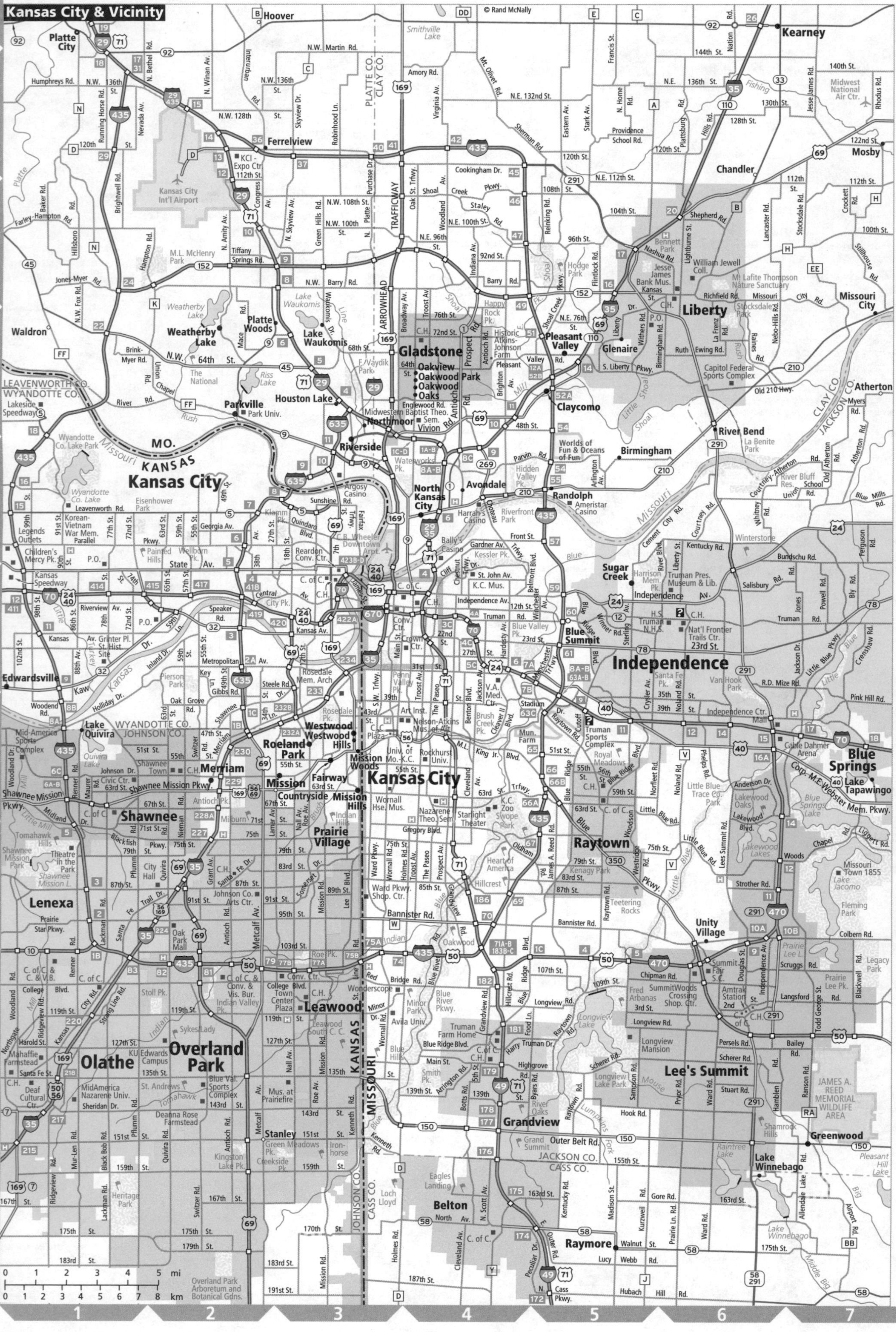

Central Kansas City

St. Joseph

Kansas City & Vicinity

Nebr. Pg. 62

Kansas Pg. 40

Okla. Pg. 82

© Rand McNally

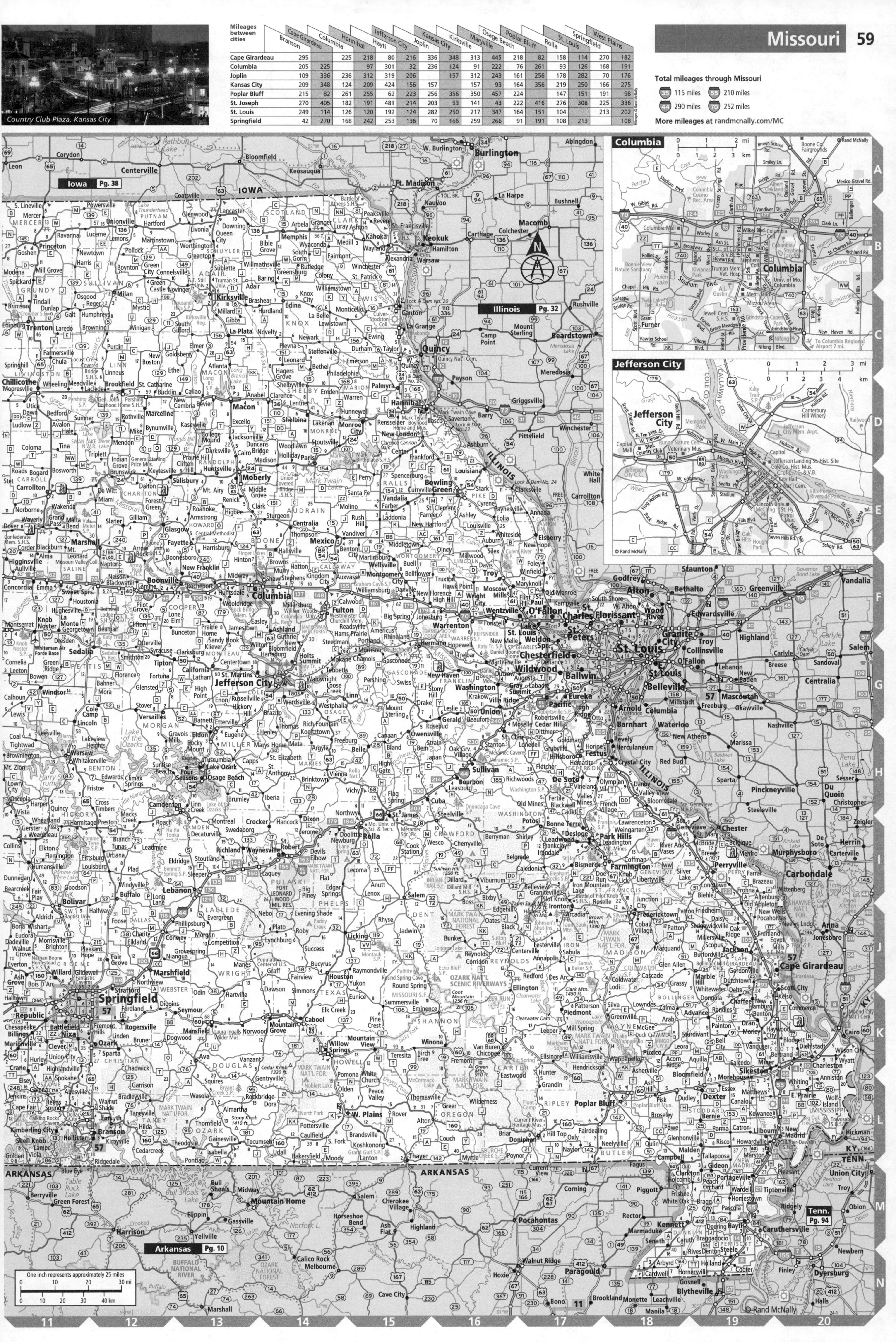

Mileages between cities

	Branson	Cape Girardeau	Columbia	Hannibal	Hayti	Jefferson City	Joplin	Kansas City	Kirksville	Maryville	Osage Beach	Poplar Bluff	Rolla	St. Louis	Springfield	West Plains
Cape Girardeau	295		225	218	80	216	336	348	313	445	218	82	158	114	270	182
Columbia	205	225		97	301	32	236	124	91	222	76	261	93	126	168	191
Joplin	109	336	236	312	319	206		157	312	243	161	256	178	282	70	176
Kansas City	209	348	124	209	424	156	157		157	93	164	356	219	250	166	275
Poplar Bluff	215	82	261	255	62	223	256	356	350	457	224		147	151	191	98
St. Joseph	270	405	182	191	481	214	203	53	141	43	222	416	276	308	225	336
St. Louis	249	114	126	120	192	124	282	250	217	347	164	151	104		213	202
Springfield	42	270	168	242	253	136	70	166	259	266	91	191	108	213		108

Total mileages through Missouri

- 35: 115 miles
- 55: 210 miles
- 44: 290 miles
- 70: 252 miles

More mileages at randmcnally.com/MC

Montana

Nickname: The Treasure State
Capital: Helena, G-7
Land area: 145,509 sq. mi. (rank: 4th)
Population: 1,084,225 (rank: 44th)
Largest city: Billings, 117,116, I-13

Index of places Pg. 132

Travel planning & on-the-road resources

Tourism Information
Montana Office of Tourism: (800) 847-4868; www.visitmt.com

Road Conditions & Construction
511, (800) 226-7623, (406) 444-6200; www.511mt.net, www.mdt.mt.gov/travinfo

Toll Road Information
No tolls on state or federal highways

Determining distances along roads

Highway distances (segments of one mile or less not shown):
Cumulative miles (red): the distance between red arrows
Intermediate miles (black): the distance between intersections & places

Interchanges and exit numbers
For most states, the mileage between interchanges may be determined by subtracting one number from the other.

B.C. Pg. 118
Alberta Pg. 119
Idaho Pg. 31

One inch represents approximately 30 miles

Waterton-Glacier Int'l Peace Park

© Rand McNally

Helena

© Rand McNally

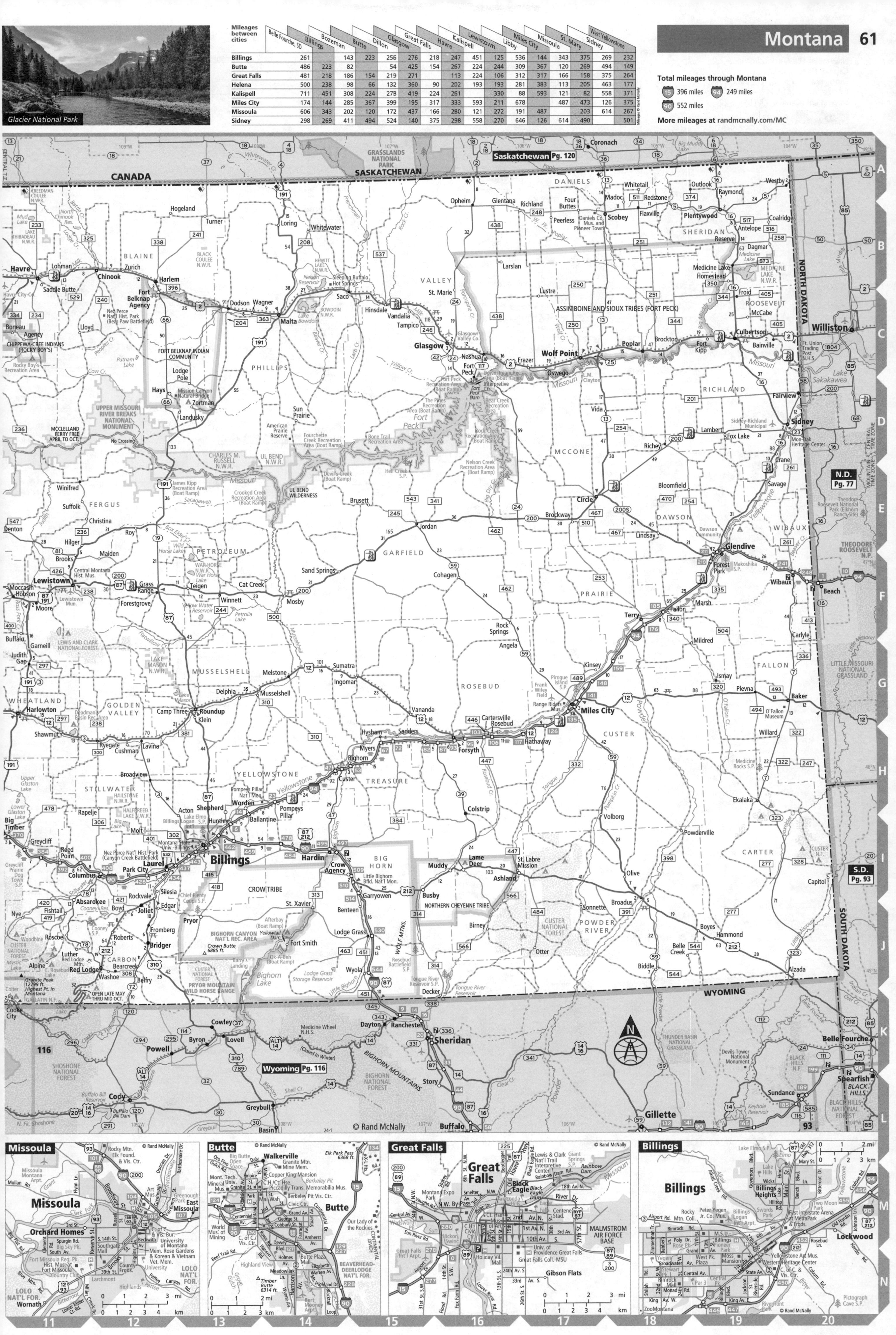

Mileages between cities	Belle Fourche, SD	Billings	Bozeman	Butte	Dillon	Glasgow	Great Falls	Havre	Kalispell	Lewistown	Libby	Miles City	Missoula	St. Mary	Sidney	West Yellowstone
Billings	261		143	223	256	276	218	247	451	125	536	144	343	375	269	232
Butte	486	223	82		54	425	154	267	224	244	309	367	120	269	494	149
Great Falls	481	218	186	154	219	271		113	224	106	312	317	166	158	375	264
Helena	500	238	98	66	132	360	90	202	193	193	281	383	113	205	463	177
Kalispell	711	451	308	224	278	419	224	261		330	88	593	121	82	558	371
Miles City	174	144	285	367	399	195	317	333	593	211	678		487	473	126	375
Missoula	606	343	202	120	172	437	166	280	121	272	191	487		203	614	267
Sidney	298	269	411	494	524	140	375	298	558	270	646	126	614	490		501

Total mileages through Montana

15: 396 miles
94: 249 miles
90: 552 miles

More mileages at randmcnally.com/MC

Nebraska

Nickname: The Cornhusker State
Capital: Lincoln, K-17
Land area: 76,796 sq. mi. (rank: 15th)
Population: 1,961,504 (rank: 37th)
Largest city: Omaha, 486,051, J-19

Index of places Pg. 132

Travel planning & on-the-road resources

Tourism Information
Nebraska Tourism Commission: (402) 471-3796; visitnebraska.com

Road Conditions & Construction
511, (800) 906-9069, (402) 471-4567; www.511.nebraska.gov, dot.nebraska.gov/travel

Toll Road Information
No tolls on state or federal highways

Determining distances along roads

Highway distances (segments of one mile or less not shown):
Cumulative miles (red): the distance between red arrows
Intermediate miles (black): the distance between intersections & places

Interchanges and exit numbers
For most states, the mileage between interchanges may be determined by subtracting one number from the other.

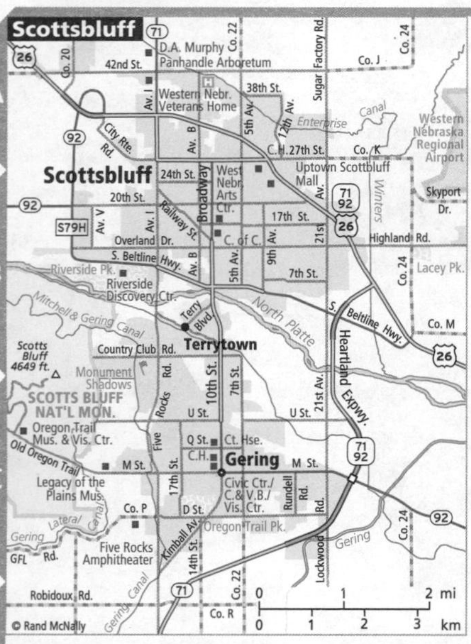

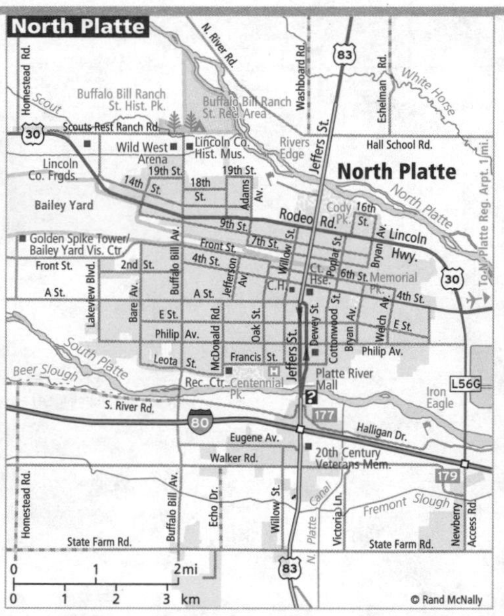

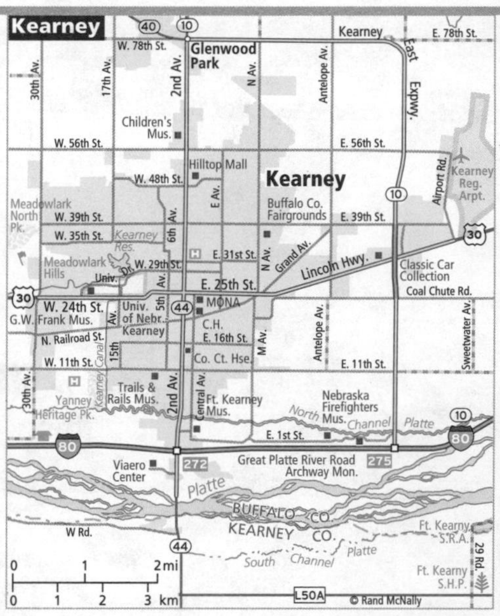

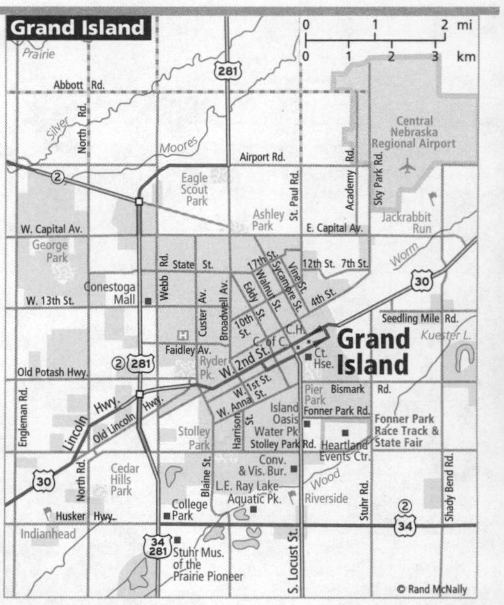

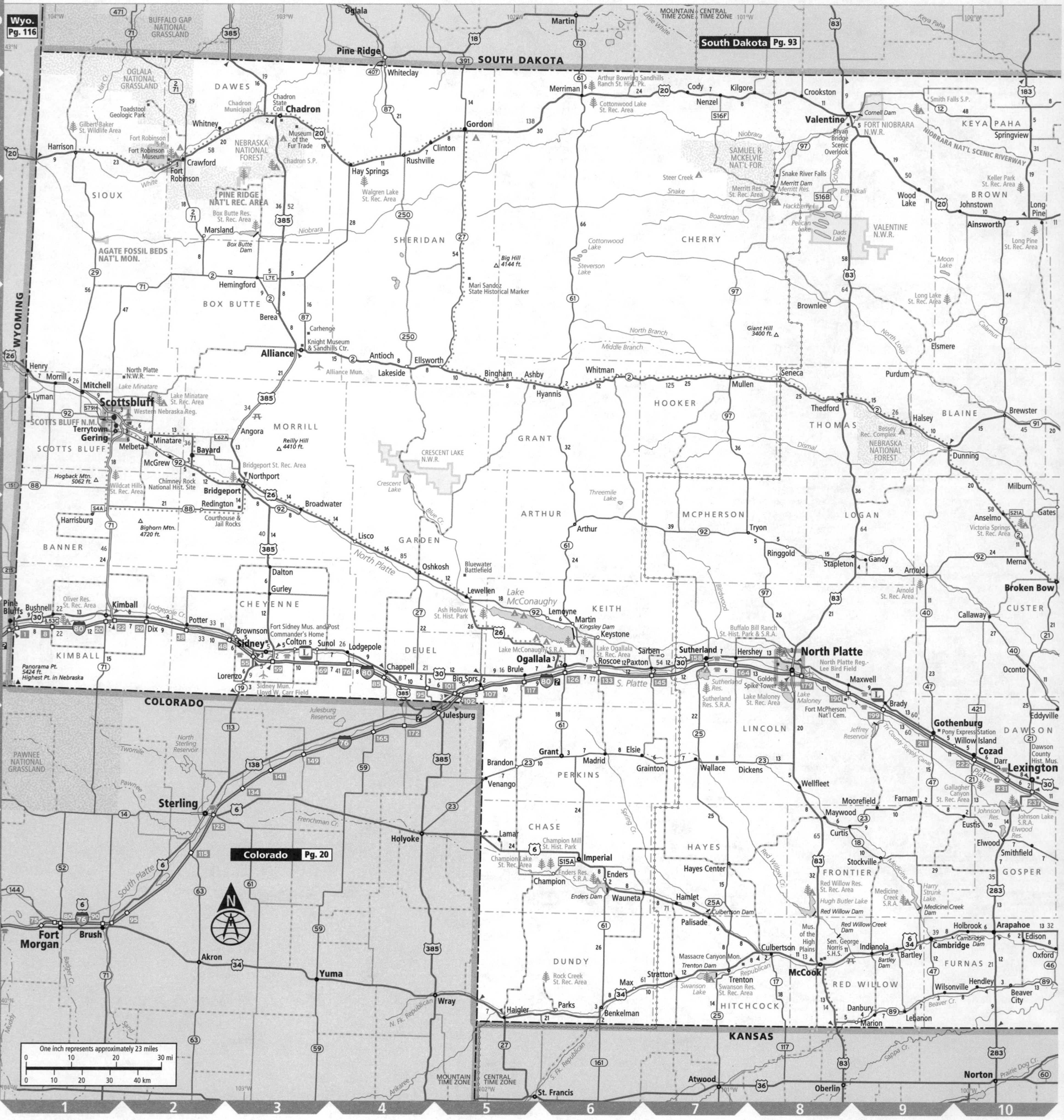

Scottsbluff

North Platte

Kearney

Grand Island

Wyo. Pg. 116

South Dakota Pg. 93

Colorado Pg. 20

One inch represents approximately 23 miles

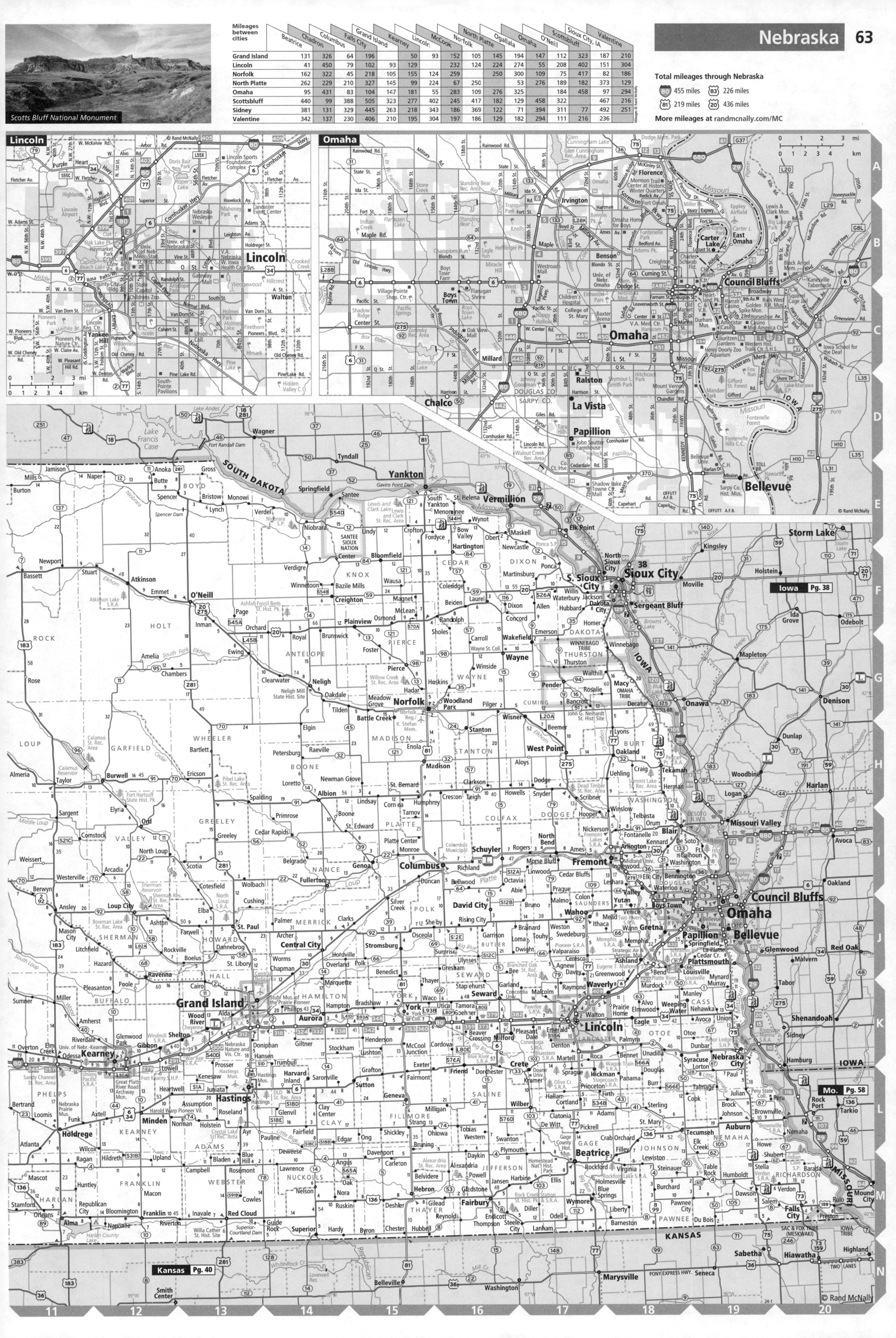

Scotts Bluff National Monument

Mileages between cities	Beatrice	Chadron	Columbus	Falls City	Grand Island	Kearney	Lincoln	McCook	Norfolk	North Platte	Ogallala	Omaha	O'Neill	Scottsbluff	Sioux City, IA	Valentine
Grand Island	131	326	64	196		50	93	152	105	145	194	147	112	323	187	210
Lincoln	41	450	79	102	93	129		232	124	224	274	55	208	402	151	304
Norfolk	162	322	45	218	105	155	124	259		250	300	109	75	417	82	186
North Platte	262	229	210	327	145	99	224	67	250		53	276	189	182	373	129
Omaha	95	431	83	104	147	181	55	283	109	276	325		184	458	97	294
Scottsbluff	440	99	388	505	323	277	402	245	417	182	129	458	322		467	216
Sidney	381	131	329	445	263	218	343	186	369	122	71	394	311	77	492	251
Valentine	342	137	230	406	210	195	304	197	186	129	182	294	111	216	236	

Total mileages through Nebraska

80: 455 miles · 83: 226 miles
81: 219 miles · 20: 436 miles

More mileages at randmcnally.com/MC

Nevada

Nickname: The Silver State
Capital: Carson City, F-2
Land area: 109,831 sq. mi. (rank: 7th)
Population: 3,104,614 (rank: 32nd)
Largest city: Las Vegas, 641,903, L-8

Index of places Pg. 132

Mileages between cities

	Carson City	Elko	Ely	Jackpot	Las Vegas	Reno	Tonopah	Winnemucca
Elko	304		188	117	429	288	252	125
Ely	319	188		205	241	319	167	271
Las Vegas	435	429	241	446		447	210	472
Reno	32	288	319	405	447		237	163
S. Lake Tahoe, CA	27	332	347	450	451	60	237	208
Tonopah	225	252	167	373	210	237		261
West Wendover	414	109	120	125	361	397	288	232
Winnemucca	179	125	271	240	472	163	261	

Total mileages through Nevada

15: 124 miles; 6: 307 miles
80: 411 miles; 95: 652 miles

More mileages at randmcnally.com/MC

Travel planning & on-the-road resources

Tourism Information
Travel Nevada:
(775) 687-4322; travelnevada.com

Road Conditions & Construction
511, (877) 687-6237, (775) 888-7000
www.nvroads.com, www.dot.nv.gov

Toll Road Information
No tolls on state or federal highways

Determining Distances
(segments of one mile or less not shown)
Cumulative miles (red): the distance between red arrows
Intermediate miles (black): the distance between intersections & places

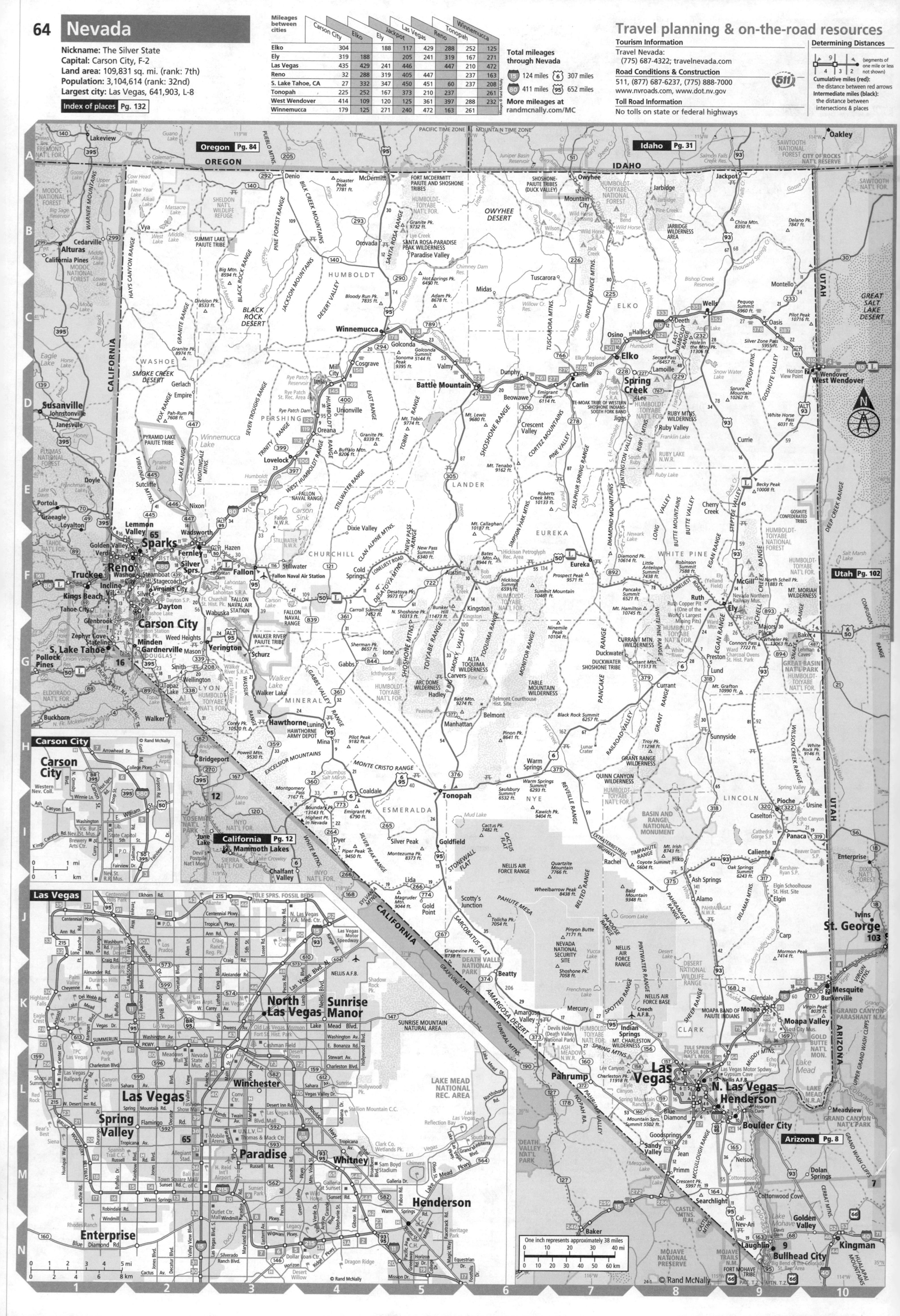

Travel planning & on-the-road resources

Tourism Information

New Hampshire Division of Travel and Tourism Development:
(603) 271-2665; www.visitnh.gov

Road Conditions & Construction

511, (603) 271-3734; newengland511.org, www.dot.nh.gov

Toll Road Information

Bureau of Turnpikes (*E-ZPass*):
(603) 485-3806; www.nh.gov/dot/org/operations/turnpikes

Total mileages through New Hampshire

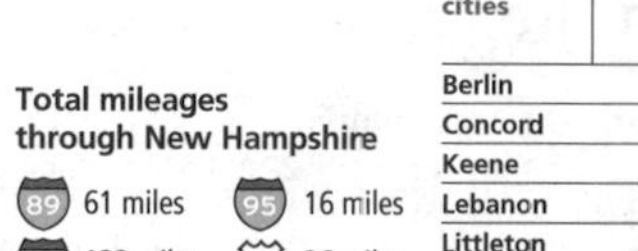

More mileages at randmcnally.com/MC

Mileages between cities	Colebrook	Concord	Conway	Keene	Laconia	Littleton	Nashua	Portsmouth
Berlin	49	115	40	168	97	42	151	117
Concord	137		77	51	27	87	36	44
Keene	181	51	130		80	136	50	99
Lebanon	128	57	88	64	58	82	89	111
Littleton	56	87	54	136	66		121	129
Manchester	155	18	95	55	45	105	18	43
Nashua	172	36	113	50	63	121		54
Portsmouth	180	44	77	99	57	129	54	

New Hampshire

Nickname: The Granite State
Capital: Concord, K-7
Land area: 8,951 sq. mi. (rank: 44th)
Population: 1,377,529 (rank: 41st)
Largest city: Manchester, 115,644, L-7

Index of places Pg. 132

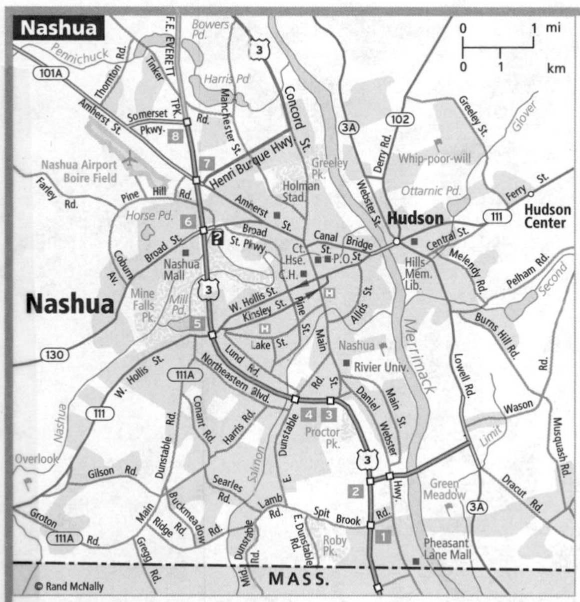

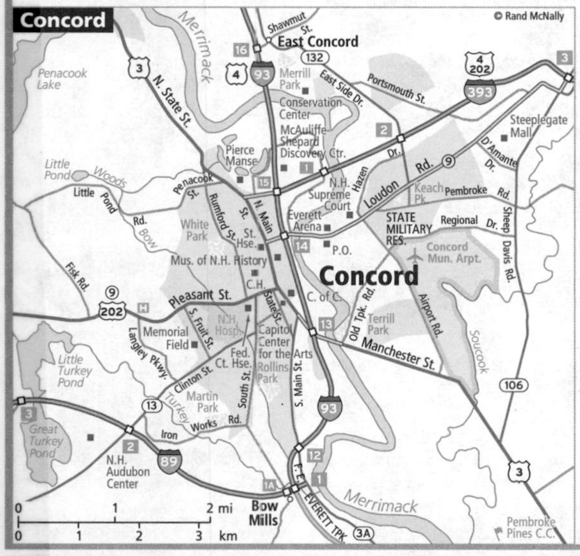

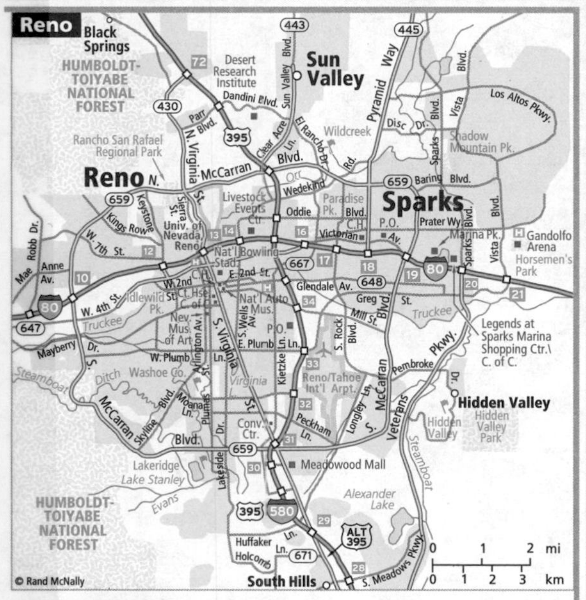

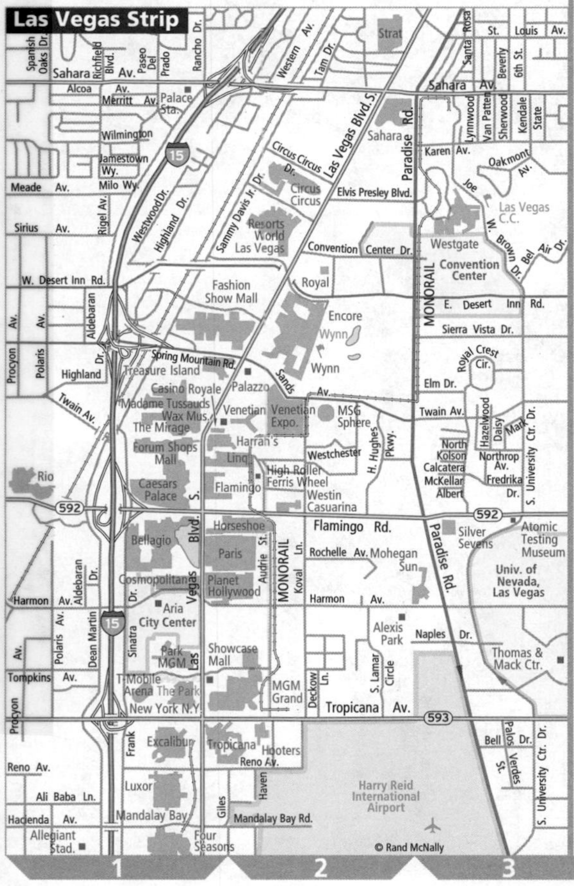

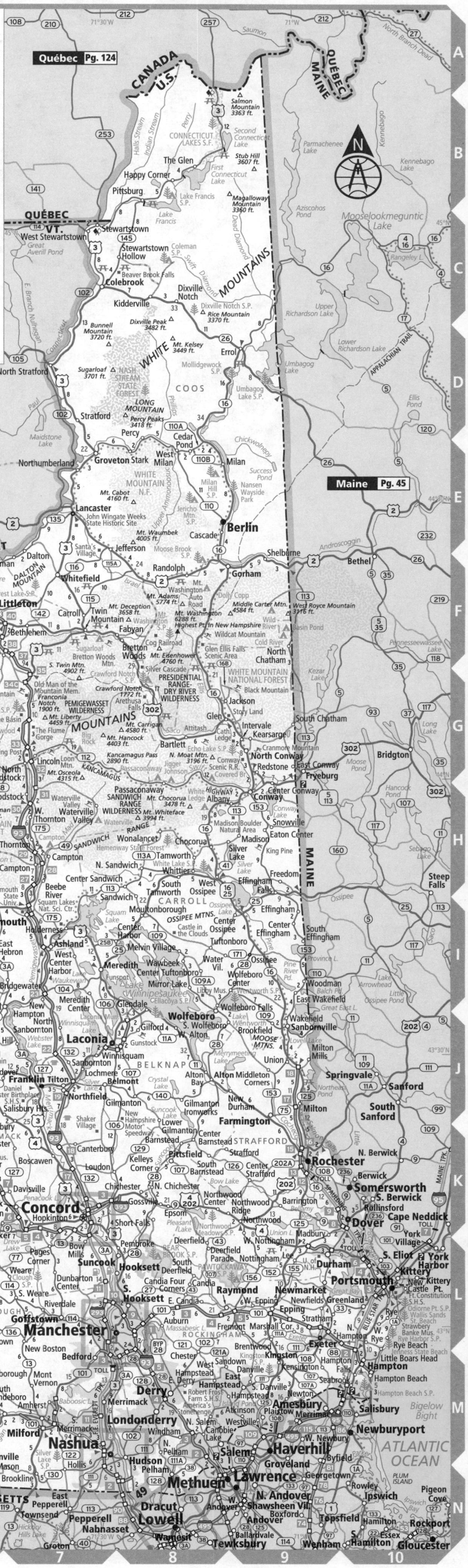

Nashua

Manchester

Concord

Reno

Las Vegas Strip

Québec Pg. 124
Maine Pg. 45
Vermont Pg. 104
Mass. Pg. 48

One inch represents approximately 14 miles

Nickname: The Garden State
Capital: Trenton, J-8
Land area: 7,353 sq. mi. (rank: 46th)
Population: 9,288,994 (rank: 11th)
Largest city: Newark, 311,549, F-12

Index of places Pg. 132

Travel planning & on-the-road resources

Tourism Information
New Jersey Div. of Travel and Tourism: (609) 599-6540; visitnj.org

Toll Road Information: *(all use E-ZPass)*
New Jersey Turnpike Authority (N.J. Turnpike, Garden St. Pkwy.): (732) 750-5300 ext. 8750; www.njta.com
South Jersey Transportation Authority (Atlantic City Expressway): (609) 965-6060; www.sjta.com

Road Conditions & Construction
511, (866) 511-6538; 511nj.org, www.state.nj.us/transportation

Toll Bridge/Tunnel Information: *(all use E-ZPass)*
Burlington County Bridge Commission: (856) 829-1900, (609) 387-1480; www.bcbridges.org
Delaware R. & Bay Auth. (Del. Mem. Br., Cape May/Lewes Fy.): (302) 571-6300; www.drba.net
Delaware R. Port Auth. (Philadelphia area bridges): (877) 567-3772, (856) 968-2000; www.drpa.org
Delaware R. Joint Toll Br. Commission (other Delaware R. bridges): (800) 363-0049; www.drjtbc.org
Port Auth. of N.Y. & N.J. (NYC area inter-state bridges & tunnels): (800) 221-9903; www.panynj.gov

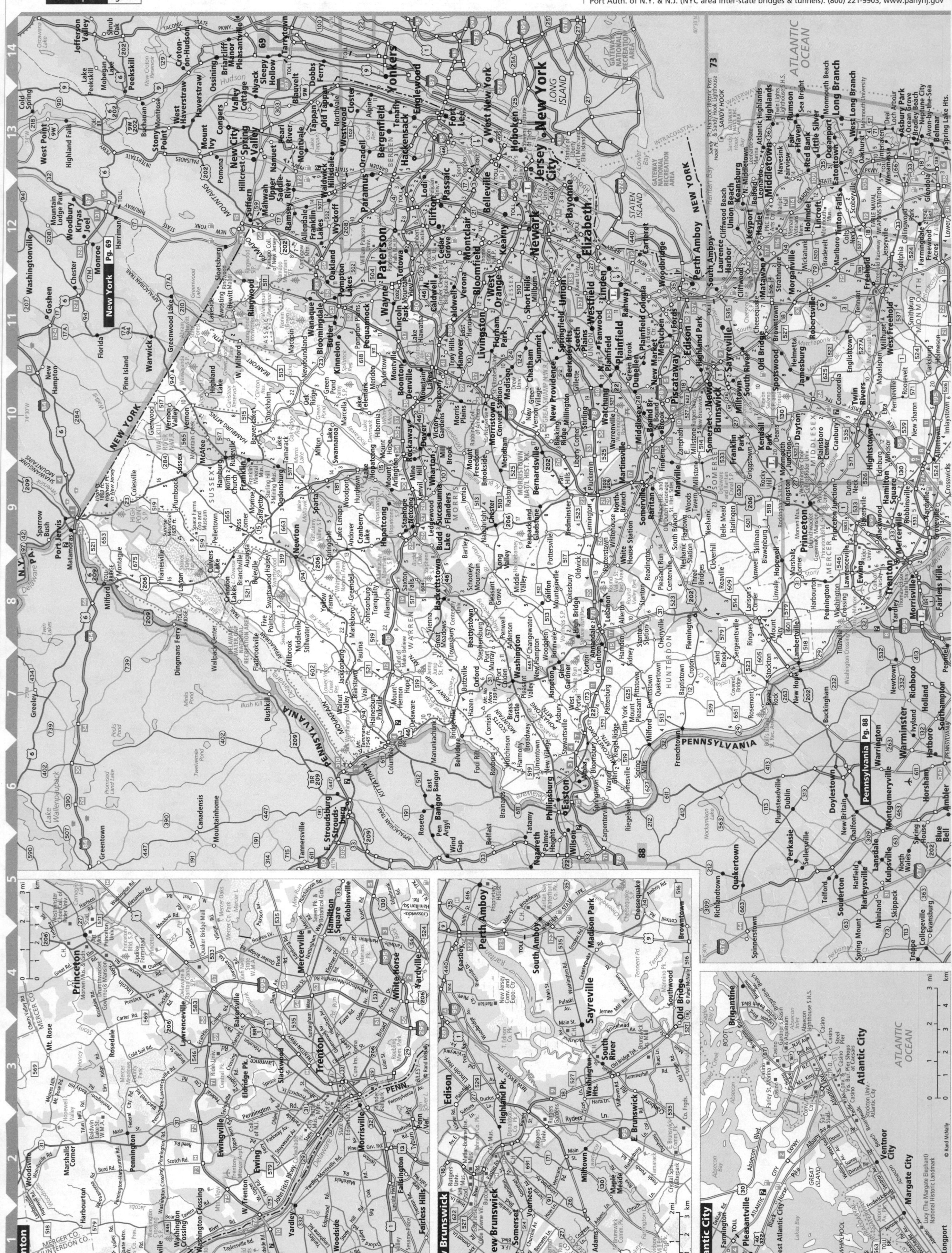

Victorians at Cape May

Mileages between cities	Atlantic City	Camden	Cape May	Jersey City	Long Branch	Newark	New Brunswick	New York, NY	Paterson	Phillipsburg	Port Jervis, NY	Princeton	Toms River	Trenton	Vineland	Wilmington, DE
Atlantic City		58	47	120	82	115	94	126	129	138	182	99	52	90	36	82
Camden	58		88	86	76	80	61	96	94	80	143	45	55	34	36	31
Cape May	47	88		151	114	147	126	157	161	170	214	131	84	121	48	98
Newark	115	80	147	6	43		25	10	15	58	74	41	63	55	114	112
New Brunswick	94	61	126	30	34	25		36	39	48	92	16	43	26	95	93
Phillipsburg	138	80	170	64	81	58	48	68	67		74	54	101	54	118	95
Port Jervis, NY	182	143	214	89	110	74	92	95	73	74		94	130	122	180	158
Trenton	90	34	121	61	52	55	26	66	69	54	122	11	47		69	61

Total mileages through New Jersey

78 — 68 miles
95 — 78 miles
80 — 68 miles

More mileages at randmcnally.com/MC

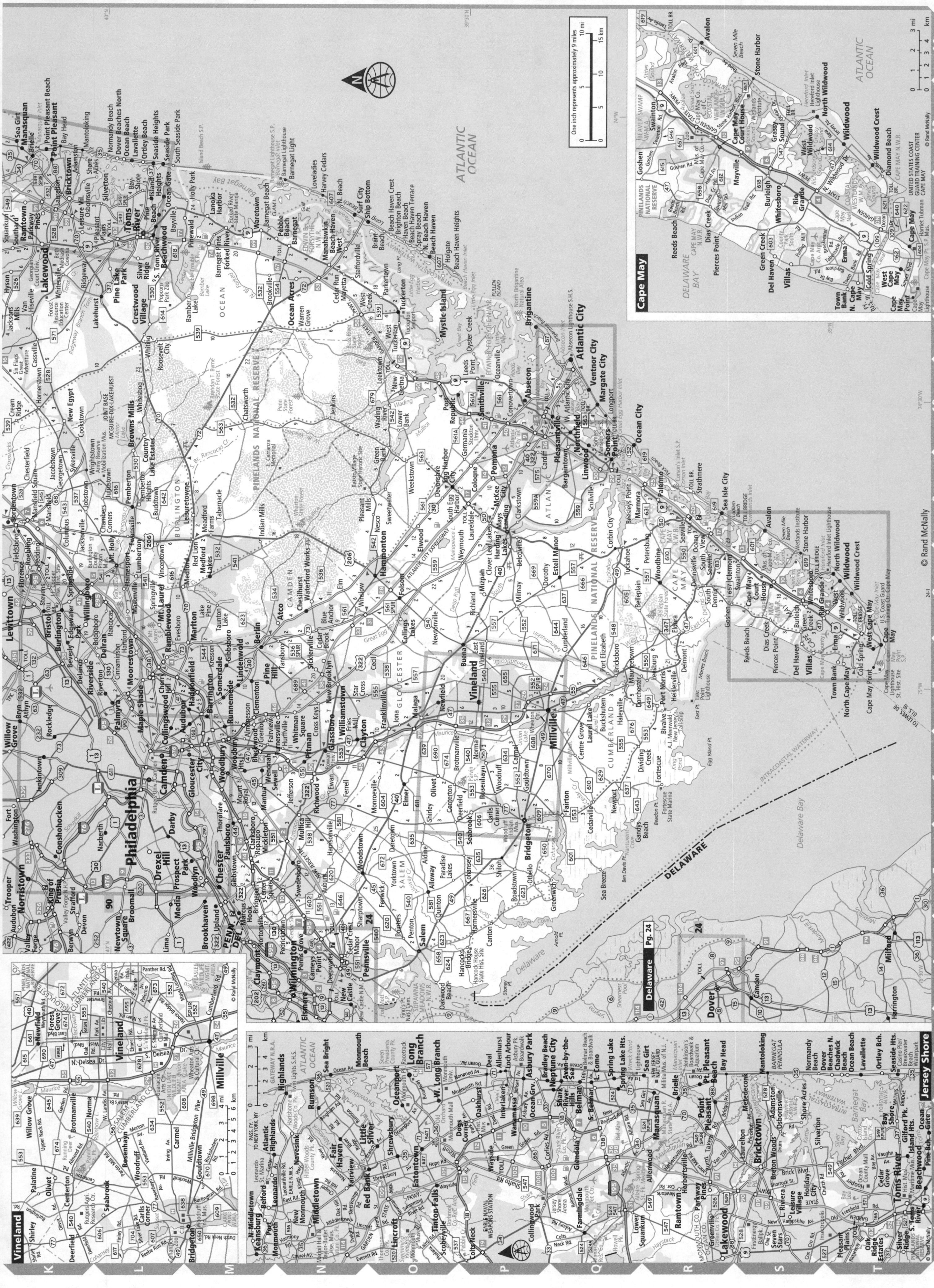

One inch represents approximately 9 miles

Cape May

Jersey Shore

Vineland

Delaware Pg. 24

New Mexico

Nickname: Land of Enchantment
Capital: Santa Fe, D-6
Land area: 121,280 sq. mi. (rank: 5th)
Population: 2,117,522 (rank: 36th)
Largest city: Albuquerque, 564,559, E-4

Index of places Pg. 133

Mileages between cities

	Albuquerque	Carlsbad	Clayton	Gallup	Las Cruces	Socorro	Taos	Tucumcari
Albuquerque		277	270	137	222	78	128	173
Carlsbad	277		374	412	206	241	336	263
Clayton	270	374		407	415	347	163	111
Clovis	219	180	168	356	292	248	246	83
Farmington	180	455	418	121	404	258	202	354
Las Cruces	222	206	415	338		146	351	303
Roswell	199	76	293	336	184	165	260	182
Santa Fe	58	268	215	197	282	136	68	166

Mileages © Rand McNally

Total mileages through New Mexico
10: 164 miles
40: 374 miles
25: 462 miles

More mileages at randmcnally.com/MC

Travel planning & on-the-road resources

Tourism Information
New Mexico Tourism Department:
(505) 795-0343; www.newmexico.org

Road Conditions & Construction
511, (800) 432-4269, (505) 795-1401
www.nmroads.com, www.dot.nm.gov

Toll Road Information
No tolls on state or federal highways

Determining Distances
(segments of one mile or less not shown)
Cumulative miles (red): the distance between red arrows
Intermediate miles (black): the distance between intersections & places

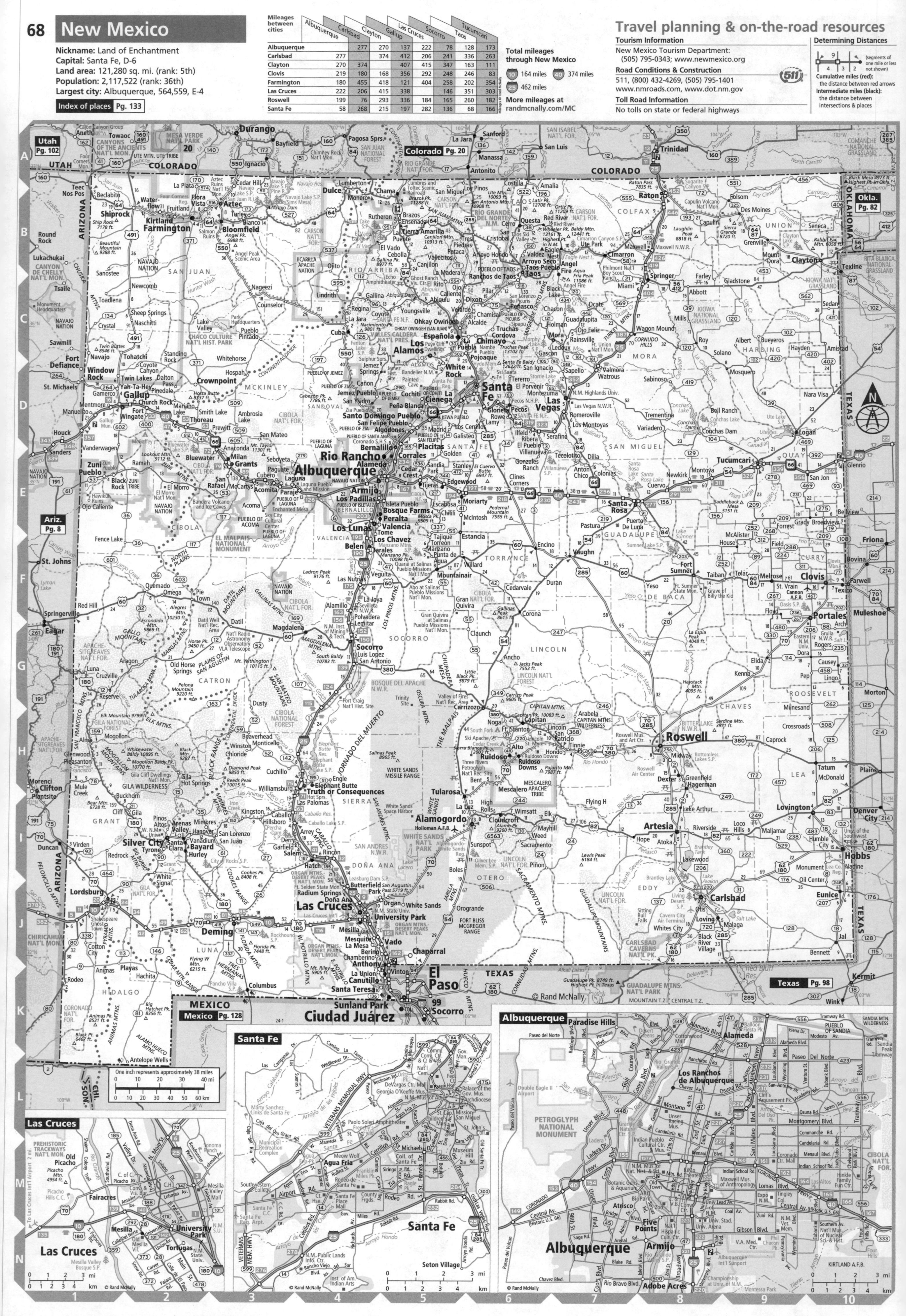

Travel planning & on-the-road resources

Tourism Information
N.Y. State Division of Tourism: (800) 225-5697; www.iloveny.com

Toll Road Info
see next page for listings

Road Conditions & Construction
511, (888) 465-1169
www.511ny.org, www.dot.ny.gov
N.Y. State Thruway: (800) 847-8929, (518) 436-2700
www.thruway.ny.gov

Determining Distances
(segments of one mile or less not shown)
Cumulative miles (red): the distance between red arrows
Intermediate miles (black): the distance between intersections & places

Total mileages through New York
84: 72 miles
95: 24 miles
87: 334 miles
495: 66 miles
More mileages at randmcnally.com/MC

Mileages between cities

	Albany	Buffalo	Hempstead	Newburgh	New York	Poughkeepsie	Riverhead	White Plains
Albany		289	167	87	156	75	219	138
Buffalo	289		423	361	395	362	471	394
Hempstead	167	423		78	12	92	59	34
Kingston	55	339	116	37	106	19	168	87
Montauk	260	513	97	172	107	184	42	126
Newburgh	87	361	78		72	19	130	49
New York	156	395	12	72		84	66	26
Poughkeepsie	75	362	92	19	84		143	60

Nickname: The Empire State
Capital: Albany, NK-19
Land area: 47,111 sq. mi. (rank: 30th)
Population: 20,201,249 (rank: 4th)
Largest city: New York, 8,804,190, SF-6

Index of places Pg. 133

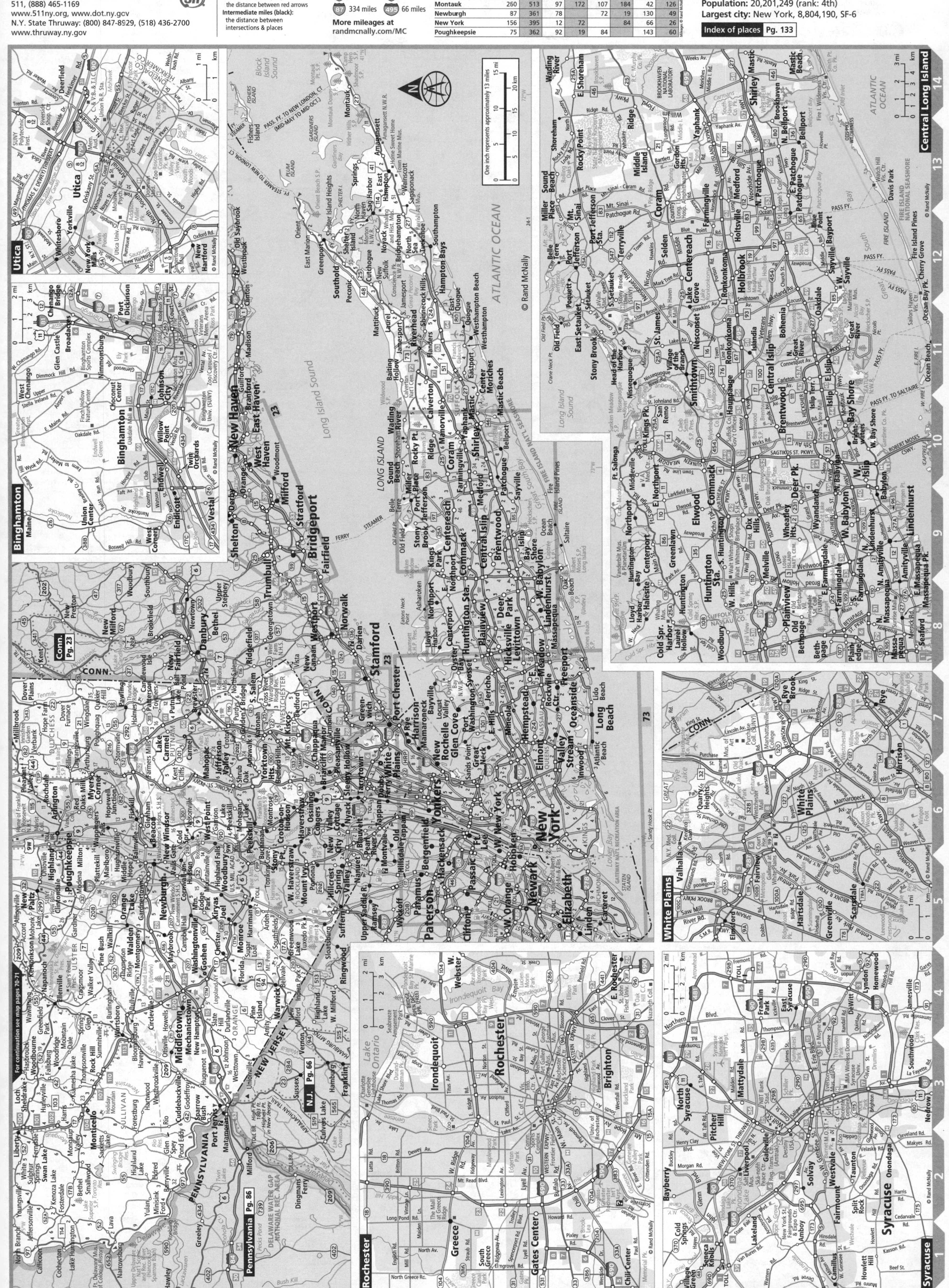

Nickname: The Empire State
Capital: Albany, NK-19
Land area: 47,111 sq. mi. (rank: 30th)
Population: 20,201,249 (rank: 4th)
Largest city: New York, 8,804,190, SF-6

Index of places Pg. 133

Travel planning & on-the-road resources

Tourism Information
New York State Division of Tourism: (800) 225-5697; www.iloveny.com

Road Conditions & Construction
511, (888) 465-1169
www.511ny.org, www.dot.ny.gov
N.Y. State Thruway: (800) 847-8929
(518) 436-2700; www.thruway.ny.gov

Toll Road Information: *(all use E-ZPass)*
New York State Thruway Authority: (518) 436-2700; www.thruway.ny.gov
MTA (N.Y. City in-state bridges & tunnels): (877) 690-5116
new.mta.info/agency/bridges-and-tunnels
New York State Bridge Authority (Hudson River bridges): (845) 691-7245; www.nysba.ny.gov

International Toll Bridge Information:
Buffalo & Ft. Erie Public Br. Auth. (Peace Br.) *(E-ZPass)*: (716) 884-6744; www.peacebridge.com
Niagara Falls Bridge Comm. *(E-ZPass or ExpressPass)*: (716) 285-6322; www.niagarafallsbridges.com
Ogdensburg Br. & Port Auth.: (315) 393-4080; www.ogdensport.com
Seaway Int'l Bridge Corp. *(Seaway Transit Card)*: (613) 932-6601; sibc.ca
Thousand Islands Br. Auth. (Alexandria Bay): (315) 482-2501; www.tibridge.com

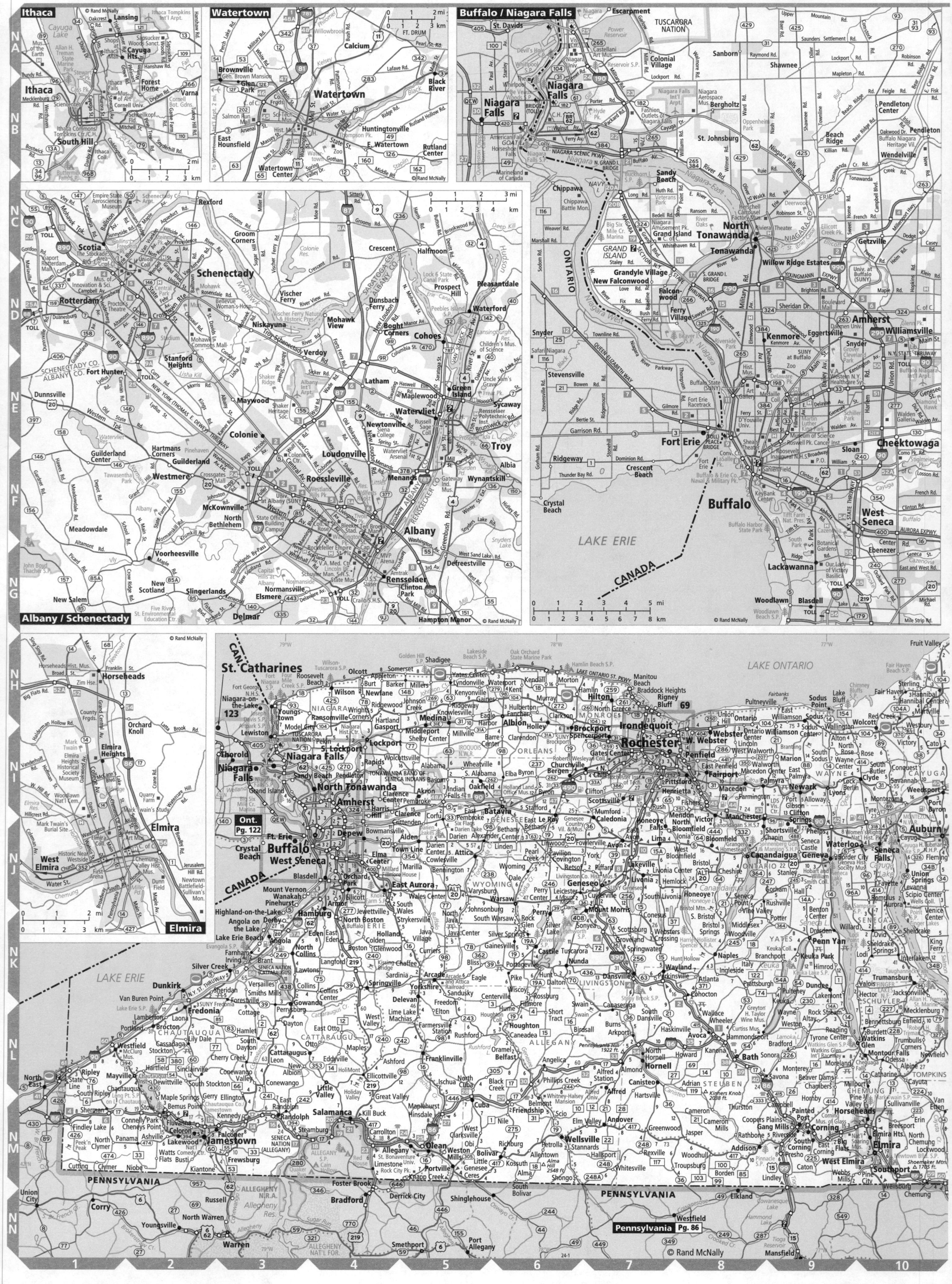

Ithaca

Watertown

Buffalo / Niagara Falls

Albany / Schenectady

Elmira

Ont. Pg. 122

Pennsylvania Pg. 86

Niagara Falls

Mileages between cities	Albany	Binghamton	Buffalo	Elmira	Glens Falls	Jamestown	Kingston	Lake Placid	Massena	New York	Niagara Falls	Plattsburgh	Rochester	Syracuse	Utica	Watertown
Albany		140	289	195	53	356	55	140	217	156	302	160	226	145	94	175
Binghamton	140		222	56	179	218	130	266	231	176	235	287	159	73	89	143
Buffalo	289	222		148	313	71	339	337	305	395	21	373	73	150	198	212
Jamestown	356	218	71	163	395		349	404	370	392	92	436	139	214	263	278
Plattsburgh	160	287	373	342	110	436	214	53	82	317	384		308	227	183	165
Rochester	226	159	73	120	248	139	277	275	242	332	87	308		86	135	149
Syracuse	145	73	150	90	160	214	195	195	159	246	162	227	86		53	70
Watertown	175	143	212	160	179	278	226	125	89	316	225	165	149	70	80	

Total mileages through New York

81: 184 miles
87: 334 miles
86: 176 miles
90: 385 miles

More mileages at randmcnally.com/MC

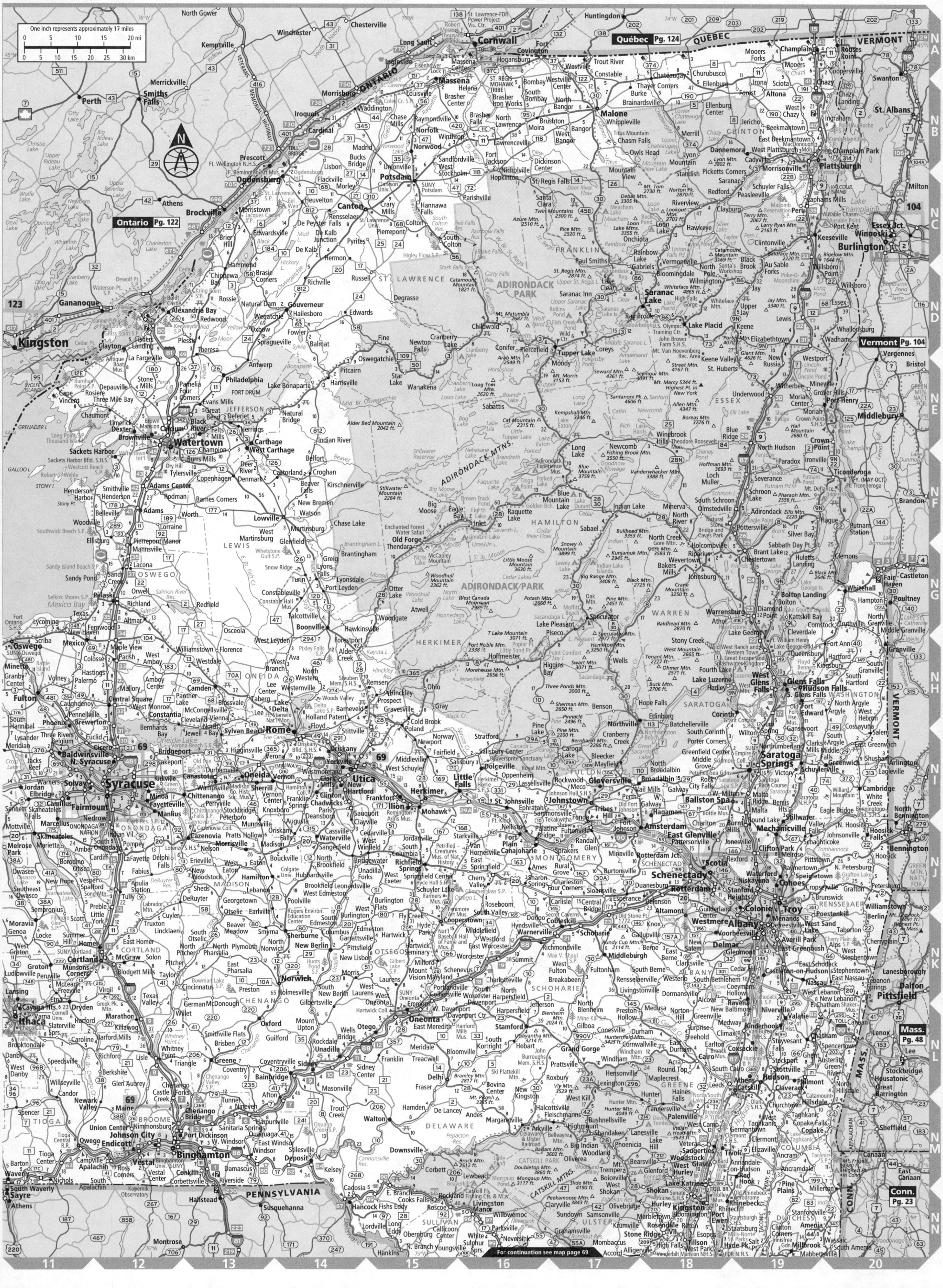

One inch represents approximately 17 miles

Ontario Pg. 122
Québec Pg. 124
Vermont Pg. 104
Mass. Pg. 48
Conn. Pg. 23
For continuation see map page 69

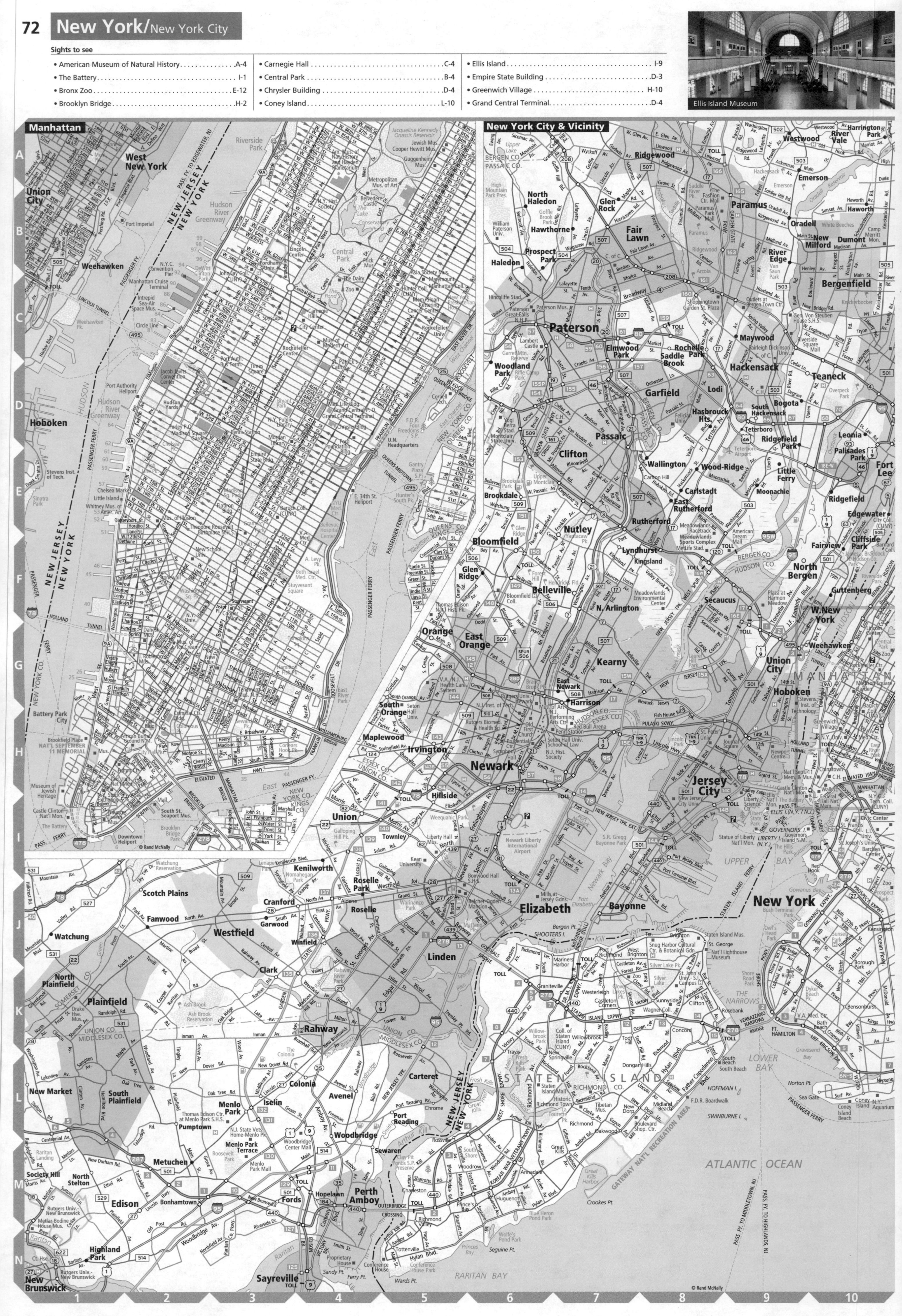

Sights to see
• American Museum of Natural History A-4
• The Battery I-1
• Bronx Zoo E-12
• Brooklyn Bridge H-2
• Carnegie Hall C-4
• Central Park B-4
• Chrysler Building D-4
• Coney Island L-10
• Ellis Island I-9
• Empire State Building D-3
• Greenwich Village H-10
• Grand Central Terminal D-4
Ellis Island Museum
Manhattan
New York City & Vicinity
West New York
Union City
Weehawken
Hoboken
Central Park
Riverside Park
Hudson River Greenway
Times Square
Rockefeller Center
Grand Central Terminal
Empire State Bldg.
U.N. Headquarters
Battery Park City
Paterson
Passaic
Clifton
Hackensack
Paramus
Ridgewood
Teaneck
Bloomfield
Belleville
Newark
Elizabeth
Jersey City
Bayonne
Irvington
Union
Linden
Rahway
Westfield
Plainfield
Edison
Woodbridge
Perth Amboy
Sayreville
New Brunswick
Staten Island
New York
Upper Bay
Lower Bay
Raritan Bay
Atlantic Ocean
© Rand McNally

Brooklyn Bridge, New York City

Sights to see

- Guggenheim Museum A-5
- Intrepid Sea-Air Space Museum C-2
- Lincoln Center B-3
- Madison Square Garden D-2
- Metropolitan Museum of Art B-5
- National September 11 Memorial H-1
- New York Stock Exchange and Wall Street H-1
- Rockefeller Center C-4
- Staten Island Ferry .... I-2 and J-8
- Statue of Liberty I-9
- Times Square D-3
- Yankee Stadium E-11

ATLANTIC OCEAN

North Carolina

Nickname: The Tar Heel State
Capital: Raleigh, E-12
Land area: 48,607 sq. mi. (rank: 29th)
Population: 10,439,388 (rank: 9th)
Largest city: Charlotte, 874,579, F-5

Index of places Pg. 133

Travel planning & on-the-road resources

Tourism Information
Visit North Carolina: (800) 847-4862; www.visitnc.com

Road Conditions & Construction
511, (877) 511-4662; drivenc.gov, www.ncdot.gov/travel-maps

Toll Road Information
I-77 Mobility Partners *(NC Quick Pass)*: (980) 337-2400; www.i77express.com
N.C. Turnpike Authority *(NC Quick Pass)*: (919) 707-2700; www.ncdot.gov/divisions/turnpike

Determining distances along roads

Highway distances (segments of one mile or less not shown):
Cumulative miles (red): the distance between red arrows
Intermediate miles (black): the distance between intersections & places

Interchanges and exit numbers
For most states, the mileage between interchanges may be determined by subtracting one number from the other.

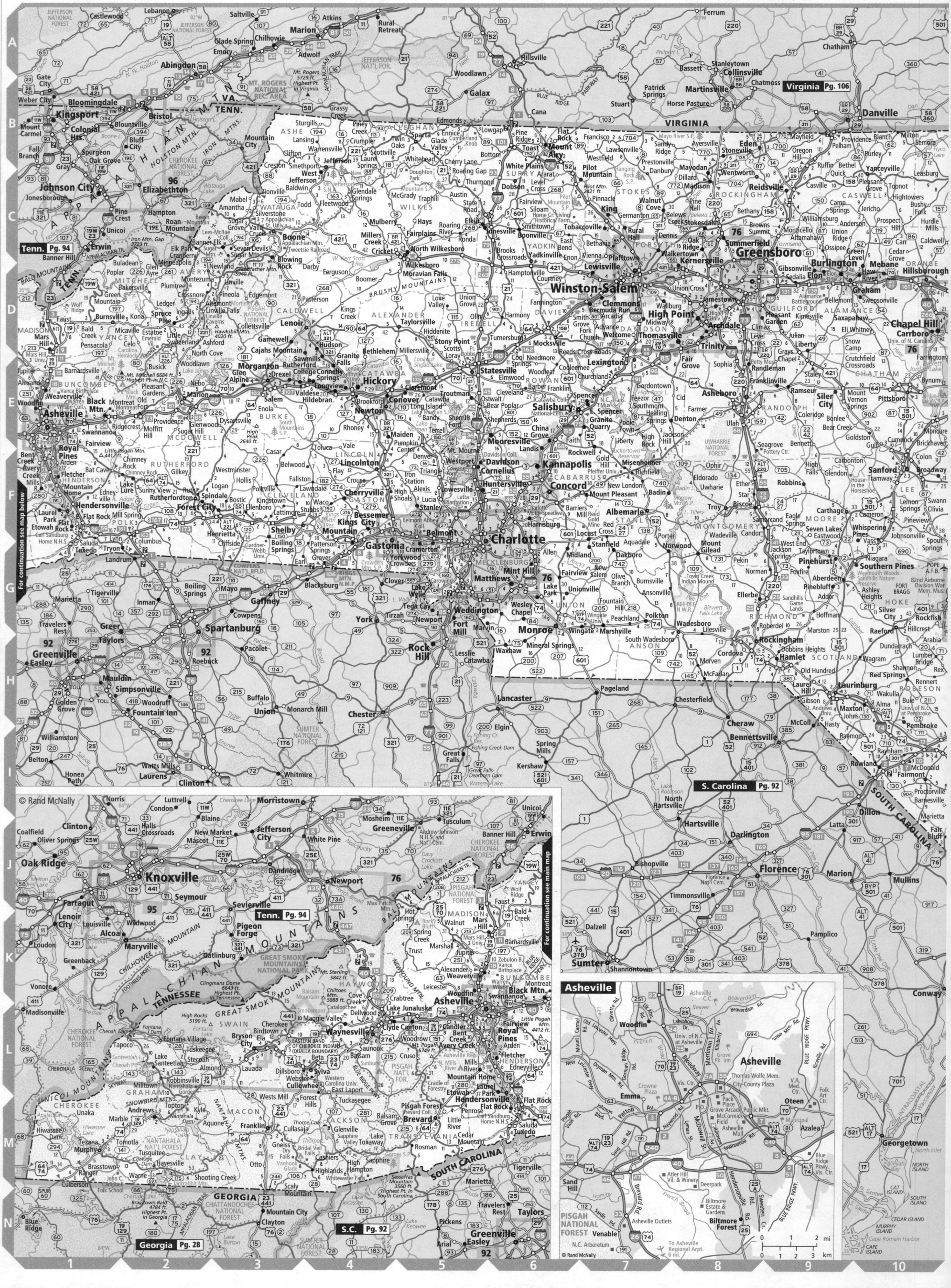

Virginia Pg. 106
Tenn. Pg. 94
S. Carolina Pg. 92
For continuation see map below
For continuation see main map
Tenn. Pg. 94
Georgia Pg. 28
S.C. Pg. 92

Asheville

Linn Cove Viaduct

Mileages between cities	Asheville	Boone	Charlotte	Durham	Elizabeth City	Greensboro	Hickory	Morehead City	Murphy	Nags Head	New Bern	Raleigh	Roanoke Rapids	Rockingham	Wilmington	Winston-Salem
Asheville		94	128	224	412	172	77	393	110	444	358	251	308	200	327	145
Charlotte	128	100		144	332	93	57	313	223	364	278	168	231	71	197	77
Elizabeth City	412	354	332	185		241	338	152	520	56	119	164	97	259	208	269
Fayetteville	261	202	137	89	203	94	189	138	369	234	130	63	127	64	89	119
Greensboro	172	113	93	53	241		98	223	279	271	188	80	138	83	207	29
Greenville	332	273	250	101	97	156	258	79	440	129	44	82	86	176	116	188
Raleigh	251	192	168	22	164	80	177	146	358	195	111		89	98	130	107
Wilmington	327	319	197	156	208	207	259	91	428	230	90	130	178	127		236

Total mileages through North Carolina

- 40: 419 miles
- 85: 233 miles
- 77: 102 miles
- 95: 182 miles

More mileages at randmcnally.com/MC

ATLANTIC OCEAN

One inch represents approximately 20 miles

0 5 10 15 20 mi

0 5 10 15 20 25 30 km

Wilmington

Fayetteville

Gastonia

Sights to see

- Discovery Place, Charlotte H-4
- Duke Homestead State Historic Site & Tobacco Museum, Durham F-9
- Historic Bethabara Park, Winston-Salem A-1
- Mint Museum of Art, Charlotte H-5
- Morehead Planetarium & Science Center, Chapel Hill H-8
- North Carolina Museum of History, Raleigh I-12
- North Carolina Museum of Life & Science, Durham F-10
- North Carolina State Capitol, Raleigh I-13
- North Carolina State University, Raleigh I-13
- Old Salem, Winston-Salem B-2
- Reynolda House, Winston-Salem B-1

Great Smoky Mountains National Park

Great Smoky Mountains National Park

Raleigh / Durham / Chapel Hill

Greensboro / Winston-Salem / High Point

Charlotte & Vicinity

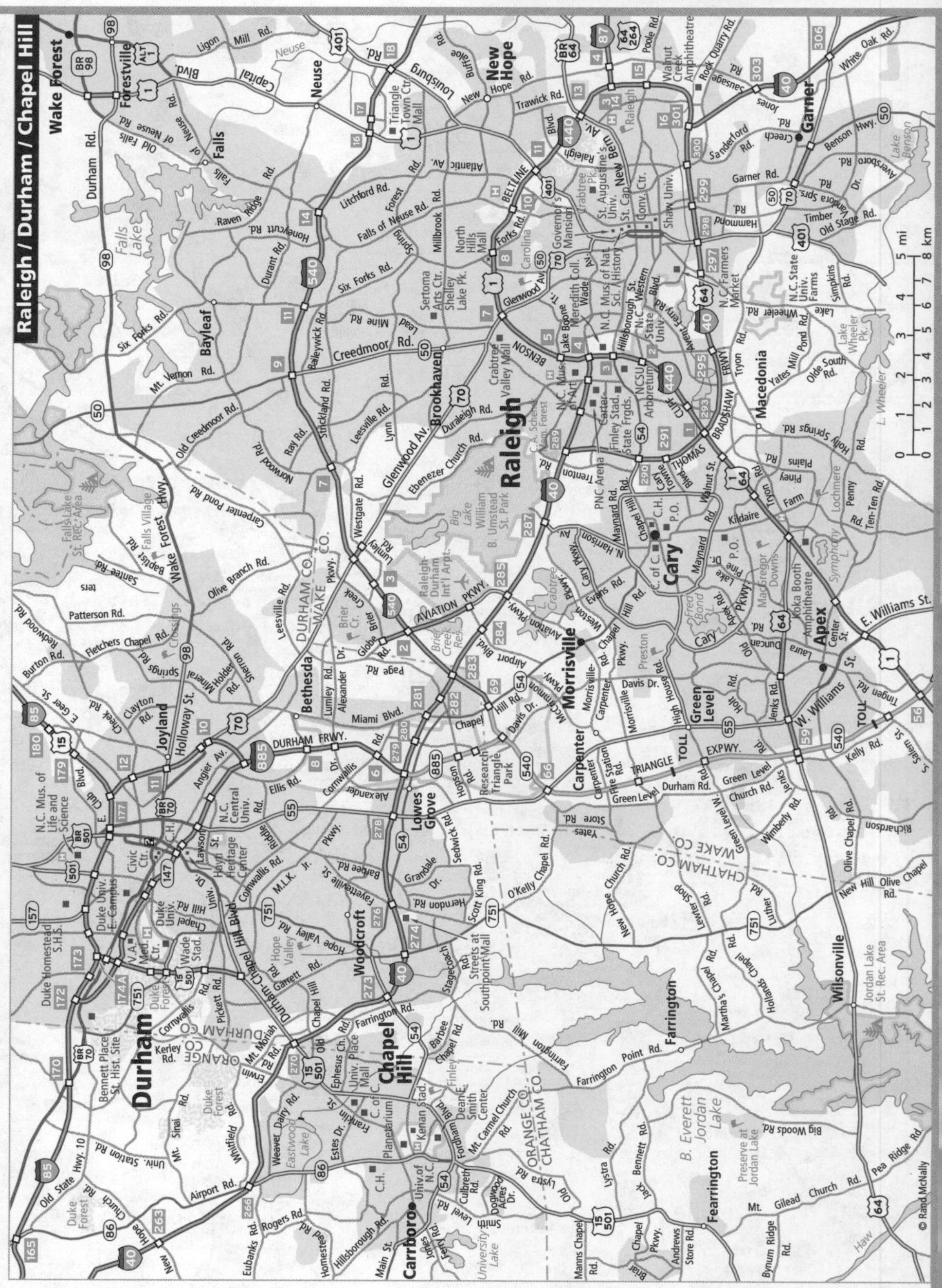

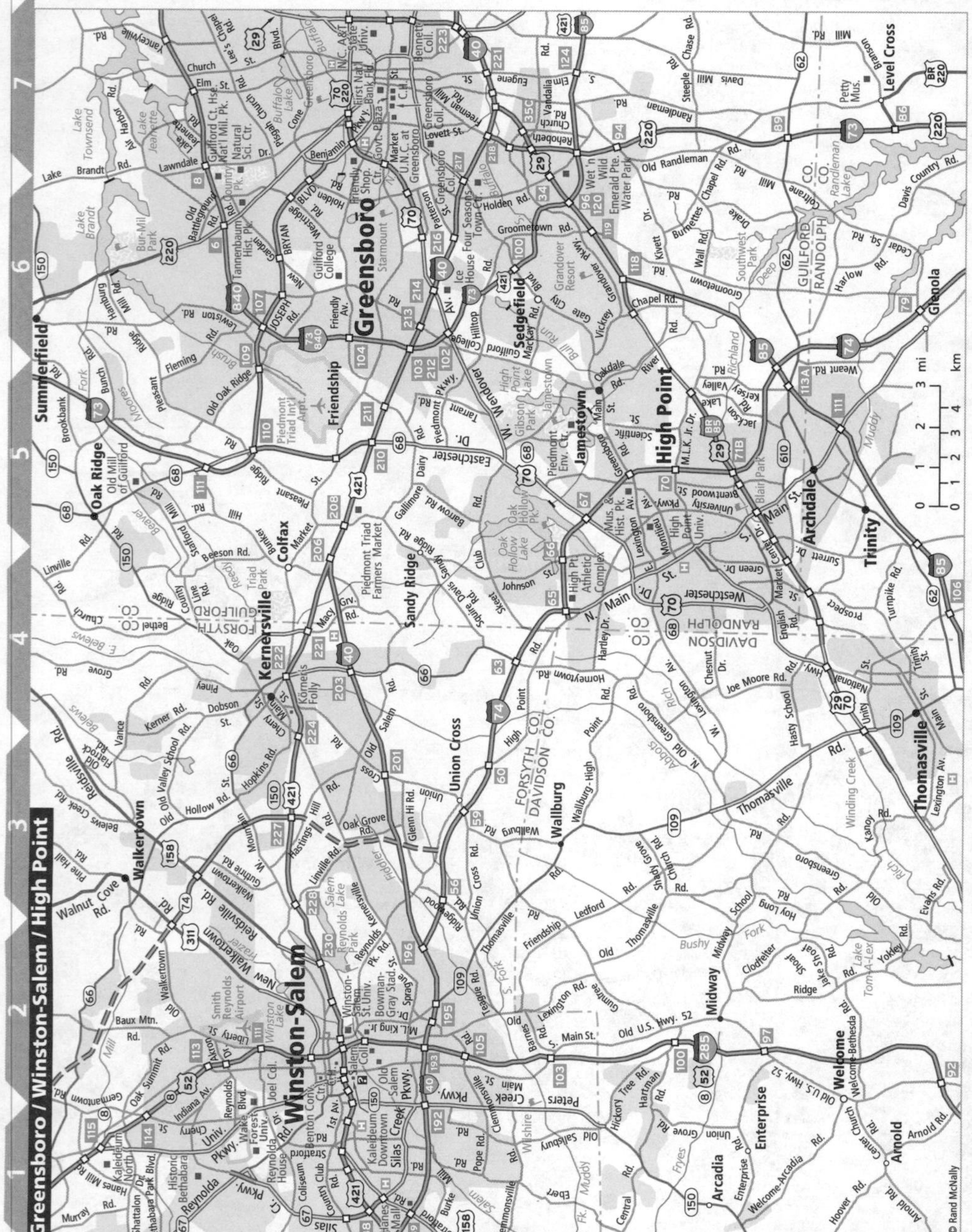

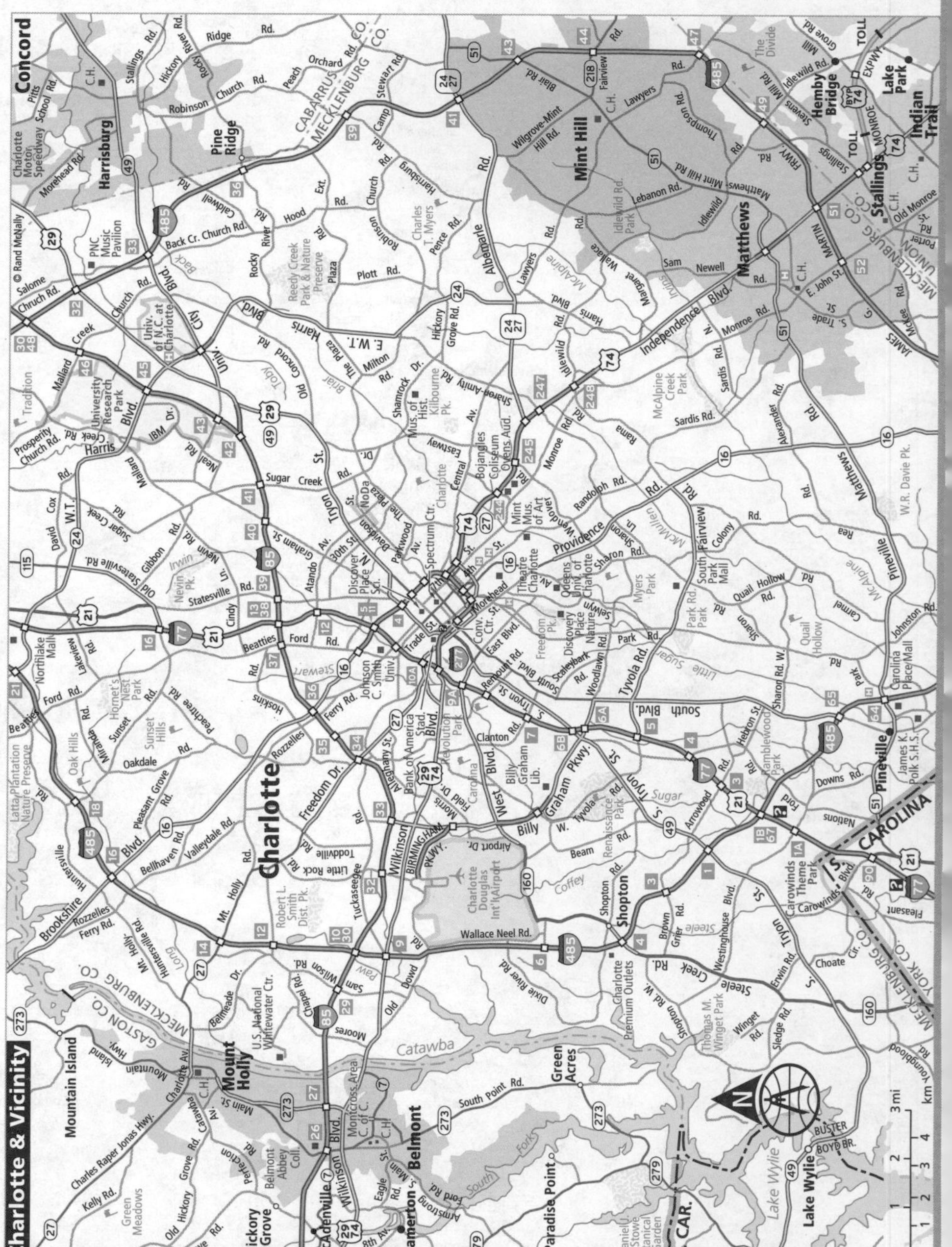

Travel planning & on-the-road resources

Tourism Information
North Dakota Tourism Division:
(800) 435-5663; www.ndtourism.com

Road Conditions & Construction
511, (866) 696-3511
travel.dot.nd.gov, www.dot.nd.gov/travel

Toll Road Information
No tolls on state or federal highways

Determining Distances
(segments of one mile or less not shown)
Cumulative miles (red): the distance between red arrows
Intermediate miles (black): the distance between intersections & places

Total mileages through North Dakota
29: 218 miles
2: 359 miles
94: 352 miles
83: 265 miles

More mileages at randmcnally.com/MC

Mileages between cities

	Bismarck	Bowman	Fargo	Garrison	Grand Forks	Jamestown	Williston	Winnipeg, MB
Bismarck		174	195	75	272	102	228	413
Devils Lake	180	354	165	167	89	99	245	230
Dickinson	97	78	292	149	368	198	132	509
Fargo	195	368		266	80	94	422	222
Grand Forks	272	444	80	256		171	334	146
Minot	110	260	268	47	210	170	124	299
Wahpeton	243	416	54	315	131	142	470	273
Williston	228	170	422	144	334	293		424

Nickname: The Peace Garden State
Capital: Bismarck, H-7
Land area: 68,977 sq. mi. (rank: 17th)
Population: 779,094 (rank: 47th)
Largest city: Fargo, 125,990, H-13

Index of places Pg. 133

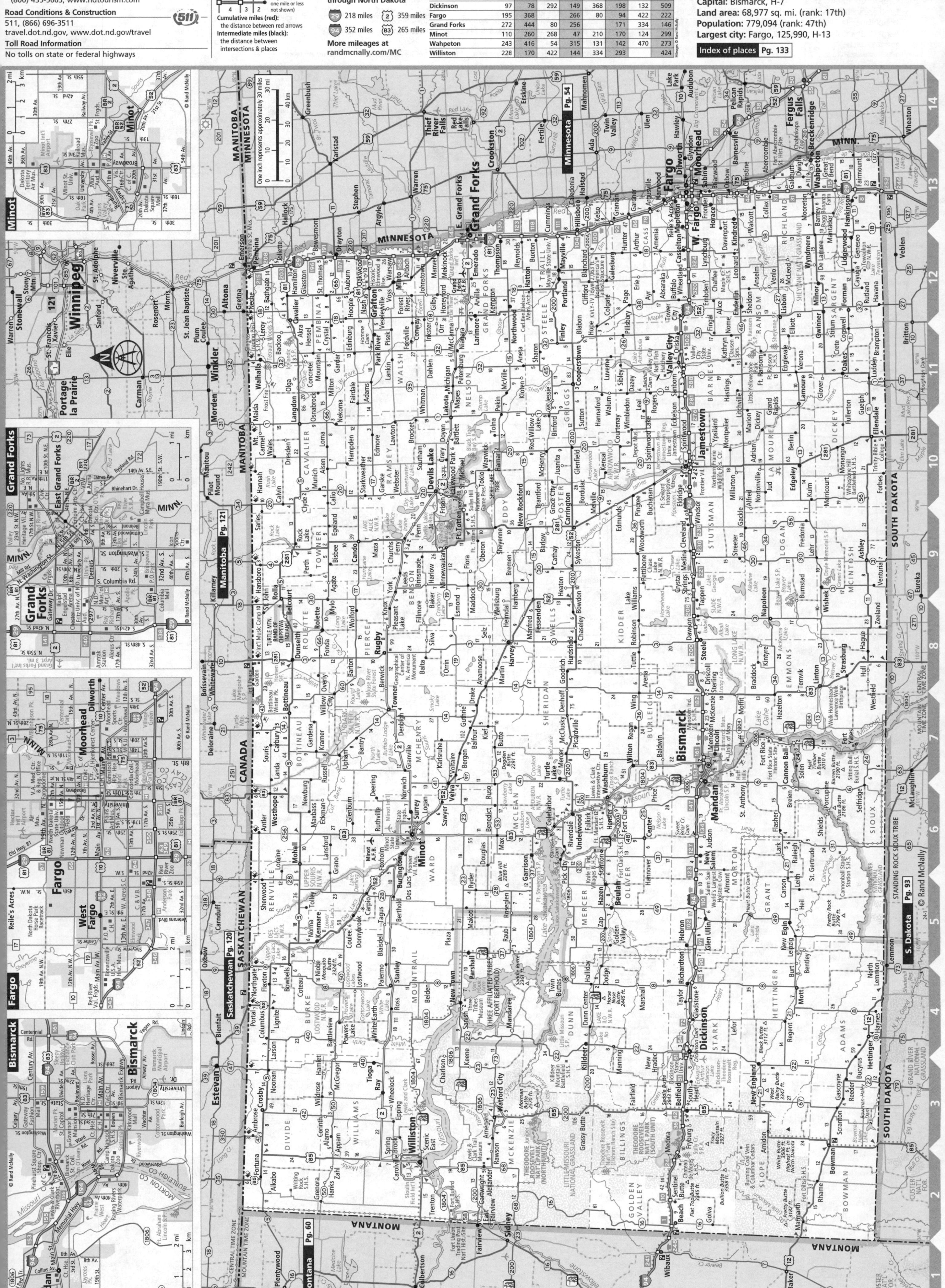

Nickname: The Buckeye State
Capital: Columbus, SB-9
Land area: 40,848 sq. mi. (rank: 35th)
Population: 11,799,448 (rank: 7th)
Largest city: Columbus, 905,748, SB-9

Index of places Pg. 133

Travel planning & on-the-road resources

Tourism Information
Tourism Ohio: (800) 282-5393; ohio.org

Road Conditions & Construction
511; (855) 511-6446; www.ohgo.com, www.transportation.ohio.gov
Ohio Turnpike: (440) 234-2081, (888) 876-7453, (440) 971-2222; www.ohioturnpike.org

Toll Road Information
Ohio Turnpike and Infrastructure Commission (*E-ZPass*): (440) 234-2081; www.ohioturnpike.org

Determining distances along roads

Highway distances (segments of one mile or less not shown):
Cumulative miles (red): the distance between red arrows
Intermediate miles (black): the distance between intersections & places

Interchanges and exit numbers
For most states, the mileage between interchanges may be determined by subtracting one number from the other.

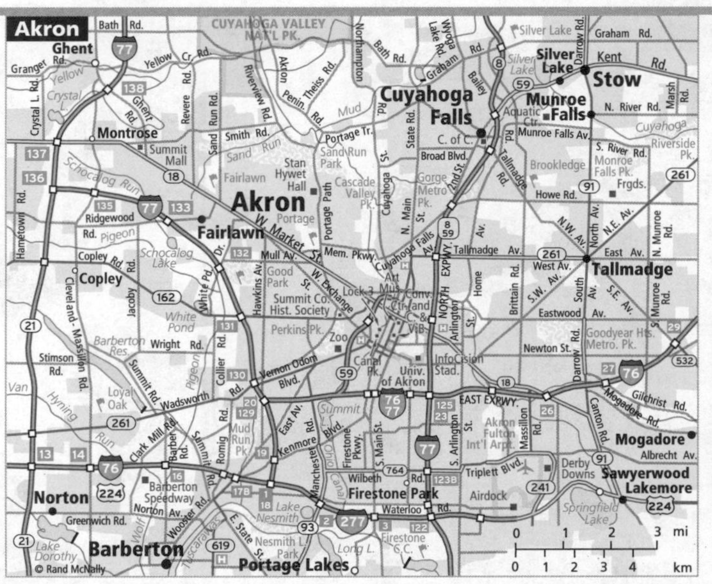

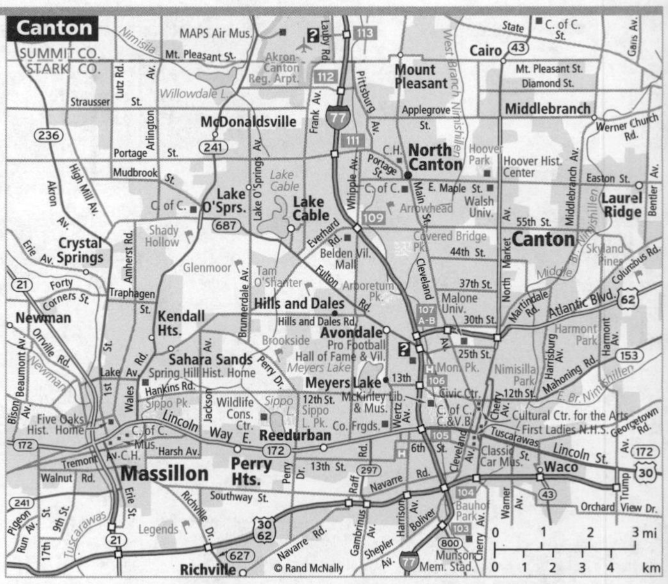

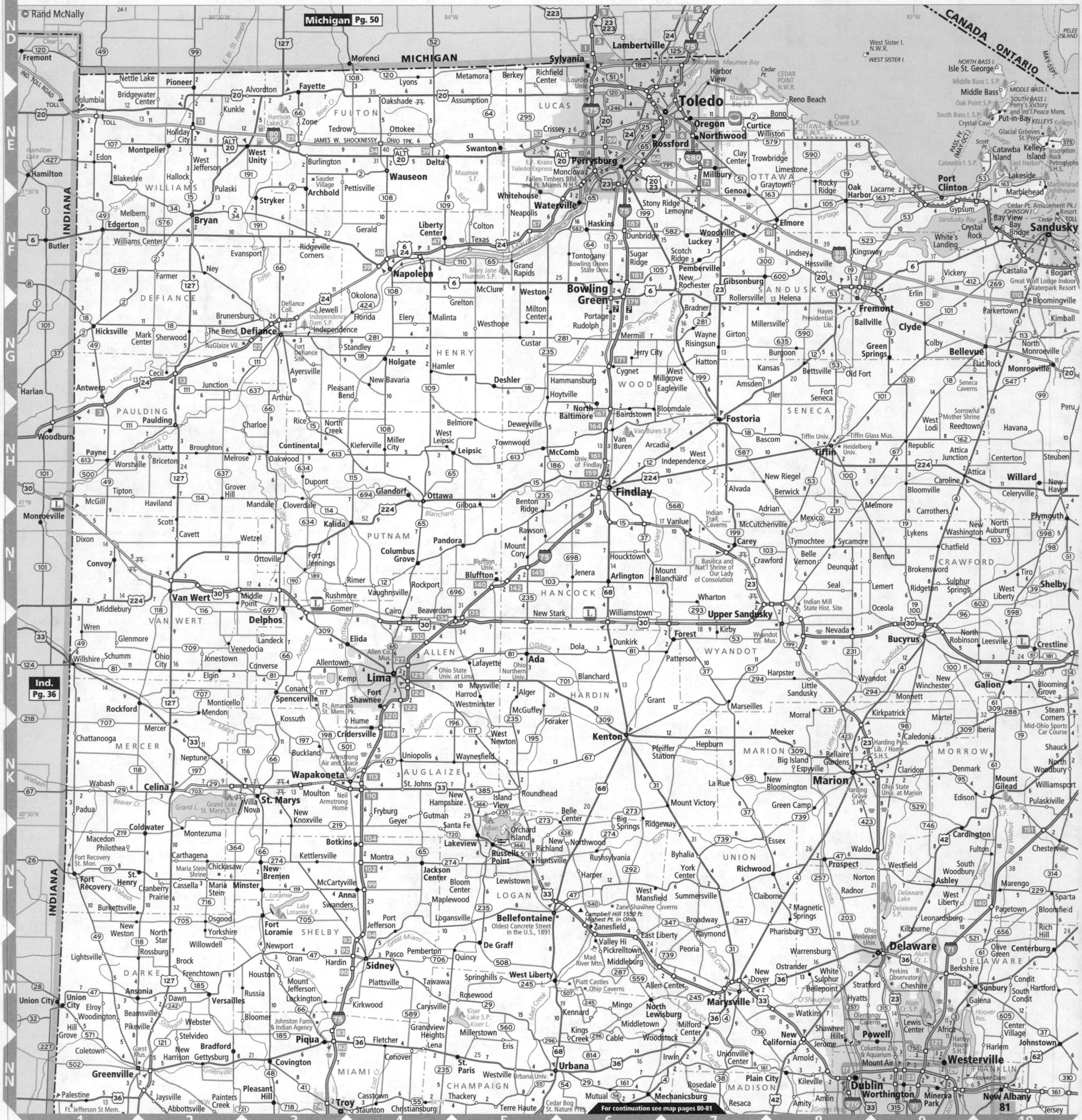

Toledo

Akron

Canton

Michigan Pg. 50

Ind. Pg. 36

For continuation see map pages 80-81

Cleveland's North Coast Harbor

Mileages between cities

	Akron	Ashtabula	Canton	Cincinnati	Cleveland	Columbus	Coshocton	Findlay	Lima	Mansfield	New Philadelphia	Pittsburgh, PA	Sandusky	Steubenville	Toledo	Youngstown
Akron		81	20	232	39	124	80	132	154	62	47	107	85	82	133	48
Cleveland	39	58	58	248		142	102	121	156	80	85	131	62	124	111	72
Columbus	124	194	126	106	142		71	96	91	66	118	184	112	150	142	172
Defiance	180	214	185	169	157	135	177	51	44	123	190	274	98	246	57	214
Lima	154	216	156	124	156	91	134	34		94	162	261	96	217	77	202
Mansfield	62	132	64	172	80	66	62	72	94		67	170	53	124	99	110
Toledo	133	171	152	200	111	142	152	44	77	99	179	228	58	221		169
Youngstown	48	57	57	279	72	172	117	180	202	110	84	67	122	66	169	

Total mileages through Ohio

- 71: 248 miles
- 75: 211 miles
- 80: 237 miles
- 90: 245 miles

More mileages at randmcnally.com/MC

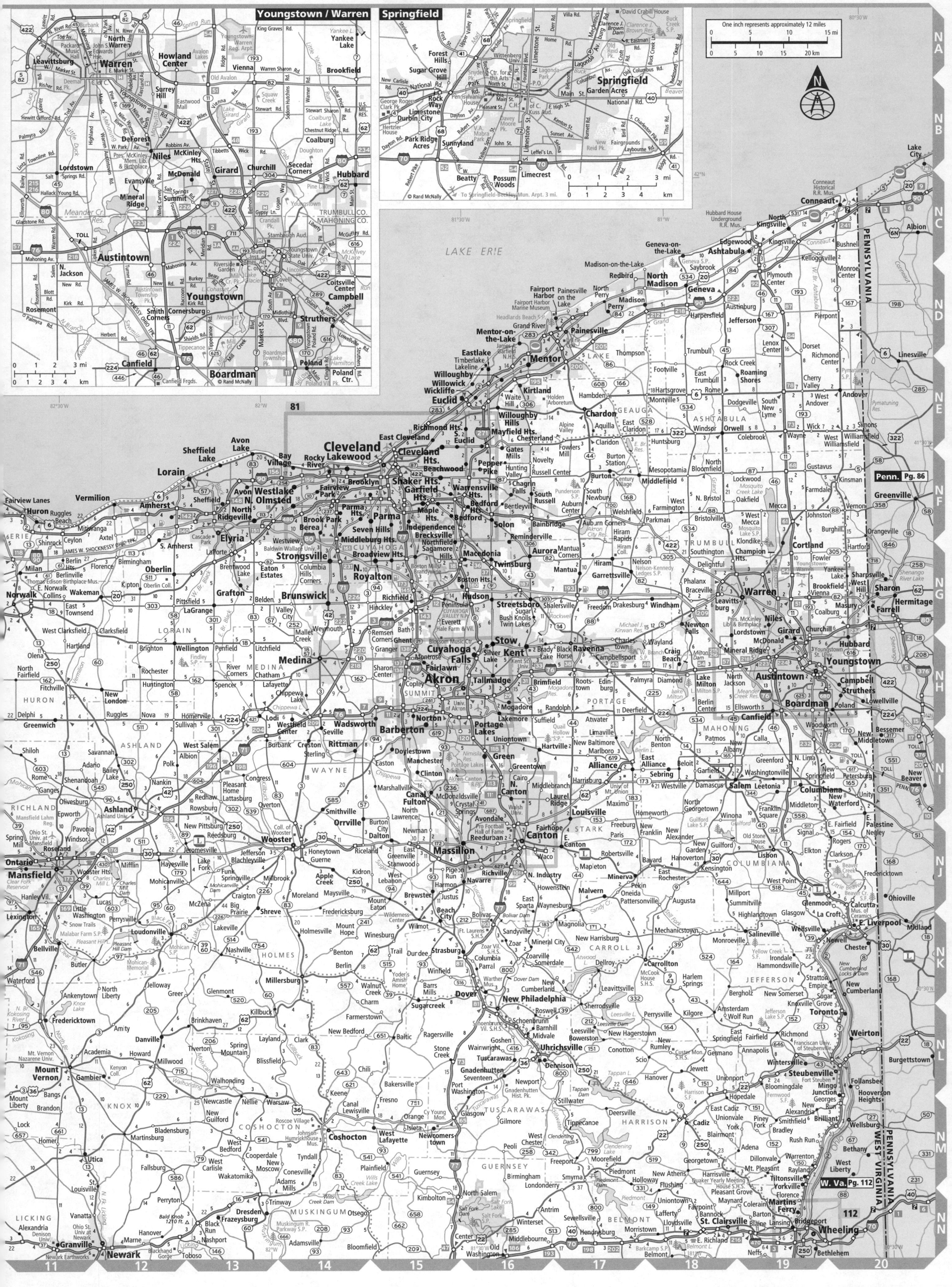

Youngstown / Warren

Springfield

To Springfield-Beckley Mun. Arpt. 3 mi.

One inch represents approximately 12 miles

LAKE ERIE

PENNSYLVANIA

WEST VIRGINIA

Penn. Pg. 86

W. Va. Pg. 112

81

Nickname: The Buckeye State
Capital: Columbus, SB-9
Land area: 40,848 sq. mi. (rank: 35th)
Population: 11,799,448 (rank: 7th)
Largest city: Columbus, 905,748, SB-9

Index of places Pg. 133

Travel planning & on-the-road resources

Tourism Information
Tourism Ohio: (800) 282-5393; ohio.org

Road Conditions & Construction
511; (855) 511-6446; www.ohgo.com, www.transportation.ohio.gov
Ohio Turnpike: (440) 234-2081, (888) 876-7453, (440) 971-2222; www.ohioturnpike.org

Toll Road Information
Ohio Turnpike and Infrastructure Commission (*E-ZPass*): (440) 234-2081; www.ohioturnpike.org

Determining distances along roads

Highway distances (segments of one mile or less not shown):
Cumulative miles (red): the distance between red arrows
Intermediate miles (black): the distance between intersections & places

Interchanges and exit numbers
For most states, the mileage between interchanges may be determined by subtracting one number from the other.

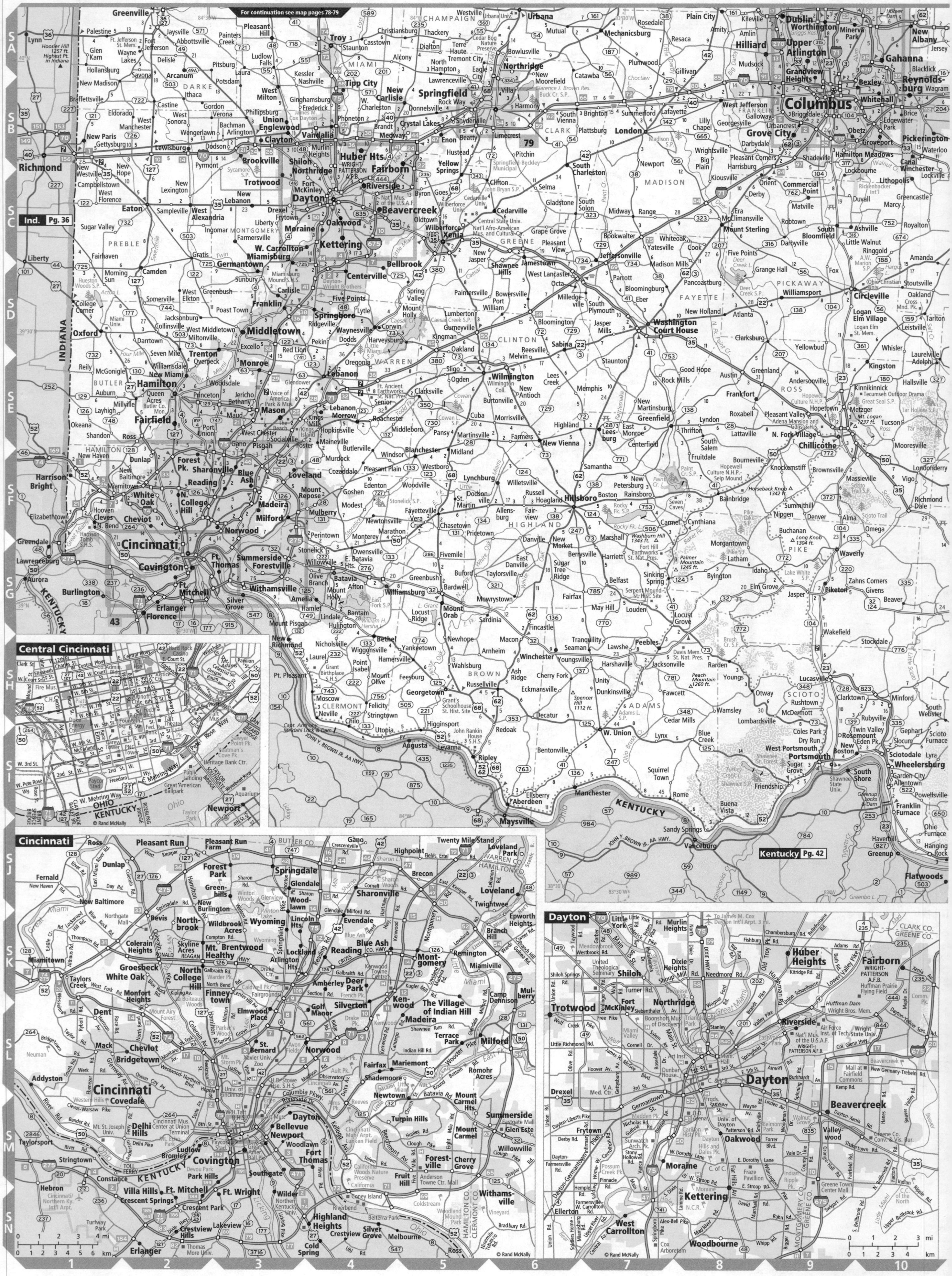

For continuation see map pages 78-79

Ind. Pg. 36

Kentucky Pg. 42

Central Cincinnati

Cincinnati

Dayton

Hocking Hills State Park

Mileages between cities

	Athens	Cambridge	Chillicothe	Cincinnati	Cleveland	Columbus	Dayton	Gallipolis	Huntington, WV	Lancaster	Marietta	Maysville, KY	Portsmouth	Wheeling, WV	Wilmington	Zanesville
Cincinnati	160	183	106		248	106	50	153	148	133	210	61	110	230	51	158
Columbus	74	79	47	106	142		71	106	137	30	124	112	91	126	62	55
Dayton	134	149	77	50	212	71		137	168	101	195	108	122	197	34	126
Gallipolis	42	114	60	153	235	106	137		39	86	66	111	55	162	112	94
Marietta	44	48	104	210	164	124	195	66	106	82		165	128	90	156	69
Portsmouth	81	162	44	110	233	91	122	55	46	80	128	52		210	79	138
Springfield	118	123	69	77	185	45	27	129	160	74	168	102	114	171	38	99
Zanesville	52	24	94	158	145	55	126	94	134	45	69	164	138	72	114	

Total mileages through Ohio

- 70: 226 miles
- 71: 248 miles
- 75: 211 miles
- 77: 160 miles

More mileages at randmcnally.com/MC

Oklahoma

Nickname: The Sooner State
Capital: Oklahoma City, F-13
Land area: 68,578 sq. mi. (rank: 19th)
Population: 3,959,353 (rank: 28th)
Largest city: Oklahoma City, 681,054, F-13

Index of places Pg. 134

Travel planning & on-the-road resources

Tourism Information
Oklahoma Tourism & Recreation Department: (800) 652-6552, (405) 522-9500; www.travelok.com

Road Conditions & Construction
(844) 465-4997; okroads.org, oklahoma.gov/odot

Toll Road Information
Oklahoma Turnpike Authority *(PIKEPASS)*: (405) 425-3600; www.pikepass.com

Determining distances along roads

Highway distances (segments of one mile or less not shown):
Cumulative miles (red): the distance between red arrows
Intermediate miles (black): the distance between intersections & places

Interchanges and exit numbers
For most states, the mileage between interchanges may be determined by subtracting one number from the other.

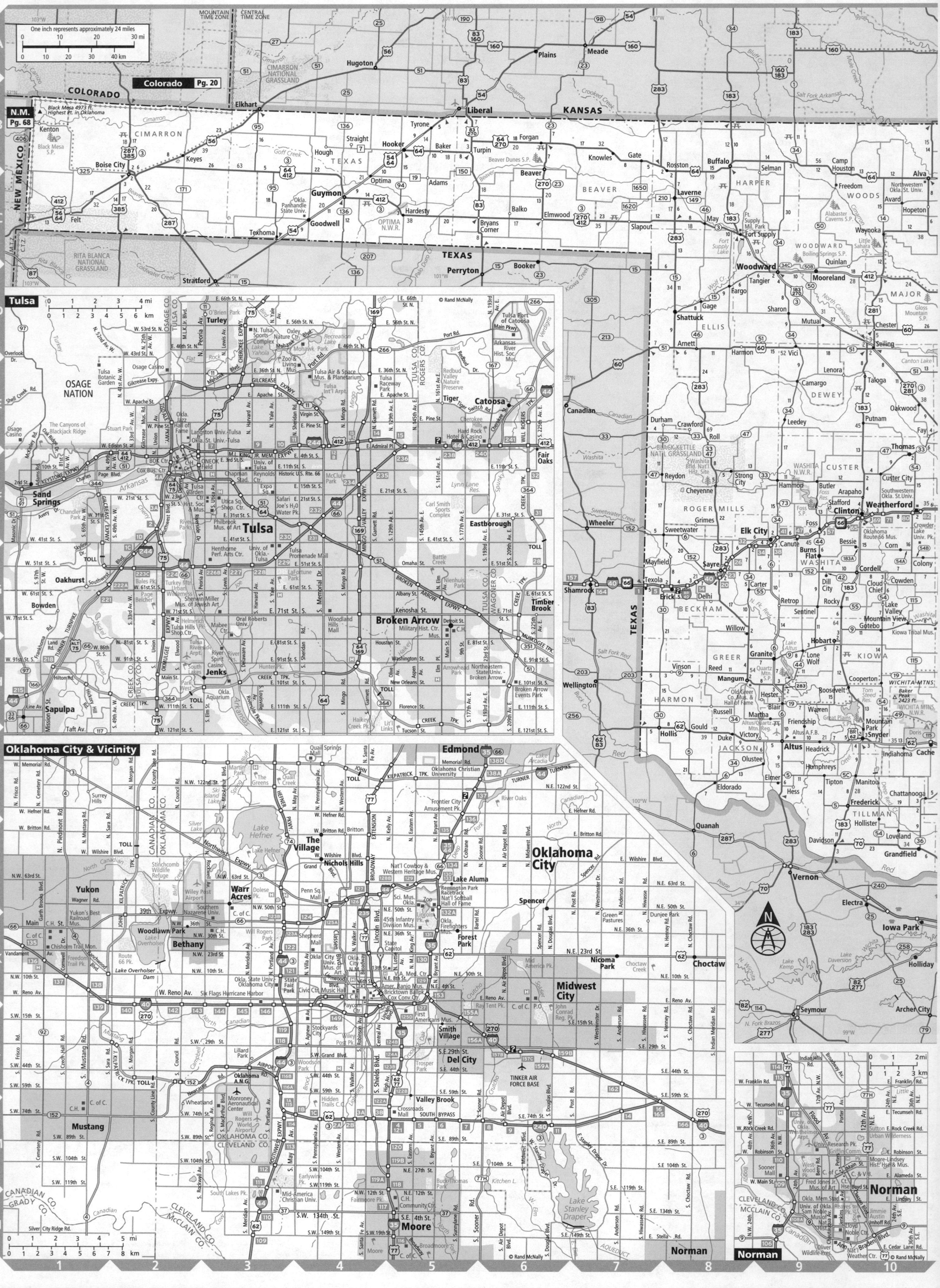

One inch represents approximately 24 miles

Colorado Pg. 20

N.M. Pg. 68

Tulsa

Oklahoma City & Vicinity

Norman

Buffalo

Mileages between cities	Ardmore	Bartlesville	Dallas, TX	Elk City	Enid	Ft. Smith, AR	Guymon	Joplin, MO	Lawton	McAlester	Muskogee	Oklahoma City	Ponca City	Tulsa	Wichita Falls, TX	Woodward
Ardmore		246	109	208	195	223	360	312	99	116	180	97	200	201	86	236
Elk City	208	260	303		148	292	184	327	108	240	249	112	216	215	143	77
Enid	195	134	302	148		232	211	227	142	204	164	99	67	114	196	87
Guymon	360	344	459	184	211	443		438	294	391	375	263	278	326	317	124
Idabel	149	248	171	352	316	136	504	295	245	116	180	240	293	203	238	380
Muskogee	180	91	236	249	164	70	375	117	218	65		137	142	50	272	251
Oklahoma City	97	149	204	112	99	180	263	216	86	128	137		105	104	140	139
Tulsa	201	45	258	215	114	118	326	113	191	91	50	104	91		244	202

Total mileages through Oklahoma

35 236 miles
44 329 miles
40 331 miles
75 227 miles

More mileages at randmcnally.com/MC

Kansas Pg. 40

Mo. Pg. 58

Ark. Pg. 10

Texas Pg. 98

Edmond

Lawton

Muskogee

Oregon

Nickname: The Beaver State
Capital: Salem, E-4
Land area: 95,963 sq. mi. (rank: 10th)
Population: 4,237,256 (rank: 27th)
Largest city: Portland, 652,503, C-5

Index of places Pg. 134

Travel planning & on-the-road resources

Tourism Information
Travel Oregon: (800) 547-7842
traveloregon.com

Road Conditions & Construction
511, (800) 977-6368, (503) 588-2941, (888) 275-6368
www.tripcheck.com, www.oregon.gov/odot

Toll Bridge Information
Bridge of the Gods (Cascade Locks) ***(BreezeBy)***: (541) 374-8619
portofcascadelocks.org/bridge-of-the-gods
Hood River Bridge ***(BreezeBy)***: (541) 386-1645; www.portofhoodriver.com/bridge

Determining distances along roads

Highway distances (segments of one mile or less not shown):
Cumulative miles (red): the distance between red arrows
Intermediate miles (black): the distance between intersections & places

Interchanges and exit numbers
For most states, the mileage between interchanges may be determined by subtracting one number from the other.

PACIFIC OCEAN

Eugene

Washington Pg. 108

California Pg. 12

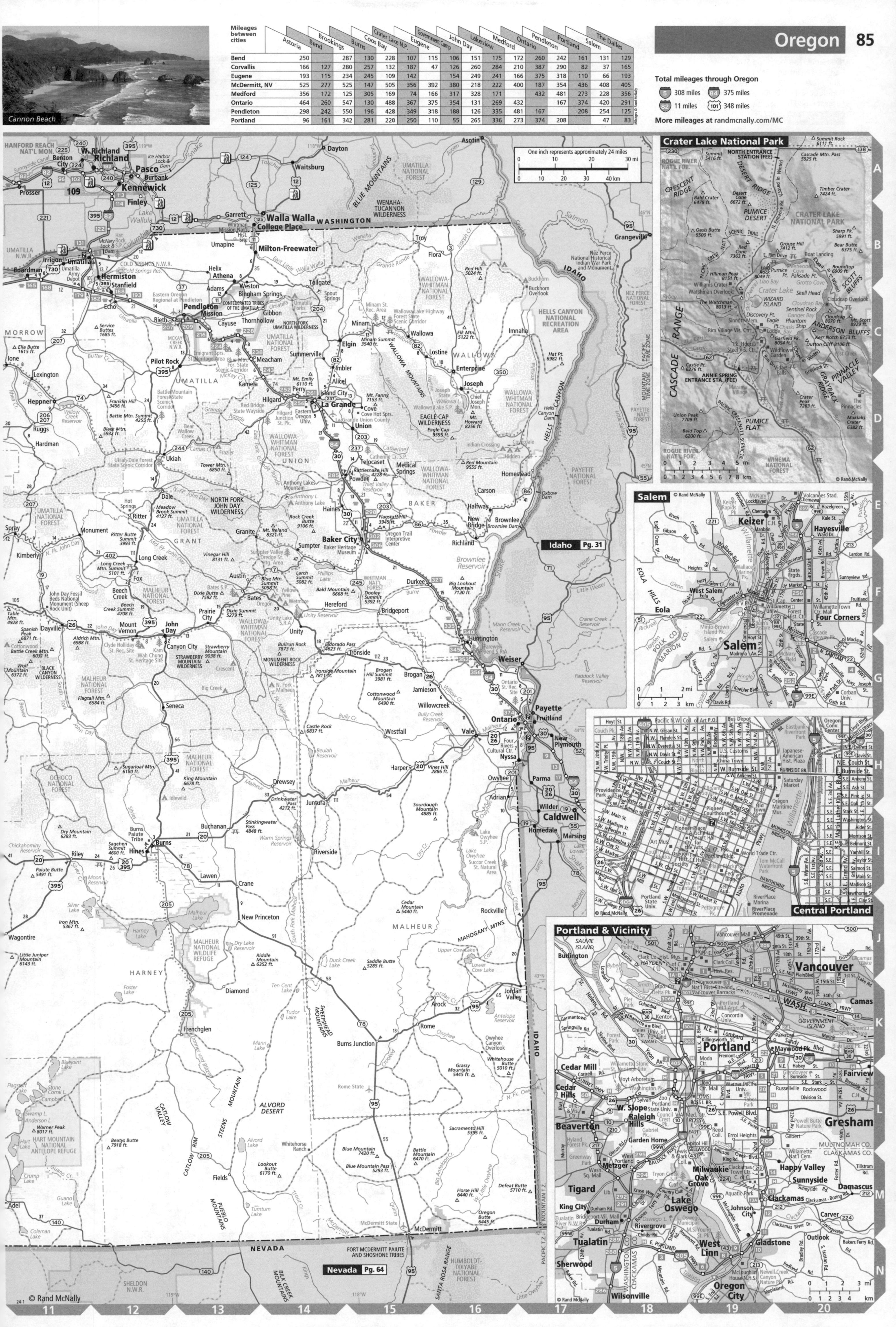

Mileages between cities	Astoria	Bend	Brookings	Burns	Coos Bay	Crater Lake N.P.	Eugene	Government Camp	John Day	Lakeview	Medford	Ontario	Pendleton	Portland	Salem	The Dalles
Bend	250		287	130	228	107	115	106	151	175	172	260	242	161	131	129
Corvallis	166	127	280	257	132	187	47	126	260	284	210	387	290	82	37	165
Eugene	193	115	234	245	109	142		154	249	241	166	375	318	110	66	193
McDermitt, NV	525	277	525	147	505	356	392	380	218	222	400	187	354	436	408	405
Medford	356	172	125	305	169	74	166	317	328	171		432	481	273	228	356
Ontario	464	260	547	130	488	367	375	354	131	269	432		167	374	420	291
Pendleton	298	242	550	196	428	349	318	188	126	335	481	167		208	254	125
Portland	96	161	342	281	220	250	110	55	265	336	273	374	208		47	83

Mileages © Rand McNally

Total mileages through Oregon

- I-5: 308 miles
- I-84: 375 miles
- I-82: 11 miles
- US 101: 348 miles

More mileages at randmcnally.com/MC

Nickname: The Keystone State
Capital: Harrisburg, EN-4
Land area: 44,730 sq. mi. (rank: 32nd)
Population: 13,002,700 (rank: 5th)
Largest city: Philadelphia, 1,603,797, EP-12

Index of places Pg. 134

Travel planning & on-the-road resources

Tourism Information
Pennsylvania Tourism Office: www.visitpa.com

Road Conditions & Construction
511, (877) 511-7366; www.511pa.com, www.penndot.pa.gov

Toll Road Information
Pennsylvania Turnpike Commission *(E-ZPass)*: (877) 736-6727, (717) 561-1522; www.paturnpike.com

Determining distances along roads

Highway distances (segments of one mile or less not shown):
Cumulative miles (red): the distance between red arrows
Intermediate miles (black): the distance between intersections & places

Interchanges and exit numbers
For most states, the mileage between interchanges may be determined by subtracting one number from the other.

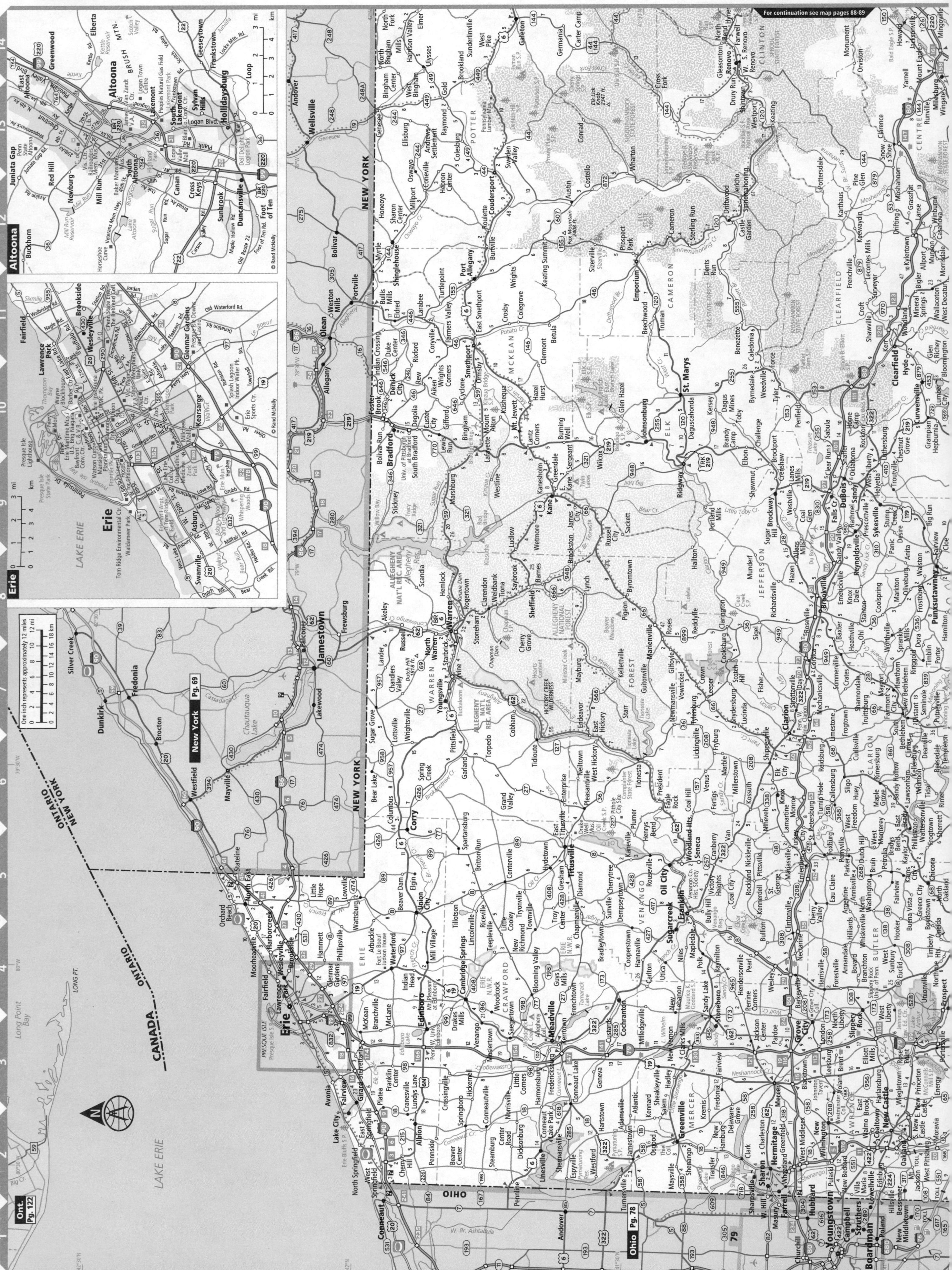
For continuation see map pages 88-89
Altoona
Erie
New York Pg. 69
Ohio Pg. 78
Ont. Pg. 122
One inch represents approximately 12 miles
LAKE ERIE
CANADA
ONTARIO
NEW YORK
OHIO
© Rand McNally

Allegheny National Forest

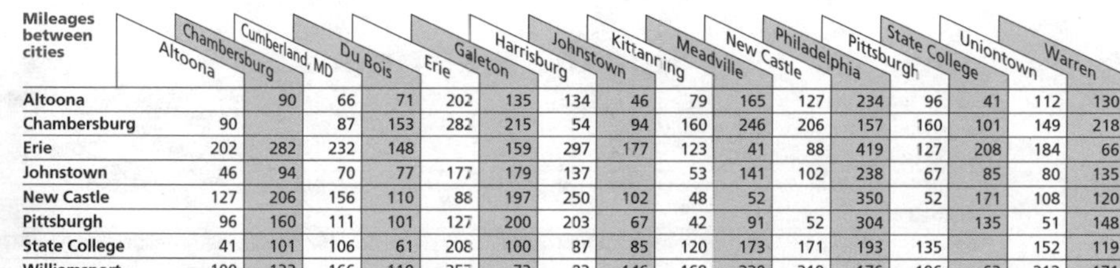

Mileages between cities	Altoona	Chambersburg	Cumberland, MD	Du Bois	Erie	Galeton	Harrisburg	Johnstown	Kittanning	Meadville	New Castle	Philadelphia	Pittsburgh	State College	Uniontown	Warren
Altoona		90	66	71	202	135	134	46	79	165	127	234	96	41	112	130
Chambersburg	90		87	153	282	215	54	94	160	246	206	157	160	101	149	218
Erie	202	282	232	148		159	297	177	123	41	88	419	127	208	184	66
Johnstown	46	94	70	77	177	179	137		53	141	102	238	67	85	80	135
New Castle	127	206	156	110	88	197	250	102	48	52		350	52	171	108	120
Pittsburgh	96	160	111	101	127	200	203	67	42	91	52	304		135	51	148
State College	41	101	106	61	208	100	87	85	120	173	171	193	135		152	119
Williamsport	100	132	166	110	257	72	83	146	168	220	219	176	196	63	212	171

Total mileages through Pennsylvania

- 70: 168 miles
- 79: 183 miles
- 80: 311 miles
- 90: 46 miles

More mileages at randmcnally.com/MC

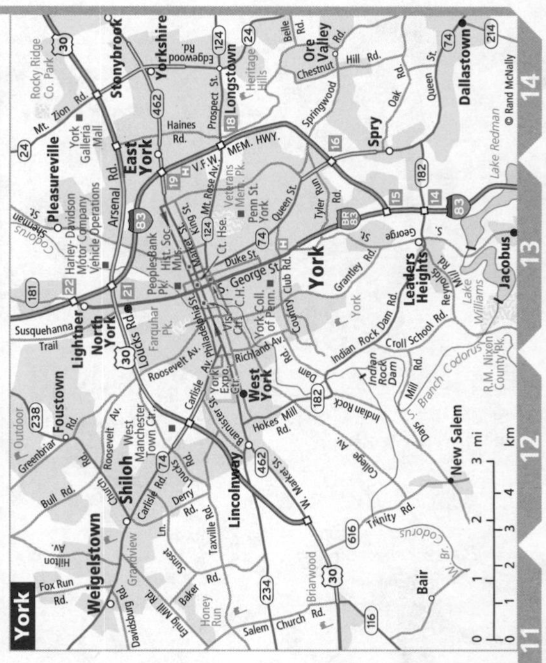

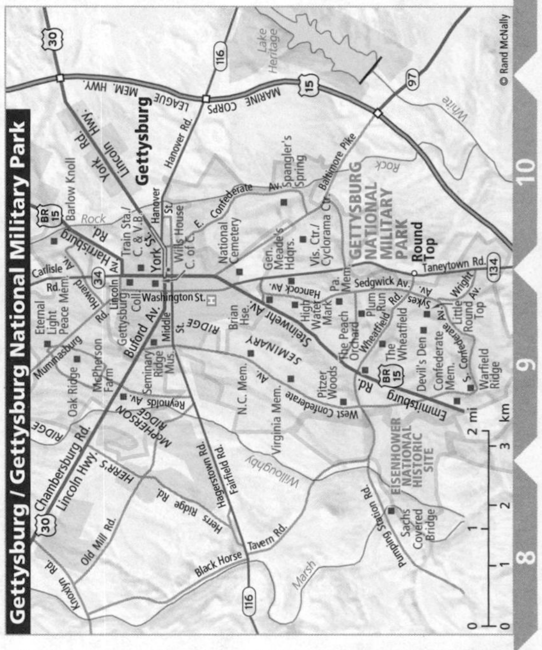

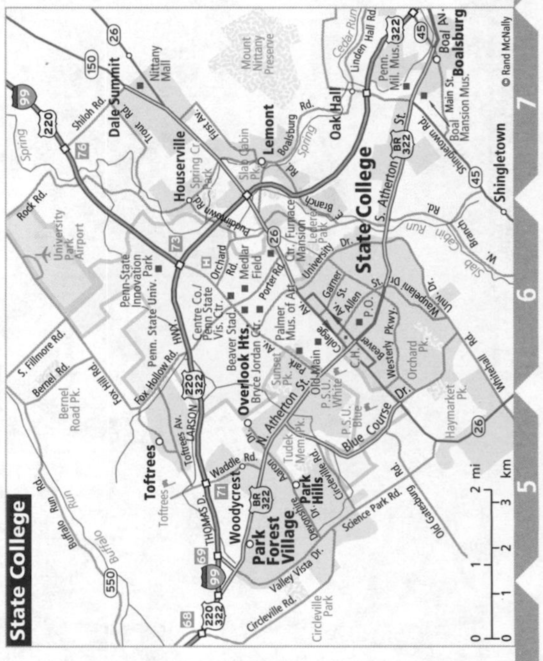

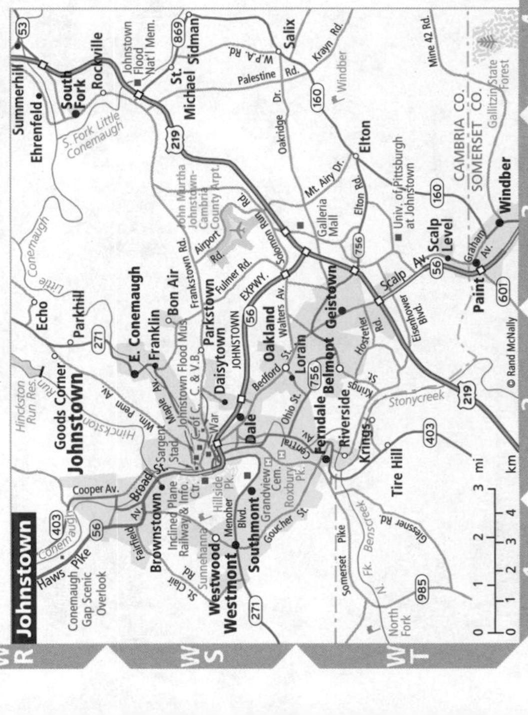

York

Gettysburg / Gettysburg National Military Park

State College

Johnstown

Md. Pg. 46

West Virginia Pg. 112

Nickname: The Keystone State
Capital: Harrisburg, EN-4
Land area: 44,730 sq. mi. (rank: 32nd)
Population: 13,002,700 (rank: 5th)
Largest city: Philadelphia, 1,603,797, EP-12

Index of places Pg. 134

Travel planning & on-the-road resources

Tourism Information
Pennsylvania Tourism Office: www.visitpa.com

Road Conditions & Construction
511, (877) 511-7366; www.511pa.com, www.penndot.pa.gov

Toll Road Information
Pennsylvania Turnpike Commission (*E-ZPass*): (877) 736-6727, (717) 561-1522; www.paturnpike.com

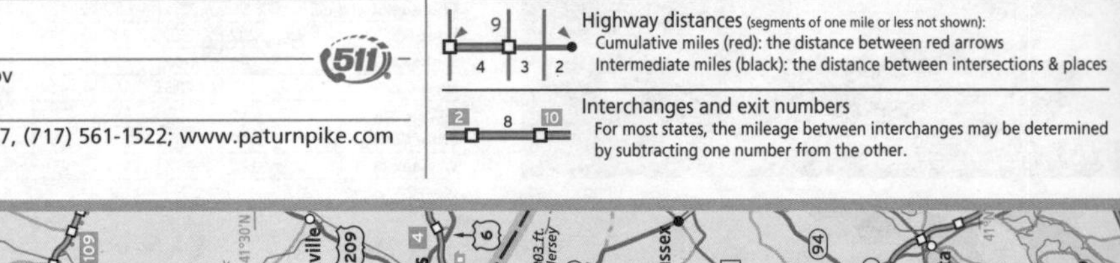

Scranton / Wilkes-Barre

Allentown / Bethlehem

For continuation see map pages 86-87

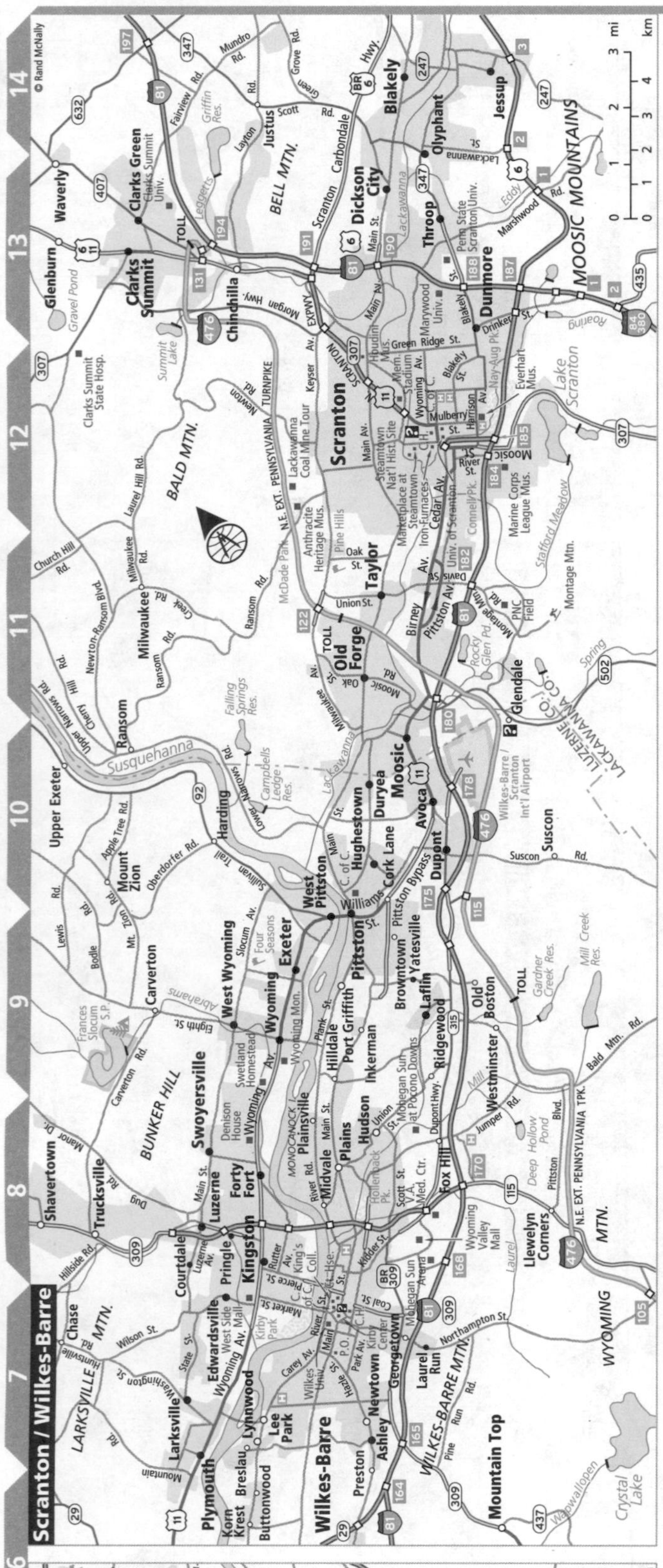

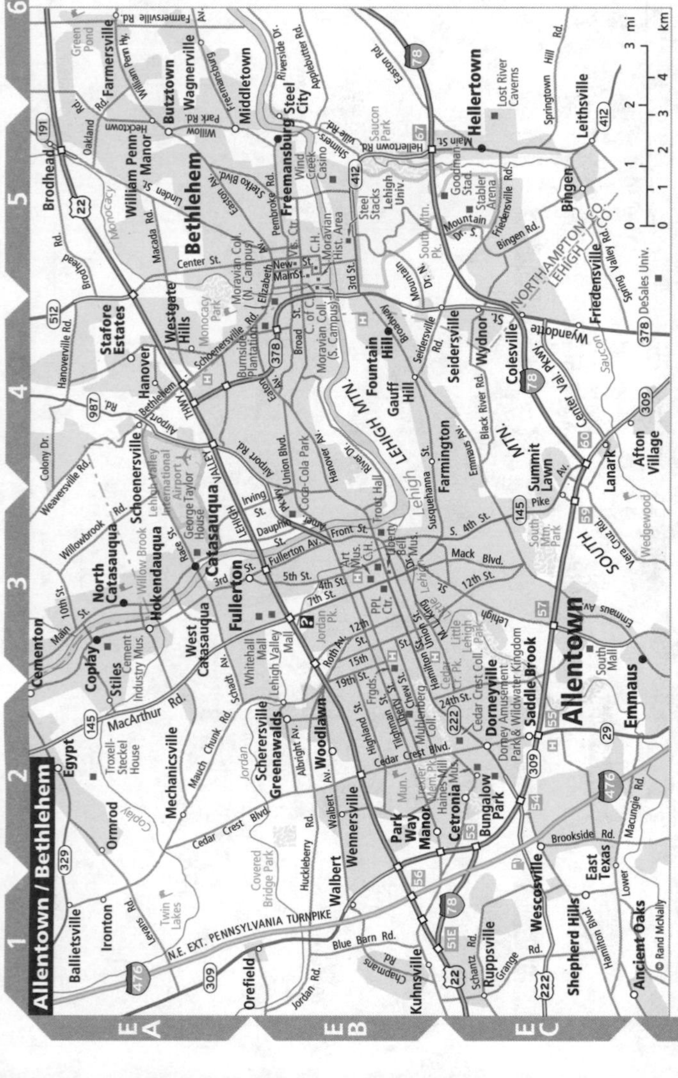

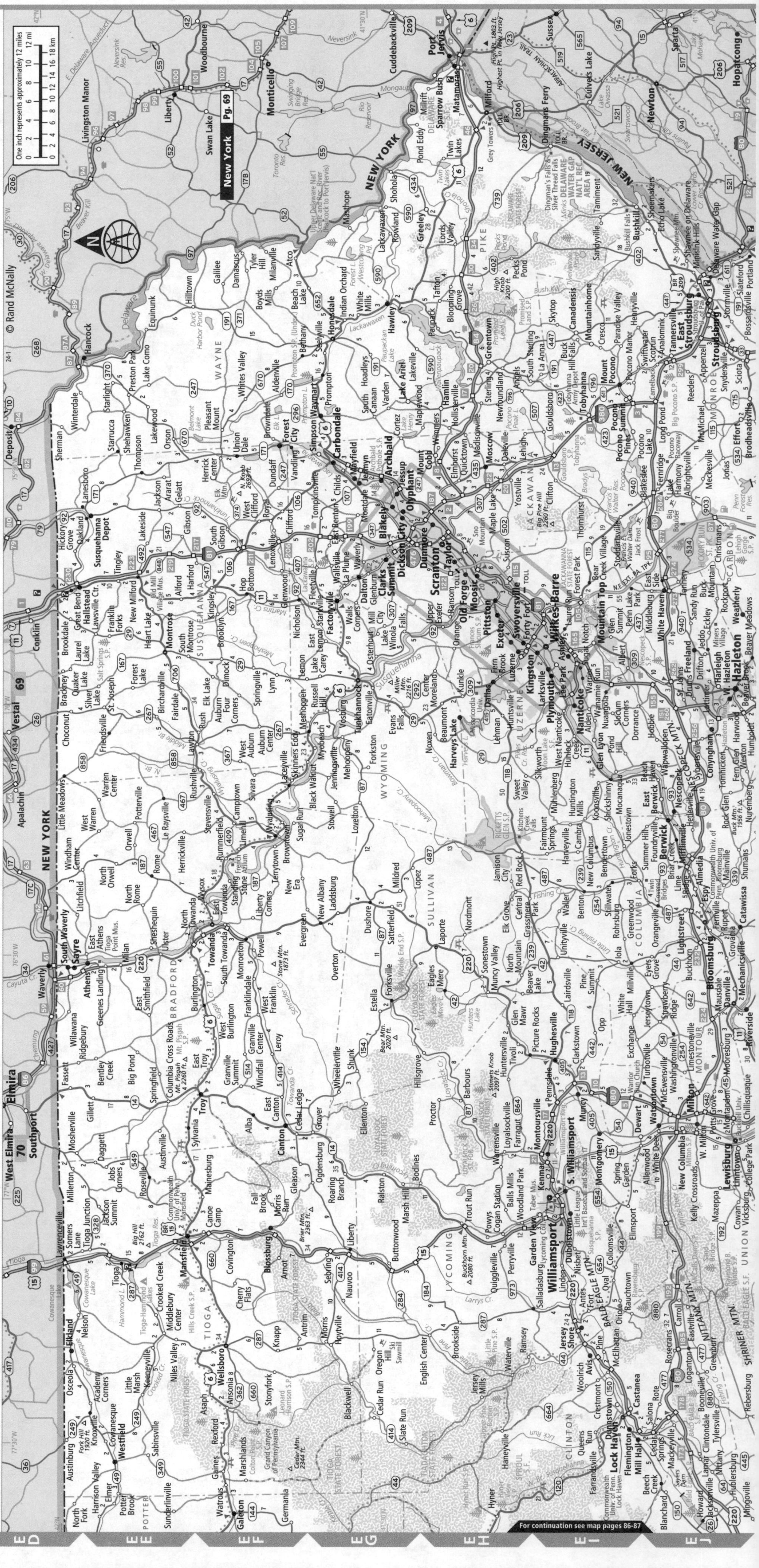

Ferry rides on the Delaware River

Mileages between cities	Allentown	Gettysburg	Harrisburg	Lancaster	Mansfield	Philadelphia	Pittsburgh	Port Jervis, NY	Scranton	State College	Stroudsburg	Towanda	Trenton, NJ	Wilkes-Barre	Williamsport	York
Allentown		121	81	67	177	62	282	81	74	175	40	126	75	60	127	92
Chambersburg	132	25	54	91	182	157	160	227	171	101	170	188	177	154	132	74
Harrisburg	81	38		39	133	107	203	176	120	87	119	139	127	104	83	26
Philadelphia	62	138	107	78	226		304	140	124	193	100	175	32	109	176	101
Reading	37	96	64	34	175	62	261	118	100	150	76	152	82	86	126	56
Scranton	74	160	120	132	102	124	279	59		150	46	64	137	16	101	146
State College	175	129	87	126	107	193	135	205	150		162	134	213	132	63	118
Williamsport	127	126	83	123	50	176	196	157	101	63	113	67	189	84		115

Total mileages through Pennsylvania

- 76: 350 miles
- 81: 232 miles
- 80: 311 miles
- 95: 51 miles

More mileages at randmcnally.com/MC

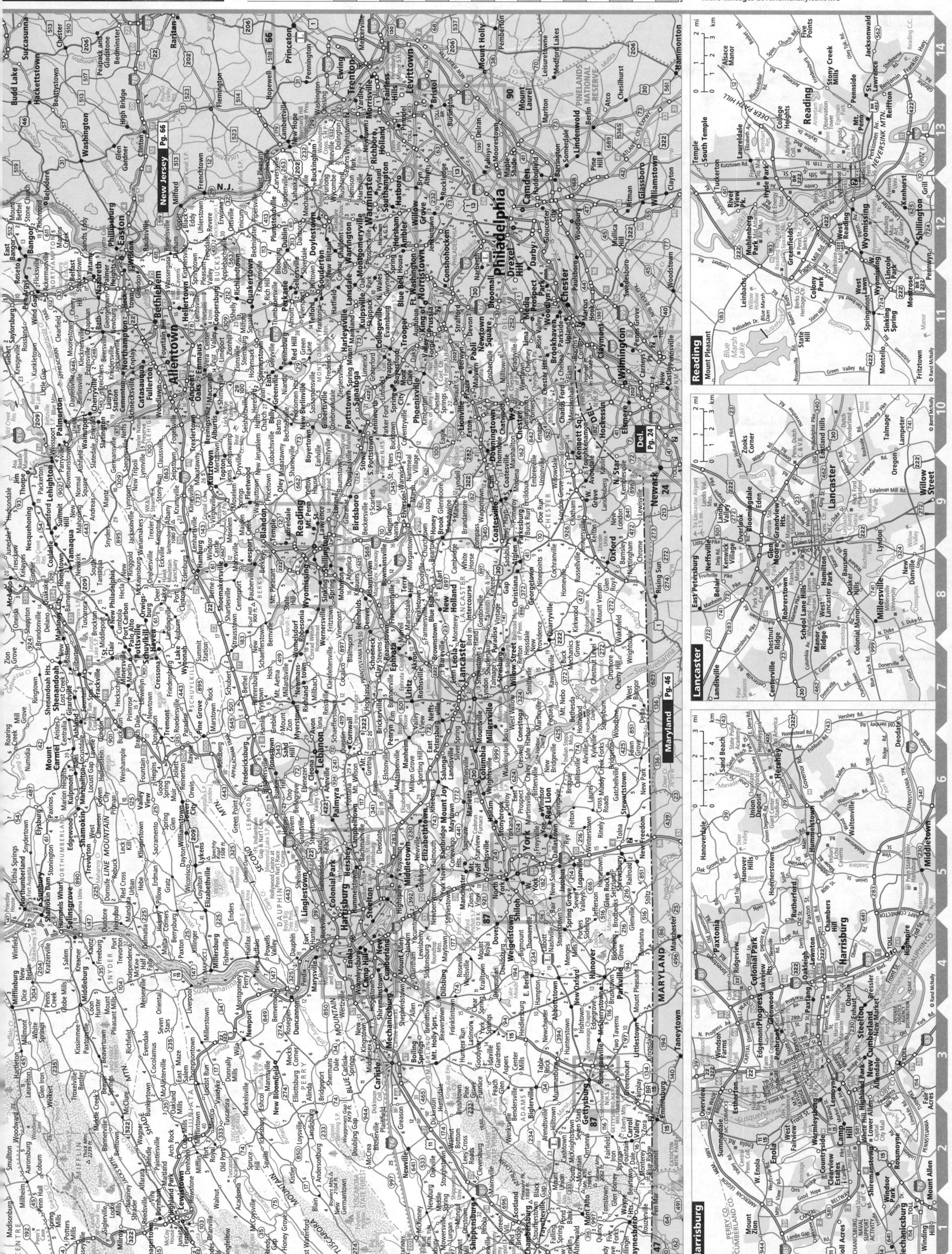

Sights to see

- Adventure Aquarium, Camden E-5
- The Andy Warhol Museum, Pittsburgh L-2
- Betsy Ross House, Philadelphia F-10
- Carnegie Science Center, Pittsburgh L-1
- Duquesne Incline, Pittsburgh M-1
- Franklin Institute Science Museum, Philadelphia F-6
- Independence Hall, Philadelphia G-9
- Liberty Bell, Philadelphia G-9
- National Constitution Center, Philadelphia F-9
- Philadelphia Museum of Art, Philadelphia E-4
- Point State Park, Pittsburgh M-1
- The Strip District, Pittsburgh..................... L-3

Independence National Historical Park

Philadelphia & Vicinity

Central Philadelphia

Pittsburgh & Vicinity

Central Pittsburgh

Travel planning & on-the-road resources

ourism Information
isit Rhode Island:
(800) 556-2484
www.visitrhodeisland.com

Toll Bridge Info (*EZ-Pass*)
Rhode Island Turnpike
& Bridge Authority:
(401) 423-0800
www.ritba.org

oad Conditions & Construction
344) 368-7623, (888) 401-4511, (401) 222-2450
www.dot.ri.gov/travel

Determining Distances
9 / 4 3 2 (segments of one mile or less not shown)
Cumulative miles (red): the distance between red arrows
Intermediate miles (black): the distance between intersections & places

Total mileages through Rhode Island
95 42 miles
6 31 miles
1 60 miles
More mileages at
randmcnally.com/MC

Mileages between cities

	Fall River, MA	Kingston	Newport	Providence	Warwick	Westerly	Woonsocket	Worcester, MA
Chepachet	35	41	45	19	23	54	13	37
Fall River, MA		35	20	16	25	58	31	56
Newport	20	16		33	26	39	47	72
Providence	16	29	33		10	42	14	40
Warwick	25	23	26	10		37	24	50
Westerly	58	23	39	42	37		56	82
Woonsocket	31	43	47	14	24	56		27
Worcester, MA	56	68	72	40	50	82	27	

Nickname: The Ocean State
Capital: Providence, D-6
Land area: 1,034 sq. mi. (rank: 50th)
Population: 1,097,379 (rank: 43rd)
Largest city: Providence, 190,934, D-6

Index of places Pg. 134

South Carolina

Nickname: The Palmetto State
Capital: Columbia, D-7
Land area: 30,056 sq. mi. (rank: 40th)
Population: 5,118,425 (rank: 23rd)
Largest city: Charleston, 150,227, H-10

Index of places Pg. 134

Mileages between cities	Anderson	Augusta, GA	Charleston	Charlotte, NC	Columbia	Hilton Head I.	Myrtle Beach	Spartanburg
Augusta, GA	92		175	160	72	151	216	120
Charleston	238	175		207	112	104	95	201
Charlotte, NC	128	160	207		93	253	176	72
Columbia	117	72	112	93		158	148	93
Florence	206	148	130	104	81	177	67	169
Myrtle Beach	273	216	95	176	148	200		237
Savannah, GA	282	134	106	251	156	34	202	246
Spartanburg	60	120	201	72	93	247	237	

Total mileages through South Carolina

20: 142 miles
85: 106 miles
26: 221 miles
95: 199 miles

More mileages at randmcnally.com/MC

Travel planning & on-the-road resources

Tourism Information
South Carolina Department of Parks, Recreation and Tourism: (803) 734-0124; discoversouthcarolina.com

Road Conditions & Construction
511, (877) 511-4672, (803) 737-1200; www.511sc.org, www.scdot.org

Toll Road Information
Southern Connector (Greenville Co.) *(Palmetto Pass)*: (864) 527-2150
www.southernconnector.com

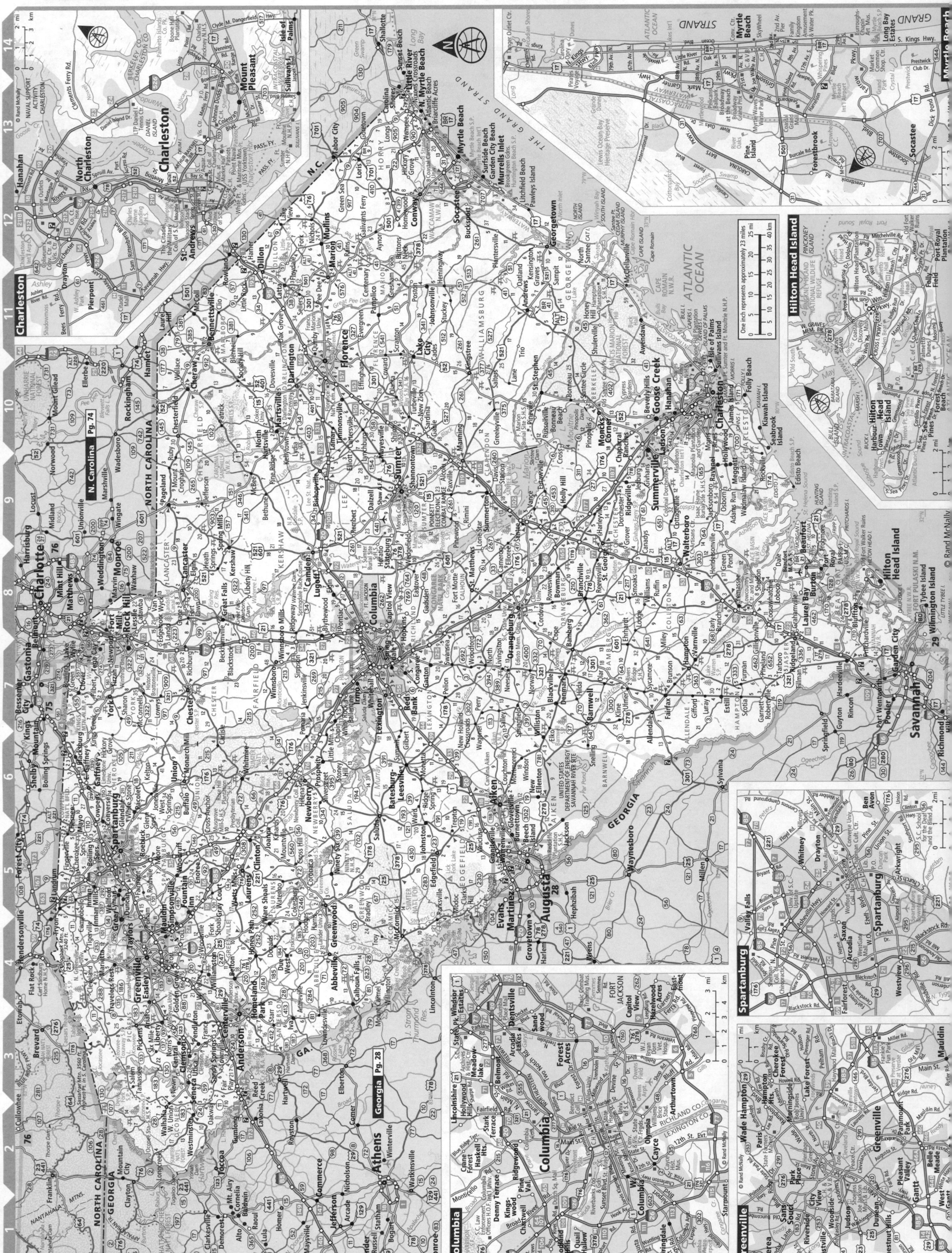

Travel planning & on-the-road resources

ourism Information

outh Dakota Department of Tourism: (605) 773-3301
www.travelsouthdakota.com

oad Conditions & Construction

11, (866) 697-3511
www.sd511.org, dot.sd.gov

oll Road Information

o tolls on state or federal highways

Determining Distances

(segments of one mile or less not shown)

Cumulative miles (red): the distance between red arrows

Intermediate miles (black): the distance between intersections & places

Total mileages through South Dakota

29: 253 miles
12: 317 miles
90: 413 miles
83: 242 miles

More mileages at randmcnally.com/MC

Mileages between cities	Aberdeen	Mobridge	Pierre	Pine Ridge	Rapid City	Sioux Falls	Watertown	Yankton
Aberdeen		100	160	360	333	203	96	236
Belle Fourche	312	212	206	172	60	403	362	421
Mobridge	100		108	308	243	303	196	332
Pierre	160	108		200	173	224	188	242
Rapid City	333	243	173	111		347	403	365
Sioux City, IA	285	384	305	358	428	85	184	63
Sioux Falls	203	303	224	356	347		103	81
Watertown	96	196	188	415	403	103		155

South Dakota

Nickname: The Mount Rushmore State
Capital: Pierre, D-7
Land area: 75,790 sq. mi. (rank: 16th)
Population: 886,667 (rank: 46th)
Largest city: Sioux Falls, 192,517, F-13

Index of places Pg. 134

Tennessee

Nickname: The Volunteer State
Capital: Nashville, C-11
Land area: 41,227 sq. mi. (rank: 34th)
Population: 6,910,840 (rank: 16th)
Largest city: Nashville, 689,447, C-11

Index of places Pg. 134

Travel planning & on-the-road resources

Tourism Information
Tennessee Department of Tourist Development: (615) 741-2159; www.tnvacation.com

Road Conditions & Construction
511, (877) 244-0065; smartway.tn.gov, www.tn.gov/tdot/welcome-to-tennessee-511

Toll Road Information
No tolls on state or federal highways

Determining distances along roads

Highway distances (segments of one mile or less not shown):
Cumulative miles (red): the distance between red arrows
Intermediate miles (black): the distance between intersections & places

Interchanges and exit numbers
For most states, the mileage between interchanges may be determined by subtracting one number from the other.

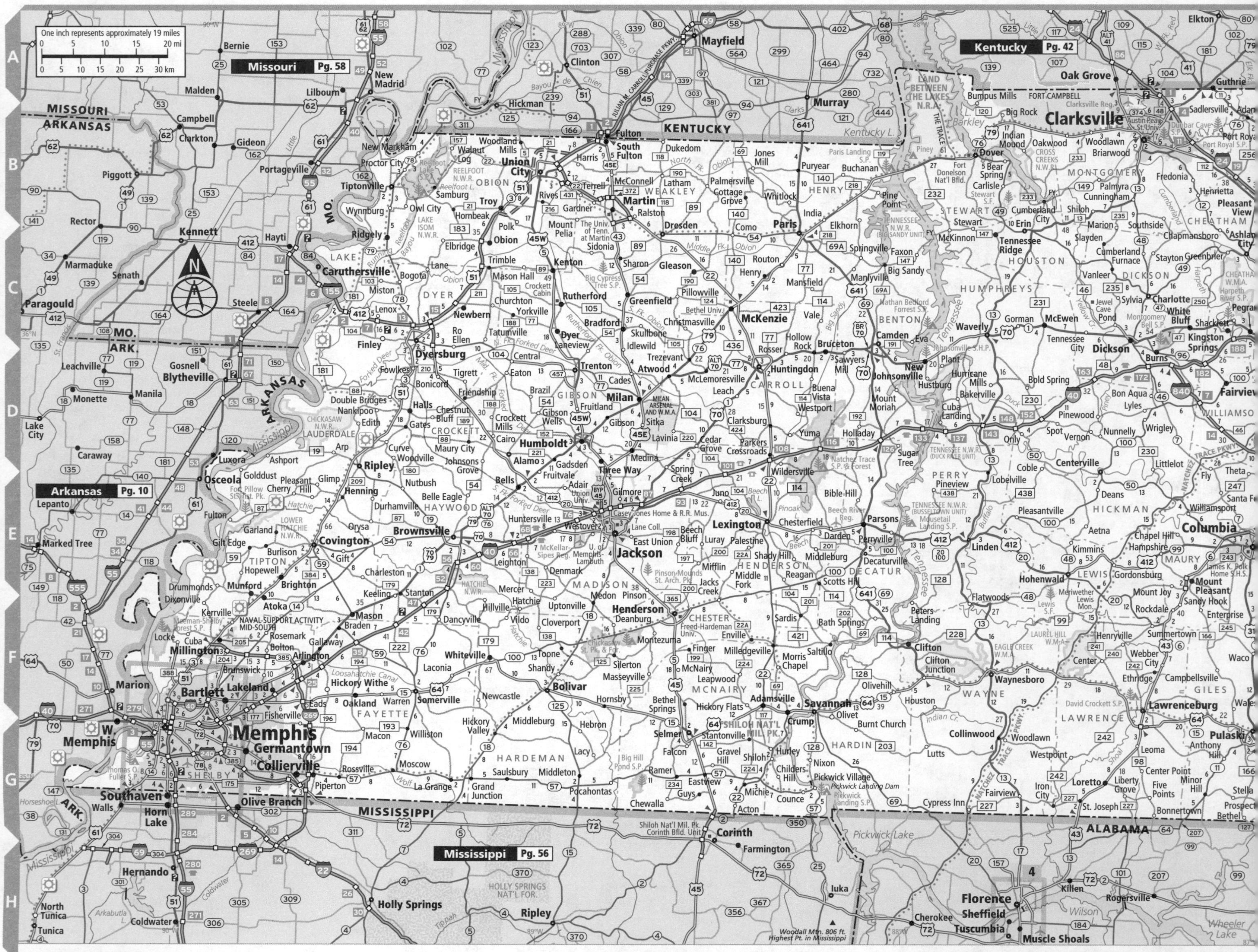
One inch represents approximately 19 miles
Missouri Pg. 58
Kentucky Pg. 42
Arkansas Pg. 10
Mississippi Pg. 56
Memphis
Nashville
Jackson
Clarksville
Columbia
Woodall Mtn. 806 ft. Highest Pt. in Mississippi

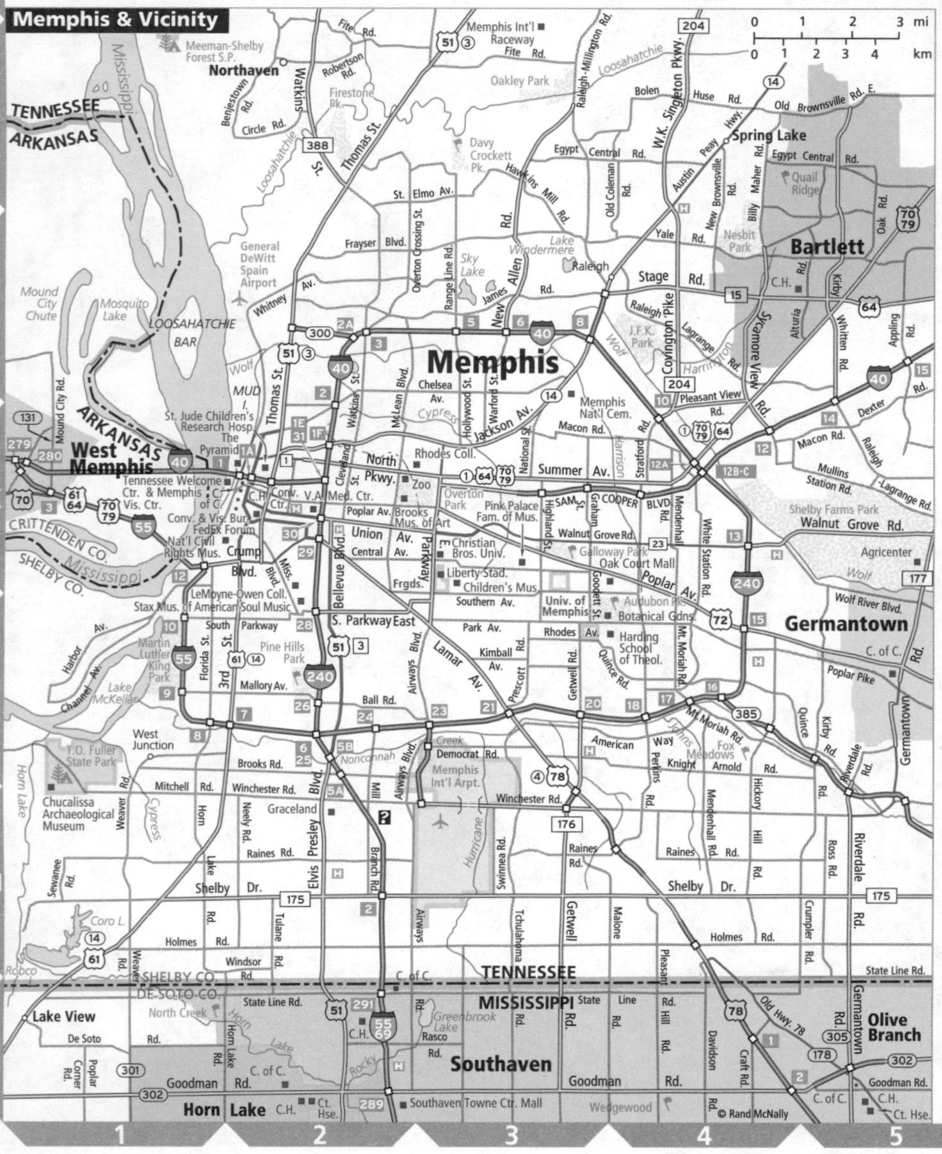
Memphis & Vicinity
Memphis
Germantown
Bartlett
Southaven
Olive Branch
TENNESSEE
MISSISSIPPI
© Rand McNally

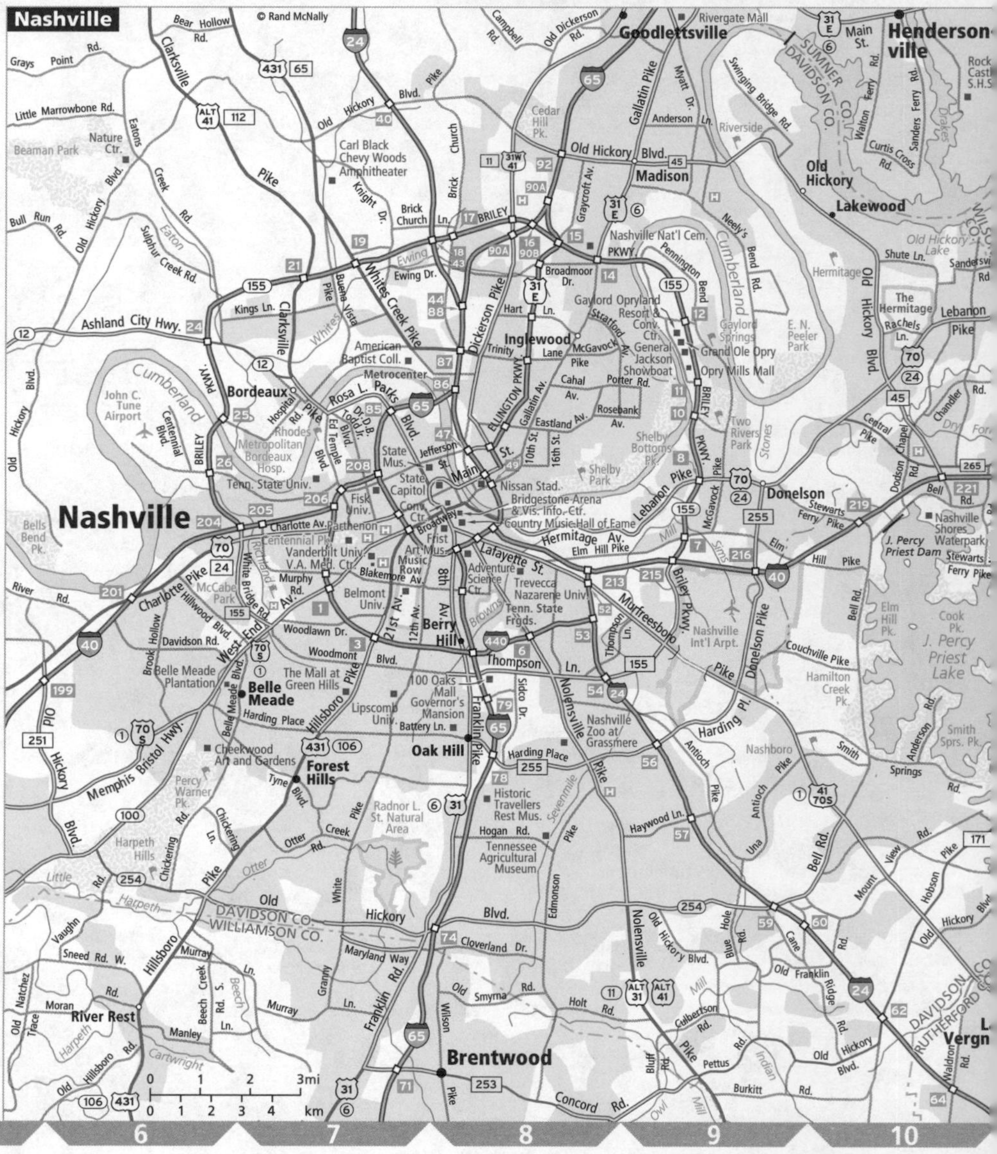
Nashville
Goodlettsville
Hendersonville
Brentwood
Oak Hill
Forest Hills
Belle Meade
© Rand McNally

Beale Street, Memphis

Mileages between cities	Atlanta, GA	Bristol	Chattanooga	Clarksville	Cookeville	Dyersburg	Fayetteville	Gatlinburg	Jackson	Johnson City	Knoxville	Memphis	Morristown	Nashville	Oak Ridge	Union City
Chattanooga	117	223		177	98	303	94	151	260	215	110	314	158	131	108	311
Clarksville	293	337	177		125	173	136	265	123	329	224	201	271	47	207	138
Dyersburg	418	463	303	173	252		229	392	47	455	351	76	398	172	334	34
Fayetteville	211	317	94	136	109	229		246	167	308	204	243	252	90	189	224
Johnson City	256	24	215	329	206	455	308	106	412		104	495	65	283	128	463
Knoxville	202	113	110	224	102	351	204	41	308	104		390	48	179	24	358
Memphis	380	502	314	201	291	76	243	431	87	495	390		437	212	373	113
Nashville	249	292	131	47	80	172	90	220	129	283	179	212	226		162	168

Total mileages through Tennessee

- 40: 455 miles
- 75: 161 miles
- 65: 121 miles
- 81: 76 miles

More mileages at randmcnally.com/MC

For continuation see map below

Alabama Pg. 4

Georgia Pg. 28

N.C. Pg. 74

Knoxville

Chattanooga

Ky. Pg. 42

Virginia Pg. 106

For continuation see main map

North Carolina Pg. 74

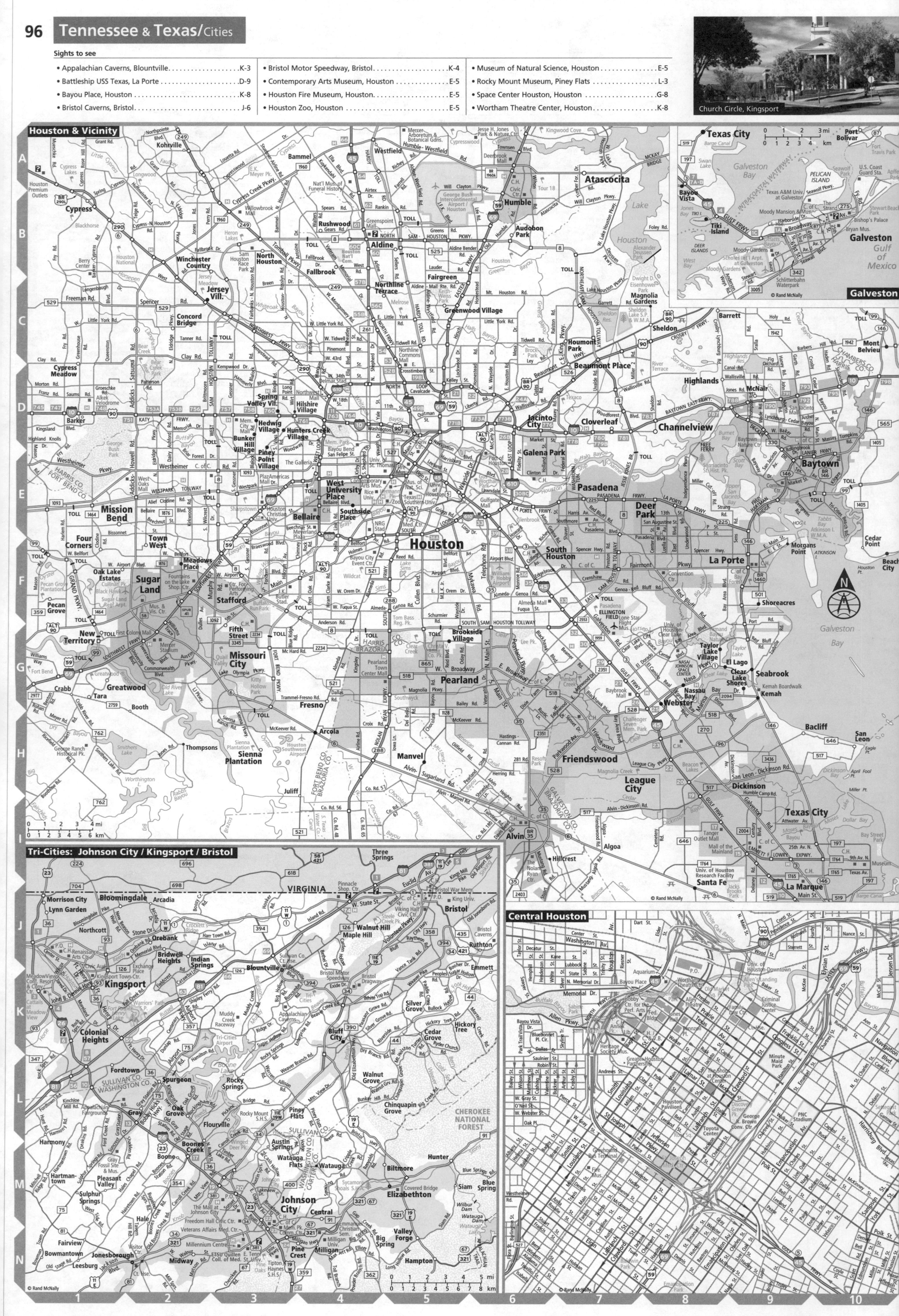
Sights to see
• Appalachian Caverns, Blountville....K-3
• Battleship USS Texas, La Porte....D-9
• Bayou Place, Houston....K-8
• Bristol Caverns, Bristol....J-6
• Bristol Motor Speedway, Bristol....K-4
• Contemporary Arts Museum, Houston....E-5
• Houston Fire Museum, Houston....E-5
• Houston Zoo, Houston....E-5
• Museum of Natural Science, Houston....E-5
• Rocky Mount Museum, Piney Flats....L-3
• Space Center Houston, Houston....G-8
• Wortham Theatre Center, Houston....K-8
Church Circle, Kingsport
Houston & Vicinity
Galveston
Tri-Cities: Johnson City / Kingsport / Bristol
Central Houston
Houston
Texas City
Galveston
Pasadena
Baytown
La Porte
Pearland
Sugar Land
Missouri City
Humble
Atascocita
Kingsport
Bristol
Johnson City
Elizabethton
VIRGINIA
CHEROKEE NATIONAL FOREST
Galveston Bay
Gulf of Mexico
© Rand McNally

Fort Worth Historic Stockyards

Sights to see

- Dallas Museum of Art, Dallas B-2
- Dallas Zoo, Dallas H-10
- Fair Park, Dallas G-11
- Fort Worth Zoo, Fort Worth H-4
- Louis Tussaud's Palace of Wax & Ripley's Believe It or Not!, Grand Prairie G-8
- Old City Park, Dallas C-3
- Six Flags over Texas, Arlington H-7
- Sixth Floor Museum at Dealey Plaza, Dallas B-1
- Stockyards Historic District, Fort Worth G-4
- Sundance Square, Fort Worth E-1
- Texas Civil War Museum, Fort Worth G-2

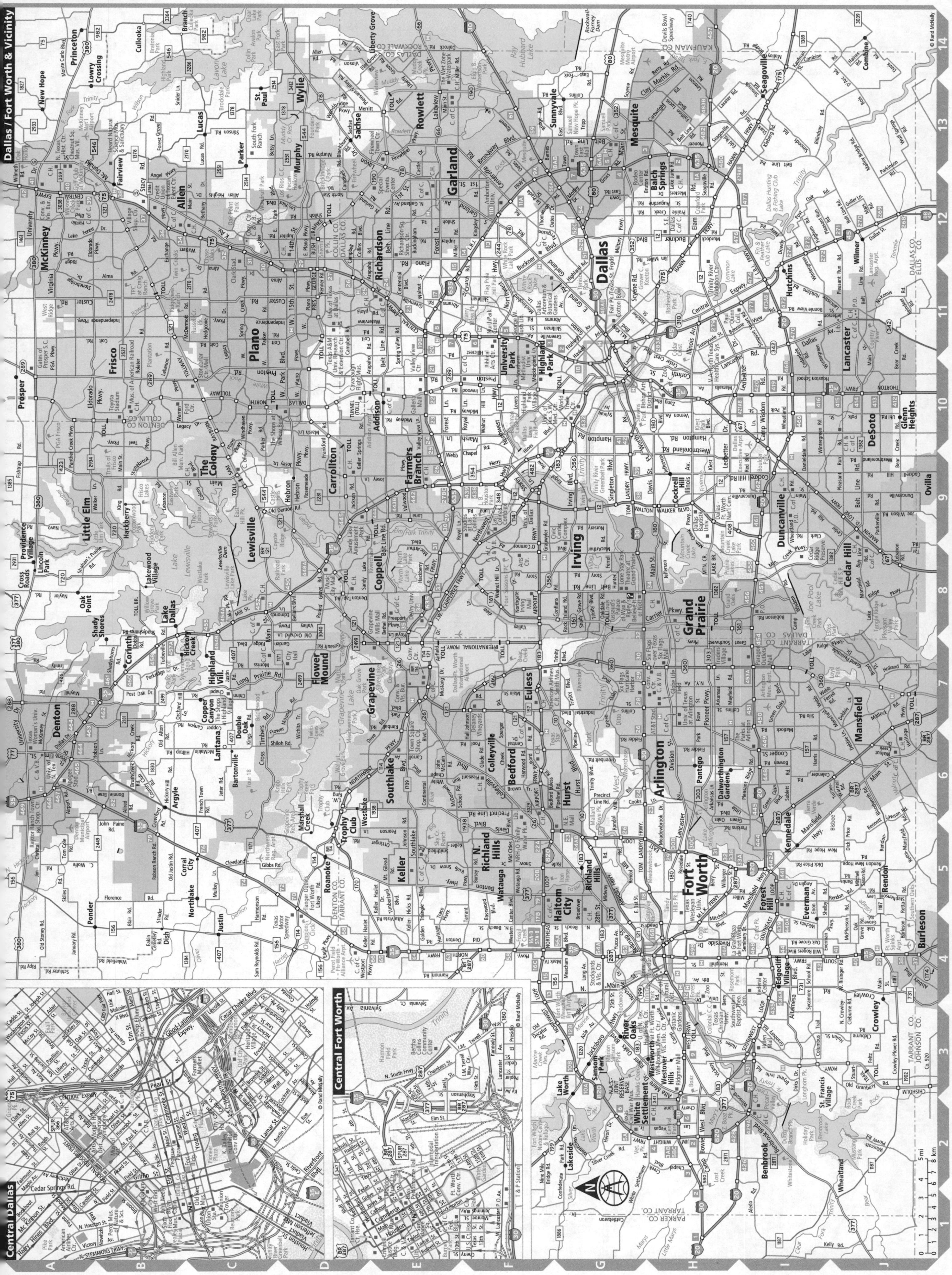

Dallas / Fort Worth & Vicinity

Central Dallas

Central Fort Worth

Nickname: The Lone Star State
Capital: Austin, EK-5
Land area: 261,194 sq. mi. (rank: 2nd)
Population: 29,145,505 (rank: 2nd)
Largest city: Houston, 2,304,580, EL-10

Index of places Pg. 135

Travel planning & on-the-road resources

Tourism Information
Texas Tourism: (512) 463-2000
www.traveltexas.com

Road Conditions & Construction
(800) 452-9292, (512) 463-8588
Dallas Metroplex: (877) 511-3255
drivetexas.org, 511dfw.org

Toll Road Information *(all use TxTag)*
Texas Department of Transportation: (888) 468-9824, (214) 210-0493; www.txtag.org
Cameron County Reg. Mobility Authority (TX 550): (956) 621-5571; ccrma.org
Harris County Toll Road Authority (Houston area) ***(also EZTAG)***:
(281) 875-3279; www.hctra.org
North Texas Tollway Authority (Dallas Metroplex) ***(also TollTag)***:
(972) 818-6882, (817) 731-6882; www.ntta.org

(list continued on page 100)

Toll Bridge Information
El Paso–Int'l Bridges: (915) 212-7500
www.elpasotexas.gov/international-bridges
Eagle Pass–Int'l Bridge System: (830) 773-2622
eaglepasstx.us/205/Bridge-I-II

(list continued on page 100)

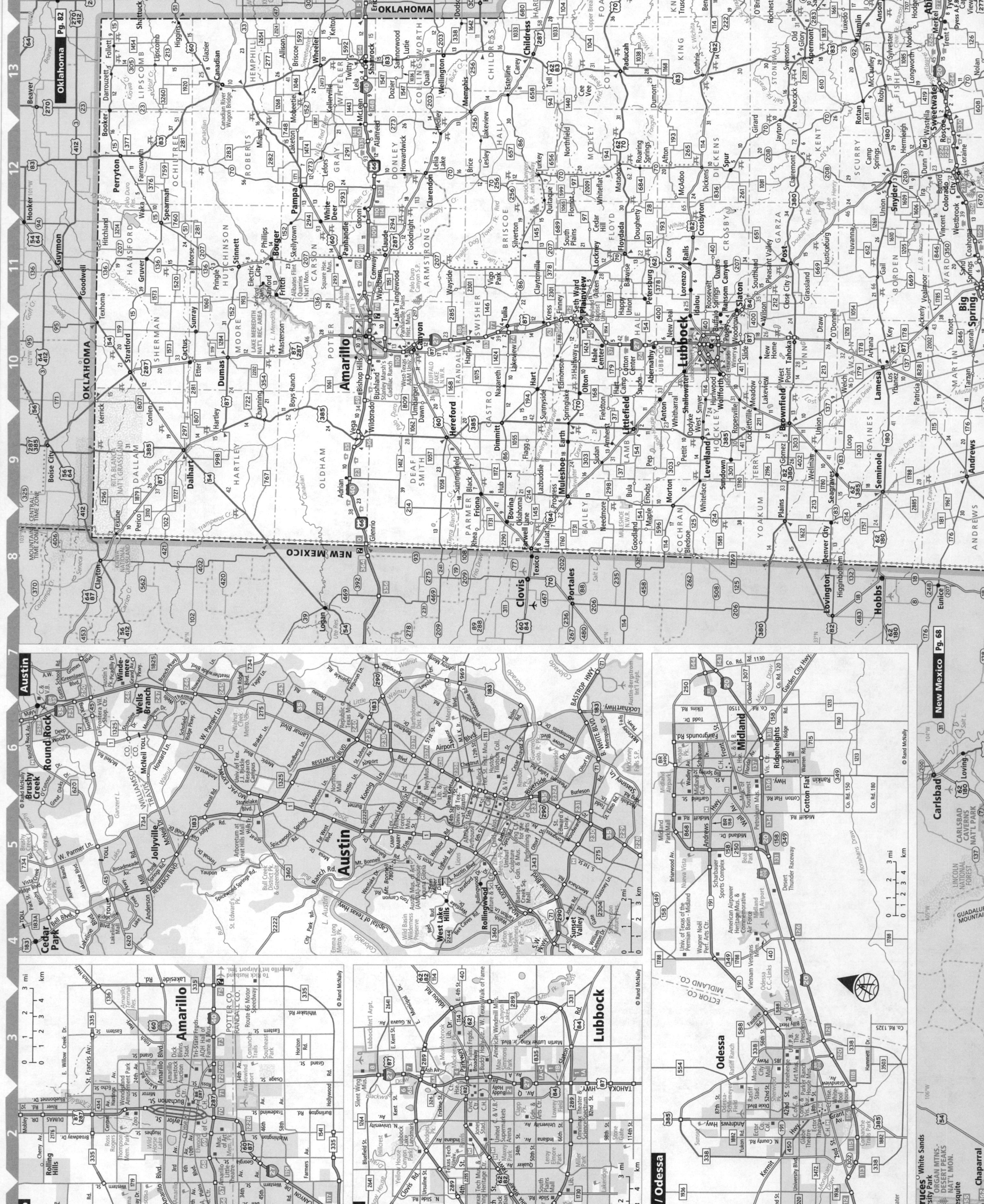

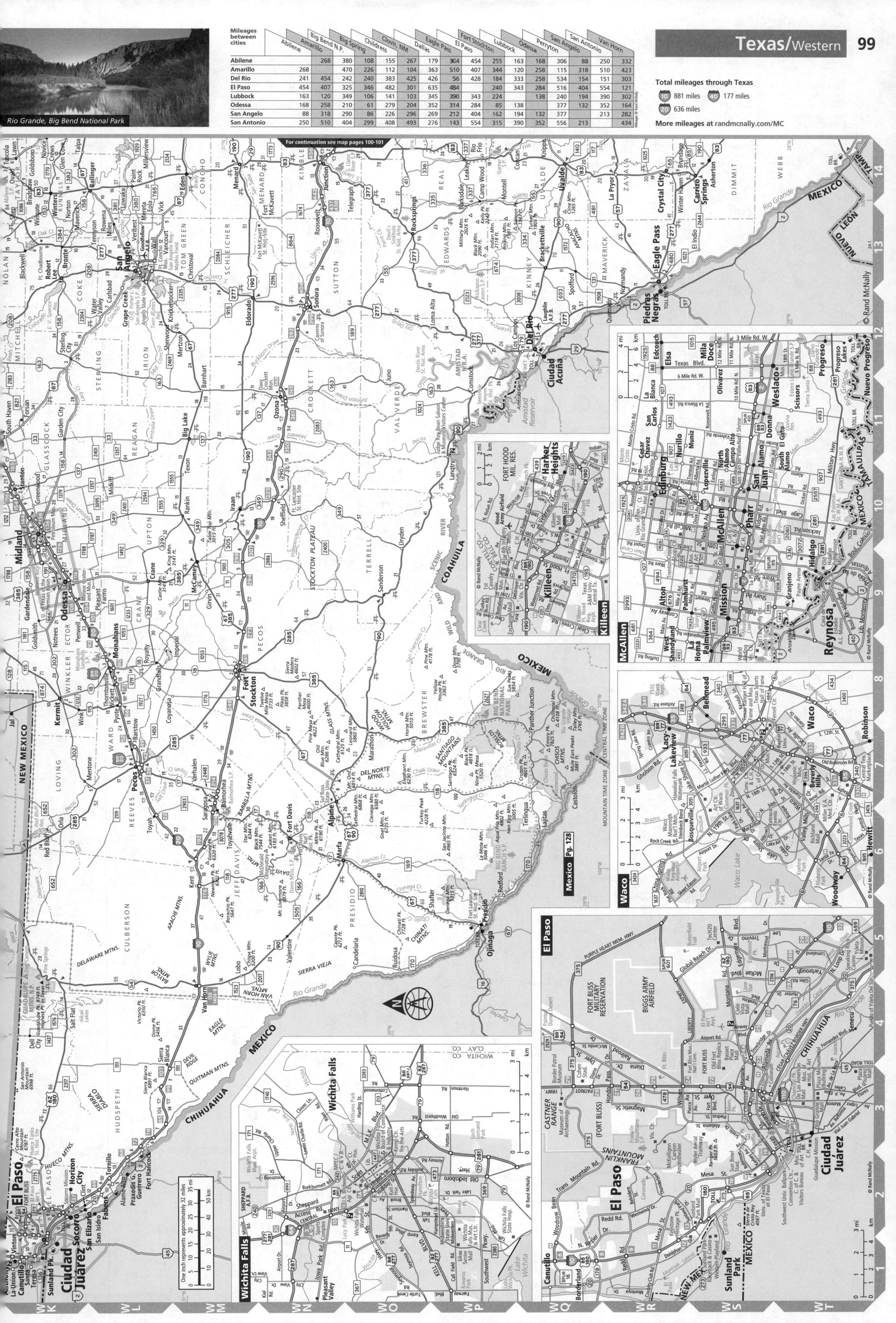

Mileages between cities	Abilene	Amarillo	Big Bend N.P.	Big Spring	Childress	Clovis, NM	Dallas	Eagle Pass	El Paso	Fort Stockton	Lubbock	Odessa	Perryton	San Angelo	San Antonio	Van Horn
Abilene		268	380	108	155	267	179	304	454	255	163	168	306	88	250	332
Amarillo	268		470	226	112	104	363	510	407	344	120	258	115	318	510	423
Del Rio	241	454	242	240	383	425	426	56	428	184	333	258	534	154	151	303
El Paso	454	407	325	346	482	301	635	484		240	343	284	516	404	554	121
Lubbock	163	120	349	106	141	103	345	390	343	224		138	240	194	390	302
Odessa	168	258	210	61	279	204	352	314	284	85	138		377	132	352	164
San Angelo	88	318	290	86	226	296	269	212	404	162	194	132	377		213	282
San Antonio	250	510	404	299	408	493	276	143	554	315	390	352	556	213		434

Total mileages through Texas

10 881 miles 40 177 miles
20 636 miles

More mileages at randmcnally.com/MC

Texas/Eastern

Nickname: The Lone Star State
Capital: Austin, EK-5
Land area: 261,194 sq. mi. (rank: 2nd)
Population: 29,145,505 (rank: 2nd)
Largest city: Houston, 2,304,580, EL-10

Index of places Pg. 135

Travel planning & on-the-road resources

Tourism Information

Texas Tourism: (512) 463-2000
www.traveltexas.com

Road Conditions & Construction

(800) 452-9292, (512) 463-8588
Dallas Metroplex: (877) 511-3255
drivetexas.org, 511dfw.org

Toll Road Information (cont. from p. 98) *(all use TxTag)*

Central Texas Regional Mobility Authority (Austin area):
(512) 996-9778; www.mobilityauthority.com
Ft. Bend County Toll Road Authority (Houston area):
(855) 999-2024, (832) 735-7385; www.fbctra.com
North East Regional Mobility Authority (TX 49):
(903) 630-7894; www.netrma.org
SH 130 Concession Co. (TX 130): (512) 371-4800; mysh130.com

Toll Bridge Info. (cont. from p. 98)

Cameron County–Int'l Bridge System:
(956) 574-8771; www.cameroncountytx.gov/international-bridge-system
Laredo–Int'l Bridge System: (956) 791-2200
www.cityoflaredo.com/bridge/
McAllen–Bridge Dept: (956) 681-1800
www.mcallen.net/departments/bridge

Determining distances

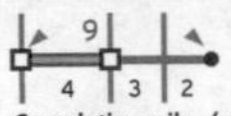

(segments of one mile or less not shown)
Cumulative miles (red): the distance between red arrows
Intermediate miles (black): the distance between intersections & places

Laredo

Corpus Christi

Tyler

Abilene

For continuation see map pages 98-99

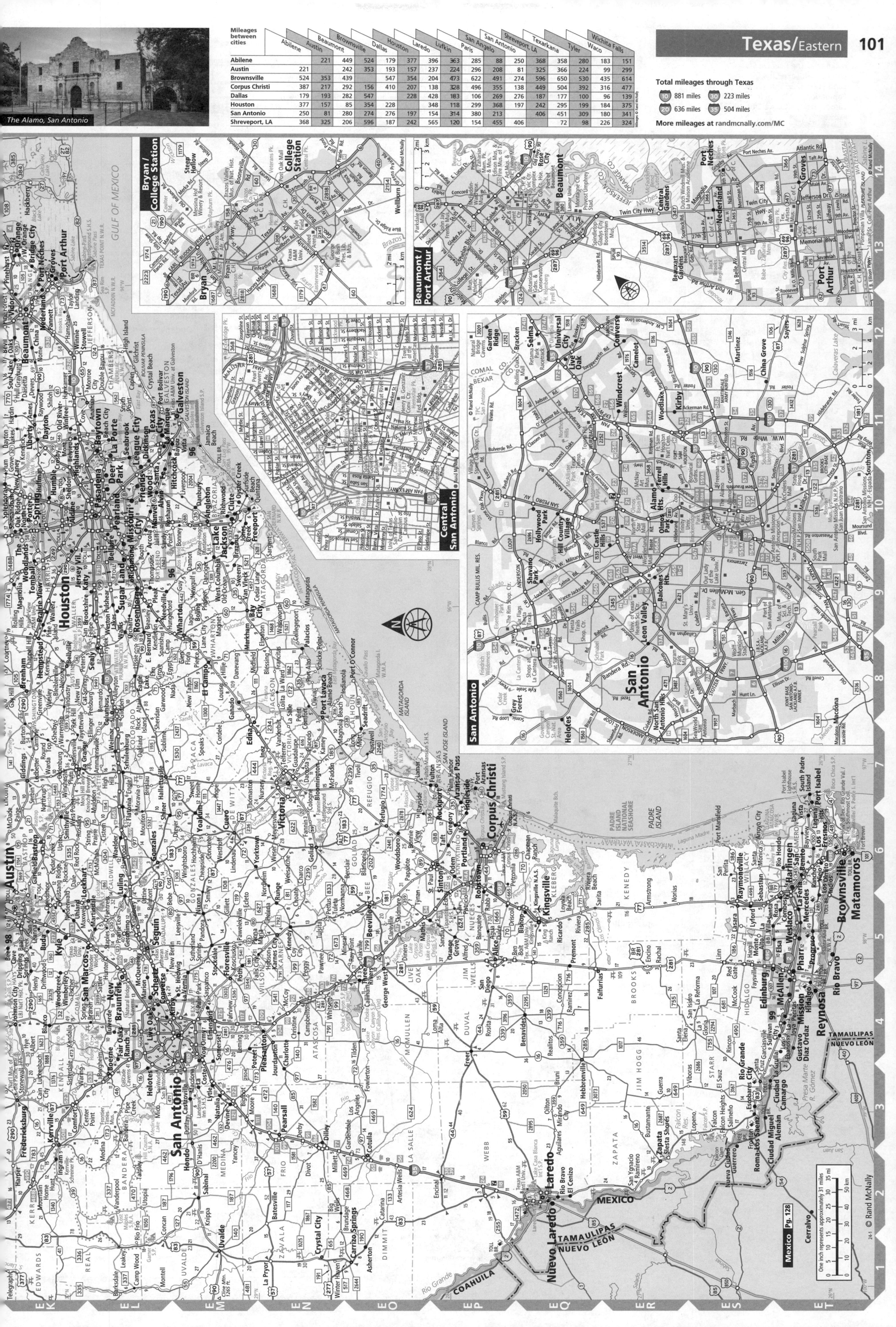

The Alamo, San Antonio

Mileages between cities	Abilene	Austin	Beaumont	Brownsville	Dallas	Houston	Laredo	Lufkin	Paris	San Angelo	San Antonio	Shreveport, LA	Texarkana	Tyler	Waco	Wichita Falls
Abilene		221	449	524	179	377	396	363	285	88	250	368	358	280	183	151
Austin	221		242	353	193	157	237	224	296	208	81	325	366	224	99	299
Brownsville	524	353	439		547	354	204	473	622	491	274	596	650	530	435	614
Corpus Christi	387	217	292	156	410	207	138	328	496	355	138	449	504	392	316	477
Dallas	179	193	282	547		228	428	183	106	269	276	187	177	100	96	139
Houston	377	157	85	354	228		348	118	299	368	197	242	295	199	184	375
San Antonio	250	81	280	274	276	197	154	314	380	213		406	451	309	180	341
Shreveport, LA	368	325	206	596	187	242	565	120	154	455	406		72	98	226	324

Total mileages through Texas

- 10: 881 miles
- 45: 223 miles
- 20: 636 miles
- 35: 504 miles

More mileages at randmcnally.com/MC

Nickname: The Beehive State
Capital: Salt Lake City, D-8
Land area: 82,355 sq. mi. (rank: 12th)
Population: 3,271,616 (rank: 30th)
Largest city: Salt Lake City, 199,723, D-8

Index of places Pg. 135

Travel planning & on-the-road resources

Tourism Information
Utah Office of Tourism: (800) 200-1160
(801) 538-1900; www.visitutah.com

Road Conditions & Construction
511, (866) 511-8824, (801) 965-4000
udottraffic.utah.gov
www.udot.utah.gov

Toll Road Information
Adams Avenue Parkway, Inc.
(Washington Terrace) *(ExpressCard)*:
(801) 475-1909; aaptoll.com
Express Lanes (Utah DOT) (I-15) *(Express Pass)*:
(801) 965-4000; site.utah.gov/connect/public/express-lanes

Determining distances along roads
Highway distances (segments of one mile or less not shown):
Cumulative miles (red): the distance between red arrows
Intermediate miles (black): the distance between intersections & places
Interchanges and exit numbers
For most states, the mileage between interchanges may be determined by subtracting one number from the other.

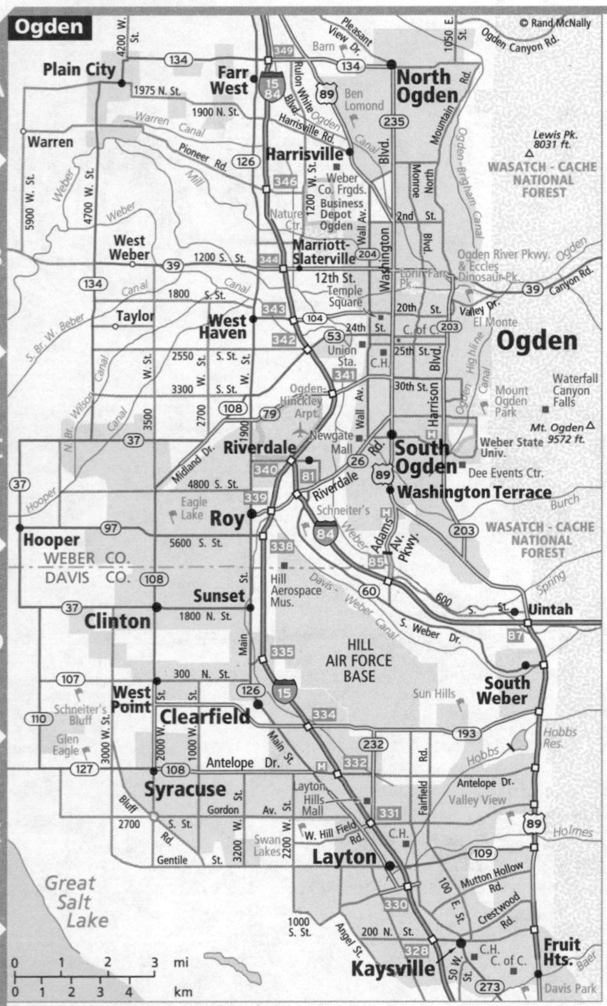

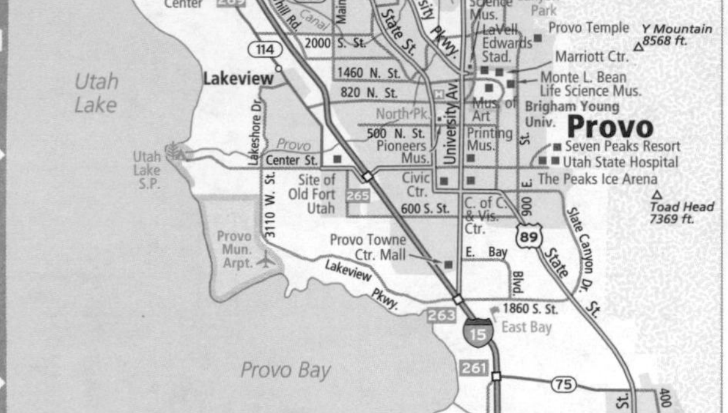

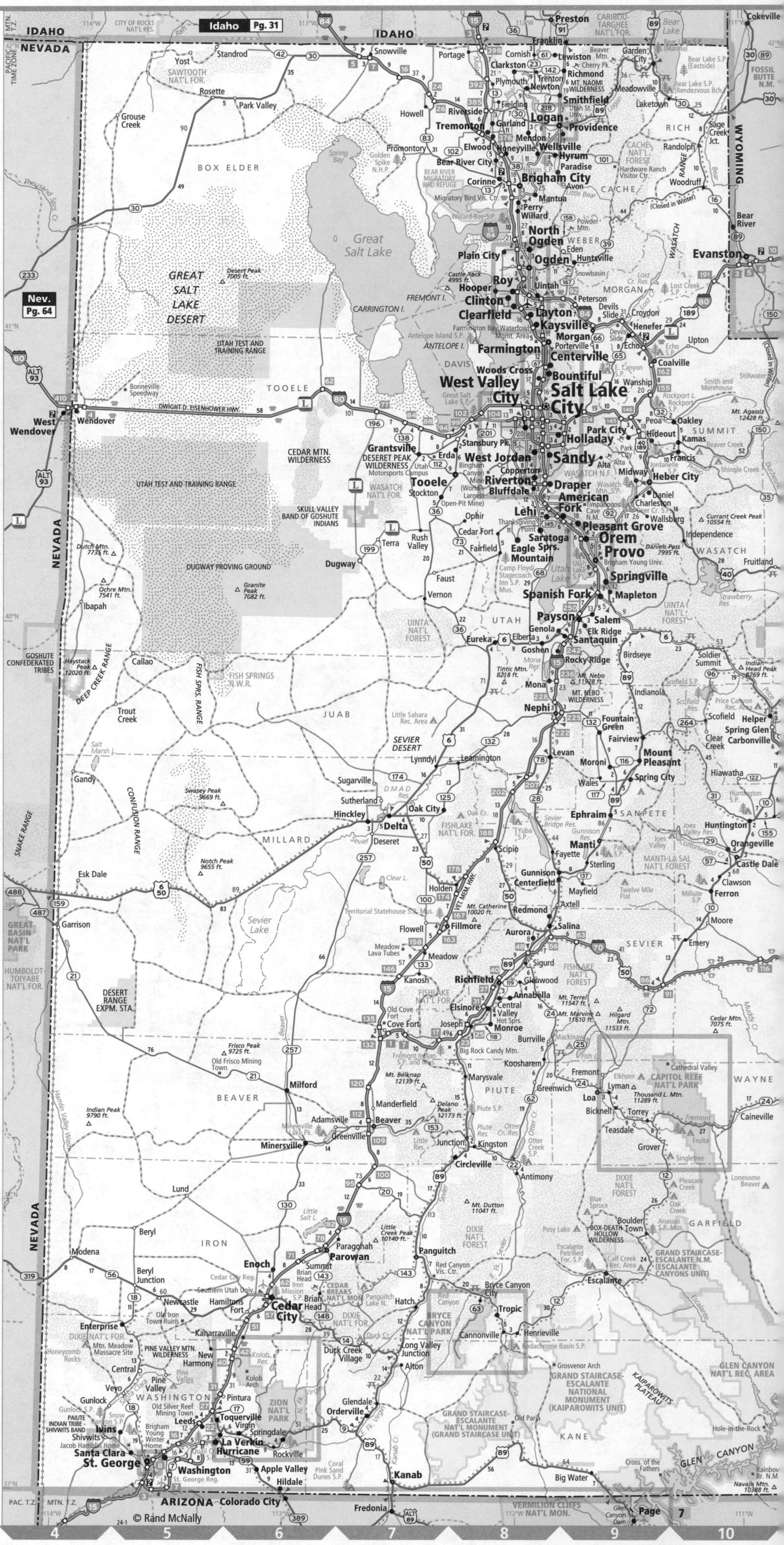

Ogden

Provo

Zion National Park

Idaho Pg. 31

Nev. Pg. 64

Delicate Arch

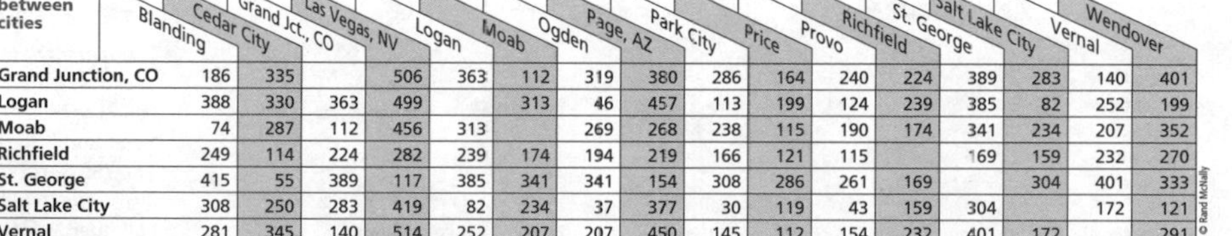

Mileages between cities	Blanding	Cedar City	Grand Jct., CO	Las Vegas, NV	Logan	Moab	Ogden	Page, AZ	Park City	Price	Provo	Richfield	St. George	Salt Lake City	Vernal	Wendover
Grand Junction, CO	186	335		506	363	112	319	380	286	164	240	224	389	283	140	401
Logan	388	330	363	499		313	46	457	113	199	124	239	385	82	252	199
Moab	74	287	112	456	313		269	268	238	115	190	174	341	234	207	352
Richfield	249	114	224	282	239	174	194	219	166	121	115		169	159	232	270
St. George	415	55	389	117	385	341	341	154	308	286	261	169		304	401	333
Salt Lake City	308	250	283	419	82	234	37	377	30	119	43	159	304		172	121
Vernal	281	345	140	514	252	207	207	450	145	112	154	232	401	172		291
Wendover	426	317	401	361	199	352	154	503	150	237	161	270	333	121	291	

Total mileages through Utah

- I-15: 401 miles
- I-70: 232 miles
- I-80: 196 miles
- I-84: 119 miles

More mileages at randmcnally.com/MC

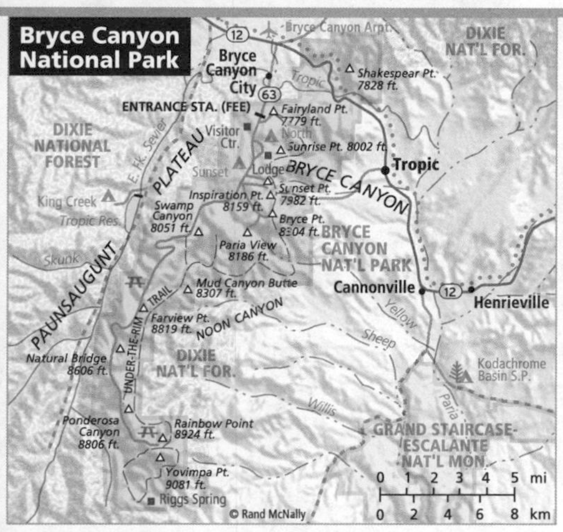

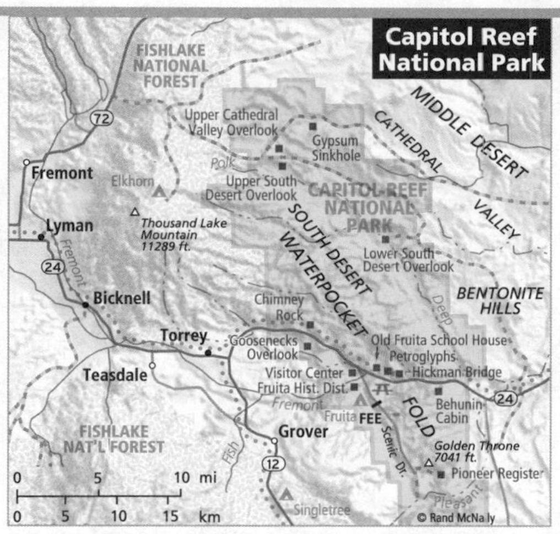

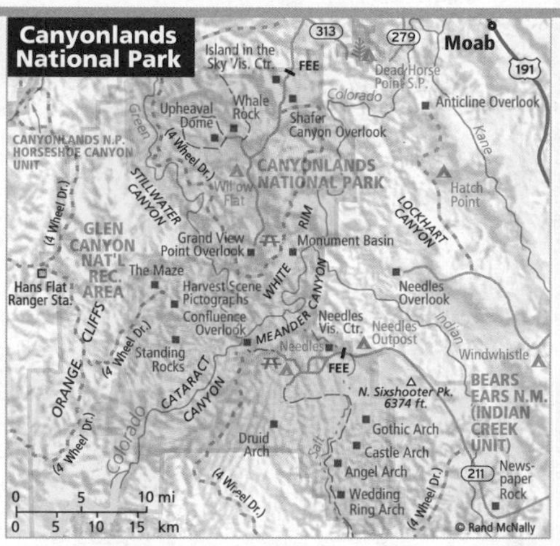

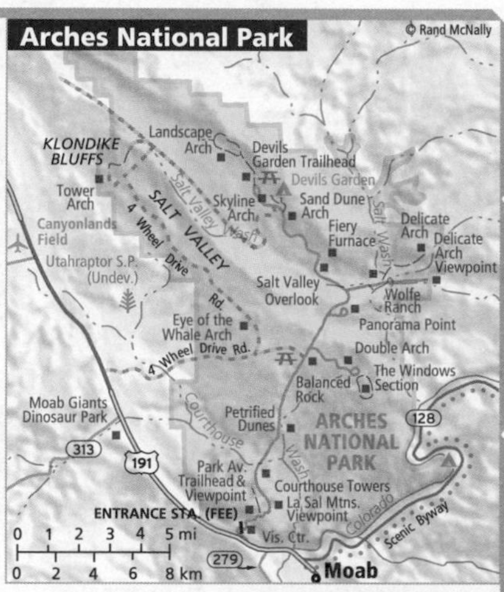

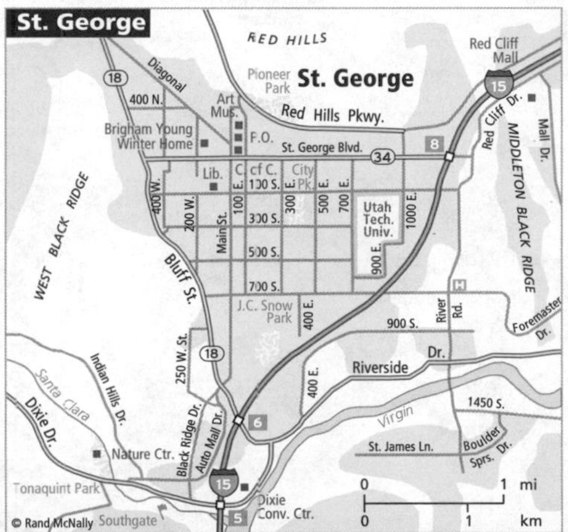

Bryce Canyon National Park

Capitol Reef National Park

Canyonlands National Park

Arches National Park

Central Salt Lake City

Salt Lake City & Vicinity

St. George

Logan

Wyoming Pg. 116

Colo. Pg. 20

Arizona Pg. 8

New Mexico Pg. 68

One inch represents approximately 27 miles

Vermont

Nickname: The Green Mountain State
Capital: Montpelier, E-5
Land area: 9,215 sq. mi. (rank: 43rd)
Population: 643,077 (rank: 49th)
Largest city: Burlington, 44,743, D-2

Index of places Pg. 135

Mileages between cities

	Albany, NY	Brattleboro	Burlington	Montpelier	Newport	Rutland	St. Johnsbury	White River Jct.
Albany, NY		78	151	156	230	90	187	128
Brattleboro	78		151	115	164	73	121	62
Burlington	151	151		39	76	67	75	90
Montpelier	156	115	39		78	66	37	54
Newport	230	164	76	78		147	43	102
Rutland	90	73	67	66	147		105	45
St. Johnsbury	187	121	75	37	43	105		60
White River Jct.	128	62	90	54	102	45	60	

Total mileages through Vermont

89: 130 miles
93: 11 miles
91: 177 miles
4: 64 miles

More mileages at randmcnally.com/MC

Travel planning & on-the-road resources

Tourism Information

Vermont Department of Tourism & Marketing:
(800) 837-6668; www.vermontvacation.com

Road Conditions & Construction

511, (802) 917-2458
newengland511.org, www.vtrans.vermont.gov

Toll Road Information

No tolls on state or federal highways

Determining Distances

(segments of one mile or less not shown)

Cumulative miles (red): the distance between red arrows
Intermediate miles (black): the distance between intersections & places

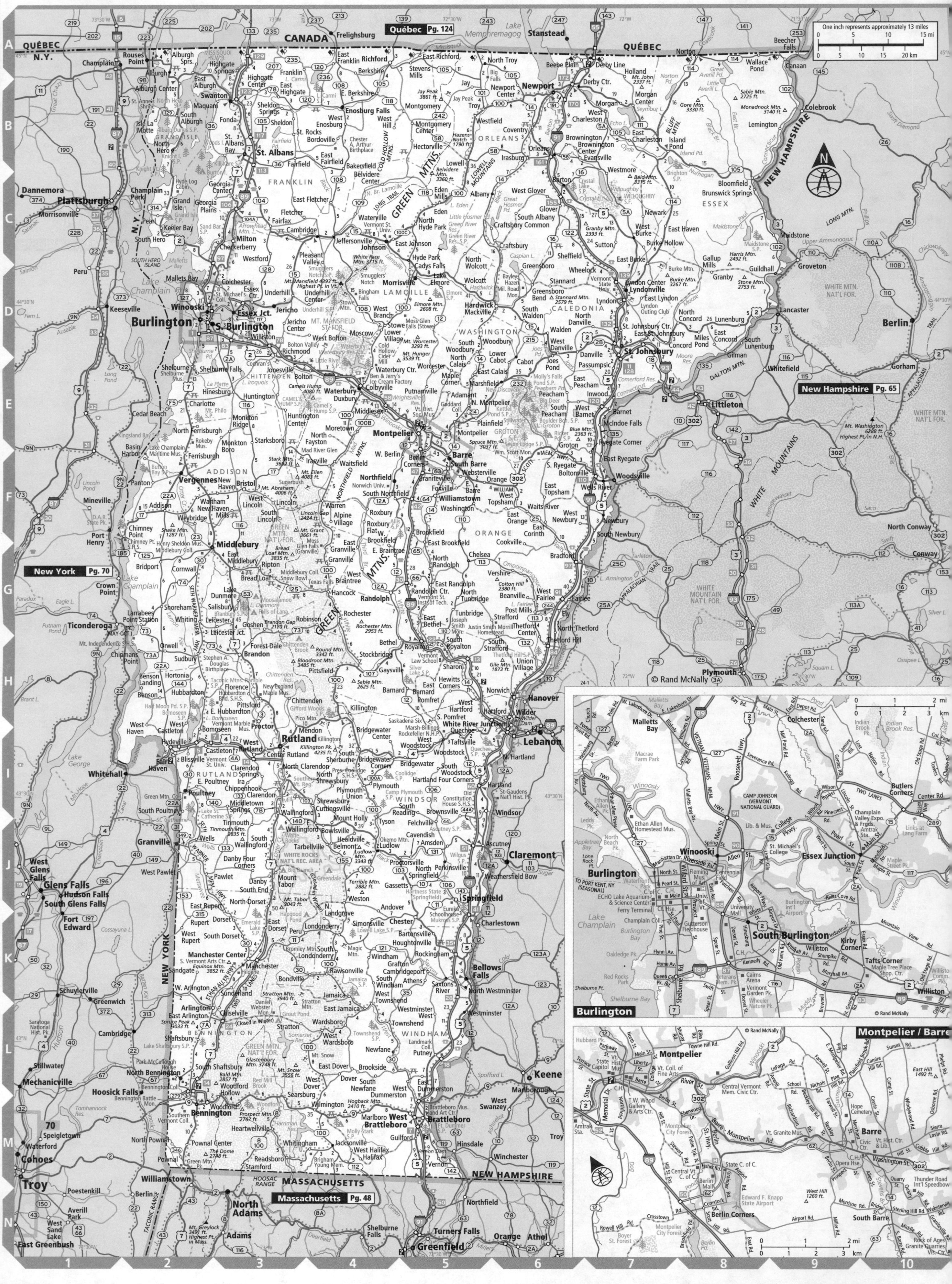

One inch represents approximately 13 miles

Québec Pg. 124

New Hampshire Pg. 65

New York Pg. 70

Massachusetts Pg. 48

Burlington

Montpelier / Barre

Historic Colonial Williamsburg

Sights to see

- Agecroft Hall and Gardens, Richmond C-7
- Children's Museum of Virginia, Portsmouth M-6
- Chrysler Museum of Art, Norfolk L-6
- Colonial Williamsburg, Williamsburg F-2
- Edgar Allan Poe Museum, Richmond C-8
- First Landing State Park, Virginia Beach L-9
- Hermitage Foundation Museum, Norfolk L-6
- Historic Jamestowne, Williamsburg G-1
- Nauticus, Norfolk L-6
- Ocean Breeze Waterpark, Virginia Beach M-10
- Old Cape Henry Lighthouse, Virginia Beach K-9
- Three Lakes Nature Center & Aquarium, Richmond . . B-8

Virginia

Nickname: Old Dominion
Capital: Richmond, J-14
Land area: 39,472 sq. mi. (rank: 37th)
Population: 8,631,393 (rank: 12th)
Largest city: Virginia Beach, 459,470, L-18

Index of places Pg. 135

Travel planning & on-the-road resources

Tourism Information
Virginia Tourism Corporation: (800) 847-4882; www.virginia.org

Road Conditions & Construction
511, (866) 695-1182, (800) 578-4111
www.511virginia.org
www.virginiadot.org/travel

Toll Road Information *(E-ZPass)*
Virginia Dept. of Transportation: (888) 860-9361, (800) 367-7623; www.tollroadsinvirginia.com
Chesapeake Expwy. (VA 168): (757) 204-0010; www.chesapeakeexpressway.com
Dulles Greenway: (703) 707-8870; www.dullesgreenway.com
ExpressLanes (Transurban Operations) (Wash. D.C. area): (855) 495-9777; www.expresslanes.com
Globalvia (Pocahontas Pkwy., Richmond): (804) 822-3458; www.pocahontas895.com
Metro. Wash. Airports Authority (Dulles Toll Rd.): (877) 762-7824; www.dullestollroad.com
Richmond Metro. Trans. Auth. (toll rds. within Richmond): (804) 523-3300; www.rmtaonline.org

Toll Bridge/Tunnel Info. *(E-ZPass)*
Chesapeake Bay Bridge-Tunnel: (757) 331-2960; www.cbbt.com
Elizabeth River Tunnels (Hampton Rds): (757) 837-0840; www.driveert.com
South Norfolk Jordan Bridge: (855) 690-7652; snjb.net

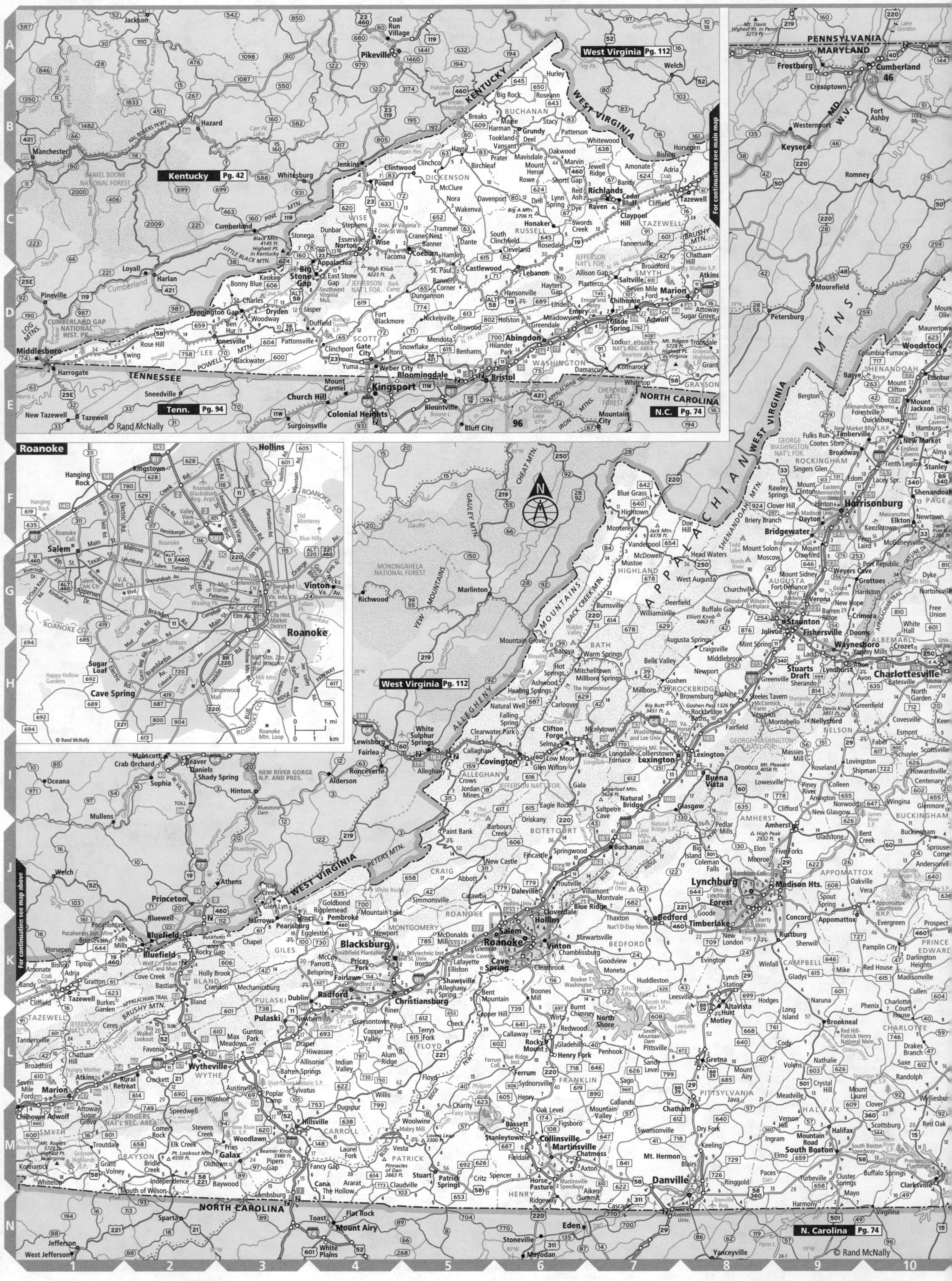

West Virginia Pg. 112
Kentucky Pg. 42
Tenn. Pg. 94
N.C. Pg. 74
For continuation see main map

Roanoke

West Virginia Pg. 112
For continuation see map above
N. Carolina Pg. 74

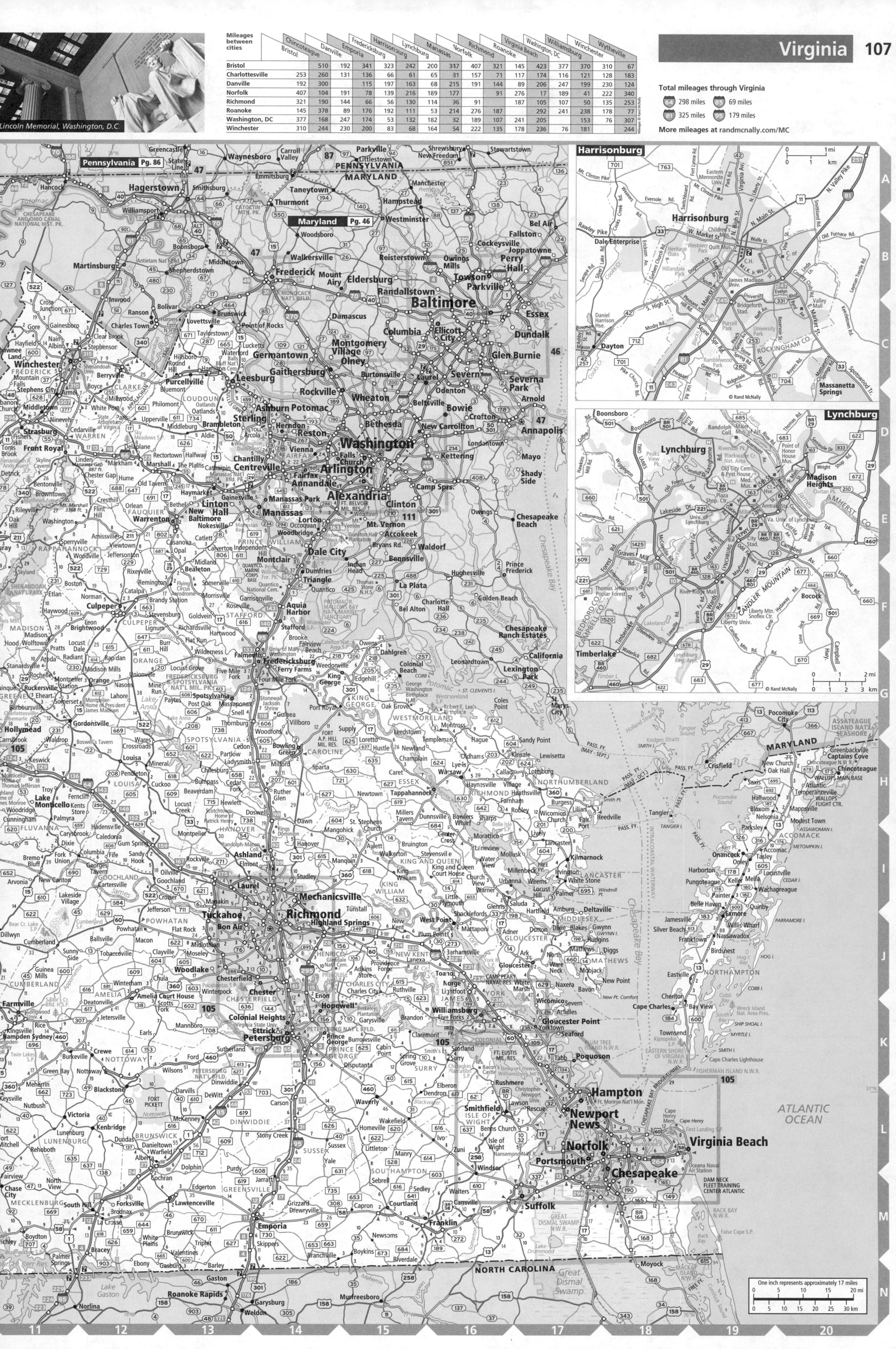

Lincoln Memorial, Washington, D.C.

Mileages between cities	Bristol	Chincoteague	Danville	Emporia	Fredericksburg	Harrisonburg	Lynchburg	Manassas	Norfolk	Richmond	Roanoke	Virginia Beach	Washington, DC	Williamsburg	Winchester	Wytheville
Bristol		510	192	341	323	242	200	347	407	321	145	423	377	370	310	67
Charlottesville	253	260	131	136	66	61	65	31	157	71	117	174	116	121	128	183
Danville	192	300		115	197	163	68	215	191	144	89	206	247	199	230	124
Norfolk	407	104	191	78	139	216	189	177		91	276	17	189	41	222	340
Richmond	321	190	144	66	56	130	114	96	91		187	105	107	50	135	253
Roanoke	145	378	89	176	192	111	53	214	276	187		292	241	238	178	77
Washington, DC	377	168	247	174	53	132	182	32	189	107	241	205		153	76	307
Winchester	310	244	230	200	83	68	164	54	222	135	178	236	76	181		244

Mileages © Rand McNally

Total mileages through Virginia

64 298 miles
85 69 miles
81 325 miles
95 179 miles

More mileages at randmcnally.com/MC

Washington

Nickname: The Evergreen State
Capital: Olympia, H-6
Land area: 66,438 sq. mi. (rank: 20th)
Population: 7,705,281 (rank: 13th)
Largest city: Seattle, 737,015, F-7

Index of places Pg. 135

Travel planning & on-the-road resources

Tourism Information
Washington Tourism Alliance: (800) 544-1800; stateofwatourism.com

Road Conditions & Construction
511, (800) 695-7623; wsdot.com/travel

Toll Bridge/Tunnel Information
Wash. St. Dept. of Trans. ***(Good to Go!)***: (360) 705-7000, (360) 705-7438; wsdot.wa.gov/travel/roads-bridges

Determining distances along roads

Highway distances (segments of one mile or less not shown):
Cumulative miles (red): the distance between red arrows
Intermediate miles (black): the distance between intersections & places

Interchanges and exit numbers
For most states, the mileage between interchanges may be determined by subtracting one number from the other.

One inch represents approximately 20 miles
0 5 10 15 20 mi
0 10 20 30 km

Olympia

Oregon Pg. 84

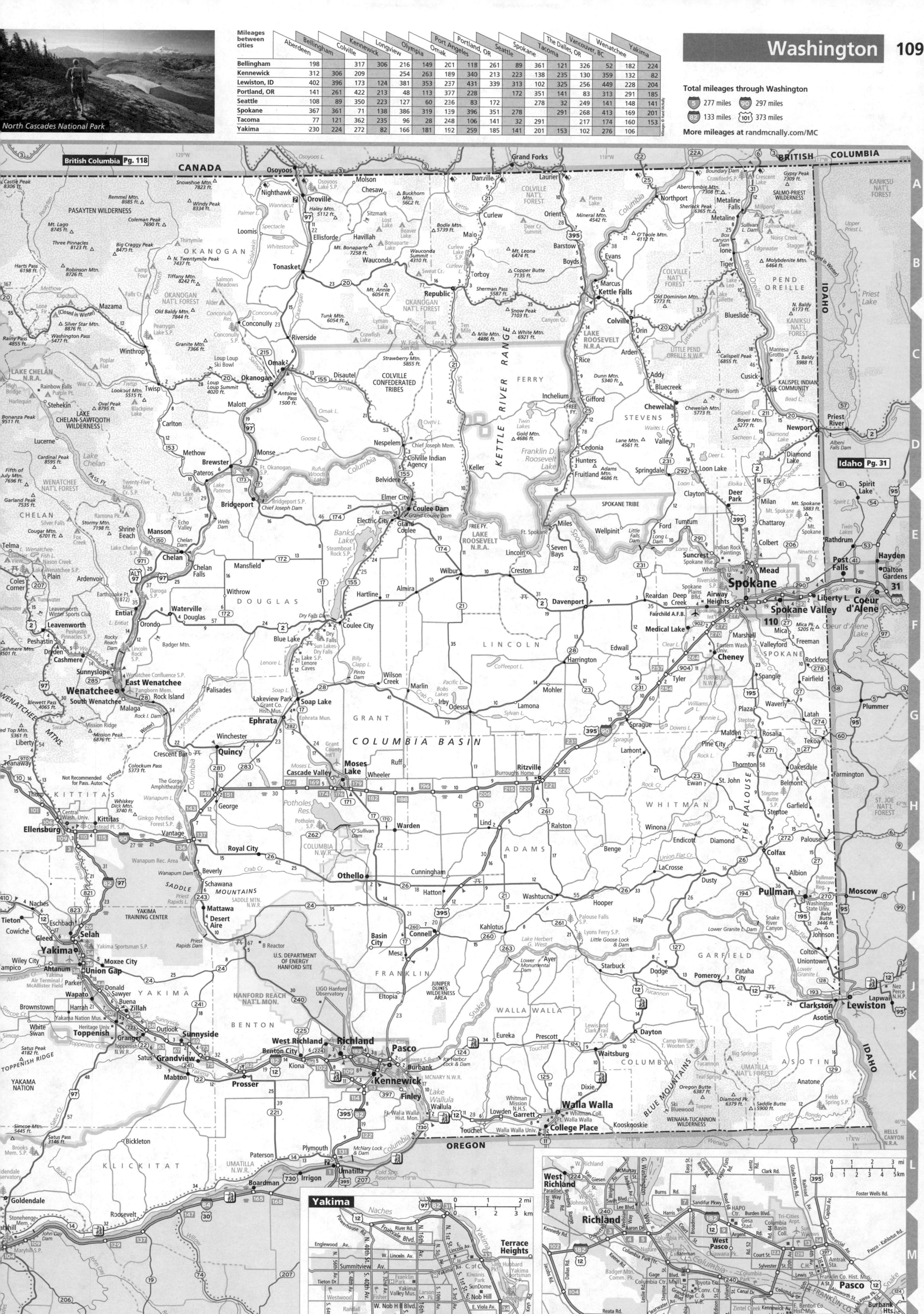

North Cascades National Park

Mileages between cities

	Aberdeen	Bellingham	Colville	Kennewick	Longview	Olympia	Omak	Port Angeles	Portland, OR	Seattle	Spokane	Tacoma	The Dalles, OR	Vancouver, BC	Wenatchee	Yakima
Bellingham	198		317	306	216	149	201	118	261	89	361	121	326	52	182	224
Kennewick	312	306	209		254	263	189	340	213	223	138	235	130	359	132	82
Lewiston, ID	402	396	173	124	381	353	237	431	339	313	102	325	256	449	228	204
Portland, OR	141	261	422	213	48	113	377	228		172	351	141	83	313	291	185
Seattle	108	89	350	223	127	60	236	83	172		278	32	249	141	148	141
Spokane	367	361	71	138	386	319	139	396	351	278		291	268	413	169	201
Tacoma	77	121	362	235	96	28	248	106	141	32	291		217	174	160	153
Yakima	230	224	272	82	166	181	192	259	185	141	201	153	102	276	106	

Total mileages through Washington

5: 277 miles
90: 297 miles
82: 133 miles
101: 373 miles

More mileages at randmcnally.com/MC

Sights to see

- Frye Art Museum, Seattle J-3
- Klondike Gold Rush National Historical Park, Seattle .. K-2
- Museum of Glass, Tacoma L-6
- Museum of Pop Culture, Seattle H-1
- National Nordic Museum, Seattle C-7
- Pacific Science Center, Seattle H-1
- Pike Place Market, Seattle J-2
- Point Defiance Zoo & Aquarium, Tacoma K-5
- Seattle Aquarium, Seattle J-1
- Space Needle, Seattle H-1
- Washington State History Museum, Tacoma L-6
- Woodland Park Zoo, Seattle C-7

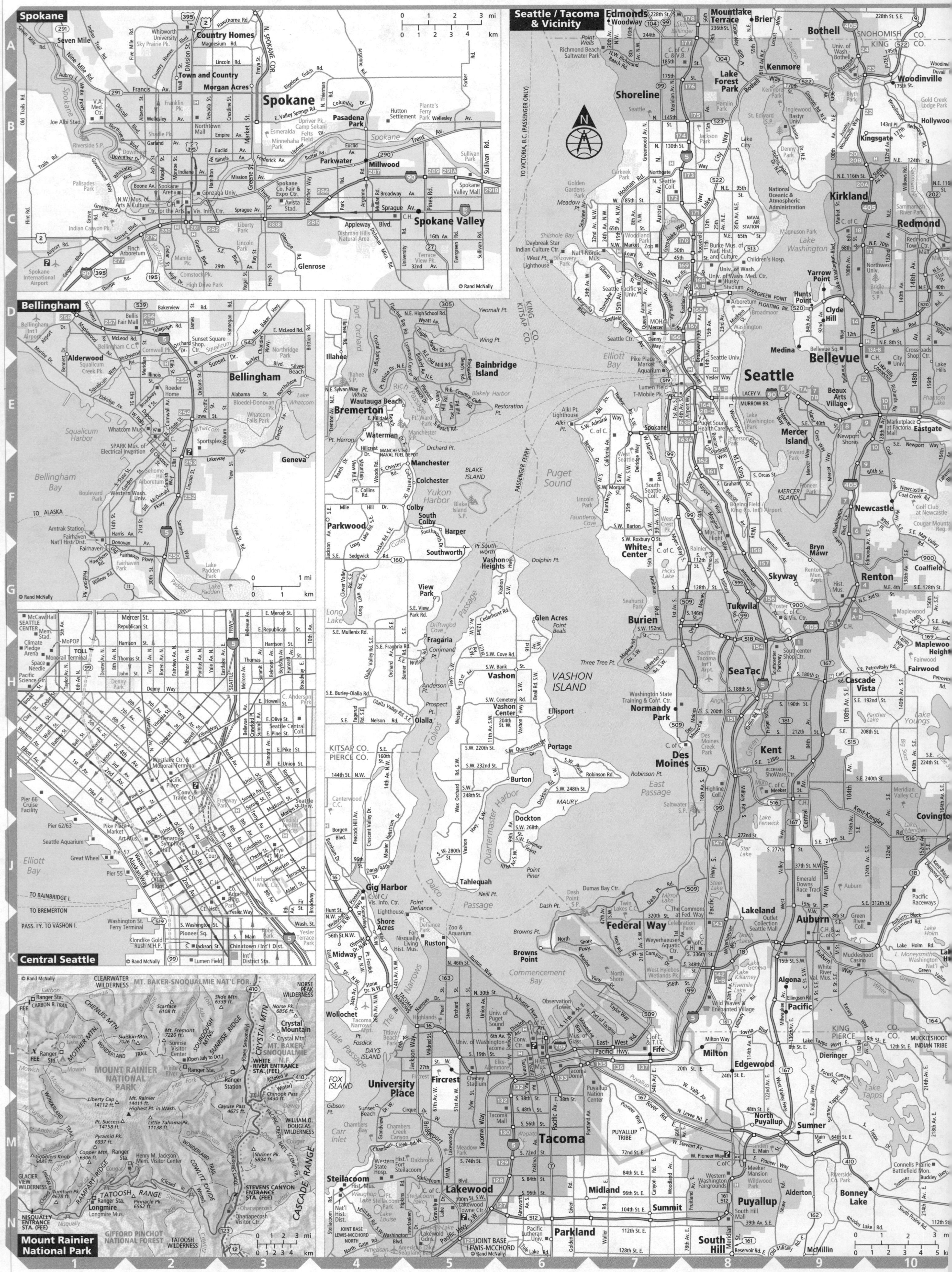

Mount Rainier National Park

Spokane

Bellingham

Central Seattle

Mount Rainier National Park

Seattle / Tacoma & Vicinity

© Rand McNally

Land area: 61 sq. mi. | Population: 689,545

On-the-road resources

ourism Information
estination DC: (202) 789-7000; washington.org

oad Conditions & Construction
11, (202) 673-6813; www.dctrafficinfo.org, ddot.dc.gov

oll Road Information
o toll roads in District of Columbia
ee Maryland or Virginia pages for toll road information

Sights to see

- Arlington National Cemetery, Arlington, VA N-1
- Frederick Douglass National Historic Site.. G-7
- John F. Kennedy Center for the Performing Arts........ L-3
- Martin Luther King Jr. Memorial.... M-4
- National African American Museum.. L-6
- National Arboretum........ F-7
- National Mall........ M-7
- National Zoological Park F-6
- The Pentagon, Arlington, VA G-6
- The Supreme Court of the United States........ M-9
- United States Botanic Garden...... M-8
- The White House K-5
- Wolf Trap National Park for the Performing Arts, Vienna, VA........ E-2

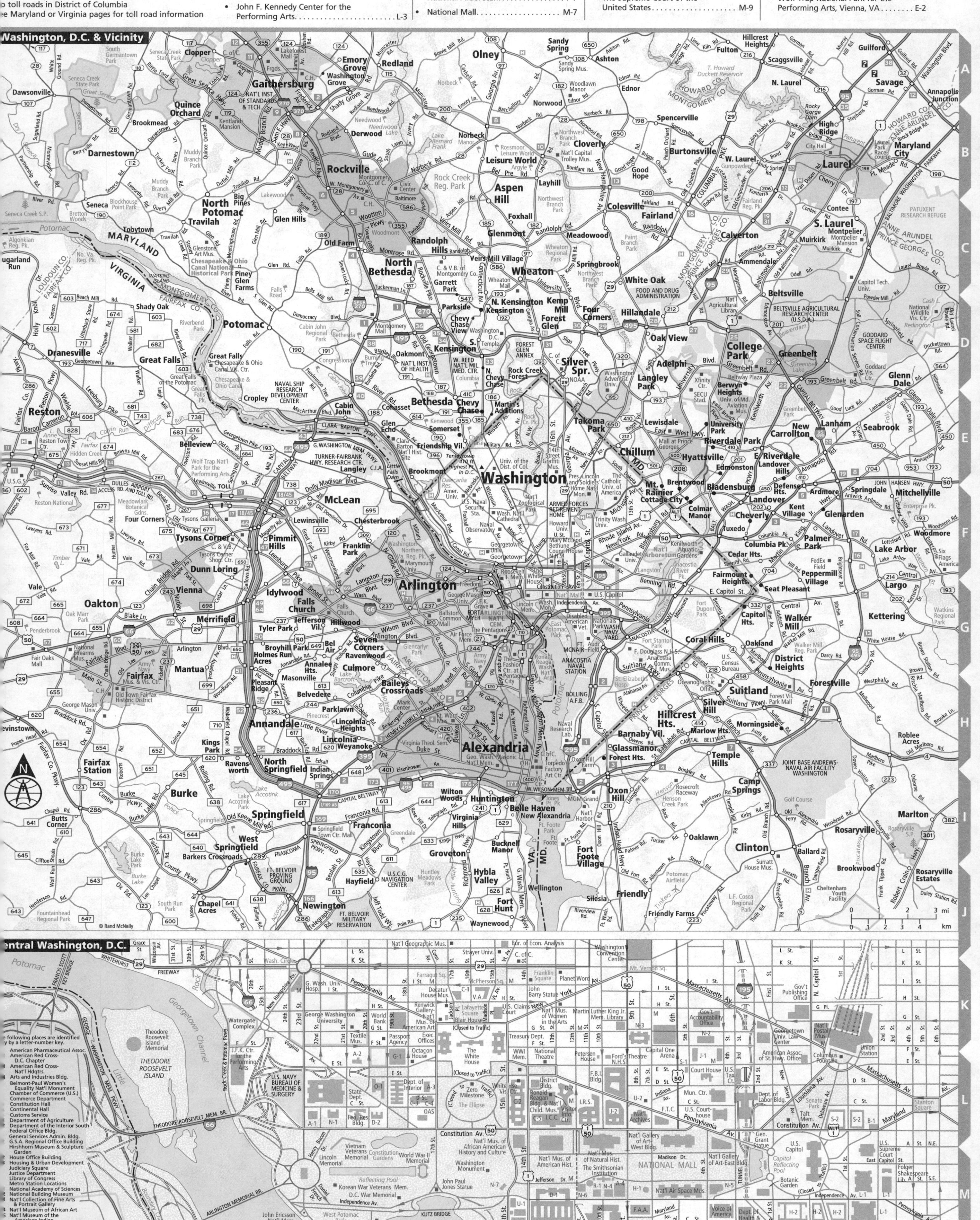

West Virginia

Nickname: The Mountain State
Capital: Charleston, J-3
Land area: 24,035 sq. mi. (rank: 41st)
Population: 1,793,716 (rank: 39th)
Largest city: Charleston, 48,864, J-3

Index of places Pg. 135

Mileages between cities	Bluefield	Charleston	Clarksburg	Cumberland, MD	Martinsburg	Petersburg	Wheeling	Wh. Sulphur Sprs.
Beckley	50	59	136	239	267	184	236	59
Charleston	106		123	225	304	193	177	120
Cumberland, MD	288	225	109		79	66	155	194
Huntington	158	51	174	276	355	244	228	172
Morgantown	218	154	38	73	151	103	78	187
Parkersburg	183	76	72	181	259	172	104	198
Wheeling	283	177	114	155	225	179		262
White Sulphur Sprs.	79	120	155	194	208	125	262	

Total mileages through West Virginia

64: 189 miles
77: 187 miles
70: 14 miles
79: 161 miles

More mileages at randmcnally.com/MC

Travel planning & on-the-road resources

Tourism Information
West Virginia Tourism Office:
(304) 558-2200; www.wvtourism.com

Road Conditions & Construction
511, (855) 699-8511; www.wv511.org, transportation.wv.gov

Toll Road Information *(E-ZPass)*
W.V. Parkways Authority: (304) 926-1900; transportation.wv.gov/turnpike

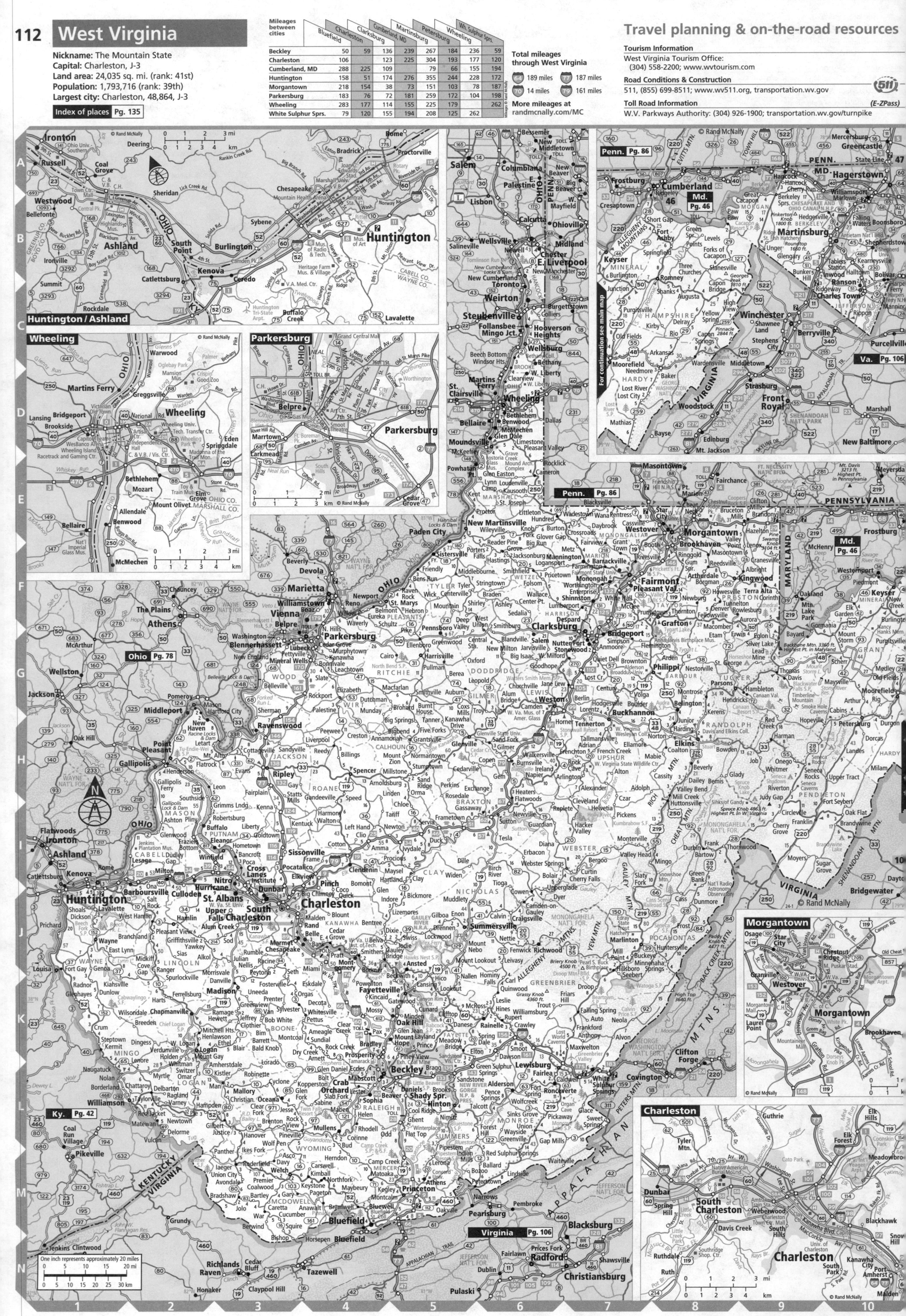

HarborPark promenade, Kenosha

Sights to see

- Bast Bell Museum, Germantown A-6
- Betty Brinn Children's Museum, Milwaukee L-9
- Golden Rondelle Theatre, Racine J-3
- Harley Davidson Museum, Milwaukee M-8
- Henry Maier Festival Park, Milwaukee M-9
- Kenosha History Center, Kenosha L-3
- Miller Brewery, Milwaukee E-9
- Milwaukee Art Museum, Milwaukee L-9
- Milwaukee Public Museum, Milwaukee L-8
- Mitchell Park Horticultural Conservatory, Milwaukee F-9
- Paul Bunyan Logging Camp, Eau Claire D-1
- Petit National Ice Center, Milwaukee F-8

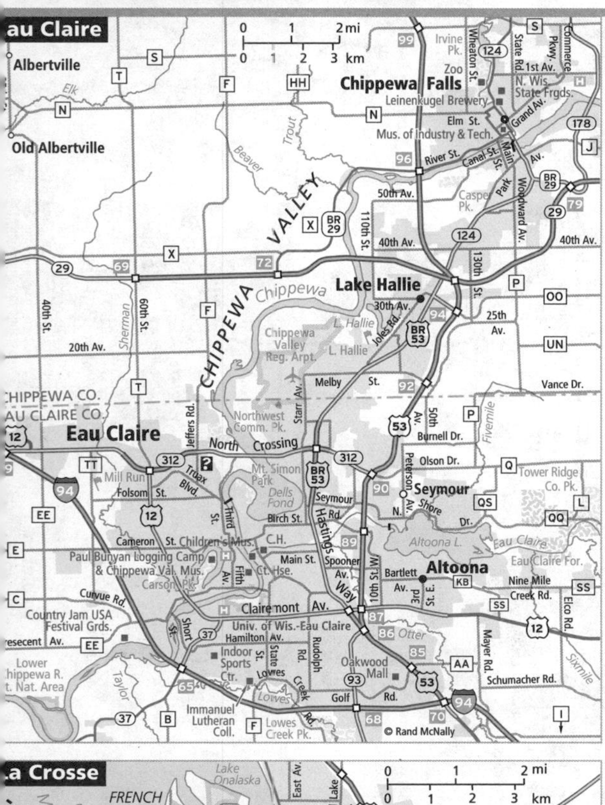

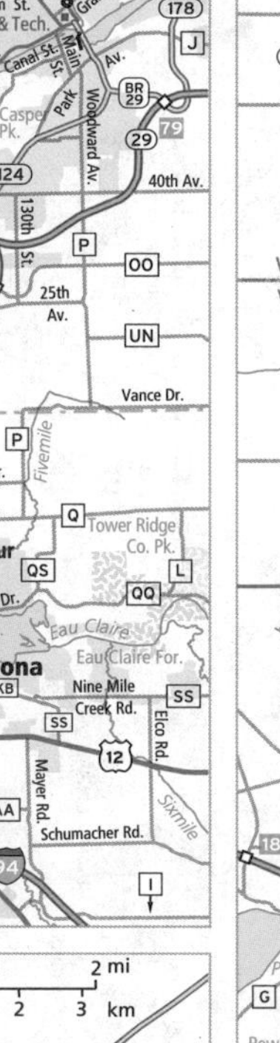

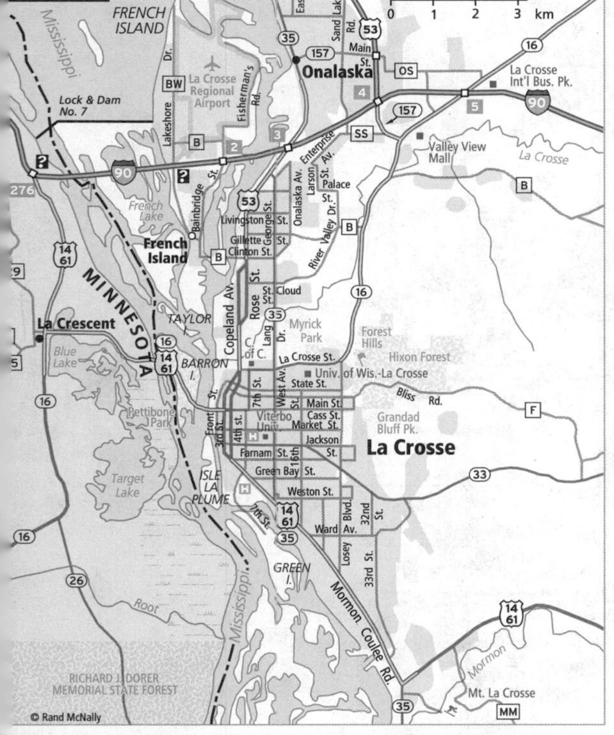

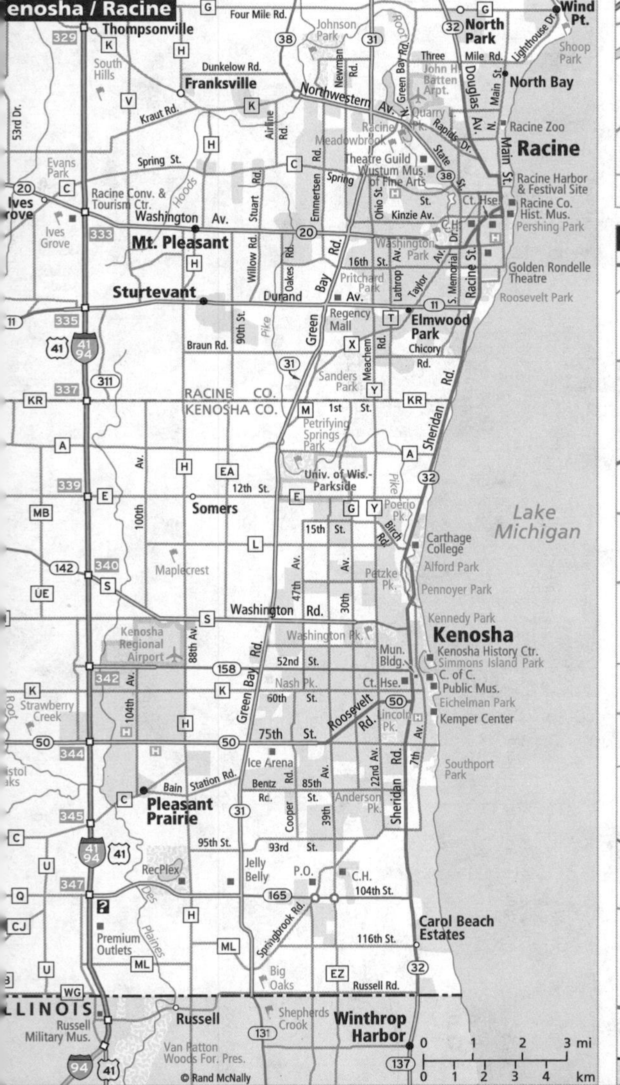

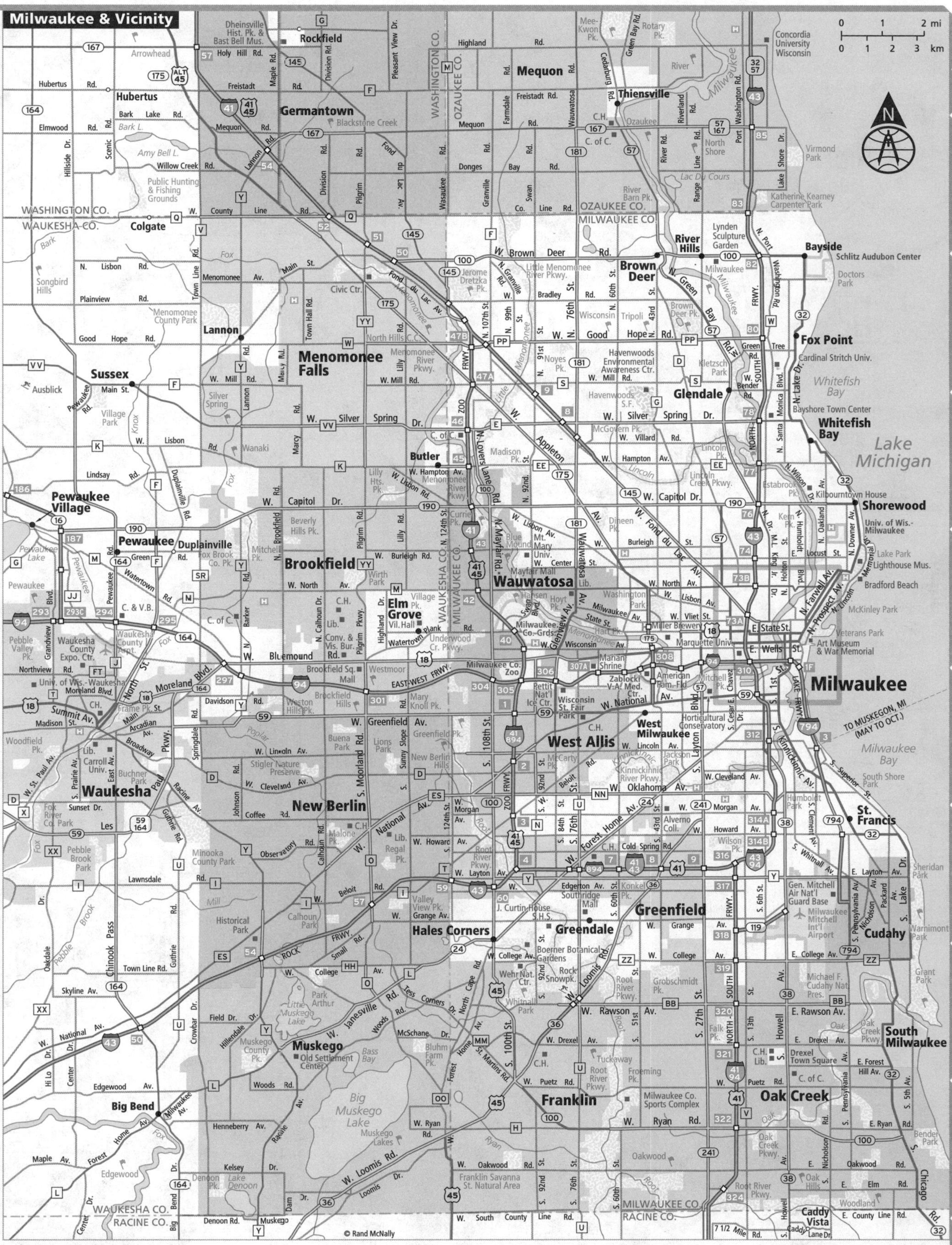

Milwaukee & Vicinity

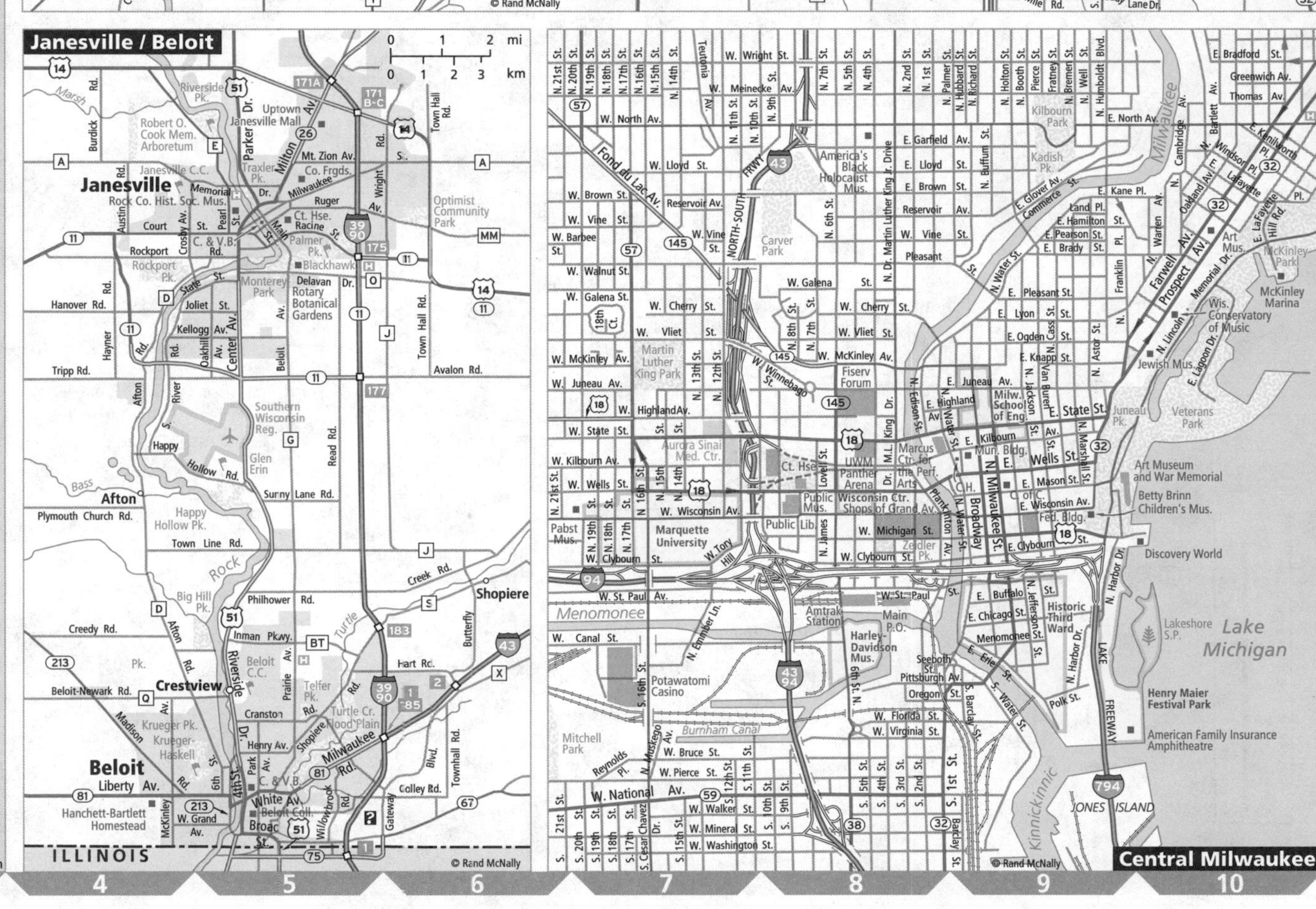

Wisconsin

Nickname: The Badger State
Capital: Madison, N-9
Land area: 54,153 sq. mi. (rank: 25th)
Population: 5,893,718 (rank: 20th)
Largest city: Milwaukee, 577,222, N-13

Index of places Pg. 136

Travel planning & on-the-road resources

Tourism Information
Wisconsin Department of Tourism: (800) 432-8747, (608) 266-2161; www.travelwisconsin.com

Road Conditions & Construction
511, (866) 511-9472; 511wi.gov

Toll Road Information
No tolls on state or federal highways

Determining distances along roads

Highway distances (segments of one mile or less not shown):
Cumulative miles (red): the distance between red arrows
Intermediate miles (black): the distance between intersections & places

Interchanges and exit numbers
For most states, the mileage between interchanges may be determined by subtracting one number from the other.

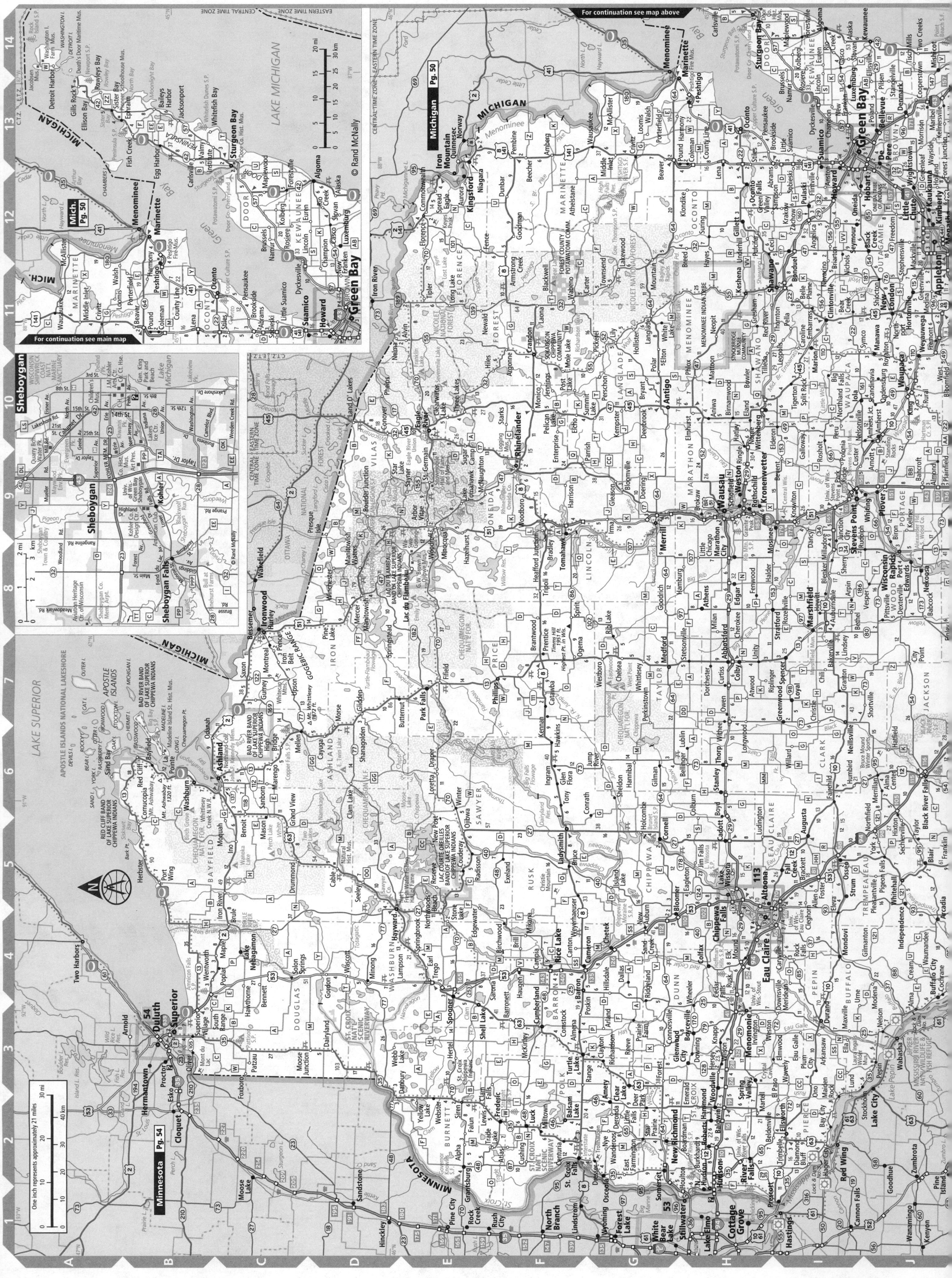

For continuation see map above

For continuation see main map

LAKE SUPERIOR

LAKE MICHIGAN

One inch represents approximately 21 miles

Lighthouse, Sand Island

Mileages between cities	Beloit	Chicago, IL	Dubuque, IA	Eau Claire	Green Bay	Hayward	La Crosse	Madison	Milwaukee	Oshkosh	Rhinelander	Sheboygan	Sturgeon Bay	Superior	Wausau	Wisconsin Dells
Chicago, IL	96		177	315	206	420	281	146	90	175	338	145	245	462	281	195
Eau Claire	223	315	192		192	106	86	177	243	181	155	228	237	149	98	124
Green Bay	184	206	233	192		283	203	138	116	52	136	64	44	326	96	132
La Crosse	188	281	119	86	203	190		143	209	153	214	195	248	233	170	90
Madison	54	146	93	177	138	282	143		78	87	200	117	185	325	143	57
Milwaukee	74	90	171	243	116	348	209	78		86	244	54	155	390	187	123
Superior	370	462	339	149	326	70	233	325	390	332	182	388	370		232	271
Wausau	189	281	239	98	96	189	170	143	187	103	59	158	141	232		112

Total mileages through Wisconsin

39 182 miles
90 189 miles
43 192 miles
94 341 miles

More mileages at randmcnally.com/MC

Wyoming

Nickname: The Equality State
Capital: Cheyenne, M-9
Land area: 97,063 sq. mi. (rank: 9th)
Population: 576,851 (rank: 50th)
Largest city: Cheyenne, 65,132, M-9

Index of places Pg. 136

Mileages between cities

	Casper	Cheyenne	Cody	Evanston	Gillette	Laramie	Sheridan	Spearfish, SD
Casper		178	213	325	126	147	148	219
Cheyenne	178		392	357	244	49	324	290
Cody	213	392		376	250	363	148	344
Jackson	283	432	177	190	411	383	325	504
Riverton	119	272	138	238	248	222	213	341
Rock Springs	225	257	278	100	351	207	373	444
Sheridan	148	324	148	473	103	294		196
Spearfish, SD	219	290	344	544	93	296	196	

Total mileages through Wyoming

25: 301 miles
90: 209 miles
80: 403 miles
20: 505 miles

More mileages at randmcnally.com/MC

Travel planning & on-the-road resources

Tourism Information

Wyoming Office of Tourism: (800) 225-5996
(307) 777-7777; travelwyoming.com

Road Conditions & Construction

511, (888) 996-7623; www.wyoroad.info

Toll Road Information

No tolls on state or federal highways

Determining Distances

(segments of one mile or less not shown)

Cumulative miles (red): the distance between red arrows

Intermediate miles (black): the distance between intersections & places

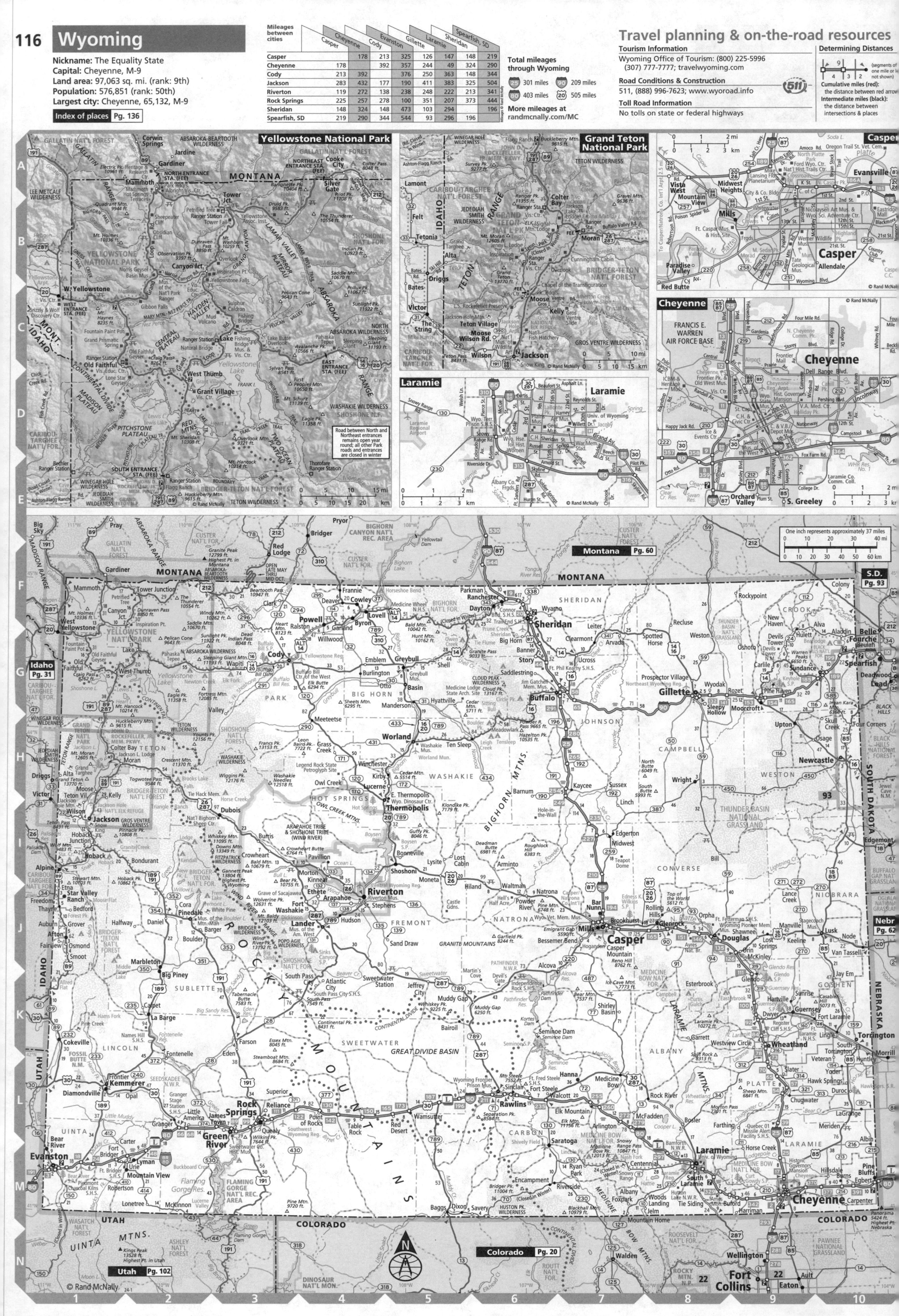

Capital: Ottawa, I-10
Land area: 3,393,322 sq. mi.
Population: 35,151,728
Largest city: Toronto, 2,794,356, I-10

Index of places Pg. 136

Selected National Park locations

- Banff National Park G-3
- Cape Breton Highlands Nat'l Park. . G-13
- Fundy National Park. H-12
- Glacier National Park G-3
- Gros Morne National Park F-13
- Jasper National Park. F-3
- Kejimkujik National Park H-12
- Kluane National Park & Reserve C-2
- Kootenay National Park G-3
- Mount Revelstoke National Park. . . G-3
- Parc national de la Mauricie H-11
- Prince Albert National Park F-5
- Prince Edward Island Nat'l Park. . . . H-12
- Pukaskwa National Park H-8
- Riding Mountain National Park. H-6
- St. Lawrence Islands National Park . . I-10

Glossary of French terms

- Aéroport . . . . Airport
- Arrondissement. . . . . District
- Baie . . . . Bay
- Barrage . . . . Dam
- Basilique. . . . . Basilica
- Bibliothèque . . . . Library
- Bois. . . . . Woods
- Cap. . . . . Cape
- Centre de recherches . . . . Research centre (or center)
- Centre des congrès . . . . Convention centre (or center)
- Chemin. . . . . Road
- Chenal . . . . Channel
- Chutes . . . . Falls
- Débarquement . . . . Landing
- Détroit . . . . Strait
- Fleuve. . . . . . Major river (that flows to the sea)
- Hippodrome . . . . Race track
- Hôtel de Ville. . . . . City or town hall
- Hôtel du Parlement. . . . . . . Parliament building
- Île . . . . Island
- Jardin . . . . Garden
- Jardin botanique. . . . . Botanical garden
- Jardin zoologique . . Zoological garden (or Zoo)
- Lac . . . . Lake
- Lieu historique . . . . Historic site
- Lieu historique national . . National historic site
- Lieu natal. . . . . Birthplace
- Mont . . . . Mountain
- Musée. . . . . Museum
- Oratoire. . . . . Oratory
- Parc. . . . . Park
- Parc marin . . . . Marine park
- Parc national . . . . National park (or provincial park in Québec)
- Pont . . . . Bridge
- Promenade . . . . Boulevard
- Réserve faunique . . . . Wildlife reserve
- Réserve indienne. . . . . Indian reserve (or Reservation)
- Rivière . . . . River
- Rue. . . . . Street
- Stade . . . . Stadium
- Tribunal . . . . Court house
- Université. . . . . University

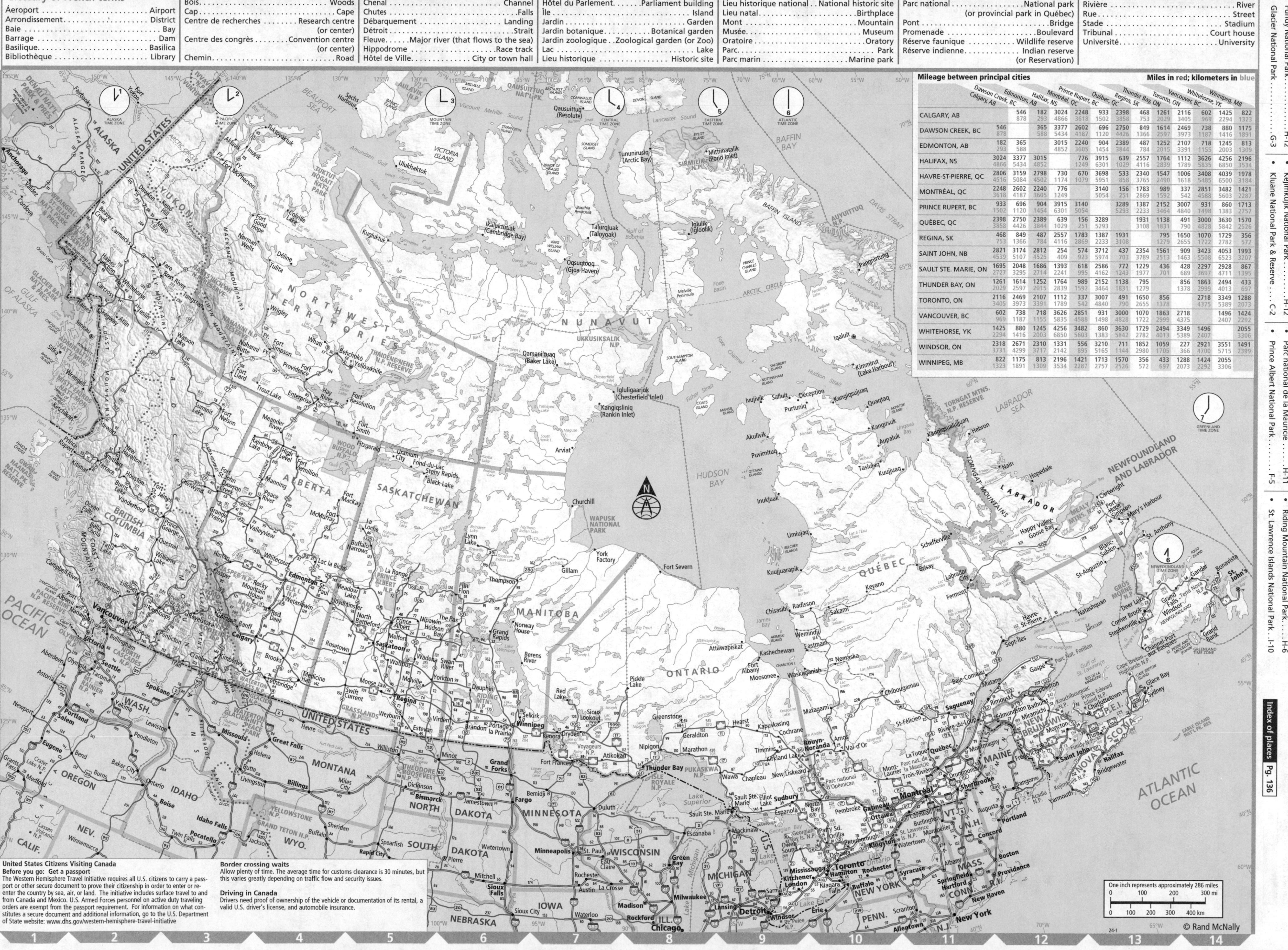

Mileage between principal cities

Miles in red; kilometers in blue

	Calgary, AB	Dawson Creek, BC	Edmonton, AB	Halifax, NS	Montréal, QC	Prince Rupert, BC	Québec, QC	Regina, SK	Thunder Bay, ON	Toronto, ON	Vancouver, BC	Whitehorse, YK	Winnipeg, MB
CALGARY, AB		546 / 878	182 / 293	3024 / 4866	2248 / 3618	933 / 1502	2398 / 3858	468 / 753	1261 / 2029	2116 / 3405	602 / 969	1425 / 2294	822 / 1323
DAWSON CREEK, BC	546 / 878		365 / 588	3377 / 5434	2602 / 4187	696 / 1120	2750 / 4426	849 / 1366	1614 / 2597	2469 / 3973	738 / 1187	880 / 1416	1175 / 1891
EDMONTON, AB	182 / 293	365 / 588		3015 / 4852	2240 / 3605	904 / 1454	2389 / 3844	487 / 784	1252 / 2015	2107 / 3391	718 / 1155	1245 / 2003	813 / 1309
HALIFAX, NS	3024 / 4866	3377 / 5434	3015 / 4852		776 / 1249	3915 / 6301	639 / 1029	2557 / 4116	1764 / 2839	1112 / 1789	3626 / 5835	4256 / 6850	2196 / 3534
HAVRE-ST-PIERRE, QC	2806 / 4516	3159 / 5084	2798 / 4502	730 / 1174	670 / 1079	3698 / 5951	533 / 858	2340 / 3765	1547 / 2490	1006 / 1618	3408 / 5485	4039 / 6500	1978 / 3184
MONTRÉAL, QC	2248 / 3618	2602 / 4187	2240 / 3605	776 / 1249		3140 / 5054	156 / 251	1783 / 2869	989 / 1592	337 / 542	2851 / 4588	3482 / 5603	1421 / 2287
PRINCE RUPERT, BC	933 / 1502	696 / 1120	904 / 1454	3915 / 6301	3140 / 5054		3289 / 5293	1387 / 2233	2152 / 3464	3007 / 4840	931 / 1498	860 / 1383	1713 / 2757
QUÉBEC, QC	2398 / 3858	2750 / 4426	2389 / 3844	639 / 1029	156 / 251	3289 / 5293		1931 / 3108	1138 / 1831	491 / 790	3000 / 4828	3630 / 5842	1570 / 2526
REGINA, SK	468 / 753	849 / 1366	487 / 784	2557 / 4116	1783 / 2869	1387 / 2233	1931 / 3108		795 / 1279	1650 / 2655	1070 / 1722	1729 / 2782	356 / 572
SAINT JOHN, NB	2821 / 4539	3174 / 5107	2812 / 4525	254 / 409	574 / 923	3712 / 5974	437 / 703	2354 / 3789	1561 / 2513	909 / 1463	3423 / 5508	4053 / 6523	1993 / 3207
SAULT STE. MARIE, ON	1695 / 2727	2048 / 3295	1686 / 2714	1393 / 2241	618 / 995	2586 / 4162	772 / 1243	1229 / 1977	436 / 701	428 / 689	2297 / 3697	2928 / 4711	867 / 1395
THUNDER BAY, ON	1261 / 2029	1614 / 2597	1252 / 2015	1764 / 2839	989 / 1592	2152 / 3464	1138 / 1831	795 / 1279		856 / 1378	1863 / 2999	2494 / 4013	433 / 697
TORONTO, ON	2116 / 3405	2469 / 3973	2107 / 3391	1112 / 1789	337 / 542	3007 / 4840	491 / 790	1650 / 2655	856 / 1378		2718 / 4375	3349 / 5389	1288 / 2073
VANCOUVER, BC	602 / 969	738 / 1187	718 / 1155	3626 / 5835	2851 / 4588	931 / 1498	3000 / 4828	1070 / 1722	1863 / 2999	2718 / 4375		1496 / 2407	1424 / 2292
WHITEHORSE, YK	1425 / 2294	880 / 1416	1245 / 2003	4256 / 6850	3482 / 5603	860 / 1383	3630 / 5842	1729 / 2782	2494 / 4013	3349 / 5389	1496 / 2407		2055 / 3306
WINDSOR, ON	2318 / 3731	2671 / 4299	2310 / 3717	1331 / 2142	556 / 895	3210 / 5165	711 / 1144	1852 / 2980	1059 / 1705	227 / 366	2921 / 4700	3551 / 5715	1491 / 2399
WINNIPEG, MB	822 / 1323	1175 / 1891	813 / 1309	2196 / 3534	1421 / 2287	1713 / 2757	1570 / 2526	356 / 572	433 / 697	1288 / 2073	1424 / 2292	2055 / 3306	

One inch represents approximately 286 miles

United States Citizens Visiting Canada

Before you go: Get a passport
The Western Hemisphere Travel Initiative requires all U.S. citizens to carry a passport or other secure document to prove their citizenship in order to enter or re-enter the country by sea, air, or land. The initiative includes surface travel to and from Canada and Mexico. U.S. Armed Forces personnel on active duty traveling orders are exempt from the passport requirement. For information on what constitutes a secure document and additional information, go to the U.S. Department of State website: www.dhs.gov/western-hemisphere-travel-initiative

Border crossing waits
Allow plenty of time. The average time for customs clearance is 30 minutes, but this varies greatly depending on traffic flow and security issues.

Driving in Canada
Drivers need proof of ownership of the vehicle or documentation of its rental, a valid U.S. driver's license, and automobile insurance.

British Columbia
Capital: Victoria, M-7
Land area: 355,477 sq. mi. (rank: 4th)
Population: 4,648,055 (rank: 3rd)
Largest city: Vancouver, 662,248, L-7

Index of places Pg. 136

Mileages between cities	Banff, AB	Dawson Creek	Jasper, AB	Port Hardy	Prince Rupert	Vancouver	Victoria	Williams Lake
Banff, AB		503	178	808*	855	524	578*	483
Cranbrook	173	638	312	806*	989	521	575*	553
Dawson Creek	503		326	1022*	696	738	791*	399
Kamloops	307	576	275	502*	769	217	271*	177
Kelowna	299	671	376	526*	865	242	295*	272
Prince George	408	250	231	772*	447	488	542*	149
Prince Rupert	855	696	677	307*		931	985*	592
Vancouver	524	738	492	285*	931		72*	339

*Via ferry

Mileages © Rand McNally

Total mileages through British Columbia
1: 538 miles
16: 658 miles

More mileages at randmcnally.com/MC

Travel planning & on-the-road resources

Tourism Information
Destination British Columbia: www.hellobc.com

Road Conditions & Construction
(800) 550-4997; www.drivebc.ca
www2.gov.bc.ca/gov/content/transportation

Toll Road Information
No tolls on provincial or federal highways

Determining Distances
(segments of one mile or less not shown)
Cumulative miles (red), km (blue): the distance between red arrows
Intermediate miles (black): the distance between intersections & places

ravel planning & on-the-road resources

urism Information
avel Alberta: (403) 648-1000; www.travelalberta.com/us

ad Conditions & Construction
1, (855) 391-9743; 511.alberta.ca

ll Road Information
tolls on provincial or federal highways

Determining Distances
(segments of one mile or less not shown)
Cumulative miles (red), km (blue): the distance between red arrows
Intermediate miles (black): the distance between intersections & places

Total mileages through Alberta
1: 332 miles
16: 397 miles
More mileages at randmcnally.com/MC

Mileages between cities	Calgary	Dawson Creek, BC	Edmonton	Fort McMurray	Grande Prairie	Jasper	Lethbridge	Red Deer
Banff	78	503	260	544	423	178	217	167
Calgary		546	182	465	463	256	139	89
Grande Prairie	463	82	283	467		246	602	376
Edmonton	182	365		281	283	226	321	95
Lethbridge	139	684	321	604	602	395		227
Medicine Hat	178	724	360	563	641	434	102	267
Peace River	480	146	299	421	123	354	618	392
Vermilion	299	481	120	321	399	342	338	211

Alberta
Capital: Edmonton, E-16
Land area: 245,042 sq. mi. (rank: 6th)
Population: 4,067,175 (rank: 4th)
Largest city: Calgary, 1,306,784, I-16

Index of places Pg. 136

Saskatchewan
Capital: Regina, K-8
Land area: 222,803 sq. mi. (rank: 7th)
Population: 1,098,352 (rank: 6th)
Largest city: Saskatoon, 266,141, G-6

Index of places Pg. 136

Mileages between cities	La Loche	La Ronge	Medicine Hat, AB	N. Battleford	Prince Albert	Regina	Saskatoon	Yorkton
Estevan	668	498	391	371	350	125	285	159
Lloydminster	331	347	289	85	214	331	171	375
Meadow Lake	217	232	370	98	162	343	183	388
Prince Albert	318	148	365	129		225	88	233
Regina	543	373	289	246	225		160	116
Saskatoon	379	236	277	86	88	160		205
Swift Current	505	403	139	190	255	151	167	266
Yorkton	551	382	405	290	233	116	205	

Mileages © Rand McNally

Total mileages through Saskatchewan
1: 413 miles
16: 437 miles

More mileages at randmcnally.com/MC

Travel planning & on-the-road resources

Tourism Information
Tourism Saskatchewan: (877) 237-2273, (306) 787-9600
www.tourismsaskatchewan.com

Road Conditions & Construction
(888) 335-7623, Saskatoon area: (306) 933-8333, Regina area: (306) 787-7623
www.saskatchewan.ca/residents/transportation/highways/highway-hotline

Toll Road Info
No tolls on provincial or federal highways

ravel planning & on-the-road resources

urism Information

avel Manitoba: (800) 665-0040, (204) 927-7800
www.travelmanitoba.com

ad Conditions & Construction

1; (877) 627-6237, (204) 945-3704
vw.manitoba511.ca/en

ll Road Information

tolls on provincial or federal highways

Determining Distances

(segments of one mile or less not shown)

Cumulative miles (red), km (blue): the distance between red arrows

Intermediate miles (black): the distance between intersections & places

Total mileages through Manitoba

1: 306 miles

16: 166 miles

More mileages at randmcnally.com/MC

Mileages between cities	Ashern	Brandon	Dauphin	Flin Flon	Grand Rapids	Pine Falls	Thompson	Winnipeg
Brandon	200		104	444	355	217	558	134
Dauphin	127	104		342	282	267	485	198
Flin Flon	368	444	342		255	546	244	483
Morden	184	129	216	552	338	167	542	87
Portage la Prairie	119	80	144	485	274	136	477	53
Swan River	233	208	106	236	211	372	385	303
Virden	245	47	148	419	399	262	568	178
Winnipeg	114	134	198	483	269	81	472	

Manitoba

Capital: Winnipeg, L-17
Land area: 208,614 sq. mi. (rank: 8th)
Population: 1,278,365 (rank: 5th)
Largest city: Winnipeg, 749,607, L-17

Index of places Pg. 136

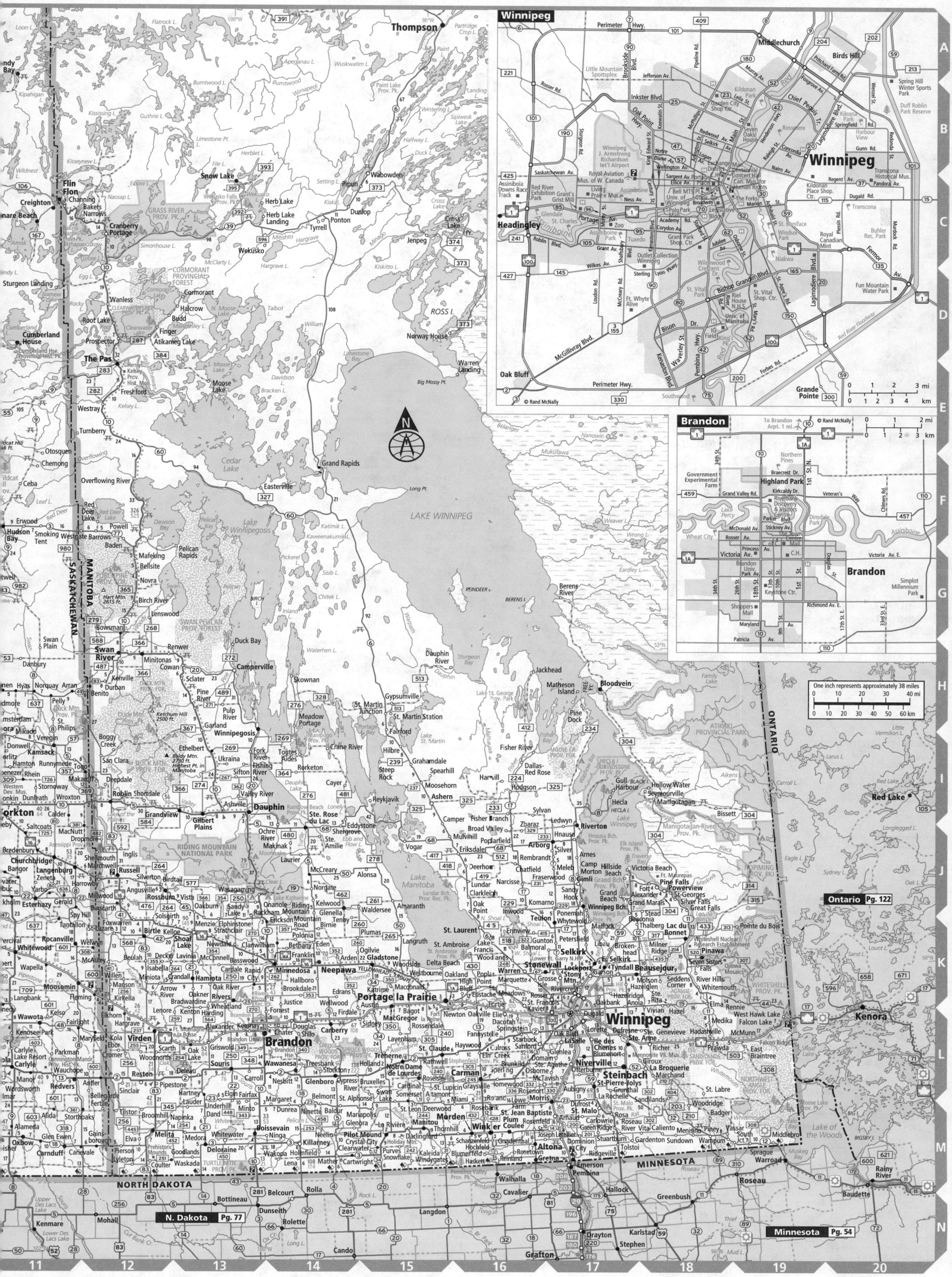

Winnipeg

0 1 2 3 mi
0 1 2 3 4 km

Brandon

0 1 2 mi
0 1 2 3 km

One inch represents approximately 38 miles
0 10 20 30 40 mi
0 10 20 30 40 50 60 km

Ontario Pg. 122

N. Dakota Pg. 77

Minnesota Pg. 54

11 12 13 14 15 16 17 18 19 20

Ontario

Capital: Toronto, I-10
Land area: 344,561 sq. mi. (rank: 5th)
Population: 13,448,494 (rank: 1st)
Largest city: Toronto, 2,794,356, I-10

Glossary of common French terms found on these maps: pg. 117

Index of places Pg. 136

Travel planning & on-the-road resources

Tourism Information
Destination Ontario: (800) 668-2746
www.destinationontario.com/en-ca

Road Conditions & Construction
511, (866) 929-4257; 511on.ca

Toll Road Information:
407 ETR (Toronto): (888) 407-0407; www.407etr.com

Ontario–Michigan Toll Bridge/Tunnel Information
Ambassador Bridge (Windsor):
www.ambassadorbridge.com
Federal Bridge Corp. (Blue Water Bridge, Sarnia):
(866) 422-6346; bluewaterbridge.ca
Detroit-Windsor Tunnel (*NEXPRESS*):
(519) 255-6100 ext. 6730, (313) 567-4422 ext. 200; www.dwtunnel.com
International Bridge Administration (Sault Ste. Marie):
(705) 942-4345, (906) 635-5255; www.saultbridge.com

Ontario–New York Toll Bridge Information
Buffalo & Ft. Erie Public Br. Authority
(Peace Bridge) *(E-ZPass)*:
(716) 884-6744; www.peacebridge.com
Niagara Falls Bridge Commission:
(E-ZPass or ExpressPass): (716) 285-6322;
www.niagarafallsbridges.com
For St. Lawrence River crossings, see New York, p. 70

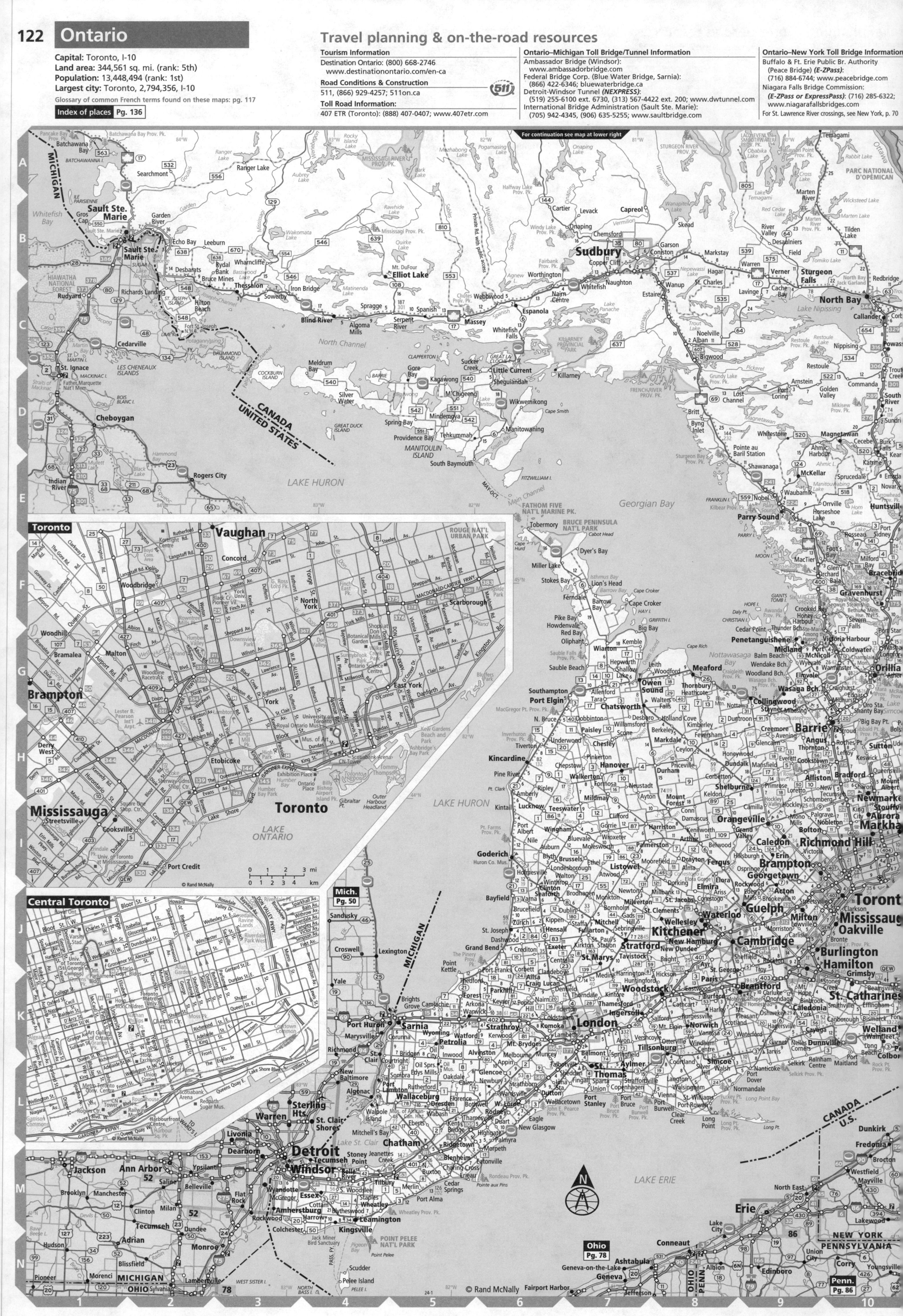

Nathan Phillips Square winter skating, Toronto

Mileages between cities	Bracebridge	Hamilton	Kenora	Kingston	Montréal, QC	Niagara Falls	Ottawa	Owen Sound	Pembroke	Sarnia	Sault Ste. Marie	Sudbury	Thunder Bay	Timmins	Toronto	Windsor
Kingston	223	204	1285		180	243	120	263	154	335	555	369	983	509	161	381
London	213	81	1255	274	450	127	360	143	360	68	525	339	953	535	121	116
Niagara Falls	185	47	1227	243	419		329	163	328	188	497	311	925	507	83	233
Ottawa	237	290	1207	120	124	329		333	91	421	494	300	905	445	247	467
Sudbury	153	272	925	369	424	311	300	233	209	401	195		623	182	242	446
Thunder Bay	767	886	303	983	989	925	905	852	814	1015	436	623		517	856	1060
Toronto	116	44	1158	161	337	83	247	118	246	182	428	242	856	438		227
Windsor	319	187	1361	381	556	233	467	259	466	96	631	445	1059	641	227	

Total mileages through Ontario

69 & 400 & QEW 323 miles

401 513 miles

17 & 417 1358 miles

More mileages at randmcnally.com/MC

Kitchener / Cambridge

Ottawa

One inch represents approximately 27 miles

Québec Pg. 124

New York Pg. 70

London

Hamilton

Sudbury

St. Catharines

Kingston

Thunder Bay

Qué. Pg. 124

Minn. Pg. 54

Wisc. Pg. 114

Mich. Pg. 50

For continuation see main map

Capital: Québec, J-11
Land area: 501,390 sq. mi. (rank: 2nd)
Population: 8,164,361 (rank: 2nd)
Largest city: Montréal, 1,762,949, M-8

Glossary of common French terms found on these maps: pg. 117

Index of places Pg. 136

Travel planning & on-the-road resources

Tourism Information
Tourisme Québec: (877) 266-5687, (514) 873-2015
www.bonjourquebec.com/en-ca

Road Conditions & Construction
511, (888) 355-0511
www.quebec511.info/en

Toll Bridge Information
Concession A25 (Pont Olivier-Charbonneau, Montréal) *(A25 Smart Link)*: (855) 766-8225, (514) 766-8225; a25.com/en
A30Express (near Montréal) *(A30 Express)*: (855) 783-3030, (514) 782-0800; a30express.com/en

Determining distances along roads
Highway distances (segments of one mile or less not shown):
Cumulative miles (red): the distance between red arrows
Cumulative kilometers (blue): the distance between red arrows
Intermediate miles (black): the distance between intersections & places

Comparative distance: 1 mile = 1.609 kilometers 1 kilometer = 0.621 mile

Mileages between cities	Baie-Comeau	Edmundston, NB	Gaspé	Mont-Laurier	Montréal	North Bay, ON	Ottawa, ON	Québec	Rimouski	Rivière-du-Loup	Rouyn-Noranda	Saguenay	Sept-Îles	Sherbrooke	Thetford Mines	Trois-Rivières
Montréal	410	336	566	145		346	124	156	331	266	389	289	534*	93	143	88
Ottawa, ON	533	459	689	122	124	222		279	454	389	323	411	657*	213	266	205
Québec	253	199	429	294	156	501	279		195	129	537	135	397*	146	72	78
Rouyn-Noranda	706	723	953	243	389	181	323	537	719	653		517	921*	481	530	461
Saguenay	196	186*	390*	427	289	634	411	135	156*	108*	517		339	279	205	211
Sept-Îles	143	306*	319*	678*	534*	879*	657*	397*	206*	268*	921*	339		524*	450*	465*
Sherbrooke	400	326	556	237	93	435	213	146	321	256	481	279	524*		65	94
Trois-Rivières	342	268	497	217	89	427	205	78	263	197	461	211	465*	94	88	

*Via ferry

Mileages © Rand McNally

Total mileages through Québec

20 / 132 / Trans-Canada: 937 miles

40 / 138: 765 miles

15 / 117 / Trans-Canada: 412 miles

More mileages at randmcnally.com/MC

New Brunswick

Capital: Fredericton, H-4
Land area: 27,509 sq. mi. (rank: 11th)
Population: 747,101 (rank: 8th)
Largest city: Moncton, 79,470, H-7

Index of places Pg. 136

Travel planning & on-the-road resources

Tourism Information

Tourism New Brunswick:
(800) 561-0123
tourismnewbrunswick.ca

Tourism Nova Scotia:
(800) 565-0000, (902) 742-0511
www.novascotia.com

Newfoundland and Labrador Tourism:
(800) 563-6353, (709) 729-2830
www.newfoundlandlabrador.com

Prince Edward Island Tourism:
(800) 463-4734, (902) 437-8570
www.tourismpei.com

Road Conditions & Construction

511

New Brunswick:
511, (800) 561-4063
www.gnb.ca/roads

Nova Scotia:
511, (888) 780-4440
511.novascotia.ca

Newfoundland & Labrador:
511, (833) 616-5511
www.511nl.ca/en
www.gov.nl.ca/ti/roads/home

Prince Edward Island:
511, (855) 241-2680
511.gov.pe.ca/en

Toll Road Information

Strait Crossing Bridge Ltd:
(Confederation Bridge) ***(StraitPass)***:
(902) 437-7300; www.confederationbridge.com

Atlantic Hwy. Management Corp. Ltd.
(Cobequid Pass, N.S. (Hwy 104)) ***(E-Pass)***:
(877) 727-7104, (902) 668-2211; www.cobequidpass.com

Halifax Harbor Bridges: ***(MACPASS)***:
(902) 463-2800; www.hdbc.ca

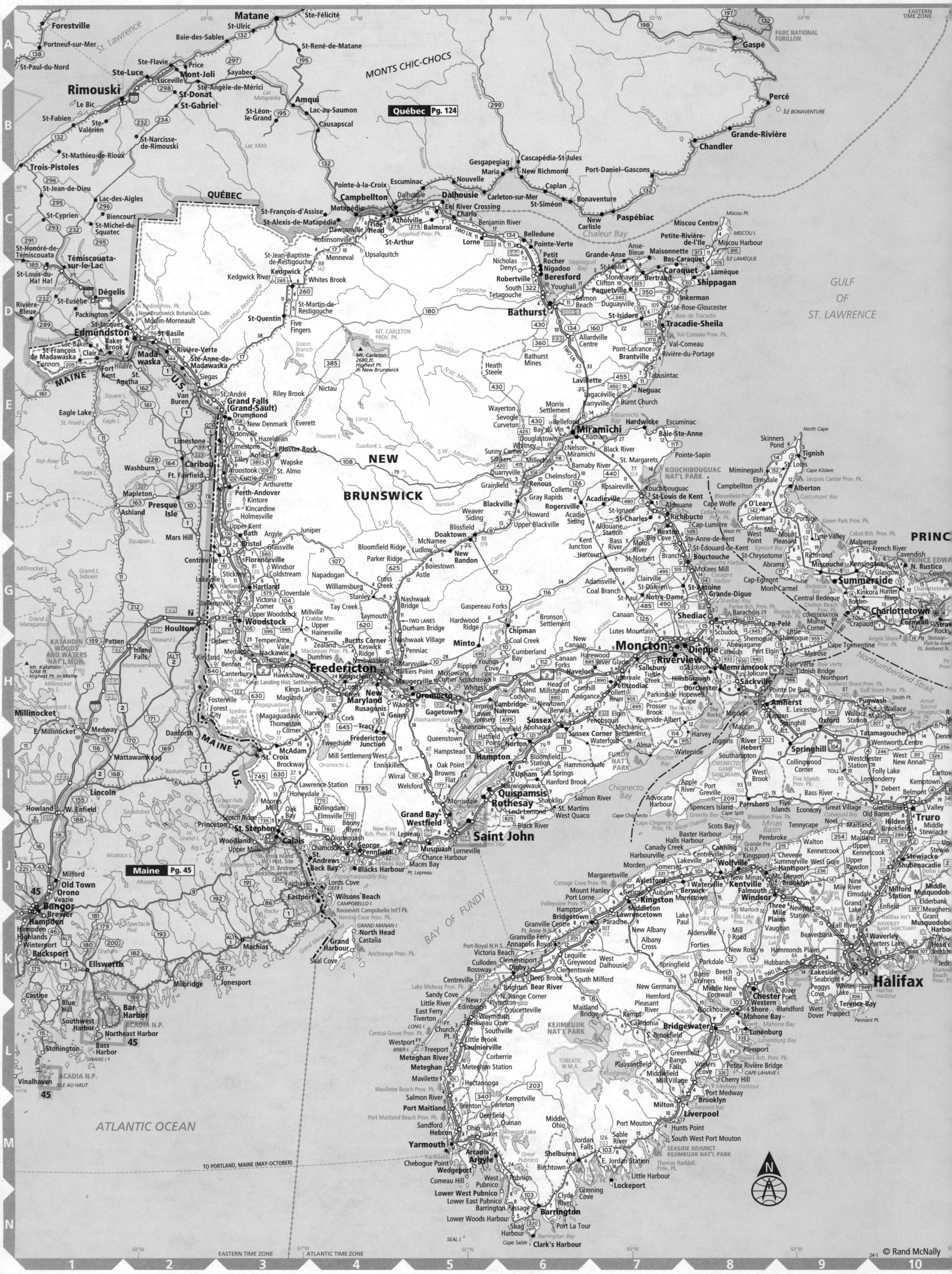

Québec Pg. 124

Maine Pg. 45

NEW BRUNSWICK

QUÉBEC

MAINE

U.S.

GULF OF ST. LAWRENCE

BAY OF FUNDY

ATLANTIC OCEAN

Northumberland Strait

Chaleur Bay

MONTS CHIC-CHOCS

EASTERN TIME ZONE

ATLANTIC TIME ZONE

TO PORTLAND, MAINE (MAY-OCTOBER)

ages veen s

*Via ferry

	Amherst, NS	Bathurst, NB	Campbellton, NB	Charlottetown, PE	Corner Brook, NL	Edmundston, NB	Fredericton, NB	Grand Falls, NB	Halifax, NS	Moncton, NB	New Glasgow, NS	Saint John, NB	St. John's, NL	St. Stephen, NB	Sydney, NS	Yarmouth, NS
lottetown, PE	82	214	280		461*	392	222	354	205	112	63	204	888*	274	215	389
undston, NB	319	160	125	392	817*		176	39	442	283	419	239	1244*	215	571	353
ericton, NB	149	160	248	222	647*	176		138	272	113	249	69	1074*	80	401	183
fax, NS	122	286	353	205	496*	442	272	403		162	98	254	923*	323	250	188
cton, NB	39	137	203	112	537*	283	113	244	162		139	95	964*	164	291	346
t John, NB	131	229	295	204	629*	239	69	201	254	95	231		1056*	69	383	114
ohn's, NL	925*	1088*	1155*	888*	433	1244*	1074*	1205*	923*	964*	825*	1056*		1125*	688*	1107*
ney, NS	252	415	482	215	261*	571	401	532	250	291	152	383	688*	452		434

Nova Scotia
Capital: Halifax, K-9
Land area: 20,396 sq. mi. (rank: 12th)
Population: 923,598 (rank: 7th)
Largest city: Halifax, 439,819, K-9

Prince Edward Island
Capital: Charlottetown, G-10
Land area: 2,194 sq. mi. (rank: 13th)
Population: 142,907 (rank: 10th)
Largest city: Charlottetown, 38,809, G-10

Newfoundland & Labrador
Capital: St. John's, F-20
Land area: 138,290 sq. mi. (rank: 10th)
Population: 519,716 (rank: 9th)
Largest city: St. John's, 110,525, F-20

More mileages at randmcnally.com/MC

Glossary of common French terms found on these maps: pg. 117

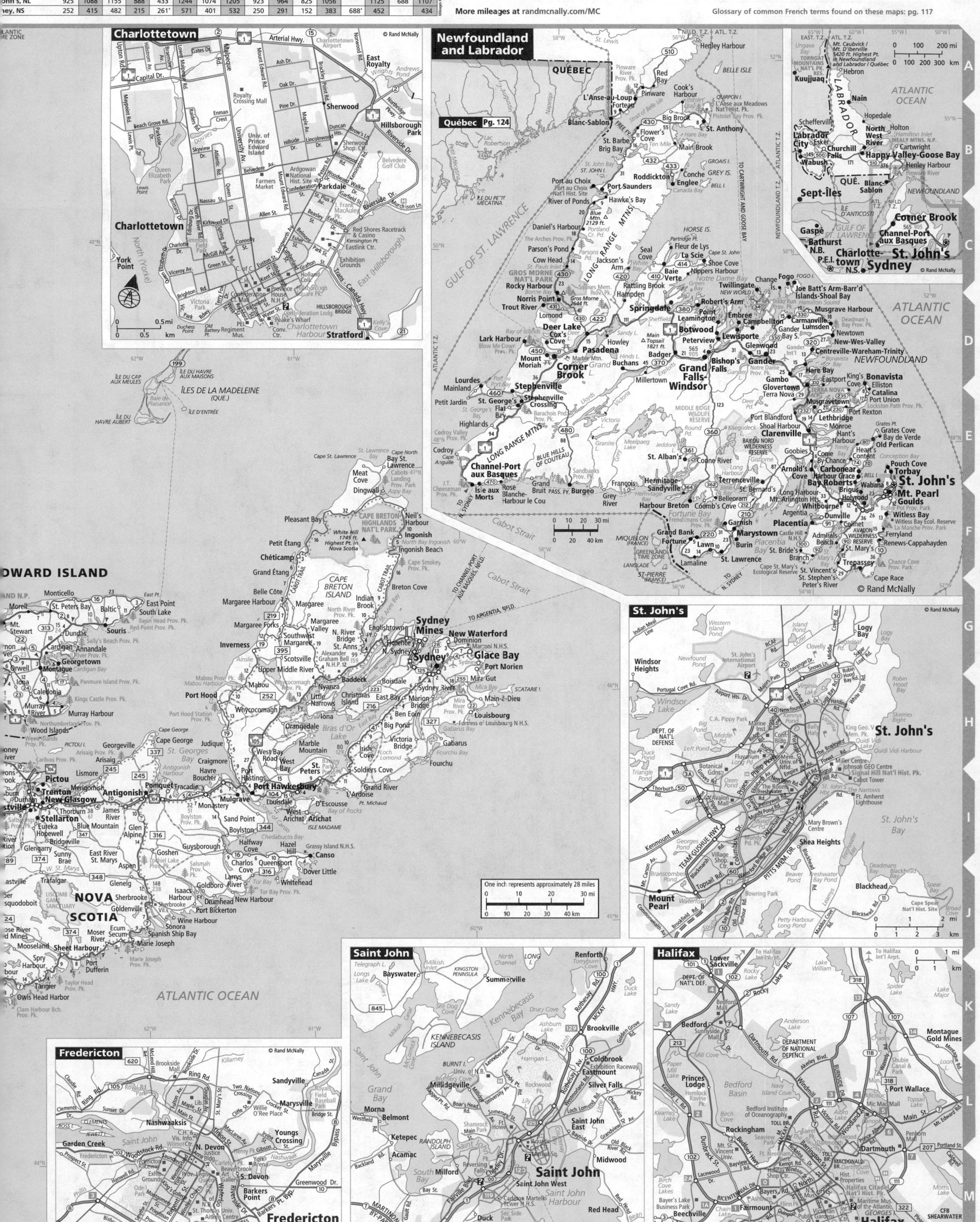

Mexico / Puerto Rico

Mexico
Capital: Mexico City, G-8
Land area: 750,558 sq. mi.
Population: 128,932,753
Largest city: Mexico City, 9,209,944, G-8

Puerto Rico (U.S.)
Capital: San Juan, A-13
Land area: 3,423 sq. mi.
Population: 3,285,874
Largest city: San Juan, 342,259, A-13

Index of places Mexico: Pg. 136; Puerto Rico: Pg. 134

Sights to see

Mexico
- Chichén Itzá Ruinas G-13
- Barranca del Cobre C-4
- Grutas de Cacahuamilpa H-8
- Parque Ecológico de Xochimilco I-3
- Parque Internacional del Río Bravo C-7
- Plaza de la Constitucion G-2
- Teotihuacán Ruinas G-8
- Tulum Ruinas G-14

Puerto Rico
- Bahía Fosforescente B-10
- Castillo del Morró A-13
- Museo de Arte de Ponce B-11
- Submarine Gardens A-13

On-the-road resources

Tourism Information
Mexico Tourism Board: visitmexico.com/eng
Discover Puerto Rico: (787) 710-8280, (787) 721-2400
www.discoverpuertorico.com, prtourism.com

Toll Information, Road Conditions, & Construction
Mexico: www.gob.mx (in Spanish)
Puerto Rico: (800) 981-3021, (787) 977-2200; its.dtop.gov.pr/en

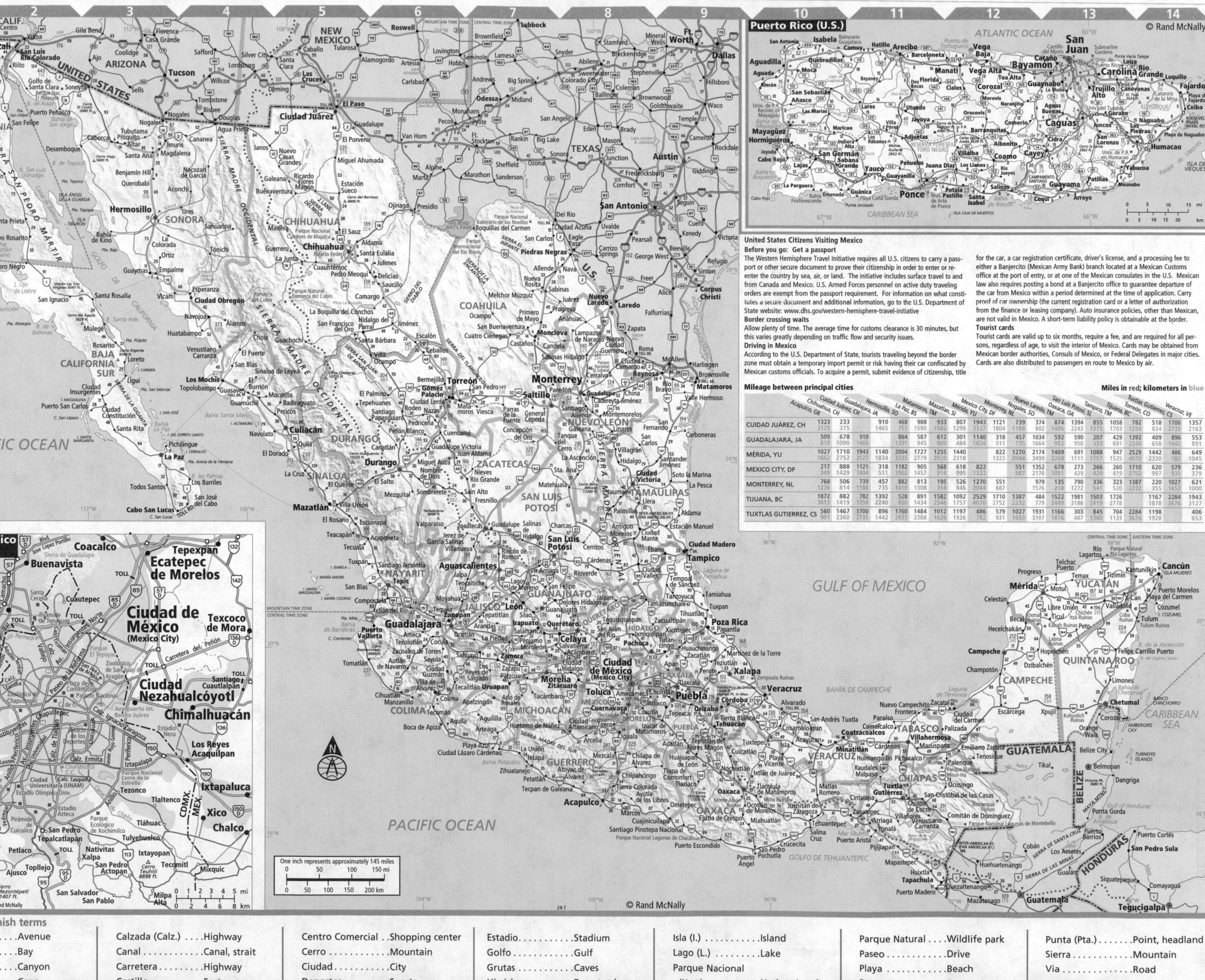

United States Citizens Visiting Mexico

Before you go: Get a passport
The Western Hemisphere Travel Initiative requires all U.S. citizens to carry a passport or other secure document to prove their citizenship in order to enter or re-enter the country by sea, air, or land. The initiative includes surface travel to and from Canada and Mexico. U.S. Armed Forces personnel on active duty traveling orders are exempt from the passport requirement. For information on what constitutes a secure document and additional information, go to the U.S. Department of State website: www.dhs.gov/western-hemisphere-travel-initiative

Border crossing waits
Allow plenty of time. The average time for customs clearance is 30 minutes, but this varies greatly depending on traffic flow and security issues.

Driving in Mexico
According to the U.S. Department of State, tourists traveling beyond the border zone must obtain a temporary import permit or risk having their car confiscated by Mexican customs officials. To acquire a permit, submit evidence of citizenship, title for the car, a car registration certificate, driver's license, and a processing fee to either a Banjercito (Mexican Army Bank) branch located at a Mexican Customs office at the port of entry, or at one of the Mexican consulates in the U.S. Mexican law also requires posting a bond at a Banjercito office to guarantee departure of the car from Mexico within a period determined at the time of application. Carry proof of car ownership (the current registration card or a letter of authorization from the finance or leasing company). Auto insurance policies, other than Mexican, are not valid in Mexico. A short-term liability policy is obtainable at the border.

Tourist cards
Tourist cards are valid up to six months, require a fee, and are required for all persons, regardless of age, to visit the interior of Mexico. Cards may be obtained from Mexican border authorities, Consuls of Mexico, or Federal Delegates in major cities. Cards are also distributed to passengers en route to Mexico by air.

Mileage between principal cities

Miles in red; kilometers in blue

	Acapulco, GR	Chihuahua, CH	Cuidad Juárez, CH	Guadalajara, JA	Hermosillo, SO	La Paz, BS	Matamoros, TM	Mazatlan, SI	Mérida, YU	Mexico City, DF	Monterrey, NL	Nogales, SO	Nuevo Laredo, TM	Oaxaca, OA	San Luis Potosí, SL	Tampico, TM	Tijuana, BC	Torreón, CO	Tuxtlas Gutierrez, CS	Veracruz, VE
CUIDAD JUÁREZ, CH	1323 / 2129	233 / 375		910 / 1465	468 / 753	988 / 1590	933 / 1502	807 / 1299	1943 / 3127	1121 / 1804	739 / 1188	374 / 602	874 / 1406	1394 / 2243	855 / 1375	1058 / 1703	782 / 1259	518 / 834	1700 / 2735	1357 / 2183
GUADALAJARA, JA	509 / 819	678 / 1090	910 / 1465		864 / 1391	587 / 945	612 / 985	301 / 484	1140 / 1834	318 / 511	457 / 735	1034 / 1664	592 / 952	590 / 950	207 / 333	429 / 691	1392 / 2240	409 / 658	896 / 1442	553 / 891
MÉRIDA, YU	1027 / 1652	1710 / 2752	1943 / 3127	1140 / 1834	2004 / 3225	1727 / 2779	1255 / 2020	1440 / 2318		822 / 1323	1270 / 2044	2174 / 3499	1409 / 2268	691 / 1111	1088 / 1751	947 / 1525	2529 / 4070	1442 / 2320	486 / 782	649 / 1045
MEXICO CITY, DF	217 / 349	888 / 1429	1121 / 1804	318 / 511	1182 / 1902	905 / 1457	568 / 914	618 / 995	822 / 1323		551 / 887	1352 / 2176	678 / 1091	273 / 439	266 / 429	260 / 419	1710 / 2752	620 / 997	579 / 931	236 / 379
MONTERREY, NL	768 / 1236	506 / 814	739 / 1188	457 / 735	882 / 1419	813 / 1308	195 / 314	526 / 846	1270 / 2044	551 / 887		979 / 1576	135 / 218	790 / 1272	336 / 541	323 / 520	1387 / 2232	220 / 355	1027 / 1653	621 / 1000
TIJUANA, BC	1872 / 3013	882 / 1419	782 / 1259	1392 / 2240	528 / 850	891 / 1434	1582 / 2546	1092 / 1757	2529 / 4070	1710 / 2752	1387 / 2232	484 / 779	1522 / 2449	1981 / 3188	1503 / 2419	1726 / 2778		1167 / 1878	2284 / 3676	1943 / 3127
TUXTLAS GUTIERREZ, CS	560 / 901	1467 / 2360	1700 / 2735	896 / 1442	1760 / 2833	1484 / 2388	1012 / 1628	1197 / 1926	486 / 782	579 / 931	1027 / 1653	1931 / 3107	1166 / 1876	303 / 487	845 / 1360	704 / 1133	2284 / 3676	1198 / 1928		406 / 653

Glossary of Spanish terms

Avenida (Av.) ..... Avenue	Calzada (Calz.) .... Highway	Centro Comercial .. Shopping center	Estadio .... Stadium
Bahía (B.) .... Bay	Canal .... Canal, strait	Cerro .... Mountain	Golfo .... Gulf
Barranca .... Canyon	Carretera .... Highway	Ciudad .... City	Grutas .... Caves
Cabo (C.) .... Cape	Castillo .... Fort	Deportes .... Sports	Hipódromo ...... Race track

Isla (I.) .... Island	Parque Natural .... Wildlife park	Punta (Pta.) ...... Point, headland
Lago (L.) .... Lake	Paseo .... Drive	Sierra .... Mountain
Parque Nacional (Nac.) .... National park	Playa .... Beach	Via .... Road
	Presa .... Reservoir	